AL GRAY
MARINE

THE EARLY YEARS
1968-1975

VOLUME 2

BY SCOTT LAIDIG

FOREWORD BY: GENERAL ANTHONY ZINNI, USMC (RET)
PREFACE BY: DR. JOHN F. GUILMARTIN, LT COL, USAF (RET)
COMMENTARY BY: GENERAL JOHN J. SHEEHAN, USMC (RET)

POTOMAC INSTITUTE PRESS

Publisher's Cataloging-in-Publication Data

Names: Laidig, Scott, author.

Title: Al Gray, Marine : the early years, 1968-1975 / by Scott Laidig ; foreword by: General Anthony Zinni;
           preface by: Dr. John F. Guilmartin; commentary by: General John J. Sheehan.

Other titles: Al Gray, marine, volume 2.

Description: Arlington, VA : Potomac Institute Press, [2017] | Includes bibliographical references and
           index. | Contents: Defense Communications Planning Group & the electronic battlefield --
           STEAM & SCAMP -- Off to school -- Finally, Infantry battalion commanding officer -- Army
           War College -- Back to the fleet Marine force -- The end of a long war -- HQMC, briefly --
           Bibliography -- Appendix -- Index.

Identifiers: ISBN: 978-0-9963960-3-5 (v. 2 ; paperback) | 978-0-9963960-8-0 (v. 2 : cloth) |
           978-0-9963960-7-3 (Kindle)

Subjects: LCSH: Gray, Alfred M. | United States. Marine Corps--Officers--Biography. | United States.
           Marine Corps--History--20th century. | Generals--United States--Biography. | Vietnam War,
           1961-1975--United States. | Vietnam War, 1961-1975--Vietnam--Ho Chi Minh City. | United
           States--Military policy. | United States--Military relations--Vietnam. | Vietnam--Military
           relations--United States.

Classification: LCC: VE25.G73 L35 2017 | DDC: 359.9/6092--dc23

This book contains information obtained from authentic and highly regarded sources, including interviews and personal collections. The author and publisher gratefully acknowledge the permission granted to reproduce copyrighted material in this book. The author has made every effort to trace copyright holders and to obtain their permission for use of this material. The author and publisher apologize for any omissions and would be grateful if notified of any corrections that should be incorporated in future reprints or editions of this book. Government-produced materials are not copyright protected (17 U.S.C. § 105). The author and publisher do not hold the copyright to works of the United States government appearing in this publication. The author and publisher cannot assume responsibility for the validity of all materials or the consequences of their use; the view and opinions expressed do not necessarily reflect those of the Institute and publisher.

Notes on formatting and usage: With respect for those who serve, capitalization has been applied to named ranks and titles throughout this work. Military terminology can vary depending on the scope, tenor, and context of usage, and every effort has been made to maintain authenticity of usage while ensuring clarity. Given myriad service acronyms, an acronym/abbreviations listing has been included in the appendix for each volume.

POTOMAC INSTITUTE FOR POLICY STUDIES
901 N. Stuart St, Suite 1200
Arlington, VA 22203
www.potomacinstitute.org
Telephone: 703.525.0770; Fax: 703.525.0299
Email: webmaster@potomacinstitute.org

The book is dedicated to the memory of Colonel George P. Slade, USMC, and all the other Magnificent Bastards of the 2nd Battalion, 4th Marines who served honorably in Vietnam from Operation Starlite *through* Operation Frequent Wind, *and to all other veterans of the Vietnam War who so honorably and heroically fought and too often died in that faraway place.*

All the net proceeds from this book will be donated to the Injured Marine Semper Fi Fund. The Semper Fi Fund (a 501(c)(3) nonprofit) and its affiliate program America's Fund are set up to provide immediate financial assistance and lifetime support for injured and critically ill post-9/11 service members from all branches of the U.S. Armed Forces and their families.

More information about the Injured Marine Semper Fi Fund can be found at: http://www.semperfifund.org.

ACKNOWLEDGEMENTS

This project has brought the author into contact with a whole host of people who otherwise would have been unknown. Most are admirers of the subject of the book, General Al Gray. However, the book would not be so rich in detail nor would it contain so much positive material about the General but for the contributions of a small group of men.

We lost Colonel George P. Slade in May 2013, before this volume was published. Colonel Slade was literally a picture poster Marine. Though a captain, the Marine Corps made him don the bars of a 1st Lieutenant before using his picture, in dress blues with his sword at the carry position, as an officer recruiting poster. But Colonel Slade was much more than a physical model for officers. He was a simply outstanding leader whose battalion performed in an exemplary fashion during the evacuations of Phnom Penh and Saigon. Much of the information in Chapters 6 and 7 came from Colonel Slade, whose modesty about his own achievements and leadership were in sharp contrast to his glowing comments about his officers and men, and in particular about General Gray. The whole Marine Corps family shall miss this quiet, self-effacing Texan.

Colonel Charles Beale, USMC, and Lieutenant Colonel Howard Alberts, USMC, were also welcomed into their final rally point during the process of writing this volume. Both made indelible impressions on General Gray when he first came to Headquarters Marine Corps in 1961. Their stories and primary contributions to this project are reflected in Volume 1, but their respect for General Gray set the tone for this effort. Though both were senior in terms of rank and experience, both conveyed the affection and respect they had for the hard-working, highly-professional young captain that Al Gray was when they first met. Those early interviews with Colonel Beale and Lieutenant Colonel Alberts convinced me that General Al Gray, whom I only knew after his retirement, had been special for his entire time as a Marine.

Sadly, we all said goodbye to Major Barney Prosser as Volume 1 was being finished. Much of the material about General Gray's impact on the Radio Battalion, and many of the pictures came from Barney. General Gray described Barney as one of the finest men he had ever met, and certainly everyone who had the privilege to know that exceptional Marine thought similarly.

No one who ever met Colonel Donald (Bear) Layne, UMSC, wonders about his nickname. We had the good fortune to meet Colonel Layne at the venerable *Globe & Laurel Restaurant* in Quantico, where he has a small group that has earned special status from the proprietor, Major Rick Spooner, USMC (Ret.) "Bear" was a great tackle at the College of William & Mary before becoming a Marine officer. He attended Communications Officer School with 1st Lieutenant Al Gray; then he was present at Guantanamo Bay when Captain Gray was doing "special" work during the Cuban Missile Crisis. Later, it was perhaps the influence of Major Layne who had Lieutenant Colonel Gray diverted for duty at the Defense Communications Project Group in early 1968, after General Gray returned to the United States on Emergency Leave. Colonel Layne was a great source of information about General Gray from all those times, and we miss him.

The late Colonel Lloyd (Jerry) Goodwine, USMC (Ret.) was also part of the special group at the *Globe & Laurel*. The possessor of a quick wit and marvelous memory, much of the information in Chapters 7 and 8 came from interviews with Colonel Goodwine. He and Colonel Slade were both junior to Al Gray during their time as Marines, but both shared unbounded respect for the man who would become Commandant. From Colonel Goodwine, who was the senior Marine on the staff of Rear Admiral Donald Whitmire during the evacuation of Saigon, came the insights regarding how the Admiral viewed Colonel Gray. Those insights are unique to this project, but reflective about how General Gray earned the respect of his bosses during times of great stress. Those chapters would have turned out much differently without Jerry's many contributions.

The special contributions made by General Anthony Zinni, USMC (Ret), the General John Sheehan, USMC (Ret), and the late Dr. Paul Otte are deeply appreciated.

For his special contributions to Volume 2, I must mention Colonel Rufus Smith, USMC (Ret). Colonel Smith served contemporaneously with General Gray, and was a great admirer of the 29th Commandant. No author had a better, or more formidable editor, than Colonel Smith. Sadly, Rufus passed before this volume was published.

Sherry Loveless of the Potomac Institute Press is solely responsible for the production of this book. Sherry is, as General Gray often says, a "superb professional"; no author has more needed her very able assistance. Thank you, Sherry!

And I must publicly thank Jan Gray for her patience and encouragement throughout this project. Jan is an exceptional person, a great Marine wife (the hardest job in the Corps) and an peerless hostess. I happily also call her a dear friend. Thank you so very much, Jan.

My good friend and mentor, Dr. John F. Guilmartin, Jr. (LtCol, USAF, Ret.) passed away before Vol. 2 was published. America has lost one of its leading historians and scholars have lost a man whose knowledge of the Vietnam War was encyclopedic. Sadly, his own history of that war will never be written.

Finally, let me acknowledge the man that many of us admire so much, the 29th Commandant of the Marine Corps, General Al Gray. Words cannot express the honor that has been mine to work on this project. No biographer ever had a more compelling subject; that we could complete these volumes with General Gray's factual contributions make the work all the more relevant. As I say to the General often, "Sir, you deserved a better author, but I am honored you permitted me to make the attempt to tell parts of your story."

To all these and many others, I owe a tremendous debt.

–Scott Laidig

AL GRAY, MARINE

THE EARLY YEARS

1968-1975

VOLUME 2

CONTENTS

FOREWORD

Every organization or institution that has a long successful history is marked by a number of legendary leaders who have shaped that success and built its reputation. The United States Marine Corps is no exception. Our remarkable history is replete with leaders whose courage, innovation, skill, and charisma made our Corps into an elite military organization steeped in pride and respect for the extraordinary service we have given to our nation. The list of these legendary leaders over our two plus centuries of dedicated service include names such as Henderson, Lejeune, Puller, Wilson, Barrow, and many others from our officer and enlisted ranks. One of these superb leaders from our more recent history is General Alfred M. Gray.

I first met General Gray in 1972 when he was a Lieutenant Colonel. At the time I was a Captain commanding a rifle company in the 2nd Marine Division at Camp Lejeune, North Carolina. A good friend and fellow company commander, Captain (later General) Jack Sheehan, kept telling me about his extraordinary battalion commander, a decorated Vietnam veteran named Al Gray. He invited me to have dinner with the two of them at the Officers' Club one evening. I quickly saw why Jack had such high regard and admiration for General Gray. That began a relationship that has lasted to this day and one that I truly cherish. General Gray became a mentor and role model for me. Despite coming from another battalion, he took me under his wing, as he did many other officers in whom he saw promise. Here was a rare senior officer who could talk the nitty-gritty of tactics and leadership issues at our level with a depth of knowledge and understanding that was far greater than his peers. He immediately connected to us junior officers because of his passion for our profession and his clear understanding of what we did. I would have the honor to serve under him several times after that. I was also able to seek his advice and counsel when I didn't. As I rose through the ranks over the remaining three decades of my military career, I knew I could call on General Gray for advice or to bounce thoughts and ideas off of him. Most impressive to me, he always sought me out, as he did many others, to ensure I was doing OK or to share his thoughts and ideas.

General Gray's legacy to our Corps is rich and varied. He is renowned for his charismatic mentoring of junior leaders; his exceptional operational skills; his dynamic approach to leader education and development; his organizational and doctrinal innovations; and his strategic vision for the role of our service in defense of our nation.

He drew young leaders to him like a powerful magnet with his approachable and personable character. They were also drawn to him by his clear understanding of their world and his common sense brilliance about every aspect of their mission and tasks. He talked fire team tactics or strategic planning with a degree of insight and detail that few other senior leaders could. His ability to communicate to, and connect to, privates as well as presidents attracted a following of loyal junior and senior leaders seeking his valuable counsel.

General Gray is credited with forging a renaissance in thinking about our profession of arms. He changed the outdated and constipated approaches to war fighting and the operational art that had evolved and were reflected in our training, organization, concepts, and doctrine. He encouraged out of the box thinking and challenges to our operational concepts and fathered the *Maneuver Warfare* conceptual basis for campaigning.

Without question he is consider the foremost leader in leader education and development in the history of our Corps. He created the Marine Corps University, Research Center, Training and Education Command, and other organizations dedicated to building strong, creative leadership. These institutions significantly changed our service by developing an officer and NCO corps with a competence and skill level fully capable to meet the challenges of 21st Century.

Arguably, General Gray's greatest contribution to our Corps was his vision for how our service best met our mission to win our country's battles. His saw a much more expansive role for us. A role that did not encroach on the roles of other services but complemented them because of the flexibility, readiness, adaptability, deployability, interoperability, and expeditionary nature of our organization. He saw the Marine Corps as a "reservoir of combat capability" that can be shaped, organized, and tasked to meet the missions assigned in the most effective and efficient manner. He did not believe in rigid structures or dogmatic organizational designs. He saw a unique contribution from our service that required the flexible and creative organization and leadership he intended to build and promote in our revitalized leader development and operational concepts.

For all of us who were fortunate enough learn at the knee of General Gray, he provided us with an exciting environment that was intellectually challenging and invited our participation in the development and decision making that shaped our service. Sergeants and Generals had a voice. His enthusiasm was infectious. His challenges were stimulating. Most of all, his total dedication and love of our Corps were inspiring.

To many, General Gray is best known for the remarkable things he accomplished as a general officer. For those of us who knew him well before he rose to flag rank, we witnessed and benefited from his exceptional talents well before that time. Scott Laidig has superbly captured that time in this excellent book. Typical of General Gray is his, Scott Laidig's, and the publisher's request that all proceeds from this book go to the Semper Fi Fund to benefit our military servicemen and women.

-General Anthony C. Zinni
US Marine Corps (Ret.)
Former Commander-in-Chief, US Central Command

PREFACE

General Alfred M. Gray, Jr., holds a special place among Commandants of the Marine Corps. Serving as the 29th Commandant from 1987 to 1991, he is widely regarded as having had a transformative influence on his service, notably in re-invigorating the Corps' warrior ethos and in replacing the existing attritional warfighting paradigm with one of maneuver warfare. That the maneuver warfare paradigm undergirded spectacular battlefield success in *Operation Desert Storm* and the initial stages of *Operation Iraqi Freedom* and proved adaptable to the challenges of asymmetrical warfare in a counter-insurgent role in Iraq and Afghanistan both underlined the thoroughness of the transformation and added lustre to the Corps' reputation.

Al Gray – as he styled himself and was widely referred to by Marines of all ranks, and to a remarkable degree still is – assumed the Commandancy at yet another difficult and challenging period in the Corps' long history. In four years he guided the Corps through what might be termed an intellectual renaissance, centerpieces of which include the publication of *Fleet Marine Force Manual 1, Warfighting*, which expounds the theory and practice of maneuver warfare based on the encouragement of low-level initiative and innovation, and on the establishment of the Marine Corps University and Marine Corps Combat Development Command. An important ingredient in Gray's transformational success was the degree to which he was perceived by field Marines as "looking out for them." Simply put, Gray inspired a remarkable degree of loyalty, not least of all among the junior officer and enlisted ranks. The degree to which he fostered this ethos and the degree to which it simply happened is open to question, but he was clearly aware of it. As evidence, consider Gray's adoption of "Papa Bear" as his personal radio call sign as the Ground Force Commander during the Saigon evacuation.

As former Marine Staff NCO-turned historian Earl Cantagnus has pointed out, what General Gray did as Commandant is generally well established.[1] The how and why of his accomplishments as Commandant are much less clear and here the volume at hand has a great deal to offer. Clearly, Al Gray's take on the profession of arms and on the proper role of the Marine Corps within it was heavily influenced by his experience in the Cold War and in Vietnam… and we should remember that the two cannot be cleanly separated. Indeed, the Vietnam War can be considered a major "hot" campaign waged within the strategic context of the Cold War. With that in mind, it is perhaps less than coincidental that the benefits of Gray's transformational impact on the Marine Corps took effect in the wake of the collapse of the Soviet Union and proved remarkably well tailored to the new strategic challenges that emerged.

Plainly, General Al Gray's belief in the warrior ethos and his unbounded confidence in Marines that accompanied him into the Commandancy were heavily shaped by his experience in Vietnam. It is that experience that Scott Laidig – who saw combat in Vietnam as a company grade Marine infantry officer before serving in intelligence billets – turns to in the following pages. Above and beyond Vietnam's shaping influence on Al Gray, what Laidig has to say is of considerable interest in its own right, for Gray saw the Vietnam War "up close and personal" as few Americans did. He was there in 1964, close to the beginning of the United States' overt military commitment to South Vietnam, commanding a Special Operations and Intelligence unit in northern I Corps that included a Marine infantry company, the first American line infantry to see combat in that country. He was there at the bitter end as a regimental commander, heavily – and critically – involved in the planning for *Operation Frequent Wind*, the helicopter evacuation of Saigon, and commanding the ground security force that secured the landing zones from which Marine and Air Force helicopters took evacuees, and eventually the ground security force, out to the ships of Navy Task Force 76.

In between, Gray served in a remarkable array of billets, serving as a regimental operations officer and unofficial intelligence advisor to high-level Marine commanders (though not by that name; despite his extensive experience in the field, particularly as a cryptologist, Gray was never actually an intelligence officer); as an artillery battalion commander in a particularly difficult situation; and serving in what amounted to a Corps-level intelligence billet during the run-up to the 1968 Tết Offensive. In between, he commanded an infantry battalion and infantry regiment in the 2nd Marine Division, and an infantry regiment (the 4th Marines) along with Camp Hansen, on Okinawa. As America's commitment to Vietnam was winding down, he found himself dealing with a host of problems involving demoralization, drugs, and race and leadership issues that plagued all the military services. His draconian prescriptions, including mandatory high school education for those lacking one, proved remarkably successful and helped point the way to a better Corps.

It is worth noting at this point that Gray's career pattern, one that exposed him to a remarkably wide range of issues and problems, would have been impossible in any other service. Testimony to the mission orientation and flexibility of the Marine Corps, he was not shoe-horned into the career progression ladder of a weapons system community (Navy), arms branch (Army) or weapons system identifier (Air Force). Although he was honored by the National Security Agency for his professional skills related to cryptology, he was never an intelligence officer per se but rather had extensive experience in the combat arms.

Al Gray had a colorful personality with seemingly contradictory facets. Unusual among general officers, he served as a sergeant in an elite amphibious reconnaissance unit that included duty aboard a submarine. He was regarded by some as an intellectual and had a flair for languages (he became fluent in Japanese and spoke some colloquial Korean, Chinese and Vietnamese as well as other Asian dialects without benefit of formal instruction), but applied for and received his college degree only after his promotion to Lieutenant General. Although not a teetotaler, he eschewed alcohol while overseas but was an inveterate tobacco chewer. Beyond his cryptologic talents, he proved to be a virtuoso artillery commander and shrewd tactician. Unusual among American officers who were not advisors, he developed close personal and professional relations with many of the South Vietnamese officers with whom he served. Committed to the Corps, he remained a bachelor until he had attained flag rank. The constants in his professional life were frightening competence, a competence on which many of his superiors commented; a willingness to take on challenging tasks; an ability to think "out of the box"; loyalty to the Corps; and always – particularly as he moved upward in rank – "his Marines."

In the pages that follow, Laidig uses Al Gray and his experience in Vietnam as an analytical lens through which to examine the Vietnam War and America's role in that war. In the process, he gives us a richer understanding of just what that war was about, interweaving the twists and turns of Gray's career with those of American politics, Vietnamese politics, the shifting strategic balance, debates within our national leadership as to how the war should be prosecuted and the news media's coverage of the war. *Al Gray, Marine: The Early Years* is more than the biography of an important figure in the history of the Marine Corps, though it is certainly that; it is an analytical examination of an institution under challenges at a critical time in its history and that of our nation, one that demonstrates that an individual can make a difference.

–John F. Guilmartin, Jr.
The Ohio State University
Columbus, Ohio

1. Stories detailing the experiences of Marines who met Gray abound on the internet and are frequent in conversations with Marines [who served] in the "Gray years," Earl Cantagnus, Jr., "Intellectual Warrior: General Alfred M. Gray's Transformational Commandancy, 1987-1991" (Annapolis, Maryland, 2009 U.S. Naval Academy Naval History Symposium Conference Paper), cited with permission.

COMMENTARY

As a young Captain assigned to Marine Barracks Washington D.C., I was "invited" by Colonel Joe Fegan to attend a reunion he had organized with 20 of his contemporaries. These Marines had served in World War II and Korea. Like Colonel Fegan, who was awarded Silver Stars at Saipan and Korea, these Marine had been decorated for valor. At the dinner, there were two Medal of Honor recipients, some seven or eight Navy Crosses, a dozen Silver Stars and more than 30 Purple Hearts (one Colonel had five Purple Hearts).

My platoon commanders and I were in awe of these legends. I do not remember eating dinner. I just sat there listening to the stories and banter.

The next day, the Colonel summoned me to his office. His first question was "what did you learn last night?" I answered, "I thought it was fascinating." He smiled and in his classic Princeton style said, "Captain, that was not my question."

After a long pause, I told him that I was surprised at the straight forward discussions. They talked mostly about what they learned from certain battles as well as the mistakes they made. They talked with feeling about the individual Marines and small units that contributed to the success of a fight.

He then asked what I learned from a discussion between two of the more senior Marines who sat next to us. It was not hard to hear the animated discussion. I replied that it was obvious that both officers had very strong opinions of events and their roles in the history of those events.

The Colonel paused and thoughtfully said, "Captain, there were two types of Marine Officers in that room last night. Although all of them served in combat, there is a fundamental difference between the first group you spoke about and the last. In the Marine Corps, you do not get to pick your commanders. If by chance, you could serve under officers like the first group; they will teach you the professional lessons they learned the hard way. In addition, they will insure that the Marines that do the heavy lifting and dying receive the credit they deserve. The Colonel continued; the latter group, especially the more senior they become, think and act like they are the Marine Corps. They spend a lot of their time and energy talking about themselves. You probably will not learn much from that group."

General Al Gray clearly belongs in the first group. Many of us have never heard General Gray say a word about his personal exploits in Korea or Vietnam. Every professional discussion with General Gray was always about the teaching/learning process. His focus was on how to fight as a Marine Air Ground Task Force. If you were a ground officer and did not know the capabilities of the Marine Air Control system then you were given a brief lesson and then sent out to learn more. There was always something else to learn about the profession of being a Marine.

To repeat General Tony Zinni "without question he (General Gray) is considered the foremost (officer) in leader education and development in the history of our Corps."

It has been our professional and personal privilege to learn from General Al Gray.

General John J. Sheehan
US Marine Corps (Ret.)
Former Commander-in-Chief, US Atlantic Command

PRELUDE: TO VOLUMES I & II

There was no historical precedent for the events of April 30, 1975.

Never in the history of the United States of America had it lost a war. Never in history had an ally of the United States, fighting for its independence with American military support, been forced to surrender.

Never in the modern era had a Congress and a President turned their backs on friends, allies, and comrades-in-arms. During the days leading up to April 30, 1975, for the first time in American history, they had.

The Democratic Republic of Vietnam (North Vietnam) had been continuously attacking the Republic of Vietnam (South Vietnam) since at least 1960. The circumstances that in 1955 had created North and South Vietnam were complex and confusing, but no more so than those that established North and South Korea, or East and West Germany. America did not sanction East German attacks against West Germany, and America fought a war to stop North Korean aggression against South Korea. And for a long while, and at great cost in national treasure and in the lives of its best young men and women, America had stood with South Vietnam, though the American military always fought with at least one arm tied behind its back. On April 30, 1975, the American commitment to South Vietnam died a painful death, and with it expired freedom for the citizens of the Republic of Vietnam and the lives of many of their patriots.

After the Paris Peace Accords had been signed in 1973, which ended the active participation of the United States in the war, the American Ambassador to South Vietnam had hoped against all hope that the country could be saved. The South Vietnamese President, buoyed by innumerable promises of endless financial and military support made by two successive American Presidents, was incapable of making the tough decisions that might have saved his nascent nation. Reality was, that without American military aid and financial resources, South Vietnam's fight against communist aggression faced extremely long odds and was almost surely doomed to failure. The North was, after all, sustained, abetted and encouraged by the two largest communist powers on Earth, the Soviet Union and China. As recently as 1972, during what was dubbed the *Easter Offensive*, South Vietnam – aided substantially by American air power and military assistance – had drubbed the invaders and inflicted tremendous casualties on the attackers. But between the end of 1974 and early 1975, the American Congress lost its resolve to assist the South, and the American Presidency, weakened by the events of Watergate, could not push back against the Congress with the will to do what was right – to defend a free people fighting for freedom.

Many Americans and other allies had remained in Saigon in April 1975, and they needed to be rescued. Three large columns of communist forces had overwhelmed the South Vietnamese defenders, who by that time lacked sufficient amounts of bullets, bandages and bombs to put up a good resistance. There were also numerous, near countless, South Vietnamese who had worked for America, and they faced certain death in the event of a communist takeover. They, too, needed rescuing – and many were.

The American commander of the ground forces that saved the Ambassador and about 8,000 others sat in the rearmost seat of a large helicopter, one that he thought was the last helicopter out of Saigon. Gazing out the open rear hatch as the aircraft flew eastward in the darkness, he felt a great sense of personal loss. After all, he had been operating and fighting in and for South Vietnam during parts of 8 of the past 13 years, and he had great admiration for the South Vietnamese people as they waged their struggle to be free-from communist oppression. He had observed first hand the North Vietnamese Army and Viet Cong forces carry out barbarous terrorist tactics and other atrocities against the Vietnamese people in hamlets and villages. Looking back at the events of April 29-30, 1975, Colonel Al Gray knew that the Sailors, Airmen, and Marines had performed brilliantly. His men had landed, carried out their mission flawlessly for over 26 hours, and now they were returning to their amphibious ships lying 50 miles off the Vietnamese coast. Like many veterans of the long conflict, he wondered how their loyal South Vietnamese military and civilian personnel left behind would survive in the future. Gray was tired from not having slept for nearly 48 hours, but he remained alert, thinking.

He was thinking mostly about the future, because that is how Al Gray lives – looking ahead. In an hour, there would be a new dawn of a new day and new challenges. Nevertheless, it was impossible for the Marine not to ponder the innumerable events, twists, and turns that brought him to this day, April 30, 1975.

CHAPTER I

DEFENSE COMMUNICATIONS PLANNING GROUP
& THE ELECTRONIC BATTLEFIELD
THE VIETNAM WAR REACHES A TURNING POINT

DEFENSE COMMUNICATIONS PLANNING GROUP & THE ELECTRONIC BATTLEFIELD

Few Washington insiders had ever heard of the Defense Communications Planning Group (DCPG). It was a super-secret organization set up by Secretary of Defense Robert Strange McNamara with the purpose of stopping the North Vietnamese infiltration into South Vietnam. To do this, the Secretary planned, inter alia, to implement an electronic fence, which soon became known as the McNamara Line; the DCPG's mission included providing the means to put into action such a fence. Located on the grounds of the Naval Observatory just off Wisconsin Avenue in Georgetown, the DCPG had a big budget, nearly non-existent congressional oversight, and no reporters thirsting after a story. It was an engineer's nirvana. Even 40 years after the conflict had ended, the DCPG's place in the history of the Vietnam War remains elusive, and its overall effectiveness open to debate.[1]

In January 1968, Lieutenant Colonel Gray returned from Vietnam on emergency leave, following the unexpected death of his primary mentor and role model, his father Alfred Mason Gray, Senior. Although Gray, along with his senior, expected his absence from command would be temporary and that he would soon be returning to Southeast Asia, the Marine Corps needed a replacement at the DCPG, and the officer from New Jersey fit the bill perfectly.

Indeed, Gray was the ideal candidate for the assignment. After all, he had recently commanded the Marine Corps' Signals Intelligence unit in Vietnam and before that had led a reinforced artillery battalion plus all U.S. forces that were physically located astride the McNamara Line at the Gio Linh Outpost. Additionally, Gray had flown countless hours as an aerial observer over precisely the ground covered by the McNamara Line. Few knew any more about the topography of the region, or the enemy hiding there, than Al Gray. Indeed, no other DCPG officer had such relevant experience; as a result, Lieutenant Colonel Gray was assigned, among other things, to give the Group's monthly briefing to President Lyndon B. Johnson's Science Board.

During one session of the Science Board, Gray was asked his opinion of the effectiveness of the centerpiece of the DCPG effort, an electronic barrier just south of the Demilitarized Zone nicknamed the McNamara Line. With his usual dynamism, Gray pulled no punches in pronouncing the project an unfortunate idea with many cons and just a few pros. When the Army brigadier general in charge of operations at the DCPG heard what Gray had said, he called the Marine to his office and delivered a verbal dressing down. After all, the organization's position was exactly the opposite of Gray's. The matter escalated to the attention of the Director of the DCPG for resolution, Air Force Lieutenant General John D. Lavelle. He listened attentively to Lieutenant Colonel Gray's explanation of his position, and promptly told the Marine to persist in testifying as he saw fit. Al Gray had survived another dustup with a general officer.

III MARINE AMPHIBIOUS FORCE HEADQUARTERS, DA NANG, JANUARY 1968

Al Gray had spent the day visiting his units in the field and conducting liaison activities. He was alone in his small office reviewing intelligence information, when he responded to a knock at the door. A very somber Force Chaplain returned his greeting; Gray knew immediately that something was wrong, and he instinctively thought was that his mother had fallen ill. After all, his father had always been in good health. But his world was suddenly and unexpectedly changed on 8 January 1968, when the Chaplain informed him that his father died of a heart attack while spending the winter in Florida.

Gray's relationship with his father was neither complex nor extraordinary. Al Junior was born in Rahway, New Jersey, but the family moved to Point Pleasant Beach, New Jersey while Al was still a young boy. He returned to Rahway briefly in the spring of 1942, playing high school varsity baseball there. The move was the result of the railroad changing his father's job assignment; that same summer, however, the family settled back into Point Pleasant Beach.[2] While growing up, Gray, Sr. was a friend, role model and confidant to his only son. It was his father who encouraged young Al to read extensively, and who tutored him in arithmetic and other subjects. Gray Sr. had played basketball and tennis in high school, and it was Gray Sr. who nurtured and encouraged young Al's love of sports, especially baseball's New York Giants. Like many young men in the New York and New Jersey area, Al idolized Giants' players like Mel Ott and Johnny Mize. The great slugger Mel Ott was a particular favorite, perhaps because his size was nearly identical to the younger Gray's. Gray Sr. pushed his son's interest as a fan, often taking his son into the city from Point Pleasant Beach to attend a game; perhaps more importantly, Gray Sr. encouraged participation in all sports. When the younger Gray became quite the local luminary, earning all-state laurels in baseball, football, and basketball, it was his father who kept him grounded.

In addition to liking team sports, Gray Sr. and his brothers were all strong swimmers, having grown up around the water on Staten Island, where their father owned a boat works. His father ensured that Al Jr. started swimming at a very early age.

It was his father who gave the young athlete the confidence to shine, but Gray Sr. also made certain that the budding star remained humble, deflected credit to his teammates, and led by working harder than anyone else on any team. Working hard, sharing and taking care of others were the hallmarks of Alfred Mason Gray, Senior.

Al Gray's two siblings, both sisters, had died at a very young age, leaving young Al to grow up as an only child. But during the depression years and throughout the 1930s, the Gray household was expanded to include grandparents, uncles, aunts and their families, all relatives who had fallen on hard times. The elder Gray had gone to work on the Pennsylvania Railroad at a very young age prior to World War I. After his military service, Gray returned to the railroad and, because of his veteran status, retained his job seniority. Consequently, Gray Sr. held his job as a railroad brakeman and later conductor throughout the period of national economic hardship. Despite the difficult times, the hardworking father was able to provide for his extended family through those difficult years. He retired in 1964, after completing 44 years of service with the Pennsylvania Railroad.

Though his father was his primary mentor, his mother and her side of the family also influenced Al Gray. His maternal grandparents came from Switzerland and settled in New York. Like many Swiss, they were multi-lingual and frequently spoke German around the house. Gray's grandfather was fluent in five languages and for three years lived along the Amazon in Brazil, where he learned several native dialects. Interestingly, his grandfather also had broad knowledge of Native American history.

Like many Depression-era families who allocated a portion of their meager incomes to relatives in order that all survived as best they could, the Gray family, close-knit, proud and hardworking during that time, provided young Al with a host of role models and life shaping experiences. Al Gray, Sr. treasured books, and each day he often brought home a variety of newspapers that had been abandoned aboard the trains. Thus, it was not unusual for young Al to read newspapers from up and down the eastern seaboard. Growing up in this environment accounts for his strong work ethic, his commitment to reading, and his love of sports.

Like his father, Al Jr. worked hard in his early years. He obtained a Social Security number at age 11 and worked part time all through his middle and high school years. His efforts at a variety of jobs helped his family, not unlike many youngsters of that era. He did yard work and other routine chores, but he also worked at a local moving and storage company, caddied at a golf course, and delivered ice to both homes and businesses. During his high school years, he packed fish nightly on the local fishing docks and spent time offshore as a scallop fisherman. It was a busy childhood for a youngster committed to work, sports, and reading.

With his uncles around, another lesson the younger Gray learned was the meaning of patriotism. Al Gray, Sr. and his four brothers had all served in the United States Navy in World War I. They were men extremely proud of their service, and they loved their country, despite the difficult economic circumstances in which the extended family found itself. Throughout his life, Al Gray, Sr. had been the rock of the family and the man Al Gray, Jr. most wanted to emulate. Before going back to Vietnam in 1965, young Al had made a solemn oath to his father to care for his mother should anything happen to the elder Gray. Thoughts of his father and pride in how Gray, Sr. had lived his life gave the 39-year-old Marine much solace as he returned to the United States on emergency leave to assist his mother and fulfill his promise to his father. The trip home was, like that experienced by many who left the war zone unexpectedly, hardly routine.

With little more than his field utility uniform and a modicum of personal civilian clothing, Gray caught a Marine logistics aircraft to Okinawa. From there, he boarded a medical evacuation flight to Tachikawa Air Force Base, Japan, which then went on to Seattle. As was his norm, he spent the flight up and about, speaking quietly with the wounded while reminiscing about his father. Military aircraft, even when transporting the wounded, hardly approach the status modern civilian aircraft with respect to creature comforts. With seats that were little more than slings, passengers were always uncomfortable, and Gray recalled being cold for the entire flight – he had shared his field jacket with one of the wounded. From Seattle, he proceeded to Florida via Chicago.

After settling the family affairs in Florida, Gray drove his mother, Emily, back home to Point Pleasant Beach, New Jersey. Al Senior was buried in the family plot in the nearby town of Brielle, overlooking the shore area that he loved.

Gray reported from emergency leave to Headquarters, Marine Corps, anxious to return as soon as possible to his command in Vietnam. Given all the recent intelligence information that Gray had been privy to, and in many cases had a hand in developing, prior to leaving on emergency leave, he was very concerned about the direction of enemy activities. Gray was personally and professionally committed to an American and South Vietnamese victory in the war, an attitude noted by many of the senior officers with whom he served.[3] While Lieutenant Colonel Gray had definite goals for his coming assignment, the Marine Corps had a different idea.

Someone at Headquarters Marine Corps (HQMC) decided that Lieutenant Colonel Gray would not be returning to Vietnam; the Marine Corps had another

Figure 1.1
This is General Gray's favorite picture of his father, Alfred Mason Gray, Sr.[4]

Figure 1.2
Alfred Mason Gray, Sr., and his brother, Charles Gray, in
their World War I U.S. Navy uniforms.[5]

Figure 1.3
Al Gray aged seven and Little Duke.[6]

Figure 1.4
Al Gray the young student.[7]

Figure 1.5
Al Gray, Sr., and Emily Gray outside their New Jersey home, circa 1954.[8]

Figure 1.6
*Al Gray, Sr., long served as a conductor on the Pennsylvania Railroad. His
job kept the entire extended family afloat during the depression, and his
work gave Al Gray, Jr. the opportunity to meet his beloved New York Giants
as they traveled on the railroad between NYC and Philadelphia.*[9]

assignment for him. While Gray was on emergency leave, an old friend and class-mate, then-Major Donald Q. Layne, sealed his future assignment. Layne and Gray first met when both were students at Communications Officer School. Subsequently, they saw each other again when each brought a detachment to the National Security Agency for technical training in the 1950s. Layne was a 1st Lieutenant from 2nd Composite Radio Company, and Gray a Captain from 1st Radio. Later they met at Guantanamo during the Cuban Missile Crisis. Layne had been sent to the DCPG for what supposedly was a three-month Temporary Additional Duty assignment in 1966. He was a huge man, an offensive lineman for the College of William and Mary. Fittingly, he was called "Bear" by most his shipmates. While everyone knew Don Layne was a fine college football player, very few identified Al Gray as such. He never mentioned it. In his mind, why would he?

Don Layne quickly had become an important part of the ground sensor develop-ment team. In fact, he was so vital that it would be 1969 before Layne was given Permanent Change of Station orders away from the secret organization. But in January 1968, while visiting HQMC, Major Layne was shown three names for possible assignment to replace Lieutenant Colonel Jerry Polakoff, who had become seriously ill and needed to be replaced. Layne immediately suggested Al Gray was the right man – after all, Gray could do anything, at least in Layne's mind! While Don Layne and Al Gray remained lifelong friends, Gray would not have been a happy camper had he known that he was chosen by his old colleague. However, Gray didn't learned the story until 40 years after the fact. Disappointed with his orders, the fact was that in early 1968, Al Gray desperately wanted to get back into the fight in Southeast Asia.[10]

NAVAL OBSERVATORY GROUNDS, WASHINGTON, D.C., JANUARY 1968

The inconspicuous, some would say ugly, three-story building on the grounds of the Naval Observatory, just off Wisconsin Avenue north of Georgetown, was a most unlikely place for the offices of high-powered, high-energy scientists and engineers to be located. Even more improbable was that this innocuous setting would be the site of a super-secret, high budget military project that was considered the Secretary of Defense's highest priority. It was a venture so large and complex that many dubbed it the "Non-nuclear Manhattan Project."

Initially organized and funded by Secretary McNamara, the DCPG continued to grow and expand even after Clark Clifford replaced McNamara. Clifford was Secretary of Defense for the last year of the Johnson Administration, and changed very little of what McNamara had been doing. The DCPG's value was seen when the Nixon Administration took over in January 1969, and the secret organization remained a focal point for research and development related to new sensors, weapons, and computer systems.[11]

By the time Lieutenant Colonel Gray arrived at the facilities at the Naval Observatory, much of the preliminary research into sensors and the means to employ and use them was well underway. What remained, however, was the need to marry the technological innovations that the engineers envisioned with the practicality needed for systems used by combat troops. Al Gray provided the ability to work both sides of the issue. His time at HQMC in the early 1960s had well prepared him for the issues related to research and development, while his recent experience in the field in Vietnam, under combat conditions, honed his already commonsense approach to what works and what might not work when given to Soldiers and Marines.

By January 1968, Air Force Lieutenant General John D. Lavelle had replaced Lieutenant General Starbird as head of the DCPG. Charismatic, handsome, and self assured, everything one would expect of a World War II fighter pilot, General Lavelle was a highly competent officer. Unfortunately, his professional life would later end in notoriety when he was relieved of command while serving as the Commander of the 7th Air Force in Vietnam.[12] But in 1968, he was an energetic, knowledgeable and a very formidable Director of the DCPG's far-flung efforts. Furthermore, he had the chutzpah to lead what was a largely unaudited, unaccountable scientific engineering effort that pushed technology into many new areas, primarily related to computers, bombs and sensors.

[Al Gray always remained a strong supporter of General Lavelle, and he was elated when Lavelle was recently (2011) exonerated by new facts that indicated Lavelle had been truthful about his role in the "secret bombings."[13] Gray lamented that he only wished General Lavelle had been alive to see the removal of the black marks against the General's reputation.]

The DCPG was an exciting place, and the MITRE-led engineers proved very adept at developing new products and taking advantage of recent advances in computer technology.[14] Their efforts were multi-faceted and also included large-scale integrated computer systems. In fact, a DCPG project nicknamed *Igloo White* contained what was most likely the largest mainframe computer system in Southeast Asia. Located in Nakhon Phanom, Thailand, the computer provided what some called a pinball game experience for its many operators. The flashing symbols and screen representations of the sensor data that was being collected as North Vietnamese Army (NVA) troops and logistics personnel traveled down the Ho Chi Minh Trail

Figure 1.7
Lieutenant General John D. Lavelle, United States Air Force, served as the Director, DCPG
and then had a controversial tour in Vietnam before retiring. He was a brilliant officer
and Al Gray had great respect for him. The inscription reads: "Al: Thanks for the constant
gung ho, can do, Marine attitude. You made our problems easier, John D. Lavelle." [15]

were among this nation's first attempts to use mainframe computers to support tactical operations. Not that everything went smoothly from the start.

When the sensors were first dropped over the Ho Chi Minh Trail, the information resulted in chaos among those trying to correlate the data. Aircraft-dropped sensors were problematic. First, the planes that dropped them did not have accurate information regarding their own positions, and then when the sensors fell to earth they further complicated the question of its precise position. It took some time to sort out the issue related to sensor location. Fast moving F-4 fighter-bombers were used to deliver the sensors, relying on long-range navigation for its navigational data. While the DCPG hoped to achieve 150-yard accuracy, many others felt knowing within a ¼ mile was optimistic. *Igloo White* was by far the most expensive and most ambitious part of the overall DCPG effort.

The original, and as it turned out, less ambitious project at the DCPG was called *Dyemarker*. *Dyemarker* was the code name for the *McNamara Line* – the effort to build an electronic fence across northern South Vietnam. In late 1965 and early 1966, the *Electronic Fence*, designed to disrupt passage of people and vehicles from North into South Vietnam, was in the concept proposed by the Jason Group of engineers and scientists that convinced McNamara to proceed. *Dyemarker* was the program that most affected the Marines. The "fence" was anchored by the combat outposts at Gio Linh and Con Tien; indeed, Al Gray had spent many months participating in the construction associated with the *McNamara Line*, though he and many others thought it an exercise in futility – as indeed it was.[16] McNamara's concept was strongly opposed by the Commander-in-Chief, Pacific, Admiral U.S. Grant Sharp. The very capable, highly professional Admiral was able to foresee the tactical and logistical issues associated with trying to create such a fence along the DMZ. However, like most military officers' debates with the powerful Secretary of Defense, Sharp lost.

By 1968, senior military officers, including General Westmoreland and the Marines, although still rejecting the idea of a *McNamara Line* had embraced the products of the DCPG efforts.

The Marine Corps, particularly, welcomed the addition of DCPG sensors to its defensive plans around the besieged artillery base at Khe Sanh. As early as 1967, the Marines enthusiastically deployed a host of DCPG-developed sensors in the mountains that ringed the base; the sensors quickly detected the presence of North Vietnamese infantry. The Marine commander, Colonel David Lownds, attributed much of the successful defense to the assistance sensors provided in targeting the enemy. By the winter 1967 into the spring of 1968, the situation around Khe Sanh could only be described as a siege.

Most of the Marine's sensors were put into position by infantry or reconnaissance patrols, and consequently their locations were generally well known. Al Gray, then commanding the Radio Battalion in Vietnam, worked closely with the Marine Amphibious Force (MAF) G-3 section on sensor employment and tactics; thus, he had gained extensive, practical experience on the battlefield with the products under development at the secret agency.

Generally, the Marines used two types of sensors: acoustic and seismic. Acoustic sensors, simply put, reproduce sounds that are made in proximity to them. The sound may be a stick breaking, or people talking or even whispering, or the wind rustling the trees. Seismic sensors, on the other hand, detect vibrations in the ground; vehicles rolling by may cause the vibrations or they might result from a water buffalo walking down a trail. Experience gained by the human operators while using the sensors is a vital part of the sensors' effectiveness, but the human aspect of sensor effectiveness was too often overlooked or ignored by would-be users.

In budgetary and development terms, the overall DCPG programs were quite successful by early 1968; indeed, that year might have marked the high water mark for the DCPG. The place was full of whirling dervishes, and it was about to get yet another. On the other hand, its founder and leading advocate, Robert Strange McNamara, was on his way out of the Pentagon. Disagreements over policy, particularly with respect to the air campaign against the North, ended the partnership between McNamara and President Johnson. By November 1967, the Defense Chief had announced his impending resignation, and by February 1968, he was gone with hardly a whimper, replaced by the ultimate Washington insider and prominent lawyer, Clark Clifford. The change had no effect on the war generally or on the DCPG, specifically.

INTELLIGENCE SECTION, DEFENSE COMMUNICATIONS PLANNING GROUP, WASHINGTON, D.C., JANUARY 1968

Since the DCPG was a super-secret organization, the people who worked there required top-secret security clearances. When one of the Marine officers assigned to the DCPG needed replacement in January 1968, the Marine Corps needed to look no farther than Lieutenant Colonel Al Gray to find a highly qualified replacement. Gray's previous assignment commanding the Gio Linh Outpost had placed him on the cutting edge of the *Dyemarker* project while his assignments as the S-3 of the

12th Marines and the Commanding Officer of the Radio Battalion element gave him important insights into the enemy situation across South Vietnam into Laos and Cambodia, the area addressed by *Igloo White*. Those assignments gave Gray something in very short supply at the DCPG, practical experience in the field. That Gray also had research, development and acquisition experience, gained during his previous AO2F tour at HQMC, was a major bonus. Lieutenant Colonel Gray was told to report to the Naval Observatory, for duty in the Intelligence Section of the DCPG. As usual, he hit the Observatory grounds running.

Gray immersed himself in his new assignment. Not only was Gray one of the few Marines who had both the appropriate clearance accesses *and* recent combat experience, he was one of the few people at the DCPG with such qualifications. Moreover, he understood the requirements of the Marine Air-Ground Intelligence System, and the Air Force's Tactical Information Processing and Interpretation Program (TIPI), both of which the DCPG's products needed to interface with and support. That he was only seven months removed from an assignment where he sat squarely on the *McNamara Line* meant he became an officer whose knowledge was sought by others throughout the organization. That combined with his wide experience as a briefing officer led to his assignment as the DCPG representative to the President's Science Board. And while briefing the President's Science Board may have been the most impressive-sounding of the numerous formal and impromptu meetings that Gray attended, they were hardly the most important. Far more relevant was the interaction Al Gray had with the men and women designing and developing the systems. According to those who closely observed him, and from information provided by Colonel Don Layne, Gray had a major impact on both the designers and their designs.

Gray's previous SIGINT-related research and development work at HQMC combined with his understanding of engineering issues made him a highly sought commodity among the designers of new sensors and the communications systems needed to support them. Thus, Gray's technical acumen coupled with his understanding for intelligence requirements and issues enhanced his ability to communicate effectively with engineers and scientists, and Gray's briefings soon affected the overall design of various DCPG products and systems. One example of how Gray affected the DCPG programs was in respect to the accuracy of the positions reported.

The engineers and scientists wanted NVA truck positions given to the closest meter. Unfortunately, 1968 long pre-dated the advent of the Global Positioning System, which was the first advancement that actually permitted such accuracy. Gray

Figure 1.8
Brigadier General Fred Haynes, Lieutenant Colonel Earnest Cheatham, Lieutenant
Colonel Al Gray, and Lieutenant Colonel Bob Burhans, Executive Officer, Marine Barracks,
Washington. General Haynes presented Cheatham with a Navy Cross earned at the Battle
of Hué and Gray with the Legion of Merit with Combat "V." Haynes had been the MAF
G–3 when Gray commanded the Radio Battalion units in Vietnam; General Haynes
would later command the 2nd Division while Gray served in that famous unit. Lieutenant
General Ernie Cheatham was a very highly respected warrior whom many, including Al
Gray, thought would be the 29th Commandant before General Gray was selected to serve
in that billet. Bob Burhans and Al Gray served together in the Pacific on numerous occa-
sions. A superb officer (also a poster Marine), Burhans and Gray remain lifelong friends. [17]

certainly appreciated the need for accuracy, but he demonstrated that the requested
location precision was well beyond the capability of the technology that existed at
that time in northern I Corps of Vietnam. It was a matter of operational reality
overcoming drawing board optimism. Gray's view prevailed, and the designers built
in a bigger probability of error into their designs. Such operational inputs affected
the implementation of *Dyemarker* as well as *Igloo White*, the large-scale integrated
computer system installed in Thailand.

Figure 1.9
Colonel Benjamin Read, Lieutenant Colonel Al Gray, Mrs. Emily Gray, Brigadier
General Fred Haynes, and Mrs. Ann Dodson, a Gray family friend. Ben Read, a
Navy Cross holder from the Chosen Reservoir in Korea, had been frustrated in his
attempts to have then–Major Gray awarded a Legion of Merit with Combat "V" for
his earlier service with the 12th Marines. Colonel Read was proud when General Fred
Haynes presented Gray with the Legion of Merit with Combat "V" for his accomplish-
ments as Commanding Officer of the Radio Battalion Sub-Unit in Vietnam.[18]

Igloo White was a massive, 1968 state-of-the-art mainframe computer that tied
together the impressively complex system that the DCPG had deployed. Vast arrays
of ground sensors were connected by data links to aircraft orbiting above. When the
acoustic or seismic sensor was activated, the unit would start broadcasting a signal.
From the planes, the data was relayed to the base in Thailand, where a dizzying
assortment of displays permitted operators to track the infiltrators. The operators
in Thailand could choose to launch ground attack aircraft or, as was often the case,

simply direct orbiting attack jets to specific target locations. When the system was working properly, the trigger of a ground sensor (usually a series of ground sensors) was answered within five minutes by bombs dropping on the suspected area. But the sensors were not just used to provide targets for bombs.

Al Gray was among the first officers to note that gathering information from the array of ground sensors could also be turned into intelligence; indeed, it was not simply useful to detect targets for bombs. Sensor information could provide a means to monitor activity, develop knowledge of the enemy's operational patterns, and fill many gaps in the enemy intelligence picture. Often, Gray theorized, gathering information would be much more beneficial to friendly forces and their commanders than simply attacking whenever and wherever the sensors were activated. Gray's unique background and recent experience in Da Nang and I Corps gave credence to his ideas, which in turn gave rise to operational manuals and procedures.

Just because Lieutenant Colonel Gray was briefing the President's Science Board did not mean he changed his approach to briefings or honestly giving his opinions. There was much interest in the value of the *McNamara Line* – the trace that had been scraped out between Gio Linh and Con Tien while Gray was with the 12th Marines. The DCPG was, of course, a major proponent of the trace. Asked his opinion while briefing the Board, Gray maintained what had always been his opinion – the trace was a mistake that tied down American forces while hardly slowing the enemy infiltration at all. When one of the Army generals assigned to the DCPG heard that the Marine Lieutenant Colonel was espousing views contrary to the institutional estimate, Gray was called on the carpet and given a thorough reprimand. But reprimands did not change Al Gray's opinion, facts based on reality did. The dispute was raised to the level of the Director, Lieutenant General Lavelle. After listening to Gray's stance, Lavelle told the Marine to continue to express his beliefs as he saw fit. It is unlikely that even Lavelle would have caused Gray to modify his views, but having the Air Force General back him up meant a lot to an officer steadfast in his beliefs and extremely thorough in his preparation. The aforementioned Army general became a loyal Al Gray supporter in later years.

Al Gray speculated that the possible geopolitical repercussions of the DCPG's activities had as much to do with the organization's secrecy as its development of new sensors and bombs did. If, for example, the world knew the extent to which the United States operated out of Thailand and the amount of bombs, bomblets and sensors dropped across a wide swath of Laos, Cambodia and North Vietnam, there may have been an international reaction. Unlike much of what is written about the DCPG, Al Gray recalls that certainly members of Congress knew of its existence as early as 1968, because he personally briefed them. Of course, the technology innovations derived from the DCPG effort surely merited close-hold, secret status.

Although brief, Al Gray's time at the DCPG was hardly boring. He maintained a very tiring personal schedule. In addition to working his customary long hours at the office, he usually went into work on Saturday mornings, using that relatively quiet time to keep up with dispatches from the war zone, prepare briefings for other sections, and whatever else required a relatively interrupted free work time. The classification of the work meant that he could not take it home, which permitted his companion, Lucky, to have more time with his master. It also permitted Gray to attend evening classes while working toward his college degree. Almost weekly, sometime after mid-day on Saturdays, Al Gray would make the long drive up to New Jersey to check in with mom. Although she was doing well, and had some relatives nearby, Gray recognized that eventually the house would be too much for her to manage. After spending Sunday in Point Pleasant Beach, Lucky and his Marine would make the trip back down the New York to Washington corridor and get ready to repeat the trip the next weekend. There was not much time for a personal life for the 40-year-old bachelor, though he could not help but notice the bevy of attractive secretaries at the DCPG who kept the organization humming.

During his eleven months in this joint military and civilian environment at the DCPG, observers repeatedly lauded Gray's briefing skills, and the positive effects such briefings had on various audiences, particularly the system and product design teams and those responsible for the employment of the devices. Gray was cited for demonstrated extraordinary military professionalism and competence in production of intelligence information that had a direct bearing on the design and development of a classified system of great national importance and urgency. Other observers commented on the quality and quantity of his briefings on a wide range of audiences including DoD, CIA, NSA, and all the action agencies of the various services.

Shortly before Gray was transferred, the organization was modified so that he became the officer in charge of all intelligence activities within the DCPG, with officers of higher grade reporting to him. Gray's leadership style made this inconsequential and the organization flourished. Certainly, whoever was in charge never really mattered in Gray's mind, so long as the mission was accomplished. He had more than earned the respect and trust of everyone at the DCPG, but it was time to return to the Marine Corps. Gray was detached from the DCPG and immediately reported to Quantico in December 1968.

As Al Gray often says, it is amazing what can be accomplished if it does not matter who gets the credit.

THE VIETNAM WAR REACHES A TURNING POINT

THE TÊT OFFENSIVE, JANUARY 1968

Al Gray had spent 28 months in Vietnam and when he left in January 1968, he thought that he might have understood the overall situation as well as any officer then serving. After all, as Commanding Officer of the Radio Battalion, and having worked closely with all aspects of the Marine intelligence apparatus in I Corps, Gray was one of the architects of what by 1968 had become a very capable, and very effective, instrument of the Marine air-ground task force.

As Lieutenant Colonel Gray left Da Nang, the Radio Battalion was at the top of its game. Through intercept, analysis, direction finding, and just plain hard work, the Marine cryptologists had broken down everything the North Vietnamese and Viet Cong were doing, and what they were planning to do. The Marines had precise insight into the impending attack that was building in I Corps. Marines knew where the NVA were building large field hospitals, where they planned to use culverts under roads; they knew in precise detail almost everything about the attacks – everything except the exact time. Thus, returning to the United States on emergency leave, Lieutenant Colonel Gray was sanguine about the prospects for destroying the enemy forces when then assault was made.

All this information had been fed to the Commanding General of III Marine Amphibious Force, Lieutenant General Robert E. Cushman, Jr. Indeed, as the Christmas, New Year's and Têt holidays approached, even General Westmoreland sensed a coming communist threat. While the communists looked at the recent history of the Allies agreeing to ceasefires during those holidays, and built their plans in anticipation of such a ceasefire, Westmoreland convinced his South Vietnamese counterparts to minimize any stand down from operations. As a result, the ARVN canceled leave and holiday passes for the majority of their forces. Such action would prove decisive in the coming engagement.

What General Cushman, and probably even General Westmoreland, did not realize was how well the communists had coordinated their political and military goals. Since the communist offensive would require a significant buildup of supplies in the South, the foremost NVA political goal was to convince the Allies to stop the bombing in North Vietnam. A communist agent was sent to secretly negotiate with the American Embassy in Saigon. His message to the Americans was simple:

stop the bombing and North Vietnam would agree to negotiate a settlement. The NVA move was music to President Lyndon Johnson's ears, and after a couple low-level contacts, Johnson agreed to halt the bombing in early 1968. Of course, Johnson did not consult with Westmoreland before agreeing to meet the NVA, so while Westmoreland was anticipating a ground threat in South Vietnam, Johnson's actions permitted an unimpeded buildup of supplies and materiel in southern North Vietnam and along the Ho Chi Minh Trail. The NVA, in the midst of advanced planning a major assault timed to begin with Têt, played the Americans like a violin. Of course, American tactical commanders had little, if any, effect on American political moves and were left holding the bag. Not that the offensive turned out badly for the Allies – except on television.

The communist offensive was led by the Viet Cong. By 1968, the communists realized that the South Vietnamese and American intelligence would have read-ily detected the presence of large numbers of NVA in the south. Why? Because the North Vietnamese spoke a distinctly different dialect – one readily identified by local villagers or by linguists monitoring NVA radio links. Consequently, the local forces were to lead the attack, with Phase II being consolidated by regular NVA units. The communists also expected large portions of the population to rise up in rebellion against their "puppet" masters. Three primary objectives headed the communist plan: Saigon, especially the American Embassy and Tan Son Nhut Airfield; Da Nang, home to major American naval and air bases; and Hué, the ancient capital.

The attack occurred on the morning of January 31. It was an unmitigated disaster for communist forces. To their credit however, the communist leadership in Hanoi got every inch of propaganda gain from the affair, aided and abetted by pictures and video from the American press. For certain, the American press did not cause the outcome of the war to change dramatically, but the reportage of Têt clearly shows how corrupt and lacking in objectivity American reporters were. Two examples are illustrative of how events were portrayed to the American public.

A communist sapper squad attacked the American Embassy in Saigon during the night. After breeching the wall with a satchel charge, the squad killed two military policemen who were defending the grounds outside the Embassy building. Evidently, however, the MPs had killed the leaders of the attacking force. The rest of the sappers milled about and made desultory assaults against the Embassy, but were repulsed by the Marine Security Guard detachment. No communist ever got inside the Embassy building, and all were killed by early morning. Yet the headlines from the Associated Press (AP) trumpeted in the newspapers in the United States words that indicated the communists had occupied portions of the American Embassy. The AP had chosen to create the most provocative possible headlines given the actual circumstances on the ground. But at least the AP had a real reporter, albeit an incompetent one, writing about events in Saigon. The United Press International (UPI), seeing that something big was happening but not having a journalist on site, simply made up dispatches; an editor in New York wrote the UPI accounts. Accuracy, objectivity, analysis, and trust were missing from the reports from both wire services; however, the UPI actions were entirely inexcusable.[19]

Only in Hué City, where there surely was some complicity from the local ARVN units, were the communists in any way successful. Hué became one of the signature battles of the war for the Marine Corps, whose infantry dislodged the attackers only after days of horrific combat with heavy losses on both sides. But the combat gave the press many days of combat footage while commentators like Walter Cronkite expressed dismay that the Americans could have been so surprised by the scale and fury of the communist assault. Al Gray, watching newscasts unfold from the sanctuary of his motel room was appalled by the interpretation of events put forth by Cronkite and his ilk. After all, if the newsmen could misinterpret, or misstate, the situation in Vietnam, what else were they misinterpreting or misstating? Cronkite's signature sign-off his television broadcast was to say, "That's the way it is" and then give the date. However, Gray, already skeptical of the press after his experience at Gio Linh, would never again pay attention to the evening newscasts.

A stunning defeat on the battlefield was turned into a propaganda victory for the communists, aided and abetted by the American press. Nevertheless, Cronkite's editorializing that the war had become at best a stalemate had a tremendous effect on President Johnson, who remarked, "If I've lost Cronkite, I've lost Middle America."[20]

Not that the American military helped the situation. General Westmoreland, outfitted in a heavily starched uniform and spit-shined boots, was photographed looking at the sappers' bodies inside the Embassy compound. The American commander never looked so out of touch. And he never again enjoyed the unfettered confidence of the military chain of command or the President. Indeed, because Tết was viewed as a defeat by the press and anti-war crowd, which included many politicians, Westmoreland's planned relief and subsequent return to the United States was delayed. Johnson thought he could not turn over command to General Creighton Abrams lest it appear that Westmoreland was relieved for cause.

After Tết, the original architects of the American war strategy, such as it was, were all soon gone from the stage. McNamara was sent to the World Bank. Maxwell

ne President of the Institute for Defense Analyses. Henry Cabot
sent to West Germany as Ambassador. And on March 31, 1968, the real
hell dropped when President Lyndon Baines Johnson announced that he
uld not seek re-election.

There were changes in the Marine Corps as well. General Wallace M. Greene, Jr.
retired and was replaced by General Leonard F. Chapman on January 1, 1968. With
the Marine role in Vietnam well established, Chapman did not have to maneuver
as much as his predecessor to make his views known to the Joint Chiefs; on the
other hand, the very limited role that the JCS had in formulating the strategy under
President Johnson remained the same. Even though some of the cast changed, the
obsequious General Earle G. Wheeler remained Chairman of the Joint Chiefs.
Johnson may have become a lame duck in March with his announcement not to
seek re-election, but he never ceded a major role for military policies to the military leaders. Future presidents could seek no worse role model for their conduct as
Commander-in-Chief than Lyndon Johnson.

AFTERMATH TO TÊT, MARCH THROUGH DECEMBER 1968

The communists did not give up easily on their plan for a major offensive in South
Vietnam. However, militarily they accomplished very little. In fact, calling the offensive a military disaster for the North Vietnamese is not at all gratuitous. The Viet
Cong's regular units inside South Vietnam were simply obliterated. After March
1968, the war was simply a North versus South affair. No longer was there any meaningful South Vietnamese component to the communist chain of command. On the
other hand, without even incurring the military losses that they would sustain later
in the year, the communists had achieved more than they could have imagined in
their wildest dreams. The American press, a significant force in shaping public opinion, had been almost entirely co-opted. More importantly, the American President,
the leading advocate for the war was badly shaken; so badly that one could say he
was psychologically beaten. After Têt, Johnson spent his remaining time in office
trying to wind down the war.

Johnson's attitude was a godsend to the communists, because after the military events of 1968 and early 1969, their forces needed time to rest, refit, reform
and retrain. All across South Vietnam the communist forces were badly beaten.
In I Corps, where the NVA attempted to go toe-to-toe with the Marines,
they were routed, although not without inflicting heavy casualties on the
Americans and ARVN. Allied firepower far exceeded anything that the North
Vietnamese had experienced; moreover, the individual American fighting man

was more resolute, dedicated and much more willing to endure hardship th the communists had calculated.

On October 31, the haphazard, usually frenetic but always disjointed direction of the war by Johnson reached its convoluted conclusion. Even as he withdrew from the Presidential race, Johnson continued to be the primary architect of the war. While ground combat, as reflected in the number of casualties, reached new levels of brutality, the President announced "the immediate cessation of all air, naval and artillery bombardment of North Vietnam effective November 1."[21] Johnson's announcement, christened the "October Surprise" and seen as a political decision meant to influence the coming Presidential election, failed. Johnson had given up his attempt to steer a middle course between all-out war and what Maxwell Taylor had called a graduated response to North Vietnamese aggression. Still, there was no progress toward a negotiated settlement of the war. Johnson would leave office a bitter and frustrated man, but he could largely blame the image in the mirror for the majority of his difficulties.[22]

As the support for the war eroded at home, as the draft became increasingly unpopular, as draft dodgers fled to Canada in larger and larger numbers, and as anti-war demonstrations increased in both number and anger, ground combat continued to intensify. The troops in the field, with few exceptions, conducted themselves admirably. But Westmoreland's request for additional troops to increase the pressure on communist forces inside South Vietnam fell on deaf ears in Washington. The man who had become the face of the war (Westmoreland was on the cover of *TIME Magazine* four times and was their "Man of the Year" in 1965) had no more cards to play. His publicity tour of the United States in late 1967, when he hinted that the war was going better and would soon be over, seemed empty after the events of Tết, especially given the media spin of the events of Tết. Had Westmoreland received the additional 200,000 troops and had Johnson not reduced the bombing pressure on the North (before stopping it altogether) who knows what might have happened? In any event, Westmoreland left the stage and General Creighton Abrams, a beloved figure to most soldiers, became the Commanding General of MAC(V) in July 1968. He would slowly but surely alter the U.S. policy; in retrospect, it was too little too late.[23]

General Abrams had been scheduled to relieve Westmoreland months before – about the time of the Tết Offensive. That attack caused Johnson to delay making the change; Johnson thought that shifting commanders might signal weakness in the American ranks. So Abrams, who arrived in May 1967 ready to go, remained Westmoreland's deputy. It gave Abrams, a former tank commander in George

...re time to learn the country, its leaders and the challenges ...gave Abrams time to muse the pros and cons of the U.S. strat- ...rst decisions was to abandon the Marine base at Khe Sanh. ...mistake; the Têt Offensive changed the war in many ways. 1968 became ...st expensive year of the war. The tempo of operations for infantry and artillery ...attalions matched or exceeded that of any previous war. The table below shows the casualty figures during 1968 for a typical infantry unit, the "Magnificent Bastards" of the 2nd Battalion, 4th Marines: keep in mind the typical infantry battalion has about 40 officers and roughly 1,000 men.[24]

Month 1968	Number officers/ men*	Wounded in Action	Killed in Action
January	73/1641	13	2
February	71/1740	59	10
March	73/1708	243	53
April	Not available	83	11
May	Not available	190	92
June	68/1631	167	22
July	68/1563	69	7
August	39/1070	43	11
September	38/1156	1	1
October	37/1229	0	0
November	37/1199	16	0
December	38/1152	42	16

Including USN. During the first several months of the year, 2/4 had Battalion Landing Team status, which meant the battalion was augmented by supporting units such as amphibious tractors, tanks and artillery, among other things.

The casualty figures for 2/4 show the Battalion was heavily engaged during the period January – May, when it occupied the northern and eastern most position of any Marine infantry unit.[25] They faced off against the NVA 324B Division, which was infiltrating into the South as part of Phase II of the Têt Offensive. For 2/4, this battle culminated during the period 30 April to 3 May, though intense combat remained in that area through June and into July. By May, the Marines were so extended that U.S. Army infantry battalions began operating in the area formerly covered by 2/4, alone. Such was the ebb and flow of combat throughout 1968. While

2/4 suffered significant casualties, the 324B Division became completely ineffecti[...] and was forced to withdraw back into North Vietnam.

While casualties are a measure of the tempo of operations of an infantry battal-ion, for the artillery a better measure is the number of fire missions delivered and rounds fired. Here are those data for a typical 105mm howitzer unit, the "C" Battery, 1st Battalion, 12th Marines:[26]

Month 1968	Missions Fired	Rounds Fired
January	812	9,355
February	n/a	n/a
March	912	6,560
April	1,072	8,218
May	957	11,351
June	371	5,151
July	115	2,332
August	949	12,5532*
September	661	7,305
October	344	5,475
November	637	19,403*
December	382	8,467

The majority of rounds fired in August and November were "Observed" missions, which means the battery fired in support of reconnais-sance or infantry units who were in contact with the enemy.

A single artillery "mission" may be as small as a single gun firing a couple rounds, or it may be all six guns firing multiple rounds. One only has to divide the number of rounds fired by 30 to see that the artillery sustained a high state of daily action throughout the year, something much more problematic for their infantry broth-ers.[27] In November, Battery "C" averaged firing 647 rounds each day, or almost 27 rounds each hour. The troops were very busy!

There was another questionable McNamara decision that affected the troops in the field by 1968. The bombastic Secretary of Defense was greatly concerned with uniformity and efficiency within his Department. He had forced the Air Force to buy the Navy's F-4 Phantom fighter-bomber, for example, as a means to reduce the logistics and maintenance as well as development costs for a new fighter. When the Marines landed in Vietnam in 1965, they were equipped with the M-14 rifle

...liber 7.62 round. While some old salts disliked the M-14, ...venerable M-1, which had been replaced in the early 1960s, ...cNamara, preferred the M-16, a weapon initially designed for ...se defense units. The M-16 fired a 5.56 caliber round; its high muzzle ..., combined with its smaller size meant that infantrymen could carry more ...mo and have a lighter, smaller weapon to use in the jungle fighting that General Westmoreland expected. Regardless, the M-16 was not ready for use in the field.

Despite protests, McNamara forced the weapons decision on the Marines by getting the President to confirm the change. When introduced into Vietnam, the ammo supplied with the M-16 was too powerful for the weapon, and the chamber would have to be re-engineered to make the rifle more reliable. Even with the eventual changes, however, the M-16 was a terrible weapon for troops actually engaged in fighting. It jammed so frequently that as late as April 1968, then-Captain James E. Livingston, who earned a Medal of Honor at Dai Do that month, required his men to go into the assault with their cleaning rods fully extended and ready for immediate use when, inevitably, the weapon malfunctioned. Facing the Marines were communists equipped with the ubiquitous AK-47. The AK-47 was more reliable, fired a heavier round, and was quite effective in units ranging from local VC guerilla to main force NVA divisions. Moreover, it did not require cleaning in the midst of a firefight. Many Marines grabbed AK-47s and used them during the Battle of Dai Do.

That Americans were fighting a war was significant enough; that American and allied infantry were fighting with a second-class, unreliable rifle was gross malfeasance. The anonymous decision-makers who led McNamara to the M-16 remained safely ensconced in Washington, living their lives without paying any price for their egregious error in prematurely fielding a subpar rifle. Tragically, too many Marines, Soldiers and ARVN troops that had been given the M-16 died or were gravely wounded while attempting to make their weapon function properly.

WASHINGTON, 1968

In the aftermath of Tết, the military calculations between the Chairman of the Joint Chiefs, General Earle Wheeler, General Westmoreland in Saigon and the White House more resembled something from a Byzantine court than high command intent on winning a war. Instead of coming together to develop a strategy to win the war, each faction seemed intent on doing what might look the best to the American public. When the public woke up to pictures of dead communists who had attacked the American Embassy, and then were given a nightly dose of cl. combat involving the Marines in Hué, public support for the war simply eroded.

One Washington change that was made in early 1968 was the resignation of Robert Strange McNamara as Secretary of Defense. The one-time principal architect of the war was gone, replaced by an old Democrat warhorse, and very able lawyer, Clark Clifford. Other than the face in the chair, altering who filled the Secretary's office had very little, if any, effect on the conduct of the war so long as Johnson remained President.

The reporters who wrote histories of the war in Vietnam, men like Karnow, Langguth, and even more recently Phillips, like to suggest that they, the reporters, did not influence public opinion, but rather they followed public reaction to the combat. Such lines of thinking are simply tripe. While some Americans might have formed their opinions based on their personal knowledge of Southeast Asia or from their close relatives, the vast majority of Americans in the 1960s got their news from television, newspapers and news magazines. If American public opinion was shifting away from support for the war, it was largely the result of what Americans read in news accounts or more importantly what they saw on television. To suggest otherwise is disingenuous, yet many commentators about the war do exactly that without providing any alternative reason for the opinion shift. Certainly it is true that the opinions of politicians may lag behind the public, but in the 1960s the opinion makers primarily were the men who gave the six o'clock evening news – led by Walter Cronkite.

The presidential election of 1968 was confusing and in many ways historical. Not since the Civil War in 1864 had a Commander-in-Chief been challenged by his own party while the country was at war. Of course, officially the country was not at war. But Lyndon Johnson was literally run from office when in early 1968 the Democratic Party's peace candidate, Senator Eugene McCarthy of Minnesota, almost beat the sitting President in the New Hampshire Primary. In early March, Senator Robert F. Kennedy of New York and the brother of the late President John Kennedy threw his hat into the ring. Two weeks later, following Johnson's surprise withdrawal, Vice President Hubert H. Humphrey entered the race. Humphrey, though a longtime insider and Vice President, had never had a leading role in the tactical or strategic decisions related to the war. In fact, it is accurate to say that Humphrey had no role in the war.

On the Republican side, Richard M. Nixon had made a remarkable political comeback. Following his defeat by John Kennedy for the Presidency in 1960, he had suffered a gallingly bitter defeat in a bid to become Governor of California in

`ts wrote his political obituary only to see him rise like a
publican primaries, which he handily won.

were engaged in a heated three-man race until Robert Kennedy
ced in Los Angeles on June 5, 1968, shortly after giving his victory
following the Golden State's primary. Kennedy's death, coming so soon
er the assassination of Martin Luther King, Jr. threw the country into turmoil.
The peace activists, together with the civil rights movement, took to the streets and
created mass confusion for the Democrats at their convention in Chicago. Eventually
Humphrey won the nomination, but he was a badly scarred candidate. Nixon won
the general election rather narrowly despite the presence of a third party candidate
who took 13% of the vote. That candidate, Governor George Wallace of Alabama,
skimmed votes away from Nixon and had as a running mate the retired Air Force
General Curtis E. LeMay, the same officer who advocated bombing Vietnam back
to the Stone Age while serving on Johnson's Joint Chiefs of Staff.

Throughout the campaign, Nixon spoke of achieving "peace with honor," but when
he failed to put forth a plan, the reporters gave it the name "Nixon's secret plan to
end the war." It turned out that not only was the plan secret, but also it was largely
imaginary. Soon after his inauguration, the new President resumed the bombing and started going after communist sanctuaries in Cambodia. *Vietnamization*
became the by-word and Nixon announced that the Marine ground units would
leave Vietnam by the end of 1969.

While using Henry Kissinger and others to cajole President Thieu, Nixon also
made a great effort to ensure that Thieu understood his everlasting support for
the Republic of Vietnam's independence. Though he withdrew troops from the
ground war, Nixon opened the air war substantially. New targets became assessable
to American Airmen, and no longer was the President of the United States developing target lists or dictating routes of ingress and egress to them.

But the American public's attitude toward the war was being influenced by
factors beyond the presidential race and the editorial slant of reporters covering the
events in Southeast Asia. The Civil Rights Act of 1964, the landmark legislation of
the Johnson Administration that passed only when Republicans joined progressive
Democrats to overcome Southern Democrat opposition, had not really ended the
quest for equality in the United States. While Martin Luther King never challenged the war on racial bases, he did eloquently speak of individual rights, respect
and humanity. The critics of the war used many of the same themes to voice their
opposition. By 1968, many of the anti-war protestors were also civil rights protestors,

though the two movements had not been merged into one. Race was a major polarizing issue by the time of the elections in 1968.

At the same time that race was becoming a primary factor in American society, the effects of a Johnson-McNamara experiment were adversely impacting the U.S. military. In 1966, McNamara had implemented *Project 100,000*. *Project 100,000* introduced into the military men and women (mostly men) who were not otherwise qualified to serve because their intelligence entry tests scores were not high enough. It was a social experiment of the worst kind. Commanders, already under pressure to hone and train their units to peak efficiency in order to meet the intense combat conditions then being encountered in Vietnam, now had the burden of integrating men with lower intelligence quotas into frontline combat units. Such men simply could not learn as fast as typical Soldiers and Marines, and the innate capabilities and adaptability of the American fighting man has always been the hallmark of the country's military services.[28]

By the end of 1968, the combination of politics, reporting, social change and *Project 100,000* were combining to affect the U.S. military, and not in a good way.

SAIGON, LATE 1968 AND EARLY 1969

With the announcement in late 1968 that the Marines would be leaving Vietnam, there should have been no doubt in President Thieu's mind that the war was changing; most assuredly, it was. But reading the Washington tea leaves was never a great strength of Vietnamese politicians, at least those not located in Hanoi. Those in the capital of the North did a remarkably good job in that regard.

When Nixon broadened the air war, and then invaded Cambodia intent on closing the Ho Chi Minh Trail, President Thieu had every reason to believe that such a man would not abandon South Vietnam. Plus, Nixon reiterated his support to the Thieu government every bit as often and with all the same stress that marked LBJ's commitment. Given that Thieu was worried first and foremost about staying in power, it is not at all surprising that he chose to take the American presidents at their word.

It was a fatal mistake.

NOTES AND REFERENCES

1. The Defense Communications Planning Group (DCPG) was later renamed the Defense Special Projects Group (DSPG).
2. General Gray has received many honors and tributes, but among his proudest is the street named in his honor in Rahway. He is a true son of New Jersey and very proud of his home state.

3. Many comments about Gray in Vietnam specifically mention his commitment to winning the war.

4. From General Gray's private collection.

5. From General Gray's private collection.

6. From General Gray's private collection.

7. From General Gray's private collection.

8. From General Gray's private collection.

9. From General Gray's private collection.

10. Interview with Colonel Donald Q. Layne, USMC (Ret) by author, December 2010.

11. By the end of 1967, McNamara was full of doubts about both the air war and the war in general. His relationship with Johnson had deteriorated as LBJ assumed a much greater role in the prosecution of the air war. The DCPG funding, however, continued unabated long after McNamara had left the scene in early 1968. See Volume 1, Chapter 5, Part B for much more about the DCPG early days.

12. "Lavelle's Private War," *Time Magazine*, June 26, 1972, http://www.time.com/time/magazine/article/0,9171,906068,00.html. In 1971, General Lavelle and his staff watched an immense buildup of North Vietnamese forces just outside the borders of South Vietnam. Troubled by orders not to bomb inside North Vietnam, Lavelle took matters into his own hands and ordered strikes against the enemy concentrations that preceded the Easter Offensive of 1972. That was bad enough (especially for people in Washington), but he also ordered reports falsified. A sergeant's letter to an Iowa senator broke the story and ended in Lavelle's retirement as a 2-star. Calls for a Lavelle court-martial were rejected. That interpretation of events was according to *Time Magazine*. However, when the Nixon Presidential Tapes were released to historians, more information became available which seems to support Lavelle's consistent contention that he had been authorized to make the strikes he directed. Casey, Aloysius and Casey, Patrick, "Lavelle, Nixon, and the White House Tapes," *Air Force Association Magazine Online*, February 2007, Volume 90, Number 2, http://www.airforce-magazine.com/MagazineArchive/Pages/2007/February%202007/0207tapes.aspx. Of course, working for men like Nixon and Melvin Laird, politicians, was not easy and so Lavelle remained quietly in retirement, consistently stating he did the right thing and it was authorized. The Lavelle affair is but another strange episode of the Vietnam War, an episode that must not be repeated in future wars. Links checked, 2011.

13. There are many sources for the General Lavalle story in 2010; here is one online site: http://www.npr.org/templates/story/story.php?storyId=129013259. Link checked, 2012.

14. MITRE is the commercial engineering arm of the Massachusetts Institute of Technology, and in the 1960s and 1970s it was an engineering and scientific powerhouse within DoD. Also see, Volume 1, Chapter 6 for more about the DCPG.

15. From General Gray's private collection.

16. See Volume 1, Chapters 5 and 6 for more about Gray's activities along the *McNamara Line*.

17. From General Gray's private collection. The whole issue of medals for senior officers is anathema to General Gray. By the time he left Vietnam in 1968, he had been personally decorated with a Silver Star and three Bronze Stars, two Vietnamese Crosses of Gallantry and three Purple Hearts. He had declined to permit nominations for a second Silver Star, a fourth Bronze Star and numerous Air Medals to be forwarded for consideration, and he took no part in any discussions about upgrading his awards – such as when the Deputy CG III MAF, the legendary General Ray Murray, wanted his third Bronze Star for heroism elevated to a Navy Cross or when Colonel Ben Read was furious that his proposed Legion of Merit for Gray turned into a Bronze Star. Of course, mention of the Joint Service Commendation Medal awarded Lieutenant Colonel Gray for his performance at the DCPG did not make

it into this text. Nothing got the author in more trouble than trying to work into the narrative information about General Gray's awards. General Gray thinks that Napoleon, early in has career, had it right: medals are for the troops and lieutenants, not senior officers, except on rare occasions.

18. From General Gray's private collection.

19. Oberdorfer, pp. 31, 26-33, gives AP's "fourth lead attack" bulletin, filed by Peter Arnett at 0730 Saigon time as the seminal reportage of the attack on the embassy. Based on an interview with "an overwrought MP," Arnett reported that the chancery was captured (there were MPs on both sides of the chancery building unknowingly exchanging fire with one another!). The information arrived in the United States just in time for the NBC television evening news, and that is how Chet Huntley reported it. Two hours later, at 0930 Saigon time, a UPI desk man in New York generated a copy cat story based on no reportage at all; more accurately, he simply plagiarized the AP account. It is interesting to note that Don Oberdorfer's book is one reason that one expert on the war, Dr. John Guilmartin, does not view the expression "honest reporter" as an oxymoron.

20. Wicker, Tom (January 26, 1997). "Broadcast News." *New York Times*, January 26, 1997. http://www.nytimes.com/books/97/01/26/reviews/970126.26wickert.html. Retrieved 2010-11-12.

21. The so-called "October Surprise" failed to end the war, thereby failing to benefit Johnson or Hubert Humphrey, the serving Vice President and Democrat nominee during the elections of 1968. The North Vietnamese may have been offered a better deal by Henry Kissinger, the representative for the Republican nominee, Richard Nixon, at the Paris Peace Talks.

22. Few historians applaud Lyndon Johnson's performance as Commander-in-Chief. Perhaps the most critical is McMaster.

23. For a detailed look at General Abrams, see Lewis Sorley's book, *A Better War*. Sorley is a West Point graduate and like Abrams was a tanker. He also was Al Gray's faculty advisor at the Army War College in 1973-1974. Sorley released a new book dealing with General Westmoreland in 2012. *Westmoreland: The General Who Lost the War* gives a highly critical view of Westmoreland, though in this author's opinion, the General had lots of civilian and military help in Washington to "lose the war."

24. Lieutenant Colonel Joseph R. (Bull) Fisher first called his men "Magnificent Bastards" in 1965 shortly after the Battalion arrived in South Vietnam. Lieutenant Colonel A.E. (Gene) Bench officially adopted the slogan for the Battalion in 1967. The slogan continues in use even through the politically correct days of 2012.

25. All figures are from *2ⁿᵈ Battalion, 4ᵗʰ Marines Command Chronologies* for each month of 1968.

26. A Marine 105 mm howitzer artillery battery is commanded by a captain and has six guns. Typically, one battery supports an infantry battalion. For example, A/1/12 might support (primarily) 1ˢᵗ Battalion, 1ˢᵗ Marines; Bravo Battery would support (primarily) 2ⁿᵈ Battalion, 1ˢᵗ Marines, and so forth. Of course, when the action is hot, any firing battery within range of the target might fire in support regardless of the unit needing help.

27. All figures are from *1ˢᵗ Battalion, 12ᵗʰ Marines Command Chronologies* for each month of 1968. If the infantry has sustained a high tempo of operations, soon casualties would reduce the combat power needed to successfully conduct missions against the enemy.

28. Almost every military historian has noted this. See, for example: http://thearmedhistorian.com/2011/07/26/the-backbone-of-the-army-how-vietnam-led-to-the-non-commissioned-officer-as-a-combat-leader/. Link checked 2012.

CHAPTER 2

STEAM & SCAMP
NIXON TAKES CHARGE

STEAM & SCAMP

Lieutenant General Herman Nickerson, Jr., Commanding General of the III Marine Amphibious Force (III MAF), Vietnam, listened attentively to Lieutenant Colonel Al Gray. The General had recently assumed his command, and the circumstances in I Corps, where the III MAF controlled all U.S. ground forces, were rapidly changing. Newly elected President Richard M. Nixon had embarked on the "Vietnamization" of the war. That meant American fighting units were to be withdrawn, starting with the Marines. By the end of 1969, no Marine combat units would remain. The Lieutenant Colonel was reporting his findings. Asked by Nickerson to evaluate the reconnaissance, intelligence and surveillance situation in I Corps, the briefer had several recommendations, but he also knew that the General would have many questions. A veteran of three wars, and despite his nickname, Herman the German, as he was commonly called, had a bright, curious mind. More important, he was not reluctant to improvise or introduce new policies or procedures, especially in the areas covered by the Lieutenant Colonel Gray's briefing. Among many things, the General wanted his Force Recon units to conduct deep reconnaissance throughout the I Corps Tactical Zone.

General Nickerson had specifically requested the outgoing, optimistic, highly proficient Gray. The younger officer had a varied service and had served in both combat arms and intelligence postings. He had already served the better part of three and a half years in Vietnam, and during his last six months he had commanded the Radio Battalion for the then III MAF Commanding General, Lieutenant General Robert E. Cushman. Previously, he had been the S-3 Operations Officer of the 12th Marines, while concurrently serving as the regiment's Senior Aerial Observer. Again extending his tour, he commanded a composite artillery battalion and all U.S. forces at the northernmost base in South Vietnam. Earlier, in 1964, he commanded a unit that conducted independent special intelligence operations in I Corps. Moreover, he had just completed an assignment at the Defense Communications Project Group (DCPG), the secret organization in Washington that had developed a series of sensors and munitions that were in widespread use in Vietnam. In addition, Gray had worked closely at the Development Center with Major Alex Lee, whom Nickerson had selected to organize and command the III MAF deep reconnaissance unit. In Nickerson's mind, the Lieutenant Colonel was the perfect officer to meet the challenge of ensuring all aspects of intelligence, reconnaissance and surveillance were streamlined, optimized and made as effective as possible.

The primary recommendation that Gray made was the establishment of a combined Surveillance, Reconnaissance, and Intelligence Center (SRIC). The SRIC was the culmination of the Lieutenant Colonel's long-held belief that all-source, fused intelligence and operations were in-separable. Located immediately adjacent to the III MAF Operations Center (classification issues precluded the merger of the two), the SRIC was staffed and organized in a way that promoted the fusion of information from each subsection in what the designer hoped would be a seamless and transparent fashion. If that could be done, then instead of 1+1+1=3, the product of the SRIC would be more like 32=9.

The Lieutenant Colonel liked being in Vietnam. Committed to an American victory, he thought his efforts paid the greatest dividends in the war zone. But his temporary duty at III MAF, originally expected to last a month, had been extended to almost five months. One afternoon Lieutenant General Henry Buse was visiting General Nickerson and he espied the Lieutenant Colonel, "Hey, spook, get over here. Spook, you better get your butt back to Quantico, they think you are UA!"[1] Given the crowd that heard the General's order, Gray had little wiggle room, though he did at least finagle a short delay. He was, of course, well aware that six months was the longest length of a temporary additional duty without a formal change of orders by Headquarters Marine Corps. It was with lots of regret and no recourse that Al Gray gave up his exciting task to return to his real assignment at the Development Center.

DEVELOPMENT CENTER, MARINE CORPS SCHOOLS, QUANTICO, VA, NOVEMBER 1968

The Marine Corps was in the midst of significant change. The elections of November 1968 swept Republican Richard M. Nixon into the Presidency. Reporters were skeptical of Nixon and his "secret plan" to end the war, but there was no doubt the new President was determined to turn the ground combat role over to the South Vietnamese. The first step was to reduce the Marine Corps presence in the war zone. The plan was to remove all Marine ground units during 1969, a plan that would have significant implications for the Commanding General, III Marine Amphibious Corps.

Lieutenant Colonel Al Gray, most recently assigned to the hush-hush Defense Communications Project Group, was posted to the Development Center at Quantico in late 1968. The intelligence section, which was part of the Ground Combat Division, received additional tasking and Gray was sent there.

The Commanding General of Marine Corps Schools, as Quantico was called in those days, was Lieutenant General James Masters, the same officer who had been the G-2 at Headquarters Marine Corps when Captain Al Gray arrived there in

1961. And Masters was the same general who had followed Gray's activities at the National Security Agency in the late 1950s. Yes, General Masters knew Al Gray very well, and he had been agitating to get Gray to the Development Center ever since the younger officer had returned from Vietnam. Finally, Masters' pleas fell on sympathetic ears and Al Gray was short toured at the DCPG. The Director there, Lieutenant General John Lavelle, USAF, seeing that Gray had orders to "Marine Corps Schools," thought his best and most experienced briefer was to be sent off to a professional school, and therefore General Lavelle did not challenge the orders. Gray, who had long ago learned to accept his assignment and get on with it, returned to the Crossroads of the Marine Corps.

General Masters, in command at Quantico, sent for Gray immediately and the two spent most of the morning together. The General outlined some ideas he had for improving operations and intelligence. He then gave Gray a multi-volume study entitled *Towards a Marine Corps War College* and told the Lieutenant Colonel to review it, and then submit recommendations. Among items Gray noted in his response was the fact that the Breckinridge Library facility did not meet the war college requirements in terms of library size and resources. Gray kept the report and it became his basic reference for the Marine Corps University initiative in 1987.[2]

The Intelligence Section of the Development Center had been tasked with urgent requirements in response to the changing conditions in I Corps and its designated new Commanding General, Herman Nickerson. For example, Nickerson needed new techniques and procedures related to long-range reconnaissance. Then-Major Alex Lee and Captain Buck Coffman were assigned to complete that task, working for an officer who recently returned from a convalescent leave, Lieutenant Colonel Jerry Polakoff – the same officer that Gray had replaced nearly a year before at the DCPG. By the end of 1968, the Marines in Vietnam were not doing long-range reconnaissance; all recon patrols occurred within the firing range of the artillery umbrella. Nickerson, knowing the artillery coverage was going to be much less given the impending drawdown in Marine units, desired to have eyes on the ground to complement sensors that the DCPG had developed, and deep recon by Force Reconnaissance units was the only answer. He relied on Lee and Coffman to come up with a plan, and then brought those officers to the war zone to implement it. But before they departed, they shared an office with Al Gray.

Major Joseph Flynn, another superb Marine well known to Al Gray, was also part of the section, working on other aspects of the intelligence problem. Though busy, the section was running smoothly, with officers who clearly knew their responsibilities. The addition of Al Gray would undoubtedly augment those already present, but there was an issue that needed addressing. Al Gray would be the senior man, but Jerry Polakoff was doing a great job and the powers to be wanted him to remain in charge. Polakoff was a very bright, highly engaged officer who had been at the Development Center for several months; he had an outstanding working relationship throughout the command structure and with his subordinates. How would Gray feel about reporting to someone his junior?[3]

Having just left a DCPG environment where colonels informally reported to him, a lieutenant colonel, Gray did not hesitate to accept the arrangement. He was well aware that Polakoff was a superb officer with a healthy curiosity, and knew they would work well together. Far from being a mark against Gray, something that many fear when asked to serve under juniors, Gray's Commanding General, Alan J. Armstrong, and Chief of Staff, Colonel Ike Fenton, applauded his acceptance of the situation that best met the needs of the Marine Corps.

Thus, Al Gray found himself assigned to Polakoff's section as the Combat Surveillance Officer, sharing office space with Polakoff, Alex Lee, Buck Coffman and Joe Flynn. It was a happy time for Gray, and he loved being back among Marines doing important work in support of the war effort. Gray's sense of humor, his abiding professionalism, hard-working personal example and unmatched knowledge of all things military complemented those already there. The unit churned out an impressive amount of work on a wide variety of intelligence-related topics and systems.

Gray's primary assignment was to finish the work related to employment of ground sensors that Alex Lee had started before turning his attention to the Nickerson requirement. The Marines in Vietnam had successfully deployed the sensors in several different ways, but there was no doctrine regarding their use. Further, given the diversity of missions that the sensors could augment, the Marine Corps knew it could use the experience and insights Gray had gained during his work on the Observatory grounds. While Al Gray was now assigned to Quantico, his contact with the DCPG did not end. Indeed, in many ways his association with the clandestine organization expanded. He quietly continued to support the overall intelligence community, usually on his own time after hours, especially whenever issues arose.

In the fall of 1968, Rear Admiral Elmo R. Zumwalt was assigned as Commander, Naval Forces, Vietnam, and the Chief of the Naval Advisory Group, Military Assistance Command (Vietnam). Zumwalt's command was mostly a brown-water outfit that conducted riverine operations in the area of the Mekong Delta, southwest of Saigon. Therefore, the Admiral became very interested in the sensor program at the DCPG and asked for more detailed briefings of the capability prior to his deployment to Vietnam. The DCPG turned to their best briefer, Al Gray. As a result of these sessions with Gray, Zumwalt asked the DCPG to plan for sensors to be sent to the Mekong Delta Region to support Riverine Force operations. Of course, he also asked for someone to go and explain their utilization. Guess who?

During the late winter and early spring of 1969, the outline of a plan slowly came together to send Al Gray back to Vietnam. He would represent the DCPG in sensor employment matters and he would assist III MAF in embellishing and expanding his old SIGINT/EW Coordination Center idea. As soon as Nickerson took command, in March 1969, Alex Lee and Buck Coffman were ordered to III MAF; Lee was given command of the 3rd Force Reconnaissance Company. Nickerson also wanted an efficient means to coordinate all-source intelligence in I Corps as Al Gray had demonstrated in late 1967; General Nickerson was well aware of Gray's previous efforts, and they seemed the perfect solution. Nickerson had been the Deputy Commanding General when Gray led the Radio Battalion. He also had been the Fiscal Director of the Marine Corps in the early 1960s when the HQMC AO2F section was developing the SIGINT/ EW capabilities and Gray (along with Colonel Beale) had briefed him many times. Unfortunately, the effectiveness of SIGINT/EW center that Gray had established at III MAF in 1967 had eroded more than a little. But given the support of the Commanding General, Gray recognized that more comprehensive and wide-ranging capability could be instituted.

In late spring 1969, Gray received temporary additional duty orders to Vietnam. He would travel with a group of senior DCPG officers, but also undertake a specific assignment at III MAF before finishing his work for Admiral Zumwalt in the area of IV Corps – the Mekong Delta. As was the DCPG fashion, the entire group had orders that gave them permission to travel first-class air all the way to Vietnam. Of course, Al Gray's travel was going to be paid for by the much more parsimonious, some would say frugal, United States Marine Corps. Gray, nevertheless, submitted a request to travel first class; he had never had that luxury and with the rest of the group going that way, he had nothing to lose by the asking for the same travel status. The result was another example of how being good to people, treating them with respect and following their advice can pay future dividends.

Gray's application for first-class travel ended up on the desk of Mr. Meade at HQMC; Meade was the senior civilian in charge of all transportation in the Marine Corps. Mr. Meade had long been an Al Gray supporter dating back to when AO2F sent several major equipment systems to Hawaii in the early 1960s. On those occasions, Captain Gray had made sure to seek Mr. Meade's counsel about how to ensure that the new SIGINT and special communication equipment reached the island in a timely fashion; they had many sessions together working the issues. Gray made sure that every "i" was dotted and every "t" crossed in the paperwork he submitted to justify the equipment's shipping expense. As a result of their interaction, he had become a Meade favorite. So now, several years later, Mr. Meade inquired, "Is this Gray fellow the same one who had been at HQMC earlier?" When assured that it was, in fact, the same officer, Meade promptly approved the request and sent Al Gray off to Vietnam in style.[4]

Within a short time, after ensuring that his mother was comfortable in Point Pleasant Beach, and after leaving Lucky II in a local kennel (one fit for the king that Lucky II had become), Gray left for Saigon.

DEFENSE COMMUNICATIONS PROJECT GROUP OFFICE, MILITARY ADVISORY COMMAND (VIETNAM), APRIL 1969

Captain James M. (Mike) Myatt, United States Marine Corps, was not a happy camper. During his first tour of duty in Vietnam, Myatt had been a platoon and company commander, and served briefly as the S-4 (logistics officer) for an infantry battalion. Now on his second tour, his undergraduate degree in physics had taken him well outside the mainstream of sought-after assignments, at least those desirable to hard-charging infantry officers. He was not ready to fall into a full fledged funk, but he was not exactly sure how a tour of duty that would have him teaching others to employ and exploit ground sensors would be very rewarding.

Enter Lieutenant Colonel Al Gray, canteen cup in hand.

Gray was in Saigon to liaise with the intelligence section of MAC(V) and visit the DCPG offices before continuing to Da Nang. While in Saigon, however, Gray continued his habit to stop by and meet Marines wherever he traveled. In addition to finding out about any new developments that the Marines might tell him about, the occasions were also used to form personal relationships. It was simply Al Gray's standard *walking around leadership* technique.

The newly arrived Captain impressed Gray, though the older officer also detected that perhaps being the sensor *sensei* was not Mike Myatt's first choice for an assignment. If anyone could understand the frustration of not getting his choice in assignments it was Al Gray. He decided to take the younger officer to dinner, something that was highly unusual for the more senior Marine. Gray had no intention of remaining overnight in Saigon; he simply never did that. But the pair enjoyed a steak at one of Saigon's best restaurants while Gray briefed Myatt about everything he ever needed, or wanted, to know about sensors.

Gray explained how sensors could be intelligence game-changers; how sensors should be employed; how sensors worked; how sensors had been used at Khe Sanh and during other battles, and more. Less than 15 minutes into the conversation, Mike Myatt, the physics major, realized that the Lieutenant Colonel knew more about the subject than anybody he had ever met, and that Gray's knowledge extended from A to Z.

Captain Myatt deduced that Lieutenant Colonel Gray undoubtedly had written the manual for employing ground sensors. Gray could explain the design in engineering terms, could describe employment in a way acceptable to Napoleon's corporal, and yet express the operational advantages to any skeptical regimental commander. Myatt was impressed; more importantly, he was energized. He was inspired to take Gray's enthusiasm and knowledge of sensors and to try to ensure that everyone he ever briefed had a reaction similar to his that night at dinner in Saigon. And Myatt never again doubted the importance of his posting.[5]

Al Gray? He was off to Tan Son Nhut Air Base's flight operations center to find return transportation to somewhere out of Saigon. In all probability, Gray would use the return flight time to sleep, thereby permitting him to hit the ground running when he arrived at his next destination. Having shed the DCPG senior officers prior to meeting Captain Myatt, Gray was free to move about the country in accordance with his own schedule.

I CORPS, NORTHERN SOUTH VIETNAM, 1968 - 1969

With the Marine forces starting to draw down, Lieutenant General Nickerson put a high priority on developing a comprehensive surveillance-reconnaissance-intelligence plan that could meet the new realities that would face commanders in I Corps. That is not to say that the situation on the ground was bad; indeed, it had not ever been better dating to the initial thrust by the Marines into northern I Corps in 1966. However, the fledgling ground-sensor operation that III MAF had established was in need of a comprehensive tactical surveillance system to optimize and integrate the effort.

Major General Raymond G. Davis arrived in Vietnam in the spring of 1968. His first assignment was to serve briefly as Deputy to Lieutenant General Richard Stilwell at the 24th Corps Headquarters at Phu Bai. General Stilwell and Davis had a very close rapport. Interestingly, it had been Stilwell who had foiled then-Major Al Gray's deception plan for the Marine Detachment, Advisory Team 1, when Gray was operating on the northwest frontier of Vietnam back in 1964. During his tour with the Army, General Davis learned very well how that service used their

Figure 2.1
General Ray Davis, shown here while serving as Assistant Commandant of the Marine Corps, and Al Gray had a close professional relationship that started in 1956, when Gray was a Captain in Japan and Davis was a Colonel in the G–2 Section of HQMC. Their relationship continued into their retirements from active duty. Like almost all Marines, General Gray held General Davis in the highest esteem. The inscription reads: "To Lt.Col Al Gray: A great Marine! With personal admiration and appreciation for many of your great contributions."[6]

helicopters for mobility. It was a lesson that he modified and then applied with vigor after taking command of the 3rd Marine Division at Phu Bai on 22 May 1968.

Davis was blessed with great regimental commanders, including Colonel Robert Barrow, a future Commandant of the Marine Corps. Barrow, who took command in July 1968, led the 9th Marines. Shortly thereafter Davis flew into Barrow's Command Post for an early meeting between the two officers. After a quick survey of the site, the Commanding General told Barrow to be ready to move. Barrow replied that, indeed, his regiment could react quickly to orders. Davis quietly retorted that when he gave the order, everyone and everything would move! Colonel Barrow chuckled to himself at that prospect; such a stirring, of course, was unheard of at the regimental command post, where some officers and even enlisted Marines seemingly had permanent beds. Despite their utter surprise at the order, when Barrow gave the command to saddle up a few days later, the entire regiment moved out – lock, stock and barrel. And for the next ten weeks it continued to change position on a moment's notice.

General Ray Davis, shown here while serving as Assistant Commandant of the Marine Corps, and Al Gray had a close professional relationship that started in 1956, when Gray was a Captain in Japan and Davis was a Colonel in the G-2 Section of HQMC. Their relationship continued into their retirements from active duty. Like almost all Marines, General Gray held General Davis in the highest esteem.

Davis had learned the lessons of mobility and maneuver well, and he intended to apply them forcefully. Barrow's 9th Regiment would participate in fighting in locations ranging from near the Demilitarized Zone to around Khe Sanh to as far south as the A Shau Valley west of Da Nang. No Marines would have any time to construct permanent beds! *Operation Dewey Canyon* was one of the most successful search and destroy operations of the entire war. Employing innovative tactics that included using CH-53s to airlift artillery into new positions, then attacking enemy artillery with Marine infantry, the 9th Regiment and supporting artillery kept the NVA completely off balance, inflicting numerous casualties and destroying vast amounts of supplies and equipment.[7]

From his assumption of command in May 1968 until he was relieved on April 14, 1969, General Davis had the entire 3rd Marine Division on the offensive and constantly in motion. The enemy, still reeling from their catastrophic defeat during the Tết Offensive in early 1968, never recovered sufficiently to challenge Davis's Marines. General Creighton Abrams, who assumed command of the Military Assistance Command (Vietnam) on 10 June 1968 and held it through June 1972, called Ray Davis the finest division commander of the 50 or so Army and Marine generals with whom he worked in Vietnam. It was high praise and well deserved for the quiet Georgian.

As a result of Davis's work, when Al Gray arrived in country in early April 1969, he found himself in much different conditions than when he left early the previous year. In fact, compared to his time at Gio Linh in 1967, the I Corps Gray encountered in 1969 was absolutely tranquil. So tranquil, in fact, that Gray's old friend from his days at Khe Sanh in 1964, now Major General Ngo Quang Truong, Commanding the ARVN 1st Division, had written a congratulatory note to General Davis in February 1969 that read in part:

> *"With your help, we have not only defeated the enemy at every turn, but have been able to rid our area of responsibility of the Communist aggressors and provide security for the people of Quang Tri and Thua Thien Province to a degree never reached heretofore.*
>
> *As a result of the sacrifices you have made, the Vietnamese people in the 11th DTA will be able to celebrate this traditional day in safety…"*

Indeed, that was the situation Al Gray found when he arrived. Gray drove throughout the region unaccompanied by anything more than an M-16 or carbine; it was quite a change from the frenzied days in 1967 and 1968 when the enemy was very actively trying to wrestle control of the I Corps Tactical Zone. Gray took the time to visit as many outposts, firebases and command posts as he could, gathering information, speaking with the officers and men, and, most of all, observing for himself the conditions throughout the area. As always, when he was without a jeep or vehicle of his own, he bummed rides.

Chief Warrant Officer-4 Don Larson was a platoon leader in the Radio Battalion's Operations Company, and was assigned to a Direction Finding (DF) site in northern I Corps. Larson recalled that on a hot and humid morning one of his men reported an old, dusty officer was approaching the radio direction finding site on foot.[8] He had been dropped off by a truck and walked the couple hundred yards to the DF site. The young Marines knew nothing of the officer, except that he was covered with grime and looked aged. Larson, who loved his self-proclaimed title as the oldest man in I Corps, hurried to see exactly who this old guy might be. He quickly, but disbelievingly, recognized Al Gray. The Radio Battalion units had been alerted that the Gray Ghost was in the area and might be visiting them, though Larson had thought the chance of that was quite remote.

The Chief Warrant Officer offered Lieutenant Colonel Gray his hooch so that the Colonel might clean up and refresh; Larson told Gray he would await him in the operation spaces. When Gray arrived at the door to the work area, which, typical of all SIGINT sites, was surrounded by lots of barbed wire and other obstacles, the Marine on duty refused him entry. After all, the Marine had not seen the necessary clearance message that would permit the visitor access. Larson quickly moved to rectify the situation, telling the Marine that Colonel Gray had been cleared for longer than any of them had been in the Marine Corps, and that without Gray, none of them would have clearances. With the administrative matter successfully dispatched, Al Gray entered and started asking questions ranging from how the technical work was going to how their chow was and how often they got mail.

Larson recalled that one aspect of the operation that Gray was interested in hearing more about was how the radio direction finding data was used to improve the artillery's harassing and interdiction fires. On his ever-present 3x5 cards Gray would record all the data he deemed important. After an hour or so, the Colonel left, walking back down the road looking to hitch a ride to the next location he wanted to visit. There had been no fanfare; no impromptu inspections (though Larson was sure Gray took in everything), and certainly no negative comments about trivial matters inconsequential to the mission. No local commander ever needed to worry about Gray acting like an officer of the Praetorian Guard, nor would he ever begin harassing the men about shaves and haircuts – though he might mention discrepancies to their commanders. Gray spent his time in the countryside evaluating the overall state of affairs and operational effectiveness – not gathering administrative trivia.

III MARINE AMPHIBIOUS FORCE HEADQUARTERS, DA NANG, APRIL - AUGUST 1969

During Al Gray's tenure as Commanding Officer of the Radio Battalion units in Vietnam (July 1967 through January 1968), he had been able to put in place many of the things he strongly believed would improve Marine intelligence operations. He had long encouraged close cooperation, indeed integration, of operations and intelligence. Al Gray thought that all aspects of intelligence, including reconnaissance and surveillance, had to be closely meshed. By using a combination of cryptologic techniques combined with a retrospective operational review of after-action reports generated by the G-3 (operations) staff, Gray and his cohort had broken the key NVA/VC tactical code in 1967. That breakthrough in turn led to a variety of significant intelligence coups during the period that followed. But without the close integration of the operations and intelligence efforts, brought about by the personal commitments of Lieutenant Colonels Veal, Kelly and Gray, the penetration of the NVA code would never have occurred. In III MAF, when Gray had served there earlier, such integration had been the result of personal commitment and hard work on the part of individual officers and staff non-commissioned officers. For General Nickerson's III MAF, Gray hoped to institutionalize the effort.

Lieutenant Colonel Gray decided to concentrate his efforts initially on the mission and area assigned to the 3rd Force Reconnaissance Company, which was supporting the 3rd Marine Division in northernmost I Corps. After all, his good friend Major Alex Lee now led 3rd Force, and Lee's plans, ideas and overall thinking meshed closely with Gray's thoughts and emerging concept. Lee had earned a Silver Star in a previous tour in Vietnam while serving in Lieutenant Colonel Leon N. Utter's 2nd Battalion, 7th Marines during *Operation Starlite*. Further, he was a brilliant officer, a Stanford graduate, and Gray had enormous respect and admiration for the younger man. The two had worked closely together prior to their arrival in at III MAF Headquarters, and others who shared their vision for future intelligence operations joined them. Lieutenant Colonel Donald Q. Layne, recently transferred from the DCPG and now assigned to the MAF G-2 section, was the staff officer responsible for Alex Lee's intelligence activities. Of course, Gray and Layne shared a friendship dating back to their time as lieutenants at the Communications Officer School, though their work together at the DCPG was more relevant to the job at hand.[9]

Alex Lee's mission was very important to General Nickerson. Earlier in the war, the Marines seldom did any deep reconnaissance patrolling. Most recon patrols took place within the range of friendly artillery. By the end of 1968 Marine artillery, supplemented and expanded by the 175mm guns of the U.S. Army's 2nd Battalion, 94th Artillery, covered almost all I Corps. Thus, operating under the "artillery fan," patrols had almost instantaneous fire support available in all types of weather, 24 hours a day, 7 days a week. With the drawdown of Marine units ordered by President Nixon by the end of 1969, that was no longer going to be the case.

Enter Major Alex Lee and Captain Clovis C. "Buck" Coffman, Jr., who served as Lee's Operations Officer. At the Development Center's Intelligence Section, Coffman blended right in with Gray and Lee. He had served in reconnaissance with Al Gray when both were enlisted men in the early 1950s. He had lost his father at a young age and General Nickerson had played an important part in raising young Buck, and surely he was influential in Coffman's desire to become a Marine. In 1966, then-Gunnery Sergeant Coffman earned a Navy Cross while leading a 13-man reconnaissance patrol; he was subsequently awarded a battlefield commission, one of the few given by the Marines during the long Vietnam conflict.[10] It did not take too long before the Lee-Coffman team executed their plan for long-range patrolling outside the artillery fan in order to provide the Commanding General with eyes and ears on the ground throughout the area.

Figure 2.2
Lieutenant Colonel Al Gray at III MAF HQ, Da Nang, 1969. Note the starched utility cover.[11]

Figure 2.3
Lt. Col. Clovis C. "Buck" Coffman, Jr., operations officer,
Third Force Reconnaissance Company.[12]

Figure 2.4
Maj. Alex Lee, commanding officer, Third Reconnaissance Company, prepares
to accompany a team to patrol in the Ashau Valley, December 1969.[13]

Figure 2.5
Major Lee (left) and Lieutenant Coffman (center) enjoy a relaxed moment
with their mentor, General Nickerson, in Vietnam in 1970.[14]

Figure 2.6
Lt. Gen. Herman Nickerson, Jr., 1870. [15]

Gray was excited to dig into the details of establishing an integrated Surveillance, Reconnaissance, and Intelligence Center (SRIC) for III MAF; it was work he had trained his entire professional life to do. As luck would have it, Major Jim Hatch, a Gray acolyte dating back to their time on the tugboat off Cuba during the crisis in 1962, commanded 1st Radio Battalion. Colonel John Canton, the very conservative MAF G-2, had foiled Hatch's efforts to keep alive Gray's SIGINT/EW Center. Happily, Canton was conveniently away on a special assignment for the U.S. Department of State.[16] With the often-intransigent G-2 gone, Gray's proposal for an innovative fusion center met with little or no resistance. Besides, General Nickerson was a strong supporter, and General Davis even more so. Canton's absence helped Gray while also freeing the reins from Hatch and his Radio Battalion.

So what exactly was done? A lot.

First, using 3rd Recon as the model, Gray laid the framework for deep reconnaissance throughout I Corps. *Second*, a sensor plan that employed both acoustic and seismic sensors was implemented as part of a Tactical Surveillance Center under the aegis of the SRIC. Gray and the Development Center had procured some computerized sensor data processing equipment and delivered it to III MAF. That equipment provided the Marines with the ability to read and analyze sensor data, which could then be collated at the SRIC. *Third*, an aerial reconnaissance program was re-established throughout I Corps and a photo-interpretative capability established as part of the SRIC. *Fourth*, ties to the Army's airborne direction finding assets were renewed and their data was linked into the SRIC as well. *Fifth*, by working with Hatch, Gray also was able to tweak the Radio Battalion production and fuse the efforts of the SIGINT/EW Center into the SRIC. Hatch was a superb officer and held in high esteem by Al Gray as perhaps the Marine Corps' finest cryptologic officer, though he lacked his mentor's knowledge of and appreciation for combat arms. Major Hatch had always been in communications or SIGINT. *Sixth*, Gray also ensured, using General Nickerson's blank check as collateral, that the SRIC had counter-intelligence linkage and that the Combat Intelligence Section of III MAF was noteworthy within the Fusion Center, as the SRIC was alternately known.

When he received Gray's briefing of SRIC operations shortly before departing the war zone, Major General Davis remarked that for the first time in the war, "Because of the intelligence he received from SIGINT and reconnaissance unit, he could fight the enemy instead of the terrain."[17] There was no better tactician than Ray Davis, and there also was no one who relied on operational intelligence more than he. Though he left Vietnam shortly after Gray's arrival in 1969, they would again work together in the not-too-distant future.

Not all of Al Gray's time was taken up with paperwork and coordination. The man Barney Prosser called "the finest field Marine he had ever seen" could not be kept from going into the field. Given the presence of equally hard charging and dedicated professionals like Alex Lee and Buck Coffman, there was no chance of keeping the enthusiastic, former recon sergeant inside friendly lines at night. Gray, knowing that his seniors would have been aghast to hear of his nocturnal activities, maintained a tight radio silence on exactly all that he had been up to.

Other aspects of Gray's work that went largely unnoticed were his efforts to bring the ARVN the sensor technology that the DCPG had developed. Using his close ties to the Commanding General of the 1st ARVN Division located in Hué City, General Ngo Quang Truong and the commander of the 2nd Regiment, Colonel Vu Vien Giai, Gray did not have to work hard to convince either ARVN officer of the advantages that the acoustic and seismic sensors provided. Giai's force was still located north of Dong Ha, strung along the Trace (the old *McNamara Line*) west toward Khe Sanh. Giai realized that he needed every technological advantage that he could collect.

The integration of ground sensors, ground radars, night vision devices and search-light Jeeps in support of ARVN/Marine/Army ground operations in the northern I Corps area was very successful. For example, the 3D Marine Division Sensor Surveillance Unit, led by Lieutenant Colonel Mel Soper, played a key role in training the ARVN Surveillance Unit. Lieutenant Colonel Soper was an innovative, highly-skilled professional, idolized by his "Sensor" Marines. Marines like Lieutenant Benny Raines, Sergeant (and later Staff Sergeant) Frank Gavaldon, Sergeant Karl Kari, and many other young Marines, were key players in training the ARVN Unit. The ARVN Sensor Unit was part of their Regimental Surveillance Company, commanded by Captain Vo Van NGHI. During the period 15-17 June 1969, five companies from the 33rd NVA Sapper Battalion (about 300 infantry and engineer explosive specialists) crossed the Ben Hai River with the mission of destroying a major artillery fire base and pave the way for a new major offensive. ARVN/Marine forces scored a major victory because sensors planted and remotely "read" by ARVN and Marine personnel alerted all forces in the area to NVA Sapper movements. Marine Major Bill Bahnmaier, Soper's assistant Surveillance Officer, was dispatched to the area to assess the situation and reported that the enemy suffered hundreds of casualties, five POWs and substantial weapons and other equipment. Later in 1969, after the 3D Marine Division exited the war zone, and well into 1971-1972, sensors would provide the northernmost ARVN commanders with much needed force multipliers.[18]

Indeed, during the final months that III MAF controlled I Corps, the capabilities of two of Al Gray's professional innovations – sensors and the Radio Battalion
– were utilized to their very best results. General Nickerson had realized that the
drawdown in Marine operational units meant changes had to be instituted. The
General's foresight had been rewarded. Mixing Alex Lee's recon teams with the
DCPG-developed sensors proved extremely successful. Concurrently, the SRIC
was the culmination of Al Gray's vision for the integration of intelligence and
surveillance. Alas, its legacy was short-lived.[19]

During the time Gray had been present at General Nickerson's Headquarters,
he had traveled extensively and had visited many units. As far as he could discern,
America's fighting men – the Soldiers and Marines – were still committed to
the jobs they were assigned to do. And as evidenced by the fine work done in
Alex Lee's recon unit, they still did dangerous jobs with skill, daring and commitment. Nevertheless, the news media's relentless attacks against the war, at least the
American-South Vietnamese side of the war was beginning to affect the troops.[20]
Instances of fragging of officers had increased, and the presence of drugs had gained
more than a foothold.[21] Gray could see that the saturation of critical news coverage was having an effect on the troops. He likened the situation to that when the
commander rallies the troops and says we are going to go out and win today, and we
will win tomorrow as well, but the troops are feeling that no matter how much they
win, they will lose in the end. It was a heck of a way to fight a war, and the people
most affected were the troops on the ground in Vietnam.

But all good things must eventually come to an end, even for Al Gray. The Gray
Ghost, the man who moved around like a silhouette, got caught in the MAF
Command Post by one of the Marine Corps's smartest generals, but someone
unlikely to catch a former recon sergeant in the field. Lieutenant General Henry
Buse, the Commanding General, Fleet Marine Force, Pacific was visiting III MAF
on business for the Commandant, General Leonard F. Chapman. General Buse
also had an additional duty. The Commanding General of Quantico, Lieutenant
General Lewis Fields, wanted Lieutenant Colonel Al Gray to return to his permanent duty station.[22] General Buse, a huge, likeable but often intimidating man, saw
Gray walking outside and captured him as described earlier in this chapter. After
ensnaring the "spook," as General Buse invariably called Gray, he did accede to
Gray's request that he be given time to visit the Navy in the Mekong Delta. After
all, that was part of his mission for the DCPG, though Gray had not yet found time
to get down there.

So off Gray went to the remote southeast corner of South Vietnam assigned to IV Corps. The Mekong Delta was the scene of riverine operations conducted jointly by the "brown-water" Navy and the Army's 9th Division. It had been one of the many questionable operational decisions of the war to assign Army units to the Delta and Marines to I Corps. The Delta was extremely important to South Vietnam, providing more than half its rice production in only about 25% the total area of the country. The Delta also was home to nearly 40% of the Vietnamese population. Instead of using the Marine Corps, the nation's amphibious force and clearly naval in character, the Department of Defense decided to reconstitute the 9th Division, and give it a riverine character.[23]

Lieutenant Colonel Gray did what we would expect by now. He conducted an extensive personal reconnaissance of the area and visited many outposts throughout the region. At each, he would give a briefing about the employment of the sensors and how they could be used to augment observation posts. Given that the pullout accelerated in the year following Gray's visit, the effectiveness of sensors in the Delta was never given an appropriate evaluation.

After Al Gray had left for Vietnam, his friend Jerry Polakoff had been sent off to Indonesia on a special project. Completing that task, Polakoff received Permanent Change of Station orders that sent him into Vietnam. Al Gray had learned of that development while still working in General Nickerson's Headquarters; he suggested to the General that Polakoff would be the perfect officer to run the SRIC that Gray had just established. Polakoff had all the requisite skills, had worked recently with Alex Lee and knew the deep reconnaissance issues; there could not have been a better choice. Nickerson accepted the recommendation and told Gray he would make the appointment.

After leaving the Delta, Gray returned to Quantico at the end of August 1969. As luck would have it, while Gray was changing planes in Hawaii at Hickam Air Force Base, who showed up but Jerry Polakoff – on his way to Vietnam. The two lieutenant colonels got the opportunity to have a turnover briefing before their planes departed – one returning to the land of the Big PX and the other going to war. It was a coincidence typical of many that occurred in Al Gray's time as a Marine. Polakoff, Hatch, Lee, Coffman, and many others went on to put in a remarkable performance in demonstrating the efficiency of an integrated fusion center co-equal with the Combat Operations Center and located in close proximity to the latter.

The success of the SRIC was not long in coming. Before its withdrawal in June 1969, the 3rd Marine Division monitored approximately 125 seismic and acoustical sensor strings that had been placed by sensor surveillance, recon, and helicopter units. Strings were assigned to specific artillery batteries, which would fire a salvo a short distance from the end of the string. The Marines got excellent results; when one string, which had been very active, suddenly went silent, a recon team was sent to investigate. The Marines were surprised to find a sign along the trail warning that it should not be used as "it led to death." The NVA had built a new trail around the first, providing a detour for their forces. The recon team readjusted the sensor string to the new route. While the 3rd Division had used the sensors as a trigger to fire artillery, the 1st Division, operating to the south, preferred to use sensor information to gather intelligence.[24]

Gray arrived back at his desk in the Development Center just in time to get a call from Lieutenant General John Lavelle at the DCPG.

BACK AT QUANTICO, EARLY SEPTEMBER 1969

In early September General Lavelle called Al Gray to congratulate him on the success of his recent trip to Vietnam; he also casually mentioned that he would like Gray to come by and see him when the opportunity arose. The Marine Lieutenant Colonel, who admired and respected the flamboyant Air Force General, made a point to get on the Director's schedule in the very near future – specifically, the Friday night of Labor Day weekend. When he arrived to be informed of what the General might have to say, Gray was astonished to hear that the DCPG was willing to turn over all the sensor and sensor technology, related displays and computers that it had developed – an approximately $100M investment – to the Marine Corps if the service was willing to accept responsibility for the program going forward. All that in exchange for the Marines developing and promulgating operational manuals related to sensor programs. Lavelle lamented the fact that the other services had shown no interest in the sensors, though the Marine Corps had already used them to great advantage in Vietnam. Gray, who earnestly believed ground sensors could make a positive impact on the battlefield, accepted on behalf of the Commandant – pending his Commandant's approval, of course.

Over the weekend, Gray put in a call to his friend Lieutenant Colonel Robert Darron, part of the G-2 office at HQMC and who was the project officer for ground sensors, to give him a heads up about the DCPG offer. On Monday – Labor Day – Gray was fortunate enough to see Lieutenant General Lewis J. "Jeff" Fields, and received that officer's endorsement for his activities. Fields also promised to call the Commandant on Tuesday recommending that the service accept Lavelle's largesse. And so it was that General Chapman officially accepted the program and all the program's assets.

It then came back to Al Gray to complete the daunting job of integrating the DCPG products into the Marine Corps. Gray became responsible for completing the near endless paperwork associated with developing the needed doctrine, allocating the resources among various units, developing Tables of Equipment and Organization for the new units, preparing operational manuals, and developing a spare parts and maintenance program. Building on the superb prior efforts of Major Alex Lee, ably assisted by Major Joe Flynn, Gray was able to draw from his earlier experience at HQMC when he had gone through the same steps while creating the Radio Battalions. The resulting program, nicknamed STEAM – Sensor Technology as Applied to the Marine Corps – became another of Al Gray's progeny. The initiative resulted in a Sensor Control and Management Platoon (SCAMP) being assigned to each division.[25] As with the Radio Battalions' Table of Organization and Table of Equipment, the Marine Support Battalion's Table of Organization, the Marine Corps' Combined Cryptologic Program, the Flyaway Teams, and the foreign language training program, Al Gray was the principal – often the only – driving force. While he completed the STEAM and SCAMP requirements, however, there were other DCPG matters that required fairly big chunks of his time.

By coincidence, the night that General Lavelle offered the sensors to the Marine Corps became a rather important date in Al Gray's personal life.

FRIDAY NIGHT, LABOR DAY WEEKEND, WISCONSIN AVENUE, GEORGETOWN, WASHINGTON, D.C. 1969

At shortly after 7 P.M., Jan Goss finished her duties as the Executive Secretary to one of the Defense Communications Project Group's most senior managers, the Deputy Chief for Technology. Both Jan and her boss worked for the MITRE Corporation, though they were assigned to the DCPG's Engineering Section on the first floor of the building on the grounds of the Naval Observatory. Jan loved her job, and she loved Washington.

She had grown up everywhere, an Air Force brat (she says angel) whose father had been a German Prisoner of War (POW) for more than 20 months during World War II. While her father was a POW, Jan and her twin brother Jackie were raised by their paternal grandparents and her Aunt Celia, her father's sister.[26] Later Celia and her husband, Bud Brand, took over responsibility. The youngsters became very devoted to both and spent many happy summers with Uncle Bud and Aunt Celia in Burlington, Vermont. Lieutenant Colonel Ralph (Jack) Goss and his wife moved Jan and her brother to a series of homes from Dayton, Ohio to Alaska, and then finally back to their New England roots. After graduation from high school, Jan completed the Katherine Gibbs Finishing School for secretaries; she then went to work for first the MITRE Corporation and then Philco-Ford, a large, defense-oriented electronics firm. While employed at Philco-Ford, she had moved briefly to Tucson; she loved both the city and her job. But given the vagaries of the defense contracting business, when the company lost its contract, Jan found herself without work. She moved back to Washington, D.C., where her father had been assigned. Knowing that her secretarial skills were in high demand at MITRE (as a typist or taking shorthand, she had few peers), she called and offered her services.

MITRE hired her immediately for an office in Falls Church, where she would pass time while awaiting her clearance to be approved. With clearance finally in hand, she was moved to the building at the Naval Observatory; at the same time, she also decided to rent a small apartment off Wisconsin Avenue in Georgetown, within easy walking distance of the office. Life was good.

The DCPG was a fast moving place, with busy people doing important work. Jan's office was one of the central hubs. Her boss was involved with the many disparate programs, and his workplace was the scene of a continuous parade of briefers, consultants, planners, engineers and military officers. Jan had access to all the secrets; indeed, she enjoyed coming in to the office early in the morning in order to read through the overnight messages from Southeast Asia and elsewhere, messages she would appropriately flag and arrange in order of importance for her boss. The comely secretary also loved the glamour of her job in Georgetown, a place to see and be seen, perhaps especially in the 1960s. Jan was a fashion plate who took lots of pride in her professional appearance, just like many other young women of that time. She might not have had enough money to eat well, but she definitely dressed well.

A young, attractive professional woman, Jan was extremely wary of developing friendships with mid-level military officers; all of them, she had resolved, were married. During the previous year, Jan had casually noticed one crew-cut Marine lieutenant colonel who often visited her boss, or most often her boss's boss, David Israel, the brilliant MIT scholar and MITRE luminary who was the senior civilian assigned to the DCPG and Head of the Engineering Department. Also in the office complex was an Army general. Debbie, the general's secretary, often chatted with Gray because Debbie's husband was also a Marine. Jan never gave the lieutenant colonel much thought, as he would sit patiently in the outer office waiting for the interminable meetings to clear and be ushered into see Mr. Israel. She simply regarded him as just another married officer who probably had several kids at home. That despite the fact that Debbie, who also knew the secretary in Gray's basement office, Mrs. Armstrong, tried to convince Jan Goss that this Marine really was a

Fig 2.7
Jan Goss and Al Gray, 1970.[27]

Fig 2.8
Here with Lucky 2,
Jan was also a dog lover.[28]

bachelor. Jan, ever the skeptic, dismissed that characterization as undoubtedly erroneous. Lieutenant Colonel Gray had left General Lavelle's office at about 7 P.M. Being in no rush to fight the traffic out of Washington to return to Quantico, and having lots to think about given Lavelle's offer, Gray decided to pass some time by seeing if he could get a haircut on Wisconsin Avenue. With the barbershop busy, he took a number and decided to go next door into a drugstore to buy a magazine.

Jan had left her office and was making the short walk to her nearby apartment, just down the hill from the Observatory. As fate would have it, the two met on the sidewalk; it was a surprised Gray who asked Jan what she was doing there. Jan said she lived nearby, and since she had no plans invited Gray to stop by her apartment for a drink. Gray refused that offer, but countered by saying he would like to take her to dinner later. The out-of-left-field dinner invitation was accepted with no hesitance at all; Jan had for the first time noticed that the Marine wore no wedding band. As the evening unfolded, Jan's anxiety was relieved and her interest piqued as she learned that Gray was not married and never had been. Indeed, by the end of the evening Jan Goss knew she had finally met the right man for her. She then made a comment that was completely out of character: she suggested that they might go canoeing on the Chesapeake and Ohio Canal the next day. Gray readily agreed, not knowing that strenuous outdoor activities were perhaps the last things Jan enjoyed doing! By the end of the weekend, Jan was in love and committed to herself that she would either marry Al Gray or no one.

As for Al, he was clearly intrigued. On the other hand, he viewed any developing romance as having serious complications. And while he remained focused on the Marine Corps and meeting his other responsibilities, Jan soon added to his already busy schedule.

DEVELOPMENT CENTER, QUANTICO, SEPTEMBER 1969 – AUGUST 1970

In addition to putting together the program for STEAM and the SCAMP platoons, Gray was also intimately involved with two broader initiatives that affected the Development Center in 1970.

Commandant Chapman wanted to return long-range planning to the Marine Corps. General Greene had started that process earlier in his Commandancy, in 1964, but the overwhelming requirements of the war in Southeast Asia had ended the Greene plan.[29] Chapman, who like his predecessor was a brilliant Commandant, had the time and resources, and certainly the will to push through his vision of how the Marine Corps should move forward. Two new organizations were created, both headed by senior colonels: a "Studies Division" and a "Doctrine Division."

Chapman tasked Quantico with providing much of the brainpower required for the studies, but some 55 officers were sent to implement the plan. "Long Range Studies" looked at the requirements 20 years in the future. "Mid-Range Plans" looked at requirements as a bridge to the future, two years out to ten years in the future. "Current Capabilities" planning included the next budget year. The new organizations each wanted and needed their own intelligence sections. The Doctrine Division also wanted its own intelligence specialists. One of the newly assigned Marine colonels had been assigned to Fort Belvoir, Virginia, working there with the U.S. Army's studies group, and he put forth a plan to organize along the same lines as the Army. Al Gray, knowing that the Marine Corps had neither the number of intelligence specialists nor the other resources needed to parallel the Army's organization, suggested to Brigadier General Alan J. Armstrong, Director of the Development Center, that a different approach was required.

General Armstrong accepted Gray's recommendation and completely revised the unit, turning the Intelligence Section into the Intelligence/Surveillance & Reconnaissance (ISR) Division. The unit grew from five to 23 officers, all directed and coordinated by Al Gray. Gray added capabilities in SIGINT, photo intelligence, sensors, reconnaissance, electronic warfare, counter-intelligence and more. The ISR Division provided the Marine Corps with a one-stop shop for anything related to any aspect of intelligence, surveillance or reconnaissance. Instead of distributing intelligence throughout the many sections of the Combat Development Center, the Intelligence Branch supported all requirements at their office.

It was the ISR Division that also provided all the support needed to finish the long and mid-range studies that General Chapman had ordered. Those were completed much to General Chapman's satisfaction, which means they were probably done well since the Commandant was a demanding taskmaster.

The Air Force at Wright-Patterson Air Force Base, Ohio, ran another joint program that Gray had learned of and supported while at the DCPG, the Tactical Information Processing and Interpretation Program (TIPI). TIPI complemented the Marine Air-Ground Intelligence System (MAGIS), one of the Marine Corps' largest computer-based systems of that time. TIPI was a wide-ranging system with tentacles reaching into every other service. Gray was the DCPG expert on the operational requirements, system utilization, and fielding of both TIPI and MAGIS, and, while at Quantico, he was a very actively involved with both the Air

Force program manager in Ohio and with the DCPG. The Air Force specifically lauded Gray's efforts to ensure that TIPI requirements were met to the satisfaction of both Air Force and Marine Corps needs. It would not be the last time that Al Gray was recognized as having tremendous insight into and command of all aspects of an intricate system being developed by a sister service.

Colonel Robert Nichols was elevated to be the Chief of Staff at Quantico during this time. As usual, the new Chief of Staff was given staff briefings by each of the sections of the Development Center and the Education Center. Anyone who had experienced such events knows it is like trying to drink from a fire hose. Each section puts all the information it can amass into a series of slides that are then fed rapid fire to the officer receiving the briefings. Al Gray was different, as one might expect by now. Instead of viewgraphs and charts, Lieutenant Colonel Gray, the head of all intelligence programs at the Development Center, invited Nichols to have a seat in his office and then, without any other officers present, briefly described his many programs. The briefing took fewer than five minutes of the quarter-hour that had been allocated for Gray's section. Gray subsequently asked Nichols if there were any issues or challenges that he wished to discuss. The Colonel's schedule for the rest of the day was promptly blown; seven hours later Colonel Robert Nichols departed Lieutenant Colonel Gray's office. The two had discussed everything from Marine Corps procurement policies to how to rebuild infantry units to how to attack the drug issues that all the services then faced.[30]

Another aspect of Al Gray's job at the Development Center involved briefings, presentations and seminars related to Marine intelligence, surveillance, reconnaissance, SIGINT, photo, and EW activities. Gray was the principal Marine participant in such affairs, and he traveled far and wide to perform his duties. Of course, he was a frequent presenter to the Amphibious Warfare School, the Communications Officer School, and the Command & Staff College – all located at Quantico. Plus, he kept his hand in things related to the National Security Agency, including briefings and teaching at the National Cryptologic School. The Commandant of the Defense Intelligence School also observed that Gray was able to integrate actual examples from Vietnam into his presentation and how clearly expert he was in all aspects of intelligence.

The new Commanding General of Marine Corps Education Command as of 1 July 1970, then-Major General Ray Davis, clearly noted Gray's activities and would draw on the Lieutenant Colonel even more in the months ahead.[31]

As a result of a briefing he gave Major General Michael Ryan of the 2nd Marine Division, Gray received this note from the General who had been his battalion commander in Korea:[32]

> *19 June 1969*
>
> *Dear Al,*
>
> *I presume that you are busy as ever conjuring up all these wierdies. It's too bad you are not down here in the Division so you can go to work again.*
>
> *I recall the briefing that you gave regarding the use of sensors. I am interested in what could be given to our battalion and regimental commanders in the 2nd Division related to sensors, possibly similar to the briefing that you gave me in the Development Center. Or, perhaps, some other information, or even training, related to sensors. Realizing your knowledge of infantry and artillery training, would you let me know what you think would be appropriate or useful within the 2nd Division. Based on what you indicate, I would submit a formal request for such assistance as might be available.*
>
> *I hope all is well at Quantico.*
>
> *Sincerely,*
>
> *M.P. Ryan, Major General, U.S. Marine Corps*
> *Lieutenant Colonel Alfred M. Gray, Jr.*
> *Development Center*
> *Marine Corps Development and Education Center*
> *Quantico, VA 22134*

Note a joke about developing, as the General calls them, "wierdies," and his comment about Gray getting back to work! But clearly the General was not joking about wanting sensor briefings for his subordinate commanders. General Gray had a very close relationship with General Ryan, the recipient of the Navy Cross from Tarawa. Long after then-1st Lieutenant Gray served as a rifle company commander in Ryan's battalion (1/7) in Korea, the two maintained a near continuous correspondence.

One of Gray's favorite briefing aids, and one most popular among the audiences, was a tape recording that he had discovered somewhere during his travels. The tape was recorded by one of the acoustic sensors dropped along the Ho Chi Minh Trail. The recording was a real crowd pleaser. Of course, acoustic sensors alarm and start transmitting as they pick up sounds. The first sound heard on the tape was that of saws being used to cut down the tree into which the sensor had fallen. It was a very happy group of North Vietnamese soldiers who collected the sensor after the tree fell. The cylindrical device was about two-feet long and weighed about 30 pounds; but the NVA soldier thought it some sort of explosive device and clearly heard on the tape is a sigh of relief when there was no blast as he scraped the dirt away from it. The NVA had made the contraption a gift to the Commanding General of the 559th Transportation Group, located in Tchepone, Laos. This was the general who coordinated all operations along the Ho Chi Minh Trail road complex. The general's memento transmitted for five long days after its arrival in his office. As a result, the Americans retrieved extraordinarily significant details about traffic moving down the trail. The tape was indeed a big hit among military audiences.

During the late winter or early spring of 1969, Lieutenant General Louis B. Robertshaw led a Marine Corps Board convened for the purpose of selecting colonels and lieutenant colonels to attend high-level schools and war colleges. It was one of the first times that lieutenant colonels were considered for top-level schools. Al Gray, and one of his contemporaries, another future General, Tom Morgan, were very junior and way down the list of lieutenant colonels.[33] But, as Gray was to learn from other generals, General Robertshaw had personally reviewed Al Gray's record, and he was appalled by what he saw. He would have liked to send Gray to a war college, but as of early 1970 Gray had not even attended a high-level school. Robertshaw wrote a personal note to the Commandant, Leonard Chapman, with Gray's name underlined. The note said, "this officer needs to attend high-level school now!" Conveniently, General Robertshaw also headed Manpower at HQMC. The note would directly affect two of Al Gray's next three assignments. His orders to school would be forthcoming.

In April 1970, Major General Alan Armstrong laughed aloud as Al Gray entered his office. He jokingly reported that Gray's avoidance of formal school was at an end. The running gag among Gray, Armstrong and several others – including Generals Kenny Houghton, Sam Jaskilka, Ray Davis, and near countless colonels – was that Gray was always too busy to go to school. There were always more important things to be done, more dragons to slay, fish to fry and, most importantly, a war in Southeast Asia to be won. Gray had twice turned down orders to school in order to extend in Vietnam; that was where the war was and that was where he wanted to be.

After all, as Gray thought at the time, why send him to school? His future was limited. Armstrong's almost giddy announcement also made it clear that neither Colonel Ike Fenton, the Chief of Staff, nor anyone else would be saving Gray from his next duty station. When Al Gray, nonetheless, went to check with Fenton, that officer just smiled and told the would-be student that it was true, he should collect his notebooks because he was going to school and that was the end of the discussion. Despite Al Gray's wide reputation as an avid reader, and despite the fact that he was forever optimistic and positive, nevertheless he was somewhat let down at the prospect of spending time away from really *doing things*.

In the summer of 1970, Al Gray was still a lieutenant colonel but had not yet completed his college degree, and he thought of his future more in terms of managing a few 7-Eleven Stores than he did anticipating his next promotion.[34] Nonetheless, he liked serving in the Corps and considered it a great honor and privilege to be a Marine. Through the years he had gained an ever-increasing appreciation for the opportunity to help people and that became a constant motivating factor. Professionally, he become qualified in three different occupational fields (artillery, infantry and special communications) and was a recognized expert in special intelligence/cryptologic matters. He had held commands at every grade, possessed considerable experience overseas, had commanded special operations activities, and he had broad knowledge of naval operations, including participation in over 14 amphibious exercises at various echelons of command. Though he was well qualified, the Marine Corps withdrawal from the war zone meant that the Corps would be reducing its size, further limiting the need for senior officers.[35] Consequently, his thinking was not the result of any self-pity or lack of confidence; Gray was just being, in his mind, objective about his prospects.

When asked how he could possibly have not realized that his future was bright, in light of his record and accomplishments, Al Gray, Marine, gave a very simple answer that explained much. He simply never read reports about him that senior officers filed. Yes, occasionally a reporting senior would show Gray how he had been evaluated, but that happened only rarely. Gray never went to the Personnel Section at HQMC and asked to see his selection board jacket, the folder that would be given to promotion boards when they considered him for advancement. Al Gray's hard work, long hours, or time spent helping his colleagues and fellow Marines were not intended to earn promotion. He did so because he was duty-bound to perform his function as the best he could regardless of the circumstances then in place. It was that simple.

In later years, Jan Gray recalled that whenever the pair spoke of future plans, they envisioned Al being a retired lieutenant colonel – just like her father was. Al and Jan had quietly been steadily seeing each other after a somewhat slow start brought about by Gray's duties and responsibilities. In fact, Jan was positive that had she known what the future would bring, she might not have clung to the dream of her ideal man as she had done for the previous year and would continue to do for another 11 years. Jan realized Al Gray was special in so many ways, and not the least was in how he juggled all his responsibilities while also taking college courses at night, caring for his mom, and providing exercise for Lucky II. It certainly helped that he thrived on 3-4 hours sleep – literally.

With the drawdown in Marine Corps combat units at the end of 1969, the Army's 24th Corps took over responsibility for directing operations throughout I Corps in early March 1970. The initial Commanding General, Melvin Zais, was a highly capable officer, but his G-2 did not understand the need for the SRIC. It was disbanded as one of the first actions taken by the new Army regime. However, the SRIC was not so soon forgotten. In July the Army requested that the "Lieutenant Colonel who had established the SRIC return and re-establish it." The Marines answered that the officer in question was doing other things. Gray, in fact, had a critical role and was in the midst of integrating a threat analysis against a new strategy that was being evaluated as part of General Chapman's studies and doctrine initiative. And when that was finished, he had new tasking.[36]

Al Gray had received orders to attend the Command and Staff College at Quantico; but before he left for school, General Armstrong made it clear that Gray's unit needed brand new operational requirements for all the intelligence-related activities and systems in the Marine Corps. That meant new requirements for amphibious reconnaissance, SIGINT/EW, combat intelligence and counter-intelligence, as well as aerial surveillance and reconnaissance. Then, because the Marine Air-Ground Intelligence System (MAGIS) was still new, systems requirements for it needed revalidation. From all the general requirements, specific requirements and needs would also flow. It was a massive undertaking, but Armstrong, who was a big supporter of Al Gray's efforts, showed no mercy on his young professional. Armstrong required the effort be completed before Gray left for school.

It was. Gray finished the task with 15 minutes to spare before he literally ran over to the convocation for Command & Staff College.

NIXON TAKES CHARGE

WASHINGTON, 1969 - 1970

The election of Richard Milhous Nixon in November 1968 heralded dramatic changes in the conduct of the Vietnam War. By the spring of 1969, when Nixon was actually in office, the war had stretched into its fourth year following the arrival of major American combat units in 1965. Notwithstanding the Chicago riots during the Democrat convention of 1968, the anti-war crowd had barely been able to keep their activism in check while a liberal Democrat served in the White House. Under a more conservative Republican there would be no half-hearted protests and constrained anti-war violence.

Nixon was never highly popular, though he did win the presidential elections of 1968 and 1972 surprisingly handily. Among the radical, anti-war student movement, Nixon remained an anathema. Moreover, the press, which was rightfully hard on Lyndon Baines Johnson about the war but strongly supported his domestic policies, never cared for any aspect of Richard Nixon's leadership. Thus, media sniping against the war began to reflect open hostility.

Candidate Nixon had campaigned on a promise to end the war, and as President he set about to do so. Something the American public has never seemed to learn, however, was that candidates could make promises that well-intentioned office holders found hard to keep. Certainly Johnson's handling of the war left much to be desired; in fact, it could not have been worse. So clearly there was room for Nixon to do things better almost immediately. It was simply not to be.

Whereas Presidents Kennedy and Johnson relied on individuals whom David Halberstam called the "best and brightest," their performance with respect to Vietnam turned out to be neither. President Nixon, instead, turned to a former back bench congressman as his Secretary of Defense, Melvin Laird. Laird was an honorable man who slowly but surely undid much of the McNamara legacy left in place by the brief tenure of Clark Clifford. But Laird was uninspiring to others, and much more a backslapping politician than someone with the intellect and vigor to deal with a host of problems that plagued the war effort by 1969. For his approach to the Vietnam War, Nixon relied more on his strongly accented and often overbearing National Security Advisor, Henry Kissinger, than he did anyone at the Pentagon.

Kissinger burst onto the national scene when Nixon appointed him to head the National Security Council. German-born, hard working, a decorated U.S. Army veteran of World War II, Kissinger was brilliant, and by the time of his appointment as one of Nixon's most trusted advisors, perhaps even arrogant. Kissinger came to dominate American foreign policy from 1969 through the election of Jimmy Carter as President in 1977. Kissinger was largely responsible for the policy of *détente* that resulted in an easing of tensions with the Soviet Union in the early 1970s. Further, Kissinger's actions resulted in a new alignment with China that put more diplomatic pressure on the Soviets even as the threat of a military confrontation had been eased. And while Nixon got the credit, rightfully so, of opening relations with China, there was no doubt that Kissinger did much, if not all, of the spadework. Even after leaving office, Kissinger was a sought-after advisor on a host of matters. He remained a highly divisive figure, though no one could doubt his influence.

Given the circumstances Nixon and Kissinger inherited in Vietnam, they had little choice but to give the Republic of Vietnam's President Nguyen Van Thieu their complete support – just as Lyndon Johnson had done before them. Exactly like Johnson, though, Vietnam was never the central focus for Nixon-Kissinger interest in foreign affairs. For all of them, Vietnam was little more than a distant third behind the Soviet Union and China. Perhaps that is why Vietnam, starting early in the Nixon Administration, was never given sufficient attention and when negotiations with North Vietnam finally did come, well, the rush to get out once and for all overcame any consideration of a prudent, trilateral settlement. By then Nixon was but a shadow of his former self, in the darkness following the events of Watergate, and Kissinger was clearly in charge – at least in charge of foreign policy. But that is getting ahead in the story.

At the Laird-led Pentagon, the Joint Chiefs of Staff received much more respect and their opinions were sought to a greater degree than they ever had been during the Kennedy/Johnson years. However, General Earle Wheeler initially remained at the helm as Chairman and Wheeler clearly had been a big part of the problem during the Johnson years. His inability to articulate a central theme for the conduct of the war meant the White House, the Commanding General in Vietnam, and the Air Force and Navy commanders in charge of the air war against North Vietnam were all working independently and often at odds with one another. Generally speaking, the troops on the ground wanted to win and go home; they did what they were ordered to do and in most cases did it very well. Unfortunately, America's military high command, under Earle Wheeler, was never so unified.

The early days of the Nixon Administration did see Mel Laird, the Wisconsin politician, win one significant victory with respect to Vietnam policy: he was adamant that the United States reduce its troop levels, and that happened largely as a result of Laird's exhortations. However, it was the former Secretary of Defense Clark Clifford, Laird's predecessor, who may have sparked the initial troop reductions. While he had been Secretary of Defense, Clifford spoke of initiating force drawdowns; however, Clifford talked one game and did another. The largest American troop levels in Vietnam occurred in the spring of 1969, soon after Clifford had left office. After the change in Administrations, writing in *Foreign Affairs*, Clifford suggested that the Americans could reduce personnel levels in South Vietnam by 100,000. Nixon, not ready to concede his political rivals the initiative for future American policy, retorted by seeing Clifford's bid and raising it. America would reduce by 100,000 men its troop level in Vietnam by the end of 1969.

Vietnamization was in full swing. Laird envisioned that by the end of Nixon's first term the number of American fighting men in South Vietnam would be the same as when Kennedy took office – in other words, only a small number of advisors and no combat units would be stationed there. Kissinger expedited the Laird vision.

If the military was going to reduce its number of combat units, then Nixon needed another way to strike back at perceived communist provocations and diplomatic slights. He quickly settled on an old, tried and true weapons system, the B-52. B-52 strikes had long been used in Vietnam, though their effectiveness was never really evaluated objectively. Certainly they blew lots of trees to smithereens and reduced jungles to little more than entanglements of dead and dying vegetation, but the North Vietnamese and Viet Cong forces in the field were seldom obliterated by B-52s; the NVA/VC feared American artillery much more. Of course, those poor souls caught in a B-52 strike would never forget their horror, though for the most part the severely restricted bombing was not nearly as effective as the airpower proponents thought. Still, American artillery could not reach into communist sanctuaries in Cambodia or Laos, or even far into North Vietnam and bombing remained the only option for those targets.

When the communists began their spring offensive in 1969, something they undertook despite a yearlong American halt in the bombing of North Vietnam, Nixon was outraged. He wanted to strike back, and forcefully. The problem was that Cambodia was neutral and the United States was not supposed to be bombing there, regardless of what the North Vietnamese communists were doing. As a result, Nixon developed an elaborate scheme to bomb across the Cambodian border without admitting it.

SAIGON, 1969 - 1970

The combination of new photo intelligence and information from a deserter gave Nixon the target he needed. Despite their losses in 1968, the Central Office for South Vietnam (COSVN) remained an elusive target for American military planners. COSVN was, supposedly, the communist coordinating arm for operations in South Vietnam; this despite the fact that after 1968's *Tết Offensive*, little remained of any South Vietnamese representation in the communist hierarchy. American efforts to locate the COSVN headquarters, thought to be deep in the jungles along the South Vietnam-Cambodia border in an area called the Fishhook, had been fruitless until the photos, backed up by the testimony from the defector, gave Americans the hard information they needed. Nixon wanted to bomb the area immediately to show the communists his resolution to negotiate from strength, though a planned Presidential trip to Europe caused a slight delay. It was determined that 48 B-52 strikes would be needed to do the job.

Flying from 30,000 feet, the crews reported hitting their targets and seeing many secondary explosions. Unfortunately, when a group of volunteers agreed to go into the area immediately following the bombing, the thinking being they could easily pick up survivors who would be shell-shocked from the explosions, the combination force of two Americans and 11 South Vietnamese were met by accurate machine gun fire from three sides of their landing zone. They lost several men before being evacuated. The White House, regrettably, probably never heard of the ground force follow-up report; they only heard of the aircrews' reports. Such was the war.[37] In Nixon's mind, he showed the enemy that he meant business.

Ever since the first B-52 strikes, the communists were very adept at knowing when and where the big bombers would be employed. Soviet "trawlers" located off the island of Guam, the major base for B-52s, reported the time of takeoff, direction of flight and number of bombers in each sortie. NVA intelligence, which quickly learned the Rules of Engagement for all American aircraft, could alert forces located in potential strike areas to move quickly to avoid the destruction wrought by the heavy bombers. Far from destroying the COSVN headquarters, it is likely all that Nixon accomplished was to verify that the new President was no more adept at carrying the war to his enemy than his predecessor had been.[38] However, Nixon would soon show that he also was not shy from also using ground forces.

While the communists knew that Nixon was bombing Cambodia, the American public and most of the Congress did not. Nixon slapped a "secret" tag on the Cambodian efforts and was determined to tell no one that it was going on. His determination that the bombing campaigns remain a secret lasted two months before a reporter for the *New York Times* wrote about it. Though the reaction of the public and Congress was rather ho-hum to the news, Nixon was infuriated by the leak. What ensued was the first of what would become many Nixonian searches for the enemies – those who leaked. While the President became obsessed with plugging unauthorized policy disclosures, things were actually looking up in Vietnam.

General Abrams had replaced Westmoreland in June 1968. He promptly turned away from Westmoreland's emphasis on *search and destroy* to the strategy long favored by the Marines, protect the population. Abrams also benefited from working for a new Administration who permitted the Commanding General more control over all aspects of the war. All the while that Westmoreland had been in charge, the Commander-in-Chief, Pacific, in Hawaii, had been ostensibly in charge of air operations against North Vietnam and even B-52 strikes inside South Vietnam. Now Abrams controlled all those, and something else - an incursion in Cambodia.[39]

1969 was a pivotal year in the war. The new Administration was given a huge, positive development in South Vietnam, but it is unlikely that Nixon, Kissinger, or Laird ever paid enough attention to their briefings to realize it. The success that General Ray Davis and the Marines had had in I Corps at the end of 1968 and into 1969 was also true elsewhere in the country.

Early in 1969, Abrams became aware of COSVN Resolution 9; it was essentially a declaration of victory – victory by the South Vietnamese and Americans![40] It called on communist forces to resort to basic guerrilla tactics in an attempt to hold on in South Vietnam. Abrams was excited to take advantage of the captured intelligence document, but his boss in Washington, General Wheeler, was completely frustrated by his inability to get his civilian chain of command engaged as to the possibilities. It was as though Nixon, Kissinger, and Laird did not expect to hear such news; therefore, instead of embracing it, they discounted it. Instead, Nixon and his effusive National Security Advisor concentrated on the aftermath of their supposed secret bombings of Cambodia. Abrams wanted to use ground forces to attack forcefully the NVA supply lines in Cambodia, not just attack by B-52s. And while Nixon would prove adaptable in going after the NVA more aggressively, it would not be until later.

Abrams realized that going after the NVA's supply routes and attacking the enemy there undoubtedly saved American lives that would have been lost if the caches were used to attack friendly positions. Thus, during *Operation Apache Snow*, attacks against the A Shau Valley and the 29th NVA Regiment cost the American many casualties, and opened American commanders to criticism that the numerous attacks against what came to be called Hamburger Hill, were senseless. Of course, those assaults eliminated any chance of additional NVA attacks against Hué and Quang Tri, and in Abrams judgment saved 5,000 casualties at a cost of 78 killed in action and 548 wounded. Senator Edward Kennedy of Massachusetts took to the floor of the Senate to excoriate against the travesty of American casualties. Thanks to television, the picture of one American killed was far more effective an anti-war tool, and far easier for a politician to understand, than 5,000 non-casualties, which, of course, cannot be shown in a video segment. To the men trying to win the war, Kennedy's reaction was outrageous. A year earlier, when the NVA struck savagely at Hué, American politicians and newsmen were highly critical of American commanders; now, with the military leadership taking the battle into enemy strong-holds, the politicians and press were equally indignant.[41] It was a classic case of damned if you do, damned if you do not.

General Abrams had more than just problems with the new Administration, American politicians and newsmen; President Thieu remained a serious hurdle to the successful prosecution of the war. Thieu made all of the appointments of the Province Chiefs and the senior military officers. The South Vietnamese equiva-lent of the Chairman of the Joint Chiefs of Staff, General Cao Van Vien, was a man that most Americans, whose number included Creighton Abrams, regarded as being highly capable. Unfortunately, General Vien had no more success leading his country's military than did Earle Wheeler and, later in the war, Admiral Thomas H. Moorer. All three suffered from having a civilian leadership that thought war too important be left to warriors. While Thieu admitted to Abrams that probably no ARVN officers, including him, had the experience required to command more than a division, he gradually improved as both a leader and in picking high-ranking officers. Yet, the changes were slow, painfully slow, in coming. Of course, the one thing that Thieu, and as it turned out, Abrams, had in very short supply was time.

Abrams truly was making a difference in Saigon, but he was getting no help from Wheeler in Washington. Regrettably, Wheeler's successor in June 1970, Admiral Moorer, also had little influence over the ground war in South Vietnam, though he did help persuade President Nixon to be more aggressive in the bomb-ing of North Vietnam.

HANOI, OCTOBER 1969

"Uncle" Ho Chi Minh lived long enough to see Richard Nixon become President. But it is doubtful that he was ever sufficiently vigorous to have responded to Nixon's personal overtures about peace negotiations. Nonetheless, in early September Nixon did receive a note signed by the communist leader, but on 9 September 1969, Ho Chi Minh died in Hanoi. Ho had not succeeded in uniting Vietnam in his lifetime, though even after the stunning military losses he had endured in 1968, he must have felt sanguine about his political and military goals. After all, the North Vietnamese were winning the public relations battles, continuing to receive all-out support from China and the Soviet Union, and they were playing American presidents as though they were concert violins.

Ho was replaced by Le Duan. Le Duan was nearly 20 years younger than Ho; he was born in 1908. He was not only healthier and very active, but even before Ho's death Le Duan had assumed a greater leadership role in the communist government. He was also just as smart, dedicated, and ruthless as his longtime leader had been. There would be no drop-off in communist resolution or will, and that did not bode well for either future negotiations with the Americans or for the prospects of Thieu's government surviving.

NOTES AND REFERENCES

1. "UA" is the Marine Corps shortcut for "Unauthorized Absence." Someone who is UA is subject to the penalties of the Uniform Code of Military Justice. No successful officer could ever be "UA."
2. One of General Gray's many initiatives when he became Commandant was to establish a Marine Corps University. When a prominent member of the staff suggested that the project needed "to be studied," Gray told him in no uncertain terms it had been studied, and now was the time to implement the project. The University was stood up on November 10, 1987. Subsequently, the Marine Corps Research Center was conceived and funding obtained; groundbreaking occurred several months before General Gray's retirement.
3. Within a few years after his retirement, Colonel Jerry Polakoff would suffer a fatal heart attack in California where he and Alex Lee (also retired) had an aviation business. It had been his heart that forced him on sick leave while at the DCPG when Gray had replaced him there. He was a brilliant man and made exceptional contributions to the Marine Corps.
4. General Alfred M. Gray Oral History, National Security Agency, 2010.
5. Author interview with Major General James M. Myatt, United States Marine Corps (Ret.), January 2011. General Myatt more than satiated his desire for action before leaving Vietnam following his DCPG assignment; he subsequently served as the senior advisor to a South Vietnamese Marine Battalion before ending a tour that lasted 16 months. Years later, then-Major Myatt would serve as then-Brigadier General Al Gray's G-3 (Operations Officer) in the 4th MEB. When General Gray was CG, II MEF, then-Colonel Myatt commanded a MEU. When General Gray was Commandant, then-Major General Myatt commanded the 1st Marine Division in Iraq during *Operation Desert Shield*.
6. From General Gray's private collection.
7. By contrast, a follow-up Army offensive, *Operation Apache Snow*, was not nearly as successful and opened the Army (and the U.S. Military, generally) to charges that it were engaged in "senseless and irresponsible" tactics by Senator Kennedy. The major

differences between *Dewey Canyon* and *Apache Snow* were related to artillery support, helicopter tactics and intelligence. In all three of those areas, General Davis's planning and execution were superb. "Vietnam Chronology, 1969" given by John F. Guilmartin, course on "The History of the Vietnam War," The Ohio State University.

8. Remember that to the average Marine, aged 19-23, anyone over 30 looked old!

9. Lieutenant Colonel Alex Lee's book, *Force Recon Command*, tells the story of his unit in Vietnam. Colonel Don Layne, the man who served with Al Gray several times believes Lee to have been the officer most like Al Gray in terms of his effectiveness, innovation and professionalism. Circumstances conspired and Lee retired as a Lieutenant Colonel, a sure reflection on the often-misunderstood vagaries of the officer promotion system. General Gray wrote the Foreword to Lee's book and it offers great insight into both the man and the events on the ground in Vietnam at that time.

10. Captain Clovis C. Coffman later served as General Nickerson's aide. Years later, after he had retired, General Nickerson looked more closely into the events that led to Coffman's Navy Cross and thought it merited an upgrade to a Medal of Honor. General Al Gray helped General Nickerson in his quest to upgrade Coffman's medal, but their efforts failed. Upon Buck Coffman's death, both Lieutenant Colonel Alex Lee and General Gray spoke at his funeral and helped dedicate a building in his honor at the Reconnaissance Training Facility at Fort Story, Virginia.

11. From General Gray's private collection.

12. Image courtesy Alex Lee.

13. Image courtesy Alex Lee.

14. Image courtesy Bruce Norton.

15. U.S. Marine Corps University Photo.

16. Colonel John Canton grew up the son of missionaries who had served in Morocco, and Canton was a special friend of the King. Indeed, Canton was credited with teaching English to the King; thus, whenever there was an issue in that North African kingdom, the State Department would request Canton's services. As a result, Canton could be away for days or weeks.

17. General Alfred M. Gray Oral History, National Security Agency, 28 April 2010. General Davis's message about the value of SIGINT and reconnaissance was a theme he repeated many times when lecturing about the war following his return to the United States.

18. This narration was written by Major Bill Bahnmaier, the Assistant Ground Surveillance Officer of the 3rd Marine Division the morning after the action. He and his boss, Lt Colonel Mel Soper, along with all their Marines, were either at the Dong Ha Combat Base or at other surveillance sites. The sensor data was read out and analyzed thereat. The late Mel Soper was assigned as the Ground Surveillance Officer for the 3rd Marine Division in 1968 and charged with developing criteria for the employment of electronic sensors in Northern I Corps and the DMZ. Upon his return to the states, he was subsequently transferred to the Defense Special Projects Group, where his duties included supervising sensor installations at Clark and Osan Air Force Bases, Subic Bay Naval Base, the presidential facility at Camp David and the berthing dock for the President's yacht, "Sequoia" at the Washington, DC Navy Yard.

19. *Marines in Vietnam: 1970 and 1971*, Chapter 14 provides much information about the Radio Battalion, the sensors and the SRIC. As with all histories, however, the accuracy of the information is only as good as the memories of those who provided the information. For example, while Colonel John Canton was a fine officer and very capable G-2, he had nothing to do with establishing or operating the SRIC. However, Gray had worked with Canton before and there was mutual respect.

20. See Sorley, p. 159. Sorley cites a report done by Dr. Ernest Lefever of the Brookings Institute, which is hardly a right-wing, pro-war organization. Lefever did a study based on content analysis during 1972-1973. CBS News, he found, provided an "overwhelming unfavorable portrayal of the U.S. Armed Forces, The Defense Department, and

their activities." Further, Lefever continued," CBS Evening News (Walter Cronkite) was far more critical of America's ally, South Vietnam, than America's enemy, North Vietnam." In the course of news coverage, CBS News "gave 48 times more coverage to critics who wanted the U.S. to end military support of South Vietnam than to critics who wanted the U.S. to step up its military action against North Vietnam." Most of this was "advocacy under the guise of straight reporting." On a personal note, the author returned from Vietnam in 1967. By 1968, CBS was no longer watched during any newscast; it is a personal decision that remains in effect to this very day.

21. "Fragging" was the practice of tossing grenades into the tents or spaces occupied by unpopular officers, Staff NCOs or even other enlisted men.

22. Lieutenant General Lewis J. Fields had replaced Lieutenant General William G. Thrash as the Commanding General. When Major General Davis left Vietnam in August 1969, he returned to Quantico to serve as Fields' Deputy for Education – in charge of all Marine Officer Schools at Quantico – before becoming Commanding General and getting his third star. It is a source of continuing wonderment to the author that Al Gray, Marine, not only knew all these high-ranking generals, but also he knew them well. That included Generals Thrash and Fields, the commander of Gray's artillery regiment in Korea, and just about every other general officer mentioned in this text.

23. *Vietnam Studies, Riverine Operations 1966-1969*, a monograph produced by the U.S. Army and available online at http://www.history.army.mil/books/vietnam/riverine/index.htm. Website checked March 2011.

24. Charles M. Smith, editor, *U.S. Marines in Vietnam, High Mobility and Standdown, 1969*. History and Museums Division, Headquarters Marine Corps. Washington, D.C. 1988. The reference to sensor employment is on p. 246. The entire series is very informative; this volume also explains the innovative tactics developed and used by General Ray Davis in late 1968 and early 1969.

25. http://www.mca-marines.org/Gazette/jun08_ground_sensor_platoon.asp (checked January 2011).

26. In another coincidence that marks the book, Jan Gray's Aunt Celia was a Burlington grammar school classmate of General Wallace M. Greene, Jr., the 25th Commandant of the Marine Corps.

27. From General Gray's private collection.

28. From General Gray's private collection.

29. Long-range planning is, briefly, the process by which the services forecast future requirements. For example, if the long-range plan envisions that some new capability will be needed – a new form of helicopter or new amphibious vehicle, for example – then the budget and the development process needs to react in order to provide the new asset at the time it will be needed. Without long-range planning, the research and development process is not focused.

30. Author telephone interviews with Lieutenant General John H. Miller, United States Marine Corps (Ret.), January and February 2011. General Miller said that General Nichols "chatted up" Al Gray at every opportunity. The meeting at the Development Center was the first time Nichols ever met Gray. It would not be the last. See Chapter 4.

31. The official names of the senior commands located at the Marine Corps Base, Quantico change often, but the official name is probably important only to a few high-ranking Marine generals. For everyone else, "Quantico" is all one needs to say. From the 1920s, and maybe earlier, Quantico has been the "Crossroads" of the Marine Corps. Its role has evolved over the years; it used to be home to all the officer schools, the Officer Candidate School, the Development Center and the Helicopter Squadron that flies the President's Marine-One helicopter. Now, as the Combat Development Center, it is also the place where the Manpower Division of HQMC, the Marine Corps Systems Command, the Warfighting Center, the Staff NCO Academy, the General Alfred M.

Gray Research Center, the Marine Corps University, the National Museum of the Marine Corps, and sundry other commands are located.

32. From General Gray's private collection.

33. All Marine officers' seniority is determined by their place on the lineal list, which goes from the most senior officer of each grade, #1, to the most junior of that grade. Gray recalled that his number was about 1395.

34. Al Gray had a close bond with 7-Eleven Convenience Stores that lasted through his time as Commandant, when the General and his Labrador Retrievers would often stroll from the Commandant's House a few blocks to the nearest 7-Eleven store. Among his friends, General Gray's fondness for 7-Elevens is the source of considerable humor. In keeping with his style, at every stop along the way, General Gray usually knew all the clerks and many of the frequent customers by name. He had visited 7-Eleven Stores from Atsugi, Japan to Istanbul, Turkey to Barcelona, Spain. In fact, when Commandant and Mrs. Gray arrived at their hotel in Barcelona, there was an invitation to visit the local 7-Eleven awaiting them. While General Gray was Commandant, Mr. John Philip Thompson, the son of 7-Eleven's founder, presented the General with a stylish 7-Eleven coffee cup.

35. In the period immediately after Vietnam, commanding an infantry battalion, especially in combat, was a near prerequisite for promotion for infantry officers, which was exactly the professional specialty that Gray desired to have.

36. The Marine SRIC was disestablished when the U. S. Army took over responsibility for combat operations in I Corps. When, after several months whatever system the Army put in place turned out not to be responsive, it was requested that the Marines send Al Gray back to show them how to set up and operate a SRIC. Gray, of course, was prepared to go, but the Marine Corps denied the request. Gray, however, did send a complete operational package to the Army.

37. The Nixon conduct of the war involved every bit as politically complex equations as Johnson's. Nixon never chose the type of bombs, routes of ingress and egress and the target details that Johnson enmeshed himself with, but Nixon's "war policies" showed only slightly more coherence than those of his predecessor. See Karnow, Langguth, and Sorley. Perhaps letting Wheeler retire and having a new Chairman would have made a positive difference – perhaps!

38. Among many sources, see Langguth, p. 544-6; Karnow, p. 591-2.

39. For the best analysis of the generalship of Creighton Abrams, see Lewis Sorley, *A Better War: The Unexamined Victories and Final Tragedy of America's Last Years in Vietnam*. Sorley's analysis basically starts when Abrams assumes command; thus, he presents much more information of the years 1968 through 1975 than either Karnow or Langguth. Karnow, for example, devotes 296 pages to the years 1963-1968 and only 104 pages to the years 1969-1975. Langguth gave the years 1963 through 1968 a total of 303 pages while covering 1969 to 1975 in 135. Keep in mind that Lieutenant Colonel Lewis Sorley, U.S. Army, would become Colonel Al Gray's faculty advisor later when Gray was assigned to the Army War College, which is discussed in Chapter 12. The two remain good friends.

40. Sorley, pp. 154-157.

41. Sorley, p. 141. Perhaps because Sorley was writing from Abrams perspective, only his account talks about the Kennedy tirade.

CHAPTER 3

OFF TO SCHOOL
VIETNAMIZATION

OFF TO SCHOOL

The Marine Corps' Command & Staff College was sometimes a contentious place in 1970-1971. The war in Vietnam had affected America's Corps of Marines in many ways, and several were not positive. The Corps had expanded from its pre-war strength of 196,000 officers and men to a wartime high of 387,000. Many of the finest staff non-commissioned officers had been promoted to the officer ranks, and there had been no reservoir of experienced Staff NCOs left to replace them. And while it had been the Marine Corps that introduced the helicopter to the battlefield during the conflict in Korea, the Vietnam War tested, and retested, the harmony of the Marines' air-ground team.

In the late 1950s into the 1960s, budgetary pressures had shaped the development and composition of Marine helicopter units. The helicopter lift capability of a Marine aircraft wing was designed to support the assault requirements for two infantry regiments; in other words, the assault requirements of four infantry battalions. But by 1967, two full divisions and a newly formed regiment, the 26th Marines, were in combat in Southeast Asia, though only the equivalent of one and a half air wings had been committed. That meant roughly 20 maneuver battalions were supported by an air command designed to sustain 12.[1] The lower one was in the chain of command, the less that fact was understood. Among junior officers, distrust of the air arm was rampant. However, the truth was that there was no lack of courage and commitment on the part of Marine aviation; there was, rather, a lack of resources.

The war left many Marines with frayed nerves and bitter memories, and that number included many officers assigned to the Corps' highest military school, the Command & Staff College (C&SC). Students at the C&SC were mostly senior majors with some junior lieutenant colonels. Their experience at the college prepared them for high-level commands or duty with joint staffs. They represented the next generation of Marine leadership. However, one indication of the operational tempo imposed on the air wing was the fact that no aviators had attended the C&SC since 1965.

The President of the C&SC Class of 1971 was Lieutenant Colonel Al Gray. Gray had been sent to the high-level school in order to qualify better him for future assignments, and he was the senior man in the class. While he understood the rationale for the assignment, he chafed at the time he had to spend in the course. Gray was a strong proponent of self-study and a voracious reader. He always had been. He read everything that might improve his professional understanding, and his curiosity extended well beyond military, paramilitary or technical topic. Blessed with a near photographic memory, Gray was a quick study who consumed briefings, presentations and lectures as though they were his favorite food.

While Al Gray was anything but bored by the coursework, he also welcomed additional assignments that helped satiate his native curiosity. Thus, while a student, Gray partici-pated in ad hoc study groups and assisted in various Development Center projects. One afternoon when the class heard a lecture by a faculty member representing Marine Air, pandemonium broke out among the students. Strong disagreement about ground-air rela-tions turned quite controversial, and the officer was unable to deliver the lecture and left the auditorium stage. Gray calmly took the podium, re-established proper decorum, and then delivered the scheduled lecture. He did that without consulting notes or using any aids other than the materials the original lecturer had left behind. At least one of his fellow students thought that Al Gray probably knew more about the subject matter at Command & Staff College than all the instructors combined. While that obviously was too much praise, there was no doubt that Gray was an exceptional student with considerable profes-sional knowledge.[2]

QUANTICO, AUGUST 1970

Major General Alan Armstrong accepted Lieutenant Colonel Al Gray's written documentation of all the general and specific intelligence, surveillance and recon-naissance requirements for all aspects of Marine Corps systems and missions, and then watched as the younger officer nearly sprinted from his office to Barrett Hall. Gray's class at the Command & Staff College would be convening in mere minutes, and he never liked being late.

Senior officers had consistently recommended that Al Gray be assigned to a formal school. He was a graduate of the Communications Officer Course (consid-ered an Intermediate Level School) in 1956, and considered it to be an outstanding program that roughly equated to the old "Junior School," which had become the Amphibious Warfare School and is now the Expeditionary Warfare School. Years later Gray would recall that the curriculum included 196 hours of tactics, and 96 hours on command and staff procedures. The course put considerable emphasis on amphibious operational planning stressing communications. Nonetheless, higher level school was regarded as a prerequisite for assignments that included increased responsibility and promotion.

But Al Gray never fussed with things related to promotion, especially schools during a time of war. He had repeatedly foiled assignment to professional schools by extending in Vietnam; then, when he returned to the United States on emergency leave, he was too late for school and assigned to the Defense Communications Planning Group, a vital job insofar as the Marine Corps was concerned. But Al Gray was committed to education, especially as far as his Marines were concerned, and he had found self-study both rewarding and exceptionally useful.

While he thought of learning as a lifelong commitment, he deemed field assignments as trumping formal instruction. After all, he had already spent countless hours reading a wide array of materials, but he had become an officer in order to lead Marines. Becoming a professional was that vital first step, and Gray's self-directed reading program had prepared him well for the challenges of leadership. Already many seniors had noted how knowledgeable he was about a wide variety of professional topics. Now, his admirers had the ammunition they needed to get him back into a schoolhouse. Generals Armstrong, Houghton, Haynes, Davis and an array of colonels, led by Ike Fenton, were delighted to find that Al Gray would be carrying books and sitting in class. Gray, far from being disappointed, accepted the task at hand just like he undertook every other project, determined to do the best he could.

At the convocation of the new class, Gray found out that he was the senior student officer, and thus the class president. By 1970, Gray was reputed to be well qualified in the artillery, infantry and communications fields; and he had, as well, a unique background in intelligence. Among the many things that his contemporaries and seniors thought they knew about him was his broad status as a military professional – well read and highly knowledgeable in a wide range of topics. The senior officer-instructors at C&SC, the so-called den daddies, anxiously awaited the chance to find out for themselves if this Gray fellow had what it took, or if he was an imposter. Unfortunately, they would have to wait to get the chance to test their new student. Before they could get a crack at the highly decorated officer who had already become a minor legend at the Development Center, the Commanding General had other ideas. He needed Gray, and what Commanding Generals need, they usually get.

Lieutenant General Raymond Davis had become the Commanding General at Quantico the summer of 1970, just before Al Gray was sent off to school. The General had a relationship with Al Gray that went back to the days when Gray was a captain in Japan and Davis a colonel, working as the Inspector General of the Marine Corps. The association between the two grew closer during the time Captain and then-Major Gray worked on cryptologic issues at HQMC. More recently, Davis had commanded the 3rd Marine Division in Vietnam and Gray had been assigned on temporary additional duty to develop a Surveillance and Reconnaissance Center for III MAF. Yes, Ray Davis and Al Gray established a long, continuous bond based on mutual respect and confidence.

Davis called the younger Marine to his office and explained that he had been assigned the duty of making a series of speeches around the country to explain the war in Vietnam; the lecture tour would be under the auspices of the Battelle Institute. Gray knew that there was no more impressive officer who could have been given that duty. Besides being a straight arrow, an inspiring speaker and highly knowledgeable of tactics and strategy, Davis wore the light blue ribbon with five stars signifying a Medal of Honor. As a battalion commander in Korea, during the 1st Marine Division heroic breakout from Chosin, Davis led his battalion to keep the evacuation route open, thereby permitting Major General O.P. Smith's Marines to reach safety. Further, while serving under the legendary Chesty Puller on Pelelieu in World War II, Davis had earned a Navy Cross. He was a genuine war hero besides being one of the Corps' best field generals. As Davis described the nature of his additional duty assignment, he also told Gray of what the younger man would be doing. Davis would discuss operations in Vietnam, while Gray would present the intelligence, reconnaissance and surveillance assessment. Gray pointed out that he was now a student at C&SC and he would be unable to do the travel that the speaking tour would require.

General Davis turned his steely-eyed gaze to the Lieutenant Colonel and said, unsmilingly, in his soft Georgia drawl, "I am the Commanding General of the Marine Corps Development and Education Command. I will decide where you need to spend your time, Lieutenant Colonel Gray." Al Gray knew the only acceptable response would be, "Yes, sir."[3]

And so during the first two months of the C&SC, Al Gray was often absent traveling with his boss. The den daddies were not happy, but they were obviously left with no recourse.

General Ray Davis and Al Gray toured the country and over an eight-week period in September and October 1970 and gave multiple lectures to various audiences speaking about the war in South Vietnam – a war with which both were very familiar and both had recent experience.

Al Gray's respect for Ray Davis grew even more during their two-man speaking journey; it is also likely that Al Gray's reputation among the senior Marine officers also grew, though that conclusion is speculation.[4] Though the General's wishes would have prevailed in any event, it helped Gray's cause with the instructor-colonels that Brigadier General Sam Jaskilka became the Director of Command & Staff College at the same time that Gray was enrolled. General Jaskilka knew of

Gray's exploits in support of General Nickerson in Vietnam, having just returned from the war zone himself. So while Al Gray neither wanted nor needed anyone running interference for him, two of the finest Marine generals of their time were on the scene and prepared to do just that.

While Gray traveled with General Davis, his 120 classmates moved forward. They were a diverse group; there were 15 allied officers from 13 different countries. Six officers from each service represented the U.S. Army and Navy, while the Air Force sent two. Of the 91 Marines, 61 were from the ground component and 30 were from aviation. The aviators included two officers who had earned the Navy Cross in Vietnam while 18 others had been awarded the Distinguished Flying Cross – they were an impressive group. Their instructor and advisors included 13 Marine lieutenant colonels, aided by three junior officers.[5] The adjunct faculty included an number of distinguished reserve officers. Perhaps the noteworthy faculty member was the renowned Dr. August Tresidder, an indefatigable Professor of English.[6]

This was the first time since the start of the Vietnam War that aviators had been sent to school; the personnel requirements for the war simply did not permit them to have assignments outside aviation. Gray was keenly aware of the rift that had developed between the air-ground team, particularly among the younger officers and Staff NCOs. There existed a strong perception that the Marine Air Wing personnel were not providing sufficient, timely helicopter support for medical evacuations, logistics support and other operational needs.

Gray also know this problem stemmed from a lack of resources. General Youngdale, his former boss in the G-2 section at HQMC in the early 1960s, had been in charge of the study that examined the whole issue of air support. Further, the General had spoken extensively with Gray about the matter and had shared the final report with the younger officer. And Gray was aware of the Hogaboom study from earlier years that placed the number of helicopters in each wing at the level required to support the assault requirements of two regiments (i.e., four battalions).

Once Al Gray returned to the classroom full-time, his facility for teamwork, his constant sharing of professional knowledge and his genuine assistance to others became his hallmark. By the mid-December Christmas break, he had gained the respect and admiration of the den daddies. After all, they respected officers who were proficient, hard working and well read – Al Gray was all those things and more. Also, as previously mentioned, after strong disagreement among the students over Marine air operations and capabilities caused the instructor to leave the stage, he restored propriety and completed the lecture. This was another way that Gray distinguished himself. Interestingly, he accomplished these things in his modest, unassuming manner without fanfare.

Late in the term, a major potential embarrassment arose when some officers were accused of cheating, committing academic fraud. General Jaskilka asked Gray, since he was the Class President, to conduct an investigation of the incident. Al Gray undertook the effort with all the energy and thoroughness that marked his regular duties. He got all those potentially involved together, and demanded their cooperation in learning what had happened. He determined that the problem, first and foremost, did not involve many officers. Second, he concluded that there had been no academic fraud; the quiz involved was no big deal and certainly the incident did not merit any formal investigation. Gray was sure that they had handled it in-house and that there would be no repetitions. Jaskilka accepted the Class President's recommendation and the matter was dropped.

When the Deputy Director of the college, a senior colonel, asked for the names of those who had been involved, Gray refused to disclose them. Gray told the colonel that if he wanted the names, he could always get them from the General. Eventually, the colonel's anger subsided and he too became a longtime admirer. After all, Al Gray probably knew more secrets than any officer of his rank then alive, and he kept them all very private unless someone had a real need to know.

Gray was quite satisfied with his time at C&SC. At the time there was a difference between the Marine philosophy about professional schools and the Army's. The Army sent captains to school to become the best captains possible. The Marine Corps sent captains to school to learn to be majors and lieutenant colonels. Thus, C&SC had hundreds of hours of instruction designed to make its students highly capable staff officers on joint, allied or very senior staffs. Not only was the curriculum very good, but also, because of the proximity of Quantico to Washington the class benefited from a variety of superb, high-powered speakers from inside the highest levels of government. For example, it was the norm for the Assistant Secretary of State for a particular region to present the lecture on that area. Looking back, Gray thought the curriculum outstanding and that it played an important part of expanding his professional knowledge.

One highlight of Gray's time at C&SC came at the Class Mess Night. Mess Night in the Marine Corps is an almost sacred affair, designed to boost the camaraderie of the members of the mess, usually a unit but in this case a class. In days past, the Mess Night featured the Marine Corps highly stylized formal uniforms and dress uniforms, though more recently Marine units have held Mess Nights in the field where those present are attired in camouflaged utilities. Customarily the evening features a variety of alcoholic beverages served around a multi-course meal. Thrown in are toasts that result from the interaction between the "President of the

Mess," typically the commanding officer, and "Mr. Vice," normally the unit adjutant and often the junior officer present.

At the C&SC Mess Night, the President was Lieutenant Colonel Al Gray, reflecting his position within the class. The Guest of Honor was the Commandant of the Marine Corps, Leonard F. Chapman. Other general officers were prominent guests, including Lieutenant General Gay Thrash,[7] Major General Alan Armstrong from the Development Center, Major General Sam Jaskilka from the Education Center, and Brigadier General George Webster, the Quantico base commander. Seated at the center of the Head Table was the Mess President, with the Commandant to his left, Generals Thrash and Webster to his right and other dignitaries all around.

During the prelude to the speeches and toasts, the normal chitchat typical of professional gatherings occurred. At one point, General Webster, who had served with Gray earlier, but not knowing the previous meetings between General Chapman and then-Major Gray at HQMC in 1963-64, leaned forward and made some comment to the Commandant about how well Gray was doing. The General Chapman replied with this observation. "George, you don't need to tell me about Lieutenant Colonel Gray. I know about him." The Commandant then turned to Gray and said, "I've been wanting to tell you that when you and I disagreed regarding the Radio Battalions in our meeting with General Greene many years ago, you were right and I was wrong."[8] For Al Gray, the Commandant's statement topped a fine evening, and he had nothing to drink except for the toasts! Far more important, Gray would never forget this class act by a distinguished Commandant of the Marine Corps.

About a month before the class graduated, the Lieutenant Colonels monitor, Colonel Robin Dickey, came to visit the class and determine where the students wanted to be posted. Of course, not all students received their first choice of duty; the needs of the service remained the most important ingredient leading to an officer's next assignment. During his discussion with Al Gray, the Colonel brought up the issue of all the military specialties that Gray had mastered. Plus, Dickey knew that Al Gray was more than qualified as an intelligence officer. So what did Gray want when he left school – artillery, cryptology or infantry? True to form, and in keeping with every request he had made since graduating from The Basic School, Al Gray said that he wanted to be an infantry officer and wanted to be assigned to the Fleet Marine Forces. The monitor was happy to oblige him and so it was that Lieutenant Colonel Alfred Mason Gray, now an infantryman with artillery, communications, cryptologic and intelligence sub-specialties, received orders to report to the 2nd Marine Division in June 1971. After almost 20 years of trying,

Al Gray finally achieved one of the goals that he had first sought upon graduating from The Basic School.

Another officer from Gray's past was the Commanding General of the 2nd Marine Division, Michael P. Ryan. Ryan had been Gray's battalion commander in Korea and had been the officer Gray had thought might earn promotion to general when Gray was asked his opinion at HQMC. It was General Ryan who had chided Gray about "getting back to work" – supposedly meaning he ought to be at the 2nd Division – when Gray was at the Development Center enmeshed in sensors. General Ryan had remained in contact with Gray prior to his graduation, and the General had indicated that the Division's Fire Support Coordination Center was not operating effectively. He thought Gray was the ideal candidate to square away that critical aspect of the Division's effectiveness, and as a result had requested that Gray be assigned to the 2nd Division.

As it turned out, however, General Ryan was moved to become Deputy Commanding General of Fleet Marine Forces, Atlantic and, in June, Al Gray would report to a new Commanding General.

Shortly before graduation, Gray received an unusual order: proceed to Washington and accompany Senator Margaret Chase Smith of Maine to Quantico. Senator Smith was the guest speaker at the graduation ceremony. Gray fondly recalled her friendly banter with her Marine host; little did the Marine realize that this was the first of many future discussions he would have with a wide range of senators and congressional representatives.

Al Gray departed Command & Staff College as an honor graduate. In addition to Gray, the class included several future generals: General Joseph P. Hoar, Lieutenant General Anthony Lukeman, Major General Gene Deegan and Brigadier General James E. Sniffen.

Yes, in the end, the den daddies were truly happy with Al Gray, Marine.

VIETNAMIZATION

NEW POLITICAL LEADERSHIP: WASHINGTON, 1969 - 1970

If there was a President who misled, or wanted to mislead the public, about Vietnam more than Lyndon Baines Johnson, it was Richard Milhous Nixon.

From the very start of his Presidency, Nixon knew he had to "do something" with respect to Vietnam. The looming anti-war riots, the increasingly negative television news reporting, and the mounting congressional criticism of the war had an effect on Nixon, and not a positive one. Nixon desperately wanted to win public approval, and despite his claims that he would pay no attention to the anti-war activists, he paid close attention to them.[9]

Almost everything Nixon did in Vietnam, except for announcing and implementing troop reductions, he did secretly. He secretly bombed Cambodia; he secretly authorized incursions into Laos; and he sent Kissinger on secret negotiations in Paris. Moreover, Nixon lied to President Thieu; despite assuring Thieu repeatedly that American aid was unequivocal —the *Nixon Doctrine* was formulated precisely for South Vietnam – but Nixon and especially his foreign policy henchman, Henry Kissinger, were willing to do almost anything to rid themselves of the political problem that was the war in Vietnam.

As early as 1970 the Nixon Administration was ready to make large concessions in order to achieve peace. There was little consideration given to South Vietnam's interests, or its future prospects.[10]

The Administration was not marching in step for the first several years it was in office. First off, Kissinger and Nixon had an unusual relationship that dated to the days before Nixon won the Republican nomination. Kissinger, while an untenured assistant professor at Harvard, had himself promoted into Governor Nelson Rockefeller's (of New York) inner circle, and he had spoken poorly of Nixon. But politics makes strange bedfellows, and after winning the nomination Nixon had reached out to the former U.S. Army intelligence sergeant for advice, and Kissinger, by providing it, dropped his allegiance to Rockefeller and won his way into the new Administration. The Secretary of State, William P. Rogers, was a patrician lawyer who did not realize until it was far too late that Kissinger aspired to his job. Kissinger was fighting to become the leading foreign policy advisor to the President. Even though Rogers had been President Dwight Eisenhower's Attorney General and had survived Nixon's first term, given Kissinger's incredible in-fighting skills, it was as though Rogers had brought a knife to a gunfight. Rogers never had any influence over any aspect of the Vietnam War or the negotiations with the communists, or discussions with the Soviet Union, or opening China – Kissinger led on all those principal questions.

Mel Laird, the former congressman turned Secretary of Defense, also had little impact on Vietnam policy. He seemed even more willing than Nixon to reduce troops strength in a desire to build public support for the Administration. Laird and Kissinger were never on the same page, not that it mattered to the National Security Advisor, who sounded more like a German speaking English than he did an American. Kissinger could bulldoze anyone; anyone, that is, but the North Vietnamese.

What was most problematic about Nixon's first several years, other than his penchant for secrecy in all matters, was that not a single figure in Washington seemed to understand the effects of reducing American troops so quickly without simultaneously giving the South Vietnamese time to fill the voids that withdrawal created. General Creighton Abrams, still Commanding in Vietnam, gave objective reports on the situation and made positive recommendations as to how to proceed, though it is doubtful that any of the civilian leadership in Washington understood, or even cared about, what he was reporting. That was surprising since a key advisor to Kissinger was then-Brigadier General Alexander Haig, U.S. Army, a highly regarded Vietnam combat veteran.

Haig made many trips back and forth to Southeast Asia, shuttling the President news and information from Abrams's Headquarters while also providing the General with the latest inside political views from inside the D.C. beltway. Perhaps though, Haig was best at taking care of Al Haig. Whereas the Johnson Administration had shown itself incapable of permitting the military professionals to conduct the air war against North Vietnam, the Nixon White House, though its intermediary Al Haig, very quickly proved that it was quite capable of meddling in the ground war in the South, and in a very big way.[11]

THE DILETTANTES WITHIN: WASHINGTON AND SAIGON, 1970

General Creighton Abrams took advantage of the death and destruction of the Viet Cong following Tết 1968 to build a new framework for the war. He did not have his major combat units out searching and destroying, though as General Ray Davis' 3rd Marine Division had proven, there was plenty of offense left on the American side. Abrams stressed cooperation with the South Vietnamese, and given President Nixon's emphasis on *Vietnamization*, he probably had no choice.

But improving performance by the ARVN and new attempts to keep the insurgents away from the population centers were bearing fruit. Further, the NVA found it increasingly difficult get supplies into the South. By late summer of 1970 the situation was looking much better than it had since President Ngo Dinh Diem's heyday of 1960. The bombing of the Ho Chi Minh Trail and Cambodian sanctuaries meant NVA operating inside South Vietnam were threatened. General Abrams wanted to add to their discomfort by attacking and destroying the supply points that dotted the cross-border region. He asked for permission to strike with ground forces into Cambodia. Regrettably Lon Nol had just overthrown Prince Sihanouk's weak government and the White House wasted valuable time trying to evaluate how Lon Nol might react.

But on April 30 and May 1, 1970, armed columns of ARVN and American ground forces thrust their way into the Fishhook area of Cambodia. The goal of the incursion was to eliminate the supply and arms caches the communists maintained in the area. The event was called an incursion before Nixon put a specific timetable on the operation. All Allied forces, declared Nixon, would be withdrawn by June 30. So Nixon's attempt to influence the anti-war crowd by saying the *incursion* was temporary really provided tactical advice to the NVA – they had to but hold out, avoid contact and on July 1 everything would be back to normal. It was another example of America fighting with one hand tied behind its back. Abrams, who knew the mission was successful and had the enemy running, grumbled about the order, but, being a good soldier, obeyed.

While Nixon tried to quench the unending demands of the anti-war crowd, it was in the Congress that the foray into Cambodia had the most repercussions. Democrats were anxious to undermine both the war and the President, while some Republicans also opposed broadening the conflict. Having South Vietnamese troops supported by Americans invade another country was more than sufficient cause for Congressional heartburn to rise to a boil. The Allied forces broke up NVA formations and supply dumps in Cambodia, the presences of which were both clear violations of that country's neutrality; but such facts were obviously inconsequential to American politicians.

Senators, led by Frank Church of Utah, introduced a resolution that cut off funding for the Cambodia operation after June 30. It passed the Senate, but not the House. Of course, all the Allied troops withdrew from Cambodia on 30 June, just as Nixon had promised; it was one of those rare times Nixon actually announced his intentions publicly. But Church – his bill co-sponsored by Republican John Sherman Cooper – reintroduced the bill that did finally get House approval; among other things it forbade armed forces of the United States from accompanying ARVN sorties outside South Vietnam. Nixon objected to the legislation, of course, which seemed to assist the nation's enemies far more than it helped United States forces in the field.[12]

Political opposition to the war had been building dating back to 1968 and the events that led President Johnson to withdraw from his re-election effort. The Nixon Administration polarized the opposition, but on May 4, 1970, the tragic killing of four anti-war students at Kent State (Ohio) University cemented the anti-war movement. The events of the situation, when Ohio National Guard troops fired into the students, remain vague and uncertain, though much has been written on the subject. Whatever happened, the graphic images on television and nearly every American saw the still photographs of the victims. The effect on the civilian-military was grievous. At the same time, anti-war activists such as Jane Fonda came to the fore of the movement, giving strong and well-known voices to the opposition.

Fonda also associated herself with the Black Panther Party, which at the time was a separatist movement. The "black power salutes" given by two American athletes at the Mexico City Olympics had brought both notoriety and publicity to the Black Panthers, and by 1970 both their membership numbers and their influence had peaked. But they surely affected the social discourse in the United States, and within the military. The anti-war movement had many factions working to disrupt the military, for example the Vietnam Veterans Against the War, whose numbers included John F. Kerry. The Black Panther Party provided a racial component.

Whatever the political opposition to the war may have been, the Church Amendment was arguably the most ill advised and unprecedented legislation ever passed by Congress in the midst of a war. It added to future American casualties while also giving aid and comfort to the enemy. Congress, especially in the midst of a war, might want to concentrate on legislation that deters America's enemies, not its allies. There were many other ways to try to influence the war without actively hurting American forces in the field. While it is true that preventing American advisors from accompanying their units in Cambodia or Laos might have saved some advisors' lives, permitting would have saved many more American lives by making the incursions be more effective militarily. The Congressional action was both shortsighted and dangerous to both our forces and, especially, our allies.

Fighting a war from the White House or Congress is fraught with danger. Abraham Lincoln certainly got it right; so did Woodrow Wilson during World War I and Franklin Roosevelt during World War II. Regrettably, Harry Truman was the President who introduced America to the notion that a war-ending stalemate is an acceptable outcome, that permitting American servicemen to be sacrificed without winning, simply to stop aggression, was permissible. That Dwight Eisenhower reinforced that approach only exacerbated the seismic change in American military policy.

The Vietnam War was the epitome of bad leadership, particularly in the White Houses of Lyndon Johnson and Richard Nixon. As bad as the executive branch leadership was, by 1970 the Congressional meddling was equally dreadful. Never in history had America, at the decisive hour, turned its back on allies who were actively involved protecting themselves from aggression. The Congresses of 1970, 1972 and 1974 earned an ignominious distinction as a gutless, spineless collection of dilettantes concerned about nothing but their own self-aggrandizement. The budgets passed by those Congresses gave the communists their goals on a silver platter. As a consequence of Nixon's foibles, reflected by Watergate, the Congress was able to make an undeterred assault on the American fighting force and on a friend reliant on America. The Administration's inability to curb the Congressional excesses cemented Nixon's place near the bottom of American wartime leaders, where he rubs elbows with LBJ.

Anyone who doubts whether or not the ARVN would fight for their country needs only look at the Cambodian expedition of April – June 1970 for their answer. The ARVN high command fought a brilliantly planned and executed operation; of course, the presence of American ground forces, and in particular U.S. air and artillery support were crucial ingredients in what amounted to a very sizeable Allied victory. With the ARVN success came, however, the loss of one of the generals who led the operation. Major General Nguyen Viet Thanh was killed when two helicopters collided. For the South Vietnamese, who had precious few commanders with corps-level experience, it was a bitter loss. Nevertheless, Abrams knew the real fight was back in South Vietnam; it was the fight for the hearts and minds, and especially the security, of the South Vietnamese people.

While some parts of Washington enjoyed basking in the success of the Cambodian incursion, the very accomplishments earned by the action led to the hatching of unrealistic schemes and plans by the Nixon White House.

THE MARINES LEAVE: I CORPS, 1970

Between January 1970 and June 1971 all major Marine Corps combat units left Vietnam. During the drawdown, the 1st Marine Division and the major elements of the 1st Marine Aircraft Wing concentrated around Da Nang. As they withdrew, Marines focused on civic action programs and assigned infantry companies into the former Combined Action Program, now called the Combined Unit Pacification Program. Even as the Marines pulled out, innovation marked their efforts.

By assigning helicopters to various infantry units, response times were reduced and reactions to enemy sightings improved. The communists had lost the initiative in and around Da Nang and there was little important that happened – unless, of course, one happened to be one of the Marines involved in a firefight or other small unit action.

Perhaps the most interesting aspect of the Marine Corps withdrawal had to do with their logistical efforts. Commandant Chapman decreed that his units would bring out every single item valued at $5 or more. The resulting harvest of equipment was distributed to Marine units throughout the Pacific area, but for logisticians it was nightmare.

The III MAF Redistribution Center coordinated the processing of over $50M of gear that represented more than 325,000 separate items. After the combat formations left in late June 1971, the 1st Air & Naval Gunfire Liaison Company, the Embassy Marines and a smattering of technicians were left. There were still Marines serving on the MAC(V) staff, but everyone else who wore an Eagle, Globe and Anchor was an advisor.[13]

NOTES AND REFERENCES

1. During the Vietnam War, each regiment had three battalions; each division had three regiments. When the 26th Marines was activated and arrived in the war zone, that meant there were 21 infantry battalions available; however, one battalion was usually refitting on Okinawa while another served as the Special Landing Force (SLF). The SLF had its own helicopter squadron assigned and it was typically aboard ship stationed offshore. That left 19 battalions conducting operations inside Vietnam. The 3rd Marine Aircraft Wing was in country, augmented by squadrons from the 1st Wing. Never, though, did the Marine Corps have enough pilots and aircraft to commit two full wings to the war. Thus, the infantry's perception that the wing was not providing adequate support was not due to anything the aviators were doing wrong; quite to the contrary, they were fully committed, and then some.
2. Author interviews with Colonel George Slade, United States Marine Corps (Ret.) during 2009 and 2010.
3. General Gray recalls that both Generals Chapman and Davis, and many other old timers, were sticklers about using the correct grade when addressing lieutenant colonels.

4. General Davis was promoted to Assistant Commandant of the Marine Corps in February 1971, and served in that capacity under General Leonard F. Chapman and briefly under General Robert Cushman before retiring in March 1972. Of course, Al Gray needed no introduction to either Commandant. One of the highlights of the author's life was having dinner with General Davis and General Gray and two other Marines one evening in Washington. The mutual respect between the two men was apparent. And, proving it is indeed a small world, the author's wife served as a judge in the same Federal Court with General Davis's son Miles. While it is tough to nail down which officers General Gray admired most during his long service, Ray Davis has to be in the top three.

5. Instructor/advisors included Lieutenant Colonels D. Deatley, P. Wichwie, W. Hammond, J. Fabey, A. Croft, J. Burice, J. Scoppa, A. Anderson, G. Dolan, B. MacLaren, R. Hagerty and M. Duke. They were assisted by 1st Lieutenants E. Kruger, E. Murphy and R. Lamb.

6. Dr. Tresidder had a reputation far and wide in Marine educational circles. At that time, many, many Marines would use the expression "and/or" in their writings. That phrase was anathema to Dr. Tresidder and he struck it down whenever he encountered it. Of course, this author is uncertain of the long-term success of Dr. Tresidder's crusade.

7. By this time, General Davis had been promoted to Assistant Commandant of the Marine Corps and General Thrash placed him as CG at Quantico, which was then the Marine Corps Development and Education Command.

8. General Chapman retired in 1972, but lived a long and useful life. He became Commissioner of the Immigration and Naturalization Service following his Marine career. He also kept close tabs on the Marine Corps, and lived to see Al Gray become Commandant. While many, perhaps most, Marines refer to lieutenant colonels as "colonel" during informal speech, Chapman never did. He always used the proper terms – lieutenant colonel – when addressing someone of that grade.

9. See, for example, Karnow, p. 599-600.

10. Karnow, Langguth and to some extent Sorley all cover Nixon's diplomatic starts and stops, and how incoherently the Nixon strategy was implemented. On one hand he offered concessions; on the other he threatened violent bombing attacks. It is highly likely that if the communists had agreed to Nixon's initial overtures, the war would have ended exactly as it did, only five years sooner. Instead, communist intransigence and miscalculation made the Nixon-Kissinger exodus take much longer, and it ended up costing the communists, and the United States, dearly.

11. Lewis Sorley is decidedly pro-Abrams; as a result he is less than favorable to Al Haig. See, for example, Sorley, p. 230 and p. 263-4.

12. Langguth, p. 568-9. Surprisingly, Sorley never mentions Senator Church.

13. Graham A. Cosmas and Lieutenant Colonel Terence P. Murray, editors, *Marines in Vietnam: Vietnamization and Redeployment, 1970 & 1971*. History and Museums Division, Headquarters, United States Marine Corps, Washington, D.C. 1986.

CHAPTER 4

FINALLY, INFANTRY BATTALION COMMANDING OFFICER VIETNAMIZATION IN FULL SWING

FINALLY, INFANTRY BATTALION COMMANDING OFFICER

QUALITY INN, QUANTICO, VA. 0630, THURSDAY, JULY 8, 1971

The Marine had been visiting the Crossroads of the Marine Corps, Quantico, from his duty station at Camp Lejeune, North Carolina. It was unusual for him to be away from his command, but there was a lot going on at Quantico and his presence there was needed. He was up early, casually dressed in civilian clothes, though his closely cropped crew cut clearly identified him as a Marine, at least to other Marines. He intended to grab a quick breakfast before returning to "Swamp Lagoon," as Marines call their sandy amphibious base on the Carolina coast. But, unexpectedly, while awaiting the dining room to open, he had been engaged in conversation by the mother of a new lieutenant who just the day before had graduated from The Basic School, where all Marine officers receive their initial professional training.

The mother knew very little about the military, and she found the stocky, well-spoken Marine to be both friendly and engaging. Her husband and daughter joined the conversation, asking various mundane questions about the service and its traditions. But soon the man was asking about their son and brother, the new lieutenant. He learned a lot, because the mother, overcoming her early aversion to the idea of her Jesuit-trained and educated son becoming a Marine, had embraced his service – helped immensely in her conversion while attending the Sunset Parade at 8th & I the previous evening – and she now wanted to learn everything she could. But she also loved to tell anyone, even this person whom she had never met, everything about a son whom she was very proud of, reflecting on his achievements in high school and college, and his pride in his nomination for a regular commission.

The lieutenant arrived shortly after 0630 to join the family breakfast. He quickly discerned that they had been talking with someone who was clearly a Marine, albeit he was in civvies. Introductions were made and the unknown Marine identified himself as a lieutenant colonel. Just then the dining room opened, and mother invited the friendly officer to join the family for breakfast; he readily accepted. To the lieutenant's delight, his mother seemed to grow silent, leaving the colonel to carry the conversation. He asked as a series of questions about the lieutenant's Basic School curriculum and experience, and then asked the lieutenant about his choice of orders and his desires for future assignments. All the questions were positive and none had the tone of senior speaking to a junior. The

Lieutenant relaxed, sort of, thinking this was more like General Lejeune's writings about seniors being mentors to juniors. Still, the young officer was wary of the potential for disaster. After all, in his very limited experience, lieutenants rarely spoke with lieutenant colonels, and never fatuously. And while he deeply loved his parents, the lieutenant realized they were completely indifferent to his perceptions of proper Marine decorum, because, indeed, they had no knowledge of the military rank structure. In response to questioning, the lieutenant stated that he knew 1st Battalion, 2nd Marines, would be the next infantry battalion that would soon head off for a cruise in the Mediterranean, or the "Med" as it was called; the lieutenant also stated he thought 1/2 would probably have already be filled with their officer complement.

The family's breakfast companion then announced that he was the Commanding Officer of 1st Battalion, 2nd Marines and that he would look forward to having the lieutenant join his battalion, which indeed shortly would deploy to the "Med." Further, the Lieutenant Colonel told a very excited lieutenant that upon his arrival he should state to the personnel section that Al Gray had indicated he would hold a spot in the battalion for the lieutenant. Unfortunately, the Lieutenant was so flustered he could not even recall the officer's name long enough to write it down. The Lieutenant Colonel bade his farewells to the family and left, leaving the lieutenant to ponder what exactly had just happened.

Four weeks later the lieutenant and three of his Basic School buddies found themselves chatting amicably with Captain Lacey, the mustang officer-in-charge of the Division's Personnel and Placement Office.[1] Captain Lacey's bonhomie had the lieutenants convinced that he was simply setting them up for a bad deal, their probable assignment to a security unit at Guantanamo Bay, Cuba – universally known within the service as" Gitmo." The Lieutenant listened listlessly to what was being said, all the while debating whether to mention his earlier breakfast meeting with the Battalion Commander of 1/2, an officer whose name remained unknown to him. He knew that bringing up that meeting would open him to possible ridicule by the Captain, and likely derision from his friends, who, after all, were just as qualified as he – all having been nominated for Regular commissions. Finally, mustering all the courage he had, the Lieutenant nervously asked if by any chance the Commanding Officer of 1/2 had mentioned holding a spot for him?

The Captain seemed genuinely surprised, but even more unexpectedly, he stated that indeed Al Gray had threatened the Captain with an assignment to Adak, Alaska if he inadvertently sent one specific lieutenant to Gitmo. He then picked up the phone and called the battalion's Executive Officer, Major Doc Smith. The lieutenants could only hear one end of the conversation which went, "Hi Doc, I've got Lieutenant Pedrick sitting in my office…. okay but you are now one over T/O so you are going to have to reassign someone… OK… OK… good morning Colonel, yeah he is sitting here in my office now, I'll send him right over.... oh, well OK, I'll have him ready." When he hung up he looked at the short (all of 5'7"), stocky and now very excited 2ⁿᵈ Lieutenant and said, "Son, I do not know what you did, or how you did it but you just hooked your star to about as fine an officer who has ever worn the uniform, he is clearly a rising star, was just deep selected for Colonel.... you better thank your good fortune and do well!" He then said that the colonel is personally coming over to pick his new lieutenant. Shortly thereafter Lieutenant Colonel Al Gray pulled up, driving his own jeep, with two Labrador retrievers in the back seat.[2]

BATTALION HEADQUARTERS, 1ˢᵗ BATTALION, 2ⁿᵈ MARINES, CAMP LEJEUNE, NORTH CAROLINA. JUNE 1971

Command & Staff College had gone quickly for Al Gray. After completing his whirlwind, two-month speaking tour with Major General Ray Davis, he had settled into the school routine well enough to become an honor graduate, enjoying the mental stimulation that the rigorous academic program had to offer. Almost as importantly, he had finally achieved a long-term objective, his primary professional specialty finally had become infantry.

Following completion of school, in June, Lieutenant Colonel Al Gray left for Camp Lejeune and the 2ⁿᵈ Marine Division. He expected that his old battalion commander from Korea would be determining his new assignment, but just before Gray's arrival, Major General Mike Ryan was transferred to become the Deputy Commanding General, Fleet Marine Force, Atlantic; it would not be he who would decide Al Gray's new duties.

Major General Robert D. Bohn had replaced Ryan as the Commanding General. The new CG was a decorated hero who had been a distinguished company commander in Korea. As a more senior officer, Bohn was tough, highly respected and a keen tactician. And the General had more pressing needs than upgrading his artillery's fire support coordination, which is what Gray thought General Ryan had in mind for him. In his initial interview with the division commander, Al Gray expressed his long-held desire to command a battalion. General Bohn was keenly aware that the 1ˢᵗ Battalion, 2ⁿᵈ Marines (1/2) was scheduled to deploy to the Mediterranean in September, and he was very concerned. The unit was well behind in all facets of training, readiness and overall preparation for deployment. Among other things, the battalion was 22 officers short and it had yet to pass any of the mandatory pre-deployment evaluations; it needed strong leadership immediately, if not sooner. General Bohn gave Al Gray the task of getting the battalion ready to deploy. In keeping with his history, Gray got right to work while wondering just how bad the situation might be.

In the months preceding Gray's arrival, the social framework of the division had been stretched to the breaking point. In all military services, not just the Marines, racial tensions ran high. The military was a microcosm of American society of the time, struggling in the areas of civil rights, drugs, and alcohol abuse. These were ongoing problems – severe and aggravated – throughout the services. Hollywood movies about Vietnam sensationalized the situation, all the while never honoring the enormous majority of Marines, Soldiers, Airmen, and Sailors who did their duty well and served just as honorably as any group who had gone before them. The social issues had been significantly exacerbated because Secretary of Defense Robert S. McNamara, in 1966, instituted a social experiment called *Project 100,000*, which permitted men not qualified intellectually or educationally to enlist.[3] When the Vietnam era ended for the Marine Corps, the problems came home with the men. Coincidentally, *Project 100,000* did not end until 1971.

One Montford Point Marine who joined the Corps in 1942, Edgar R. Huff, had risen to be the Sergeant Major of the III Marine Amphibious Force in Vietnam.[4] In fact, Sergeant Major Huff held that position twice, including the year that Marine ground forces departed the country. By the last year of the war for the Marines, 1971, the effects of society, and the personnel experiment of Secretary McNamara, had combined to have a huge impact. Huff specifically noted the McNamara project when he said, "...of the quality of some of our enlisted Marines was deficient in terms of education."[5] Still, Marines in infantry and artillery battalions, aviation and many other units, performed well, smashing the popular notion that everyone in Vietnam was high on drugs or alcohol, and that there was no discipline. Sergeant Major Huff, and every other good Marine leader, recognized that their personal attention to the issue was required.

Sergeant Major Huff specifically addressed the racial issues facing the Corps and other services head on, without pretext, when he was quoted as saying:

> *"The fact that our line units performed with little of the racial problems seen in the rear area is a tribute to the officers and staff NCOs of those units. It is interesting to note that most the black officers and staff NCOs are in the line units. In my opinion, their presence there and the common bond they shared with their white counterparts helped sustain the combat effectiveness of those commands."*[6]

Despite all the unrest in III MAF during the latter stages of the war, Huff summarized the issue from his perspective when he stated, "... the majority of the Marines I met in Vietnam met the challenge presented them in stride; no one knows that better than General Giap of the NVA."[7]

That, from the III MAF Sergeant Major, is in direct contradiction to the sensationalized scenes in Vietnam movies such as *Platoon* or *The Deer Hunter*. Sergeant Major Huff's remarks notwithstanding, there indeed were a large number of troublemakers and many had been assigned to Camp Lejeune before Gray's arrival.

In the 6th Marines, which was one of the 2nd Marines' sister regiments in the division, the Regimental Commander had been held hostage for a few days in his own headquarters. Gray knew that Colonel very well, for it had been he who had recommended Gray for a commission - his old recon platoon commander, Colonel "Bull" Kraince. That situation developed despite the fact that Kraince was a tough, no-nonsense, experienced and widely respected leader.

In those days in Jacksonville, just outside Camp Lejeune, it was well known that outside money was being sent into town for distribution to those Marines and Sailors who would instigate trouble. The problem was not just simple racial hatred; it was racial tension provoked and flamed by external sources. Regrettably, the civilian authorities never really went after the masterminds and the ability of the Marine commanders to investigate off base was severely limited. But that is not to say that old-fashioned leadership could not be effective; indeed it could be, as Al Gray was determined to prove. It was not with his eyes closed that Gray went into his new assignment.

Upon his arrival at battalion headquarters after the formal change of command, he first entered the Commanding Officer's office to see what information he could gather. It would forever be easy for Gray to recall the date, for it was his birthday, June 22. The first two desk drawers that he opened provided pretty much everything he needed to know. There he found a stack of service record books reflecting the fact that three dozen of his Marines were awaiting special courts-martial!

The Marine Corps of 1971 was much different from that of today in that summary courts-martial and special courts-martial were handled mostly by line officers, supported by lawyers. Now, such matters in the Staff Judge Advocate system are exclusively within the purview of trained attorneys. Indeed, in the 1970s, it was an unusual circumstance that a lawyer was found in an infantry battalion. A summary court-martial had a single officer serve as prosecuting attorney, defense attorney, judge and jury. A summary court-martial was used when the offense alleged was more serious than the battalion commander wanted to handle at office hours, which is also called non-judicial punishment or NJP. A special court-martial was used for even more serious crimes, and required separate officers to serve as the prosecutor and defense attorney, and three or more to serve as the jury; the senior officer on the jury was also the President of the Court and functioned as the Judge. All these courts-martial were additional duties for the officers involved, and they were not welcomed assignments.

Gray was well familiar with what had to be done. During his time in Korea he had been assigned as defense counsel for a Marine subjected to a courts-martial, and while commanding officer of the 4.2 mortar company in Vieques, Puerto Rico, he had been a member of several Special Courts-Martial.[8] To have 36 Marines, from a battalion of about 1,200, awaiting special courts-martial was far beyond the normal situation, and it gave Gray pause to consider what else awaited him. Not that it took too long before he found out.

Gray was told that "A" company was in Vieques training, a portion of "B" Company was in Panama, "C" company and part of Headquarters company were out in the Pisgah National Forest training, while "D" company had but one officer and 16 Marines. He was surprised to hear that the remnants of "B" Company was called "brig company." Previously designated the Regimental Discharge Company, until just before Gray's arrival Bravo had been the division's holding unit for troops who should have been in the brig, but for whom there was no room. The actual Bravo Company had left for jungle training in Panama, leaving the lurkers, shirkers, and others awaiting discharge behind. There were 1,214 Marines on the rolls of 1/2, but that number included many deserters, men gone on Unauthorized Absence (UA), and other "sick, lame, and lazy" – as Marines not fit for duty have forever been called. The Battalion Sergeant Major, John Murphy, greeted Gray and told him that if the battalion could muster 400 for a battalion formation, it would be a surprise; getting 500 to formation would make the Commanding Officer a magician.

Unfortunately, as Gray already knew but soon confirmed, the higher one went in the chain of command, the fewer understood the real situation. Since the regiment and the division records would show 1,214 Marines on the rolls, the officers at those headquarters thought there should be no reason for 1/2 not to achieve full personnel readiness prior to deployment. Indeed, in the opinion of many, the battalion had a training challenge, not a personnel problem.

But the issues Gray and other battalion commanders faced were not simply limited to the local leadership. In those days the number of four-star billets was determined by the total end strength of the service, so there was a great reluctance even to discharge men who simply should not have been Marines. Thus, efforts to get rid of people – for example, repeat offenders who had been the subject of numerous special courts-martial – were resisted at HQMC, which placed a strict quota with respect to the number of Marines who could be administratively discharged from the service. Consequently, local commanders had little or no latitude to discharge men on their own authority and strict quotas were enforced. As a result, as the old saying goes, the "brown stuff" flows downhill.

But late in the afternoon of June 22, after leafing through the stack of records for Marines awaiting special courts-martial, Gray decided that his first stop outside his headquarters would be to what the Marines still called "Brig" company. As he entered the barracks, a large African-American Marine wearing corporal stripes approached him. "What are you doing here? This is off limits," asked the corporal. "I'm the new Battalion Commander, and more importantly," replied Gray, "who are you?" The Marine announced that he was Corporal Bowman and that he was in charge. Gray informed the corporal that actually he, as the Battalion Commander, was now in charge. He told Bowman to have his men ready for inspection at 0700 in the following morning, or that he would have them out of the Marine Corps the following evening.

It was, of course, not an empty threat, at least not one that even the most unkempt Marine could afford to ignore. Most of the men, even those in perpetual trouble, had nowhere else to go, and certainly their mothers and families did not want them home. Most likely they had joined the Marine Corps looking for a place to improve themselves, a place where they would receive good training and leadership. Unfortunately, they had not found it, though for many the reasons were of their own making.

That a corporal was "in charge" of the barracks reflected the poor state of affairs in 1/2. Officers left the battalion area as soon as possible to return to their billets far from trouble. Staff non-commissioned officers did not live in the barracks; and given the fact that discipline was not being enforced, the Staff NCOs were seldom in the battalion area except when their duties required them to be. Both the junior officers and the Staff NCOs suffered from low morale. This was not the Marine Corps they had joined, but no one was taking charge to, as Al Gray would say, "take what you get and make what you want." The junior NCOs, i.e., sergeants and corporals, were left without proper leadership and they struggled to keep the situation in hand. Abetting the situation was the fact that the 2nd Division was nearly destitute itself. For example, officers and Staff NCOs chipped in to buy toilet paper for the troops in their barracks. When units did engage in training exercises, there were no blank cartridges to fire in their rifles and machine guns; instead, combat-hardened men back from Vietnam were forced to say, "bang, bang" to simulate firing their weapons.

This was a time when, throughout the Marine Corps, too many officers and Staff NCOs only spent time in the battalion area at night when they had the duty, and even then, too many stayed in the duty office, watching television and hoping nothing bad happened "on their watch." And it was a rare field grade officer (major and above) who performed walking around leadership after hours. Corporal Bowman, as it turned out, was a natural leader, albeit one with a very long record of courts-martial. Of course, there were many others who were unconverted recalcitrants; but they would soon, as Gray had promised, change or be gone.

The next morning, Lieutenant Colonel Gray announced in no uncertain terms how affairs were to be conducted. He specifically addressed the racial situation, telling the men that division among blacks, whites, Hispanics and others would not be permitted – it was all one Marine Corps, after all. While every Marine did not, in fact, last long enough to make the deployment, many did, including Corporal Bowman. During the coming deployment, Corporal Bowman could be heard on the fantail of his ship telling his men exactly how they would conduct themselves, all in accordance with Gray's dictates.

Several days after Gray's "meeting" with Brig Company, the other companies had returned from training, and a battalion inspection was held on the parade deck. Of course, not everyone in the companies that had been gone got the word about the new Battalion Commander's ways. Initially, only about 400 men had fallen into place to be inspected. Gray stopped the proceeding and had the officers and Staff NCOs go into the barracks and get the stragglers, the men not prepared for inspection. That effort swelled the ranks by almost another 400, still well short of the 1,214 on the rolls. The battalion was gathered, but it appeared more like Coxey's Army than a frontline Marine Corps fighting unit.[9]

During the inspection, each man not ready was reduced in rank by one grade. As Gray went through and announced such actions, the Regimental Commander, Colonel Charles B. Redman and his Sergeant Major, came along immediately after and heard each man's appeal right on the spot. Unsurprisingly, none were successful. Gray had achieved his objective; he had the full attention of both his officers and his men. But that is not to say that everyone was happy. During his interviews with his various officers, he found several that had no desire to deploy – they had had enough of the leadership challenges they had been dealing with, and they did not share their new commander's enthusiasm for the future. Gray quickly arranged for those officers to be transferred to other units. While he could commiserate with their feelings, to Al Gray there was no higher calling than to lead Marines and he had little empathy for those who disavowed the opportunity to do so.

Among the troops, the n'er-do-wells were marched over to the regimental headquarters and left there for future assignment. They would no longer be part of 1/2. Throughout the process, even though the division staff officers maintained that Gray had conducted a "reign of terror" at the morning formation, Colonel Redman, the Regimental Commander, gave Gray his full backing. Redman was a distinguished, combat-proven professional who had Gray's greatest respect. General Bohn quietly supported his efforts.

As his Executive Officer, Lieutenant Colonel Gray was happy to have Major Malcolm E. (Doc) Smith, Jr. Doc Smith had been a classmate of Gray's at Command & Staff College, though the two did not spend much time together. Having learned that Gray had been assigned to 1st Battalion, 2nd Marines as Commanding Officer (CO), Smith asked his class President if he might be assigned as Gray's XO. Smith thought Gray gave a somewhat ambivalent response, but he was excited to learn upon his arrival at Camp Lejeune that he would, in fact, be the XO of Battalion Landing Team 1/2.

When he arrived at Battalion Headquarters and met with the CO, Smith was surprised at his first assignment: he was ordered to get over to battalion supply and square it away! Through the years, Gray had observed that experienced commanders always pay attention to supply operations and logistics matters. And for Smith, it was far from a bitter experience. Several years later, when then-Lieutenant Colonel Smith assumed command of 2nd Battalion, 4th Marines on Okinawa, his first act was to send his new XO to the supply section with orders not to return until it was squared away! That was not the only lesson Doc Smith learned from Al Gray, however. Doc recalled, "Everything Al Gray did was electric." [10]

The rest of the Battalion's officer slate soon was filled. Captain John (Jack) Sheehan, who years later as a General would become the first Marine named Supreme Allied Commander, Atlantic and Commander-in-Chief, U.S. Atlantic Command, was a consummate professional and soon after Gray's arrival assumed command of Alpha Company. Captains James Magee and Erv Martin were the company commanders held over from the previous staff; Magee had Bravo Company, the former "brig" company, while Martin, who had earned a Silver Star in Vietnam, had Charlie. Typical of the state of the companies (Delta was not formed until less than a month before embarkation) was the fact that Magee was short four lieutenants and some 60 men. He had gone to Panama with one lieutenant, Norm "Rock" Chandler, an expert marksman who later became the weapons platoon leader.[11] Adding to the leadership void, Magee's company had almost no sergeants or corporals. Of course, there were many "former" sergeants and corporals who were now serving as Lance Corporals and Privates First Class; they had been busted for various offenses, usually related to unauthorized leave or drugs. Panama and the U.S. Army jungle training course at Fort Sherman proved to be somewhat of an elixir for Magee's Marines. The troops enjoyed doing real training and learning new skills, and when they got to match wits with 200 new Army 2nd lieutenants who provided the opposing force for an exercise, Magee watched as his company's morale improved. Not until later, however, when the battalion received men straight from boot camp and the Infantry Training Regiment did morale improve even more – the lance corporal fire team leaders finally had men to train and lead. With the men came new officers; 2nd Lieutenant Bill Pedrick would lead Magee's First Platoon. Corporal M. Bowman was retained and became a machine gun team leader in Magee's Weapons Platoon. Delta Company, which had mustered 16 Marines when Gray assumed command, was finally formed in mid-August under the command of Captain Dan Gardner. By then additional officers and men returning from Okinawa joined the battalion and filled its ranks.

Gray liked having captains to command companies, and insisted on that arrangement throughout his time in 1/2. The Headquarters and Service Company, for example, was under the command of the Communications Officer, Captain Jim Bailey. And when later in the cruise, Jack Sheehan was promoted to major, the Air Officer, Captain George McKay, was installed as the Alpha Company Commander. Seldom do Marine aviators get the opportunity to lead an infantry company, but McKay performed exceptionally.

Magee recalled that at one of Gray's first meetings with the company commanders he gave very clear guidance about future training and operations. Gray was intent on a successful deployment; he told the assembled officers and Staff NCOs, "We are going to do everything OK, and probably nothing great. We don't have time to learn to do things great. We will work on those things during the deployment."[12] Magee also noticed how the new CO emphasized that 1/2 would be a Battalion Landing Team (BLT), not just an infantry battalion. Though there were no division or force guidelines for incorporating the attached units into the BLT organization, Gray immediately made contact with those officers and Staff NCOs who would be deploying with his unit. As a result, the infantry commanders almost immediately got to know their aviation, artillery, tank, reconnaissance, amphibious tractor and logistics support unit counterparts. This interaction early on reinforced the team concept and had everyone in 1/2 oriented toward BLT operations, not just infantry battalion day-to-day training and affairs. Moreover, it was obvious to Smith, Sheehan, Magee, Martin, Gardner and others that Gray had an unusually in-depth knowledge about things that many infantry commanders know little. His questions to the reconnaissance commander, the artillery CO, and the communications officer revealed a side of Gray that others found highly professional, and even exciting. This was an officer, they all thought, from whom much could be learned.

Gray and Sheehan especially formed a close bond. Both men worked long hours, and Gray, a bachelor, would often find himself invited to eat leftovers or something warmed up late in the evening by Sheehan's wife, who would leave the two officers talking tactics and training well into the night. Given the highly professional Corps of Marines that the nation enjoys in this second decade of the 21st Century, it is difficult to imagine the turmoil, apprehension, lack of motivation and commitment, and general malaise that typified the Marine Corps after Vietnam and before President Ronald Reagan revitalized the military in the mid-1980s.

The Marine Corps of the early 1970s was hardly alone in facing daunting personnel challenges. All the military services, many civilian institutions and American society as a whole shared the tumultuous effects of drug and alcohol abuse, racism and the absence of strong leadership at the top of the chain of command. Adding to the racial tensions, drug problems, extensive numbers of men who were absent by unauthorized absence and desertion, were the Marine Corps personnel policies of the time.

Due to the pressures of the day, HQMC placed far too much emphasis on personnel end strength, and not nearly enough on unit efficiency and effectiveness. There was tremendous significance placed on keeping enough Marines on active duty to ensure the Assistant Commandant maintained four stars, for example.[13] However, there was no attempt to maintain unit cohesion. Battalions and their companies might receive orders to send 25 or 35 Marines to the 3rd Marine Division; new privates arriving straight from boot camp would replace those transferred – and in those days there was no School of Infantry.[14] And it made no difference where the battalion was in its training and deployment cycle. Thus, it often occurred that significant chunks of the battalion would be effectively brand new, never having been part of previous unit training evolutions. Despite the presence of men who wanted to do well, and who were committed to honorable service, often they lacked the professional knowledge or training essential to success.

But personnel policies aside, a deeper issue remained. It was a simple fact that many Marine officers were not knowledgeable in most complex tactical operations. In Vietnam, except for infrequent major operations such as *Dewey Canyon*, most infantry combat took place at the company level or below. Marines knew little or nothing about, for example, a tactical withdrawal from a beach, or making a helicopter tactical landing ready to start the movement to contact phase immediately. And finally, too many officers were spending minimal time in the field leading troops; instead they preferred hanging out in staff billets or hiding in non-command assignments. Too many officers were using command time to simply to get their ticket for promotion punched. Many of that ilk believed the politically correct notion that there were no bad Marines, just Marines who had not been loved enough by their leaders. Men like Al Gray, Doc Smith, Ernie Cook, Jack Sheehan, Jim Magee and Tony Zinni knew better. They also knew that Marines needed to be led, that there was no substitute for leadership.

Soon after Al Gray assumed command, Marines started doing the little things that built unit morale and pride, and fostered unit cohesion. When two Marines walked together, they walked in step and one was in charge. Marines marched to the chow hall in company, platoon, section or team formation. Whatever the size of the unit, the unit marched. There would be no groups of white Marines assembling on their own and strolling to the mess hall; similarly, there would not be congregations of black Marines who meandered on their own to eat. Too often the result of such racially segregated alignments were chow hall confrontations. When unit integrity was enforced, and Marines marched together to and from chow, there was little chance for arguments and disagreements to arise.

Exacerbating the personnel issues facing the battalion was the fact that the Marine Corps had decided to experiment with two issues related to administration of battalions that were deploying. The first was the idea of "battalion administration." Instead of each Rifle Company and Headquarters & Service Company keeping the record books for their Marines, the battalion S-1 (personnel) would be charged with that responsibility. The second, and the one more problematic as it turned out, was the idea of a trickle draft. But that was still in the future.

In August, while in the field training with his men, Gray received a surprising phone call from General Bohn. "Congratulations, Al, you've been deep selected for promotion," intoned the Commanding General.[15] Gray expressed his amazement, for his number was well below the zone; rather, he replied, it was probably a mistake or reflected the selection of one of the several other Grays who then served in the Marine Corps. The General took a few minutes to check and then called his battalion commander a second time, saying, "No, it's you, Al. Why don't you come by and see me when you get back from the field." The next morning found Gray in the Commanding General's office engaged in a short, but again for Gray, unanticipated conversation. "What do you want to do, Al?" asked the General. As a colonel selectee, Gray could have asked for a different assignment, one befitting his new status even though the official promotion would not occur for some time. "What do you mean, sir?" replied Gray, "I have the best assignment that I could ever want." And thus Gray stayed on at 1/2 to take the battalion to the Med. It was another learning opportunity for Gray. The others selected for colonel, all senior to Gray, asked for new billets and got them; but none of those officers ever was given command of a regiment by General Bohn. Not that it mattered to Gray; he was having the time of his life doing exactly what he wanted to do, and was up to his elbows training and equipping his BLT. [16]

With new officers who arrived after Gray, with recharged staff non-commissioned officers again willing to take on the morale or disciplinary problems and now fully engaged, and with young NCOs aware of the fact that the chain of command would back them up, the battalion's transformation was both rapid and complete. The training went very well and troops were enthusiastic, and the battalion passed the tactical test required before deployment. Led by the Battalion Commander, officers and Staff NCOs could be found in the battalion area at any time, weekends, days or nights. Being a Marine in 1/2 was fun again, and challenging for all the right reasons.

However, Al Gray did not limit his influence to simply his own Battalion. Captain Anthony C. Zinni, who the world would later know as General Tony Zinni, was then a company commander in the 8th Marines. His friend Captain John Sheehan was then Gray's Alpha Company Commander. Sheehan repeatedly told Zinni about his smart, aggressive, involved Battalion Commander. He said that Gray was the kind of officer that both Sheehan and Zinni were looking for, someone who appreciated tactics as much as administration, someone who was concerned about leadership and ways to make the Marine Corps better, someone who could relate to the troops, NCOs and Staff NCOs while also mentoring the junior officers. The three finally had dinner at the Officer's

Club one evening, and Zinni immediately understood his friend's enthusiasm for Lieutenant Colonel Gray.

Captain Zinni, at that point, had commanded seven different companies. Indeed, his repeated experience in command was proof positive that others were shirking the opportunity to lead Marines. Zinni had learned that every commander had bad apples from time to time, but that units that had good leadership never fell into the abyss that captured many units during those times, the abyss that 1/2 found itself in when Al Gray arrived. Zinni realized that any officer who could turn a whole battalion around so rapidly could do so only by being an exceptional leader. About that time the Assistant Commanding General, A.J. Poillon needed an aide, and over his personal reluctance to leave his command, Captain Tony Zinni was the choice. [17]

A general's aide is mostly to be seen and not heard, but aides are often given access to otherwise private conversations between his general and others, including other generals. After all, one of the reasons young officers are selected as aides is to give them insights into how senior officers operate. While Poillon's, and subsequently Major General Fred Haynes's aide, Tony Zinni learned even more about Al Gray. He considered Lieutenant Colonel Gray the model for the old television commercial by the brokerage firm, E.F. Hutton: "When Al Gray speaks, everyone listens." [18]

It is not unusual for senior officers to actively seek out the advice and counsel of juniors, but Zinni was stunned to the extent to which seniors sought Gray's advice on almost every imaginable topic, but especially leadership. And Al Gray, the officer who served so long in artillery and cryptologic billets in Vietnam, was known *by everybody*, at least that is what Tony Zinni thought. All the general officers knew him; they not only spoke well of him, they actively sought his recommendations on most important matters; in fact, the more significant the issue, the greater the likelihood that Al Gray would be part of the decision-making process. Seeking the approval of his seniors was not Al Gray's motivation. The Lieutenant Colonel was much more likely to seek out young enlisted men or junior officers, or meet with former comrades-in-arms of any rank, than he was to try to converse with generals.

The Assistant Commanding General of the 2nd Marine Division had his office on the second deck of the Headquarters building, and Zinni's cubbyhole was near by. Zinni soon learned to recognize when Al Gray had entered the Headquarters.

There was, according to Zinni, a noticeable buzz that arose. "Lieutenant Colonel Gray was like Santa Claus, he naturally attracted a crowd of young Marines, all clamoring to speak with him." Gray would wander about the Headquarters, almost aimlessly, bantering with one and all, while thumping the troops or young officers on their shoulders and generally making everyone smile. The general's junior aide was a former football college player, and Zinni recalled that one time Gray had the young man assume a three-point stance. Then Gray likewise got down and smashed into the Lieutenant to the enjoyment of all. Of course, what Zinni appreciated was that all this was done with the goal to improve morale, foster a sense of family between relatively senior officers and "the troops," and create a healthy atmosphere conducive to building a professional military force. All the while Gray was learning about the people, their problems and their issues, and getting a sense of their professional capabilities. Zinni also recognized that he could approach his mentor no matter what the circumstances and no matter what Gray's duties at the time were. That was also true for anybody else; Gray did not play favorites.

Even though Al Gray was charismatic, not everyone wanted to deploy to the Mediterranean. Prior to such deployments there would be many, many Marines who thought they had perfectly good reasons not to leave their families, or their friends, or their girlfriends or whomever for whatever the reason. It is the right of each Marine, feeling that way, to "Request Mast" with his Commanding Officer in order to plead his case, usually – but not always – without success. If commanders did not plan ahead, they would find that requests for mast would take up their entire days. Gray went in another direction; he announced that the Commanding Officer would hear all Request Masts at midnight on selected days. Such action dramatically reduced the number of Marines anxious to speak with their commander. But that did not take care of all the ways Marines might try to avoid deploying for six months.

Gray maintained a frenetic personal schedule getting his unit ready to deploy. Colonel Redman was amazed at all the new Battalion Commander accomplished. Not only did the Battalion go through Inspector General inspections, pass tactical tests, conduct the normal division requirements for training, but he also led 1/2 in the human relations area, improving morale, getting new off-duty recreational opportunities for the troops, etc. The importance of human relations in those days cannot be over-emphasized; how an officer did in human relations required a specific entry in the narrative section of each officer's evaluation. Gray unfailingly did superbly in the eyes of his commanders.

Though Gray faced a myriad of training requirements imposed by higher headquarters, he also took no shortcuts while also ensuring his battalion was properly prepared in areas important to him. One example of Gray's attention to detail occurred at the rifle range. Remembering General David Shoup's emphasis on permitting small units to train together, Gray extended his battalion's time at the rifle range by two additional weeks in order to allow squads, platoons and companies to fire as a single unit. Besides honing the combat skills of his men, such training was important in building both morale and small unit cohesion; things Al Gray did at every opportunity.

Lieutenant Colonel Al Gray, the man who applied cover and deception to every possible tactical situation, had one more trick up his sleeve before the battalion departed from Morehead City, North Carolina, its embarkation port. It was all together normal in those days that many Marines, not wanting to leave the United States for a variety of reasons, would go simply go UA just before a unit embarked aboard ship. After the ships disappeared over the horizon, such men would return to their base and report for duty. They might receive NJP but their punishment was usually not too severe while their goal, not having to deploy, was satisfied.

Gray announced that the unit would leave for Morehead City on September 14. Typically, the BLT would immediately go aboard ship and sail the next day. In this case, however, Gray had arranged for the men to be billeted in various buildings near the port. Once the BLT was buttoned down at the port, the Commanding Officer and many of his officers and Staff NCOs returned to Camp Lejeune, and there snagged many of the men who had returned to the base, content in their belief that the battalion was long gone. Several dozen Marines, who had planned for a quiet fall and winter in North Carolina, unexpectedly found themselves bound for the Mediterranean along with their buddies. Once again the value of cover and deception operations was proven for all to see. Finally, on September 17, 1971, the BLT 1/2 and the 34th MAU left North Carolina for Rota, Spain.

BATTALION LANDING TEAM I/2, AFLOAT IN
THE MEDITERRANEAN, 1971 – 1972

Soon after leaving for the Med, Al Gray heard from one of officers he most respected. The Deputy Commanding General of Fleet Marine Force, Atlantic (FMFLANT), Michael Ryan, sent this note:

7 October 1971

Deputy Commander
Fleet Marine Force, Atlantic
Norfolk, Virginia 23511

Dear Al,

Well, I see that you finally got underway and are
off for the R&R in the Mediterranean.

I'm well aware of the difficulties that you faced in getting the outfit
ready to go and the tremendous efforts that the battalion has made.
Now that you are in the Med, I'm sure BLT 1/2 will add to our
reputation in that area. I don't have to tell you of the interest in
this Headquarters and at HQMC in the efforts of BLT 1/2.

I want to wish you every success and I will be
following your progress with great interest.

Good luck.

Sincerely,

M.P. Ryan
Major General, U.S. Marine Corps

LtCol A.M. Gray, Jr.
Commanding Officer, BLT 1/2
1st Battalion, 2nd Marines
FPO New York 09502

Congratulations again on the selection if the promotion
comes in while you are out I'll see if we can't hold it up
until you return. Can't have too many Cols on R&R.

(Al Gray has a great sense of humor and clearly enjoyed sharing some levity with General Ryan – who also enjoyed a sense of humor while respecting hard work.)[20]

But Gray was doing far more than reading notes from General Ryan. Almost as soon as the ships had cleared the area around Morehead City, Gray called for a meeting of the company executive officers. The XOs were told that they should identify the 68 worst Marines remaining in 1/2; while there had been a thinning of those who did not deserve to be Marines before the battalion left Camp Lejeune, Al Gray was well aware that there were numerous remaining men in the ranks whose presence would be a detriment to the rest of his battalion. The XOs put together their lists that Gray and the Sergeant Major then combed through. Since Captain Magee's company included many of the former "brig company" cohort, his was the unit that provided the most names – 23 to be exact. But there was no doubt in Magee's mind that his unit, and the remainder of his men, were much better off without those notorious individuals. As soon as the BLT arrived in Rota, Spain, the 68 on the list were placed on an aircraft for return to Camp Lejeune. Undoubtedly there was more grumbling among certain staff officers within the 2nd Marine Division, but Al Gray never heard a word about the action he had taken. Without the infamous 68, morale went up and the company officers and Staff NCOs were able to concentrate more on small unit tactics and operations while worrying less about enforcing discipline; not that challenges did not remain in that area.

Perhaps a less aggressive officer would have gone to the Med (as Marines unfailingly call the Mediterranean Sea) and rested on his laurels. After all, having turned around the battalion personnel wise and administratively, some might not try too hard to push their luck tactically. Gray was anything but content. He bought into a very challenging operational schedule, one that would have the BLT make seven separate landings, open new training areas in Italy, participate in exercises with a variety of NATO allies including the French Foreign Legion, and he would make sure everyone had fun doing it.

The Commanding Officer of the 34th Marine Amphibious Unit (MAU) and Gray's immediate senior was Lemuel C. Shepherd, III. Colonel "Bo" Shepherd was the son of the legendary former Commandant.[21] General Shepherd was the man who recommended Al Gray for a regular commission upon Gray's graduation from The Basic School. Further, it was General Shepherd who had treated Gray's parents with such respect and dignity after the graduation ceremonies were concluded. The General, through his actions, provided a great role model for the new Lieutenant while also deeply impressing both Al Gray, Sr., and his wife, Emily. It was an example of personal conduct that Al Gray, Jr. never forgot. While Bo Shepherd did not reach the Marine Corps heights that his famous father did, he too was a fine professional and Gray was happy to serve in his command.

Figure 4.1
Colonel Lemuel C. Shephard, III. Commanding Officer of the
34th Marine Amphibious Unit and son of a former Commandant.[22]

Shepherd's counterpart, the Commander of the Amphibious Squadron 10, was Navy Captain Lawrence E. Stahl. The Commanding Officer of the Air contingent for 34th MAU was Major Robert K. Goforth, an exceptional airman who was a great friend of Al Gray. The two shared many laughs together while also performing their respective missions. The third sub-unit of the MAU was the Logistics Support Unit, commanded by Captain Thomas E. Peachey, a fine professional who quickly earned the trust and respect of everyone in the MAU.

Doc Smith was Gray's XO and had a ringside seat while watching intently as Gray carried out his duties. Professionalism was the by-word for officers and Staff NCOs in the Battalion. But professionalism did not mean that fun was to be avoided, or that lengths were to be taken to avoid conflict with Captain Stahl, United States Navy.

On one occasion, the Amphibious Squadron Commander announced that the BLT Chaplain would be needed to serve as duty chaplain during a French port visit. Gray, always alert to his officers or men being used to satisfy the whims of others, objected. Gray's Chaplain was a Roman Catholic, one of the few in the service and the only one in the Squadron, and evidently the Captain thought he needed a Catholic chaplain on duty for the port visit to a largely Roman Catholic country. Gray objected to anyone, even the Squadron Commander, assigning his officers to port duty. The Captain was insistent. Gray finally said that he had previously given the chaplain permission to go to the Vatican while in port, there to have an audience with the Pope. And that's exactly what chaplain ended up doing.

Despite their occasional disagreements over officer usage, Captain Stahl was a fine fellow who also had a sense of humor. Stahl kept a large framed picture of himself in his sea cabin. Knowing that there would be a mess night, or other some other affair when joking would be appropriate, Gray arranged to surreptitiously borrow the Captain's picture when he knew there would be time to return it without it being missed. Given to the Major Goforth's photo experts, who quickly copied and returned the original, the outline of a dartboard was superimposed over Captain Stahl's face. At the appropriate time, the resulting board, along with a set of darts, was presented to the skipper as a gift entitled, "Captain's Planning Process."[23] After their initial shock, both the Commodore and Colonel Shepherd were amused.

In one of the many coincidences that took place during Gray's long active duty service, Commodore Stahl had been one of the submarine officers aboard the USS *Perch*, the submarine that carried the Amphibious Reconnaissance Platoon during Gray's enlisted days.

Doc Smith quickly took to Gray's ways of running things, and why not? Gray gave his Executive Officer broad latitude and often permitted him to actually run things. On one exercise, Gray had himself declared a casualty, to the great surprise of all his officers. Of course, in combat that might actually happen, though in peacetime maneuvers such decisions by commanding officers occur very infrequently. Gray wanted to see how his staff would react, and he was pleased that they did just fine. Smith also recalled that during port visits, when most everyone except the men on duty were off enjoying liberty in exotic, foreign ports, it was Doc Smith who was left to run the Battalion.

Smith loved that he was given such authority and that Gray had such confidence in his XO. Doc knew that Al Gray had embarked with a footlocker full of books. He also knew that during the various exercises and even while steaming between exercises, when planning, coordination and taking care of the myriad administrative duties could drain anyone, Gray was on continuous duty. Thus, he soon recognized that his Commanding Officer liked to retreat to the sanctuary of his stateroom and pass hours uninterrupted, using the time to read. And exactly what did Al Gray read?

Gray's footlocker held pretty much anything of use to a professional Marine; it did not include any works of fiction. Gray's dedication to tactical and technical publications is legendary; but he also availed himself of the chance – while in the Med – to learn Islamic history, Muslim religious and cultural traditions, and a little something about each country they would be visiting. His reading encompassed anything he thought might come in useful in the future. And one could be almost certain that if Al Gray knew his unit would be operating with NATO or other Allied forces, he would know something of the background and traditions of those allies. Gray enjoyed reading in the solace of his cabin, not that he never went ashore.

Lieutenant Pedrick recalled being on shore patrol in Nice, France. He was walking the city with a Staff NCO and another Marine, mostly day-dreaming about his future. He had enjoyed the cruise tremendously, and had decided a future profession as a Marine officer made sense. He recalled turning the corner at the intersection of some alleys, and bumping into his Battalion Commander. Gray put his arm around the younger man's shoulder, and asked how things were going. During the conversation, Pedrick admitted that he was concerned because he had not received the paperwork that would permit him to augment as a Regular Officer. Gray quickly allayed the Lieutenant's anxiety and strolled along with him and his shore patrol party for nearly an hour before departing to find other Marines on liberty. The Gray Ghost had struck yet again, but not for the last time.

It turned out that going on liberty in Nice and Cannes came only after a standoff with the local authorities. In 1971, African-American Marines were not welcomed into the French ports for reasons never made clear to Al Gray. The Commanding Officer of BLT 1/2, however, had a ready response: if African-American Marines were not welcomed ashore, then none of his Marines would be permitted ashore. After two days, the howls of the local merchants were heard loudly and clearly by whomever had made the decision to ban the African Americans, and the BLT went on liberty – all the BLT went on liberty, except, of course, the duty sections. The end result, and one predictable given the outcomes previously seen during the cruise, was that all had a good time, and there was not a single incident that involved Marines. The only loss was two days of merchants' revenues.

Usually, in those days, a battalion would deploy and come back as a complete unit. Men had to have at least four months service remaining upon the battalion's planned return date in order to have time to muster out administratively. Battalion Landing Team 1/2, Gray learned, was going to receive drafts of men to replace those whose end-of-service dates occurred during the deployment. Gray, who had seen most of what might happen under such circumstances, anticipated the problem.

The first trickle draft of new men arrived in Naples, Italy about halfway through the deployment. Two planes full of replacement Marines were found lacking by the Battalion Commander and his Sergeant Major. There was evidence of drugs. Gray and the Sergeant Major arranged for the men to get food, and they were bedded down in the area of the hangar. After the aircrews had received their mandatory rest following the long flight, instead of accepting the draft, less than 48 hours after they arrived, Gray had all the Marines sent back to the 2nd Division on the same planes that had flown them across the Atlantic. Some of the other men who were due to rotate were also sent back, though many others had chosen to re-enlist or extend their service; as a consequence, the numerical deficiency in the BLT was not nearly as significant as it might have been. Gray's message to higher headquarters was clear, "we don't need such men and are better off without them." [24]

While he later heard that his actions were the cause for kicking and screaming among the division staff, Gray had one important backer – General Bohn. The Commanding General seemed to understand the reasons his Battalion Commander had done what he did. Lieutenant Colonel Gray never heard another word officially about the incident. Clearly, the actions Gray took in weeding men out of his battalion before the cruise got underway, and his handling of the trickle draft, were trend-setting and many in the chain of command took note.

While it took some time before the Marine Corps officially adopted a personnel position close to that put into practice in 1971 by the Battalion Commander of 1st Battalion, 2nd Marines, eventually it would.

SAROS BAY, TURKEY, 12-18 OCTOBER 1971

After arriving in Rota on September 30, the 34th MAU left for Turkey. Dubbed *Operation Deep Furrow*, the MAU with its BLT and other supporting units were tasked to conduct a NATO exercise in the Thrace area of Turkey. Then-Brigadier General Thomas Miller, the Assistant Wing Commander of the 2nd Marine Aircraft Wing, came out to serve as the Brigade Commander for what was designated the 8th Marine Amphibious Brigade. Miller was a formidable personality. Large and extremely active, Miller had set a world speed record flying an F-4 on a closed course. He later rose to Lieutenant General and was a highly capable, if impetuous, officer. Included in the exercise with the Marines were Turkish Marines, Greek Naval Forces and some Royal Marines, making it truly a NATO operation. The helicopter contingent consisted of CH-46s, Cobra gunships and a UH1E for use as a Command and Control aircraft. Right from the start of planning, however, the exercise did not unfold smoothly.

First, there was the subject of maps. The Turks were very sensitive about their maps, because all of their maps had actual Turkish positions that would be used in the event of a war with the Soviet Union. Building on his experience as a Forward Observer for the Turkish Brigade in Korea, Gray was able to win approval to receive 10 maps, all classified Top Secret. By mortgaging his social capital with the host country, Gray signed his life away in the return for the much-needed maps. Alas, when Gray unfolded the maps that were so dearly acquired, major portions of the exercise area had been cut from the map – they were essentially useless to the Marines. Consequently, Gray directed that the recon teams be sent in advance to make sketch maps of the area; with the sketches in hand, the operation moved forward.

As a prelude to the real landing, an elaborate rehearsal of the operation took place in full view of high-ranking NATO officers. Everything went fine, though Gray had noted that the UH1E flew continuously up and down over the beach, often dipping to what seemed like mere feet over the heads of the infantry who had come ashore. General Miller had also observed the UH1E's flagrant disregard for flight safety guidelines, and was steaming mad. After putting down on top the hill that was the landing force's initial objective, Miller started down in search of the BLT Commander, whose command and control helicopter had been hot-dogging above the beach.

Figure 4.2
Pinning Major Malcom "Doc" Smith (lft) , General Gray
promoting Captain Sheehan to Major in the field. [25]

Figure 4.3
Al Gray congratulates newly-promoted Major Jack Sheehan while on
maneuvers in Turkey. Sheehan commanded A Company and was oper-
ating within the British Royal Commandos at the time.[26]

The Brigade and BLT Commanders met halfway up the hill, Miller screaming and yelling to the top of his lungs about Gray's disregard for flight safety. Gray, figuring if he were going to be relieved that it would be on the high ground, kept walking up the hill, after saluting the General. Finally, on the top, Gray turned to the General and said, "With all due respect, General, I don't know what you are talking about." The G-3 of the Brigade, Colonel Ivins, spoke for a bit with the General, but he was still screaming and yelling. Gray could only retort, "Again, with all due respect, it was not our helicopter. I wasn't anywhere near the area, but if that's the way you feel, fine." Miller replied, "You'll never fly in another helicopter again as long as I am in the Marine Corps." Gray could only say, "Well, okay, I understand that."

It turned out that the Navy Public Affairs Officer, seeking to get good pictures of the exercise, had commandeered the UH1E. And, by coincidence, the pilot was a problematic 1st lieutenant who was, perhaps, not the best Marine officer, but who could handle a UH1E better than 99.9% of UH1E pilots then alive. 1st Lieutenant G. Olshfski had won considerable acclaim in Vietnam, though, regrettably his Marine service ended soon after the deployment. When General Miller learned of the actual circumstances surrounding the episode is not known, but he never again mentioned the incident to Gray, and in keeping with Al Gray's longstanding attitude, he also let the subject drop. Clearly, however, he did not forget it.

After the confrontation with the Brigade Commander, Gray's BLT 1/2 continued the exercise inland some 50 miles. All units put in a great performance, but the artillery outdid itself. During the course of the exercise Captain E. Campbell's men displaced 26 times without missing a beat. During the movement, more sketch maps were made and used; of course, having Major Goforth's helicopters in the area also helped the ground units. Describing the operation, Colonel Shepherd noted that, "Throughout this demanding operation Lieutenant Colonel Gray exhibited exceptional leadership, professional expertise and personal stamina… His personal drive was the major factor in the outstanding performance which his BLT made… Lieutenant Colonel Gray is an unusually conscientious officer, a natural leader and one of the most able Marines I have ever encountered."[27]

Lieutenant General Tom Miller eventually came to admire Al Gray, and in the not-too-distant future. At that time there were three generals named Miller, each of whom rose to the rank of lieutenant general. Besides Tom Miller, E.J. Miller was the President of the Promotion Board that selected Al Gray for Brigadier General in 1976, and John G. Miller, though slightly junior to the other two Millers, served as Gray's immediate boss for five years while Al Gray was a general officer. Yes, advancing in the 1970s Marine Corps would have been difficult if one did not get along with higher-ranking officers named Miller. Interestingly, as Al Gray became more senior, it was Tom Miller who often assigned him to do things related to Marine aviation.

The exercise, while highly successful, was marked by humorous (only in retro-spect) equipment breakdowns that tested the Marines ability to improvise and jury-rig components. The breakdown of a tank led to what the cruise book described as *Operation Elephant Dance* – the impromptu name associated with Al Gray's frequent requests to Captain Sylvester R. (Bob) Foley, the Commanding Officer of the command ship, about the status of the BLT's tank. [28]

BLT 1/2 also used motorcycles for reconnaissance and communications tasks, and when one of 1st Lieutenant Caire's tanks broke down well inland, two motor-cycles were jury-rigged to carry the drive train back to the beach. It was quite a feat; however, dragging the tank itself back, using two Landing Crafts Utility (LCUs) – back to back – to get the monster unit to sea and aboard ship was also quite note-worthy. The LCUs were being used for the first time – they were craft that would become a vital cog in future amphibious operations for years to come. The cruise book reveals details about the humorous communications exchanged between the BLT commander and the Sixth Fleet admiral about the status of repairs.[29] Of course, Gray never actually communicated directly to the Commander of 6th Fleet, Vice Admiral Gerald E. Miller (yes, yet another Miller) about the maintenance status of a tank, though it provided a great story for the cruise book!

The exercise also saw the Marines use the Amphibious Support and Intelligence System (ASIS) and the Seaborne Mobile Logistics System (SMLS) systems for the first time.[30] These computer-based systems marked the early attempts by the Naval Services to actually use computers to assist during exercises and eventually operations. SMLS, in particular, represented a significant milestone in the evolu-tion of logistics.

By loading the ships in accordance with what units ashore were anticipated to need, the requirement for the buildup a major logistics position ashore was eliminated. From time immemorial, military forces invading from the sea were required to establish ashore a logistics base from which units would draw supplies. Infantrymen, for example, rarely carried more than 3-4 days worth of food rations. When resupply was needed, the attacking forces drew new rations from the logis-tics base (or supply dump in common parlance.) The same was true for resupply of ammunition, spare parts, gas and oil for trucks, tanks and rolling stock, and other supplies not carried ashore by the attackers. A major drawback from this approach was the fact that the logistics base required troops to defend it from possible enemy attack. And, as the assaulting units moved inland, away from the sea, the lines of supply became more distant and much more vulnerable, and time needed to obtain resupply increasingly longer. SMLS changed the entire situation.

The operation in Turkey was a great proving ground for the SMLS approach, since the scheme of maneuver adopted by Gray's unit involved rapid transit inland, up to 50 miles from the sea. In a nutshell, SMLS permitted the units to anticipate their logistical needs ahead of time, and have needed supplies delivered by helicopter directly to them, wherever they were located. Thus, all the supplies remained stored aboard ship. The computers permitted the logisticians to quickly identify where specific parts were located and they could be retrieved as necessary. Further, Gray was not required to leave behind any of his maneuver force in order to defend a fixed location. BLT 1/2 proved the SMLS capability significantly enhanced amphibious operations and provided an invaluable adjunct to maneuver warfare, though in 1971 Gray's tactics had not yet be given that moniker.

Figure 4.4
Al Gray mans his left
seat in the UH1E. [31]

Both Admiral Miller and General Miller had long since departed the area while the 34th MAU were back loading and making ready to set sail for Greece when Gray was alerted that one of his communications relay teams was not accounted for. Gray was usually among the last to leave the beach or training area because he wanted to personally assure the host nation, and the chain of command, that the areas were clean of litter or discarded gear or equipment, and that the area appeared in better shape than when the Marines first landed. So the BLT commander had just arrived when the call came of the problem with the lost communications team. Several teams had been deployed onto mountaintops in order to ensure reliable radio links among the entire 8th MAB during the movement inland, and one was not back aboard ship. Gray wasted no time calling for his UH1E.

Al Gray hated requiring men do a job that others were fully qualified to do, especially when he could save a seat on an aircraft. Early on, Gray received familiarization training that permitted him to ride in the left rear seat of the UH1E and act as a crewman and door gunner. Thus, when Gray flew on the UH1E, one crewman could stay behind. The Air Wing was perfectly happy with the arrangement; after all, Gray had been checked out and was fully qualified. That Lieutenant Colonel Gray assumed air crewman duties meant another Marine could also go along, while leaving sufficient room for the lost communications relay team when they were found.

As the extra man, Gray took the reconnaissance platoon leader, 1st Lieutenant Joseph Crockett. Crockett had earned a Navy Cross in Vietnam while a corporal, and Gray valued the young officer's field skills. The UH1E flew to where the team was supposed to be, but found no one. Gray had the helicopter land so he and Crockett could check out the area. As luck would have it, Gray found what seemed to be footprints indicating that team had tried to get off the mountain; alas, they were going inland instead of toward the sea. Gray and Crockett left the aircrew and helicopter and started following what they hoped were tracks left by the missing Marines. About two miles from their assigned position, the team was found huddled up in a small sheltered area. They were confused and disoriented, and had no idea what to do. Gray gathered them up and radioed for the helicopter.

The UH1E pilot, the resourceful Lieutenant Olshfski, was the same officer who had done the stunt flying over the beach during the landing. Gray was happy they had him because getting back to the ship would require all the skill a pilot could muster. The weather had turned really ugly and the ships – they were headed for the USS *Inchon*, an LPH, - were 30 or 35 miles out to sea. With the Marines aboard and talking excitedly, Olshfski told everyone to shut up! And all obeyed instantly. The pilot then took off slowly circled up and up until he thought they were at an altitude high enough to clear any mountains. He then turned toward the sea and using the ship's TACAN found the *Inchon*. The communications relay team was safely home.

Figure 4.5
Al Gray and Captain Joe Crockett, taken after their return to Camp Lejeune.[32]

Given how much the BLT Commanding Officer stressed safety, and given the fact that there had been no accidents during the deployment, a happy but unusual occurrence, the overall situation reinforced Gray's belief that if his Marines were properly trained, well led, and treated like adults they would respond positively, and safely. The tactical, operational and logistical improvements made during the cruise made Al Gray very proud of all his officers, Staff NCOs, NCOs and men. Their accomplishments, conduct and safety record were noted throughout the chain of command.

Figure 4.6
Al Gray and his good friend, Bobby Goforth, Helecopter
Squadron Commander, en route to Greece.[33]

Figure 4.7
Al Gray with one of the command and control helicopters.[34]

While Gray and his BLT had performed well in Turkey, Gray had also been carrying out an additional duty, a highly unusual one tasked by the Department of State before he had ever left North Carolina. Turkey has long held the distinction of having among the toughest, least tolerant, drug laws anywhere. An American Sailor had been sentenced to life imprisonment for violating those laws. Gray, perhaps because someone knew of his ties as forward observer to the Turks during the Korean War, was asked if he could intercede on behalf of the Sailor. Beginning at his initial meeting with the Turkish exercise commander, and working his through the chain of command, including finally a trip to Ankara, Gray was able to obtain the Sailor's release. Needless to say, the Department of State was pleased, and remembered the help given by the Marine.

TIMBAKION, CRETE, 2-10 NOVEMBER 1971

Crete became the scene of a new kind of training for the subordinate unit leaders. There was plenty of real estate available for any kind of tactical maneuvers and so Lieutenant Colonel Gray gave his subordinates a chance to do whatever they thought was important for their troops. Between training directives issued by HQMC, force and division commanders, company commanders throughout the Marine Corps never had time to do what they considered important. However, the resulting exercises ashore became a model that Gray would replicate in future operations. The company commanders, the tank platoon leader, the artillery battery and every other type of specialized unit were unbound from any battalion supervision for several days. It was a great success. The free-form training was followed by practicing evacuation procedures; and then everyone took part in a period of extensive service support and equipment maintenance. The BLT left Crete is fine shape for future operations. The Air Wing units? They also had fun.

In the course of flying around in his UH1E observing what was happening, Gray noticed that the CH-46s and Cobras seemed to be boring holes in the sky above a remote part of the island. He got together with Major Goforth and went to investigate. It turned out that the red-blooded aviators, being naval aviators, had discovered a nudist colony; they were practicing approaches and other various flying skills, probably to the great amusement of the locals. Goforth and Gray had a great relationship and that fact added significantly to the success of the MAU's operations. Al Gray never asked the helicopter unit to do more than they were capable of, or comfortable, doing; in return, the aviators tried hard to satisfy all the very professional BLT Commander's wishes.

Figure 4.8
Major Bob Goforth, Commanding Officer of Marine Medium Helicopter Squadron 364
(HMM 364) with Al Gray aboard USS Inchon *in the Mediterranean preparing to celebrate*
the Marine Corps Birthday in November of 1971. Goforth was a superb leader and mentor to
his Marines. Interestingly, three of his Lieutenants rose to be General officers with one being
the Assistant Commandant of the Marine Corps and one former head of Marine Aviation.)[35]

Figure 4.9
The BLT Commander delivers remarks at the festivities marking the Marine Corps Birthday.
November 10 is an important day for all Marines, regardless of where they are or what
uniforms they have to wear. Note the Marine in utilities behind Lieutenant Colonel Gray.[36]

Figure 4.10
The BLT Commander gives the first slice of birthday cake to Captain Brown, Commanding
Officer of USS Inchon, *LPH12. Gray later worked with Brown when he was an admiral*
assigned to duty in London. The Marine officer on the right is Major Bobby Goforth.[37]

PORTO SCUDO, SARDINIA, 14-21 DECEMBER 1971 &
MONTE ROMANO, ITALY, 11-17 JANUARY 1972

The MAU's next stop was Sardinia. And again Gray and his Company Commanders provided innovative training for the small unit leaders. At the beginning of the training evolution each company's first platoon reported to an assigned area. They were, in sequence, each given a mission; the missions were similar, but each varied just a little. The company commanders and S-3 then evaluated each platoon's conduct of the exercise. How well did the platoon leaders give their Five-Paragraph Orders? How well did squad leaders give their orders? How well was the Platoon Guide used to ensure the necessary supplies and equipment were drawn? How well did the leaders inspect the weapons and field gear? Did the leaders maintain control during the movement to contact? Was the assault/ambush handled properly? How was the objective consolidated? Every aspect of the small unit's operation, and everything done by the leaders were graded. At the end of the day, one platoon was declared the winner. The next day the second platoons of each company participated, and on the third day each of the 3rd platoons were exercised.

On the final day of this sequence, all the winners from each day's competition got to go head-to-head against each other, with the winners earning an early return to steak dinners aboard ship. Lieutenant Bill Pedrick's 1st Platoon, Bravo Company, was judged the overall winner. Not a bad performance for one of the few 2nd Lieutenants in the battalion; the young platoon leader hoped that it began to repay his Commanding Officer's early trust in him.

The MAU subsequently conducted live fire exercises under the watchful eye of the Division Commanding General, Fred Haynes, who came to observe. Haynes had long known Al Gray, and he realized just how well Colonel Shepherd's men were doing operationally. Haynes and his fellow Major General, Michael Ryan, were particularly pleased with the positive response the Marines were getting while on liberty. After winding down operations in Sardinia, the 34th MAU moved on to Italy.

Throughout the cruise the Shore Patrol functioned as a key partner in keeping things well under control while Marines and Sailors were on liberty. Jim Magee commented that it was Al Gray's philosophy for the conduct of the shore patrol that added significantly to the BLT's success. Many, but certainly not all, commanders shared Gray's view that the shore patrol was there to ensure that men on liberty were safe, secure and well taken care of. The shore patrol is a highly organized function that is used to provide security for troops ashore since the earliest days of the sea services. Usually, a shore patrol party consists of both Marines and Sailors. There are typically several groups of such parties roving around the port city at any given time. Participation in the shore patrol is limited to experienced NCOs and petty officers, which are led by junior officers and senior Staff NCOs. For example, a company commander or staff captain or Navy lieutenant may be the senior shore patrol officer for the evening, or the weekend, assisted by a 1st Sergeant or Master Sergeant – usually the Navy provides a Master Chief Petty Officer or Senior Chief, often from the Master at Arms rating. Under the senior officer, there may be, depending on the port being visited, multiple shore party detachments each of which include a lieutenant, staff sergeant and two or more sergeants or even corporals. These detachments roam around freely, often entering bars or potential hot spots (but never drinking alcohol) or just being seen on the streets. They are always in the service uniform of the day. Depending on the attitude of the senior shore patrol officer, they can either choose to assist the troops or harass the troops. Al Gray always insisted on the former approach. Backing up the walking detachments were shore party vans or jeeps that could be called to carry men back to the docks for transportation to the ships. Every officer and almost every Staff NCO could count on being assigned to the shore patrol at some point in the deployment. Though the shore patrol system is age old, its execution varies from commander to commander.

Figure 4.11
Lieutenant Colonel Gray and George McKay discussing training concepts for Timbakion.[38]

In BLT 1/2, and indeed throughout the 34th MAU, the Marines and Sailors knew that if they had overdone things, all they had to do was find one of the omnipresent shore patrol parties or get to a corner and flag down a passing shore patrol jeep or van. The shore patrol would then ensure that the individual, or multiple individuals, returned to their ship without incident. No charges were brought and no harassment was permitted; it was truly a no harm-no foul situation. By stressing that Marines and Sailors needed to take care of each other, or ask the shore patrol for help whenever they felt poorly or uncertain about how or where to proceed, incidents ashore were not eliminated, but certainly minimized.

In Italy, the men enjoyed not only good liberty, but also excellent training. The extensive training area at Monte Romano had never been opened to any unit of the armed forces of the United States. Gray was determined to ensure that not only did the Marines take full advantage of such a spectacular training site, but also that they set the example for future users. In every area where 1/2 trained, Gray was usually the last person to leave the area, trying hard to ensure each location was left in better condition than when the Marines arrived. By setting such a precedent at Monte Romano in both training and troop conduct, it meant subsequent units deployed to the Mediterranean were able to enjoy the fruits of 1/2's hard work.

The mountainous terrain permitted a wide range of training opportunities that led to, perhaps for most the Marines, one of the most memorable events of the cruise, The March to the Sea. Typically, after the conclusion of exercises ashore the Marines would conduct a tactical withdrawal while helicoptering back to the ships. Recall that Gray and Sheehan had already plotted long before the cruise began that every evolution would be done tactically, so as to provide training. So while the companies formed themselves into formation that anticipated the arrival of helicopters, the Battalion Commander and his small command group marched past, not slowing down to offer any explanation of the coming event. By this time the Company Commanders were used to Lieutenant Colonel Gray's often-unusual practices, and they decided that they better follow in trace as the old football player strode purposefully toward the sea.

Figure 4.12
The start of the "March to the Sea." Lt Col Gray, walking stick in hand, came down off the mountain and simply kept walking. His commanders and staff scurried to get behind him.[39]

Five and a half hours later Al Gray and his Marines reached the point where the landing craft and helicopters could pick them up to return to their ships. More than 19 miles were covered in that time, and while the march was mostly downhill, full packs and all their field gear burdened each Marine. It was hardly a stroll in the park. Before the march had begun, there was considerable speculation, even betting, about how the Marines would be returning to the ships. Captain Magee recalled the odds were 9-1 that the CO would call in helicopters. He also recalled that the troops' name for the event was "the death march to the sea." Although only 19 miles as the crow flies, the winding small trails made it feel like the 900-odd Marines had walked at least 30.

It turned out that Al Gray's old mentor, General Mike Ryan had called Gray before the exercise. While Ryan congratulated the younger officer on all that had been accomplished during the cruise, particularly the helicopter-borne assaults and amphibious operations, the General chided Gray that probably these "modern Marines" had forgotten how to conduct forced marches. Gray simply took the chance to show the ever-observant and most interested General that his Marines, indeed, still knew how to advance the old-fashioned way, on foot.

Figure 4.13
Colonel Bill Maloney (6th Fleet Marine Air Officer – and later, Lieutenant General –
and longtime colleague of Gray), reviewing training plans in Timbakion.[40]

In February, General Ryan again showed his interest in what was going on in the Med by writing this note to Colonel Shepherd (re-printed here with permission):

3 February 1972

Deputy Commander
Fleet Marine Force, Atlantic
Norfolk, Virginia 23511

Dear Bo,

I've read with great interest your last two post liberty reports. I was particularly impressed by the obvious care that the 34th MAU is taking to insure that our Marines make a good appearance in the European area. In each of your reports, I noted the people-to-people efforts on the part of our Marines. I know you realize how much I personally appreciate the efforts that you and all Marines

*of the 34th MAU are making. I would like you to know that we
here at FMFLANT Headquarters have been very impressed with
all the actions of the outfit since it has been in the Mediterranean.*

*I know you'll be pleased to return home soon.
Please give my regards to your family.*

Sincerely,

*M.P. Ryan
Major General, U.S. Marine Corps*

*Col. L.C. Shepherd III
Commander, 34th Marine Amphibious Unit
Headquarters, 34th MAU, Det "M"
FPO New York 09502*

Colonel Bo Shepherd passed that note along to Al Gray with the following attachment:

*34th MARINE AMPHIBIOUS UNIT
LANDING FORCE SIXTH FLEET 2-71*

MEMO

DATE _____

FROM: COMMANDING OFFICER

TO: Al,

*I thought you would be interested in reading this letter I recently
received from MGen Ryan. I was pleased to hear that FMFLANT
appreciates the effort you and your outfit are making to enhance the
reputation of the Marine Corps in the Med. Keep it up!*

LCS III

Later, during the training on Corsica, Al Gray, Marine, was excited to be able to operate with one of the oldest and most storied military units in Europe – the French Foreign Legion. He had read about the Legion and admired its professionalism, its respect for its traditions, and its focus on fulfilling its mission. Gray, in the course of his long service, established close ties with any number of allied military units and the Foreign Legion was one.

There was a period when each company trained along with a platoon of Legionnaires. Captain Jim Magee and his counterpart, Lieutenant Leonelli of the Legion, became good friends who remained in contact for many years. At the beginning of the training, the Legionnaires arrived during the evening hours, and when morning came Magee's Marines were stunned to see that the Legion platoon had carefully and meticulously leveled the field where they encamped, and their tents were aligned in perfection. This was is sharp contrast to the Marines, whose hooches and tents resembled a Vietnam-style Marine encampment. The two forces got along well and there was obvious mutual respect. And the end of the exercise, Magee and Leonelli exchanged headgear, as did many of the Marines and Legionnaires. After the period of company-sized training, the Legion had served as opposing force against the Marines. The Americans were invited to visit the Legion's Headquarters at Toulon during a port call; an outing to the Legion's Museum, where displays were made from highly polished ammunition cases, was one of the highlights of the deployment for Gray. The officers and men of BLT 1/2 never forgot the treatment given them by the Legionnaires, and cherished the variety of mementoes they exchanged with one of the world's true multi-national forces. [41]

A final exercise with Spanish troops wrapped up the cruise. Significantly, the training included the *first* night helicopter-borne assault. The operation was accomplished in a manner befitting the nation's premier fighting force, and it made a very positive impact on the NATO dignitaries who were present to observe.

The Assistant Commandant had published an order prohibiting nighttime helicopter operations as part of a safety push. However, Major Goforth's squadron, encouraged and abetted by Gray, had been flying at night throughout the deployment. For the final exercise in Spain, the nighttime operation involved all the MAU's helicopter assets. Launching from 23½ miles off shore, hours after the Amtracs and LCUs had hit the water, the entire BLT came ashore simultaneously at L-Hour, 0400 in the morning. A coordinated attack from over the horizon proved the Marines could strike targets quite suddenly and in overwhelming strength at multiple landing points. Yes, indeed, the NATO observers were impressed.

The exercise also got the very positive attention of senior Marine leaders. Though still a lieutenant colonel, Gray was quickly becoming one of the Corps' foremost experts on amphibious operations. Then-Captain Jim Magee recalls that the officers in the BLT and throughout the MAU had little understanding of exactly how Al Gray came to command an infantry battalion and a BLT, though they all agreed he was unique, in an extremely competent way.

A much less compelling incident caught the attention of most of the BLT, while providing ammunition for the BLT's resident cartoonist. Gray had been attending the hot wash up, as the Navy calls exercise debriefs, while his driver waited outside. The Spanish hosts offered the young Marine some wine, and he gladly accepted. Then he drank a little more, and a little more. At the end of the briefings, Gray and Commodore Stahl climbed into the jeep for the ride back to the beach, Stahl in the front seat and Gray perched on the back. It was a rocky road, and the driver's reactions were not up to par. The jeep hit a big bump that propelled Gray out of the jeep onto the ground. He was not injured, but was more than a little put out at the turn of events. The BLT Commander climbed into the driver's seat and relegated his former driver to the back. The young Marine was a fine fellow, but a new driver had to be found. Upon the return to Morehead City, a large 2 foot by 3 foot cartoon was on display. It showed Gray, in tank goggles with an aviation headset flipped out of the jeep onto a boulder, exclaiming, "All I want is a little professionalism!" Gray encouraged the men to have fun, and this would not be the last time that a cruise ended with cartoons about Gray prominently displayed. [42]

Unbeknownst to most his officers, Gray also had kept his hand in SIGINT while in the Med. His Radio Battalion detachment conducted operations against targets that came within range during the cruise. In that regard, the Marines were ahead of the Navy because amphibious ships had no SIGINT capabilities; indeed, many surface combatants in the early 1970s lacked SIGINT resources. Gray was also able to work with Major Goforth to provide photo intelligence of targets that could be seen from helicopters, including the ubiquitous Soviet trawlers that performed SIGINT throughout the Med. By keeping his hand in SIGINT and intelligence generally, Gray maintained his close ties with NSA, and the Radio Battalion cryptologists were able to operate against live targets.

While operations were the primary focus of Al Gray, even if he had wanted to he could not overlook the importance of Marine conduct during liberty. Racial incidents, riots and lawlessness filled the news media accounts of the anti-war crowd, and the entire American chain of command spotlighted their interest in ensuring the troops were on their best behavior ashore. Impressing NATO officials with first-rate dog and pony shows about amphibious operations was not sufficient. General Ryan, fulfilling the one of his prime responsibilities as the Deputy Commanding General, FMFLANT– i.e., tracking what was happening in Europe and the Med

– was obviously happy with the overall performance of the 34th MAU. It had been only the second MAU deployment; Colonel Bull Kraince (the officer who recommended Gray for a commission) and Lieutenant Colonel Ted Willis (Gray's friend from Vietnam) had deployed the first MAU in February 1971.

After the operations in Spain, the BLT had to make one more stop. Back to Livorno, Italy, went the Amphibious Ready Group (ARG) and its embarked Marines; one final maneuver, a most important one, had to be performed. All the equipment – Navy and Marine Corps – had to be checked for snails. Certainly it would not be right to permit the snails of the Mediterranean to return to America and upset the native population of snails in Morehead City, North Carolina. The Sea Services of 1971-1972 were doing their part to maintain the environment.

LEADERSHIP CHALLENGES

In addition to operations and training issues, Gray faced a myriad of administrative duties, capably assisted by Doc Smith. Looking back, he had demonstrated that adherence to principles, taking care of and trusting the troops, encouraging officers and Staff NCOs to take the initiative while trying to have fun as much as possible paid dividends. Part of taking care of the troops meant emphasizing safety; not playing it safe, but being alert to follow instructions, be professional and attentive to detail meant that the safety record of the BLT was just as impressive as its operational achievements. That meant a lot to the former recon sergeant; something he had learned long ago was that troops need to have the confidence to complete assignments while not endangering themselves or others. His daily, often hourly, encouragement ensured that everyone knew the boss cared about their safety, while also expecting their best. Usually Gray got it. He turned the normal 5-paragraph order into a 6-paragraph order; the last paragraph was safety. [43]

But that is not to say that Gray's Marines, for all the good works they did and all the public relations good will that they had produced during the cruise, had turned into angelic choirboys incapable of creating mischief. Captain Jack Sheehan and his gunnery sergeant stayed on top the leadership problem by having thorough inspections of the troop areas after each liberty port visit. When the ships were back at sea, Sheehan and the gunny would have the men line up in their living quarters. One at a time, the Captain or the gunny would carefully search each man and collect any contraband that they might have obtained ashore – switch blade knives, small bottles of liquor, pornography or anything else Sheehan thought might be detrimental to the good order and discipline of the unit. Once each man was searched, they were led topside and remained there until all the men had been examined.

Then Sheehan and the gunny would do a detailed inspection of the personal lockers, footlockers and any potential hiding places and seize any other prohibited items might be found.

Captain Sheehan would then collect all the contraband into a pile and, in front of the entire company, conduct a burial at sea. While the amount of paraphernalia gathered for burial was reduced after each port visit as the cruise continued, so long as he commanded the company Sheehan inevitably conducted such investigations after every port call. The absence of such items no doubt contributed to the lack of disciplinary problems the BLT encountered.[44]

One of the key leadership traits demonstrated throughout 1/2 was the fact that officers and particularly Staff NCOs routinely entered the troops' berthing areas. At the height of the racial and disciplinary problems that plagued the Marine Corps in those days, oftentimes the would-be leaders were simply afraid to enter the troop areas that are typically deep in the bowels of the ship. If the leadership did not periodically and unpredictably inspect, even casually, what was happening in those quarters, then almost inevitably things would turn bad, or worse. The troops never knew when the Gray Ghost, or Doc Smith, or their company officers might appear unexpectedly. And even though the BLT was spread among five amphibious ships, no one was out of the reach of their peripatetic Commanding Officer.

Sheehan had been promoted to major during the cruise, and when the original S-3 was ordered home into a logistics billet at Camp Lejeune, Gray happily made his Alpha Company Commander the Operations Officer. Sheehan enjoyed learning from his commander and found the little extras that Gray brought into field exercises to be things that most infantry commanders did not emphasize or even address. For example, Gray made sure that his men knew how their communications could be exploited by the enemy while ensuring that, to the extent security considerations permitted, his officers were aware of the important advantages that the tactical use of SIGINT offered. Gray also used his artillery background to emphasize the use of supporting arms, ensuring that everyone could call for and adjust mortars and artillery, and that all knew when to use supporting arms in the course of their maneuvers. Sheehan took the opportunity to learn all he could, with enthusiasm.

All the officers in Gray's command benefited from his leadership. Jim Magee recalled that no sooner had the MAU entered the Med than Gray directed their attention toward possible operations in and around a north African city. The officers were not sure whether the potential operation was real, or something Gray had concocted. They all realized that Gray seemed to have access to intelligence that other officers were unfamiliar with. In the case of the unnamed city, Gray required each commander and staff officer to consider events that would have the host nation friendly to the Marines, unfriendly to the Marines, or even invaded by a third nation. Gray patiently led his staff and subordinate commanders through the planning process, correcting, congratulating, cajoling and chastising as appropriate. Magee recalled the whole exercise was a precursor to the Rapid Planning Process the Marine Corps would adopt in later years as part of the Marine Expeditionary Unit (Special Operations Capable) program that Gray was instrumental in initiating. Importantly, Gray stressed that all the officers had to become intimately familiar with logistics and fire support coordination; true professional officers had to know much more than tactics.

The planning, re-planning and continuous adjustments, Magee added, was very effective in keeping anyone from becoming bored while the ships plowed through the sea.

It was an assignment that benefited both the new Major and his commander. Gray, Doc Smith, Sheehan and Magee would remain close for the rest of their active service and even long into all their retirements.

Among all the accomplishments of the battalion during the cruise, perhaps the most impressive was the fact that there was not a single incident related to lack of discipline, fighting, or racial tensions. Luck? Perhaps, but good leadership uniformly applied was a more probable answer.

REGIMENTAL HEADQUARTERS, 2nd MARINES, CAMP LEJEUNE, NORTH CAROLINA, 21 APRIL 1972

Soon after his return to Camp Lejeune, Gray lost the billet he had so long aspired to, being an infantry battalion commander, but gained a new one equally desirable. Still a lieutenant colonel and months away from promotion, Al Gray assumed command of the 2nd Marine Regiment, becoming the 93rd commanding officer of the regiment. His decision to stay with 1/2 rather than go for a colonel's billet was now repaid in spades. Commanding a regiment has represented the professional zenith of many fine officers, and now Gray led one while still a lieutenant colonel. It was perhaps apropos that his battalion commanders at the 2nd Marines would be three majors – though each was exceptional. They were future Lieutenant General Ernest T. Cook who had the 2nd Battalion, while Major Doc Smith fleeted up to Commanding Officer of the 1st and Major John Adams commanded the 3rd. Competence, not rank or seniority, drove Gray.

For the next nine months, until Gray moved up to the division staff to be the G3, the 2nd Marines participated in every exercise conducted by the 2nd Marine

Divison. During May, Regimental Landing Team 2 (RLT-2) served as the helicopter-born ground combat element for exercised Exotic Dancer V, the largest amphibious exercise on the east coast.

It turned out that the 2nd Marines would soon be exposed to all professionalism and expertise that Gray and his battalion commanders could bring to bear. In 1972, regimental commanders were largely content to supervise the activities of their subordinate battalions; but Gray sought things to do that would permit the 2nd Marines to operate as a regimental unit, especially at Camp Lejeune where battalions were often away on independent operations like those from which Gray had just returned. Plus, in accordance with the Division's long-term schedule, the 2nd Marines would be giving up the responsibility to provide the Med battalion, something that rotated among the three regiments about every 18 months. Gray was also looking for ways to challenge his men and his subordinate leaders; so when the Development Center at Quantico asked for a regiment to test and formulate new weapons systems and new troop organizations in Exercise Spartan Forest, Gray jumped at the opportunity to volunteer the 2nd Marines. Majors Ron Christmas and Chuck Meadows, both of whom had earned a Navy Cross in Vietnam and were well known among Marines, provided the liaison duties for the Development Center.

Figure 4.14
Major Malcom "Doc" Smith relieves Lt Col Al Gray 28 April 1972.[45]

Figure 4.15
Colonel Redman relinquishes command of the 2nd Marines to Lt Col Al Gray.[46]

Few, if any, of Gray's company commanders at Camp Lejeune had led units populated by more than 130 or 140 Marines. 135-150 men, or fewer, was the norm for infantry companies dating back to the Vietnam War. In contrast, Gray as a company commander in Korea led upwards of 240 men – companies and attached units of that era were simply much larger. Working with the Development Center's testing program would, therefore, be an enjoyable yet challenging effort for every level of the regiment's command structure. Three new tables of organization (T/O) – each battalion's would be different – were to be tested, and each T/O provided for larger units than was then in existence in the Marine Corps. The new T/O would give company commanders, platoon leaders, company 1st Sergeants and gunnery sergeants the chance to work with much larger numbers – invaluable experience in Gray's mind. The Regiment would do the evaluations of each test.

Figure 4.16
Ernie Cook, shown here as a Lieutenant General, was a brilliant officer whom
Al Gray held in highest esteem. General Cook's service culminated when he
was designated Commanding General of the Marine Corps Development
and Education Command when General Gray was Commandant. [47]

Besides involvement with the T/O tests, the Marine Corps was in the process
of testing the DRAGON weapons system and the "TOW" weapons systems, and
the 2nd Marines became immersed in that effort.[48] Gray's Marines were the first
to actually fire the new systems while implementing the test program. While
shooting new anti-tank weapons was fun, the regiment was also used to test operational procedures for an entirely new class of aircraft, the AV-8 Harrier. Adapted
from a British design, the Harrier was a "jump jet" capable of taking off vertically,
hover like a helicopter but then provide close air support for ground Marines. The
concept of operations envisioned Harriers operating close to the front lines from

makeshift airfields. It was the 2nd Marines who first tested the concept, provided the advanced (in terms of battle space, not construction) landing areas and the first test of direct support procedures for the new aircraft – one unique to the Marines among U.S. forces.[49]

Figure 4.17
The 2nd Marine Regiment's newly promoted commander, Colonel Al Gray, meets with Major Doc Smith, the Commanding Officer of 1st Battalion, 2nd Marines.[50]

Another unusual thing that Gray did was help the Marine Reserves put on a MAU exercise at Camp Lejeune. The Commandant, General Cushman, had written a letter to all officers asking that they help the reserves in any way they could. Gray, of course, took the Commandant's request to heart, and when a request was made to the 2nd Division to assist in a two-week exercise for reserve units, Gray volunteered. After all, it gave more experience to his officers and men who were assigned to augment the exercise, which was built around a reserve Marine Amphibious

Force and included a brigadier general in command. This effort supported by the 2nd Marines provided much more meaningful use of the reservists time than, say, reading training manuals or washing trucks! As with many things in Al Gray's professional life, this simple thing would be of assistance to Gray a few years later. It was amazing how those coincidences worked out – do something to assist others and it turns out to help you! [51]

One more innovation that Gray introduced to the regiment involved re-orientation training for sergeants and corporals who were returning to the Fleet Marine Force after periods away in assignments such as the Marine Security Guard Battalion (where they guarded embassies around the world.) Such NCOs were typically rusty with respect to their troop leading skills or their small unit tactical skills needed refreshing. Too often, when such Marines were returned to line units, other NCOs met them with skepticism or even derision. Gray knew these were fine men; that, after all, is exactly why they had been selected to serve outside the Fleet Marine Force. Thus, instead of assigning them directly to line companies, Gray and his regimental staff ran a "leadership and tactical refresher course" for such Marines. It typically lasted two weeks, during which time the men could work on their shortcomings, receive indoctrination and basic skills training, and generally become prepared for what would meet them in the line companies.

There was another benefit to Gray's approach. He seldom had to suggest that lower ranking commanders follow his lead. At every level of command, from his days as a company commander until the time he led the 2nd Marine Division years later, Gray realized that setting the example was usually all he had to do. The old saying that "success has many fathers but failure is an orphan" was particularly true in Al Gray's Marine Corps. Besides taking the time to speak with every Marine newly assigned to the 2nd Regiment, Gray and his staff took the time to make them feel comfortable, know what was expected of them, what was in store for them in the near future, and where they could look if they needed help in any way. The frosty reception given to him in Korea when he was a second lieutenant was seared in his memory. He would try to ensure no Marine in his units ever had such an experience.

Gray's bachelor status had always been at least a little unusual, since by the time an officer reached field grade rank he was typically married. His long bachelorhood would, over the years, give rise to many stories alluding to the fact that Gray either misunderstood the necessities of marriage or he just ignored them. Interestingly, the facts dispute such assertions. During the '70s and well into the '80s, the role of Marine Officers' Wives' Clubs as semi-official organizations was something no commanding officer could neglect, though many were indifferent to the value of such groups. Nearly all battalions, regiments, squadrons and air groups had wives' clubs. The commanding officer's lady was typically the president of the local group. Since Gray was a bachelor, he asked the senior officer in the regiment, who turned out to be the Navy dentist, if his wife would serve in that capacity.

Lieutenant Colonel Al Gray had not anticipated the near rebellion that his decision caused. Several of the more senior Marine wives were upset that the dentist's wife was given the honor; they got over their indigestion soon enough, however. So long as Gray was the Commanding Officer, he periodically briefed all the wives, not just the officers' wives, on various aspects of the regiment's mission, its plans, and what exactly their husbands were doing. In the course of those briefings, Gray learned a lot that he could use to make things better. His listening skills were excellent, and the wives were hardly shy about expressing their concerns.

Professionalism involved more than briefing wives, nonetheless. There was little sitting around redoing basic map reading exercises if you were in the 2nd Marines. Mowing grass, often done five times a week, or painting rocks soon became lost skills.[52]

A new Assistant Division Commander, Brigadier General Herbert L. Beckington, arrived at Camp Lejeune in 1972. Major General Fred Haynes, who had briefly commanded the division while 1/2 was in the Med, was unexpectedly appointed to command United States Forces, Korea, a billet that the Marine Corps traded every four years with the U.S. Army. With Haynes's surprising departure, leadership of the Division changed. Brigadier General Arthur Jacques Poillon was elevated into command while General Beckington came and assumed the Assistant Division Commander slot. Beckington had at least one pet peeve, that being the lack of control that deployed unit's maintained over their "sub-units." When battalion or larger commands deployed outside Camp Lejeune, they established "sub-units" that remained on the base and cared for various buildings, equipment and personnel who stayed behind. The sub-units tended to become disorganized and were often treated like poor step-children – both out of sight and out of mind of their deployed commanders. Beckington loved to visit these sub-units at a very early hour, then take steps to ensure they operated more efficiently and effectively in the future.

Figure 4.18
General Haynes Commanding General of the 2ⁿᵈ Marine Division and Lieutenant
Colonel Al Gray, CO of the 2ⁿᵈ Marines sharing a meal with enlisted Marines in the 2ⁿᵈ
Marines mess hall. General Haynes and Gray had served together much earlier in intel-
ligence duties when Gray was a Captain and then later on one of Gray's tours in Vietnam.
Haynes, a veteran of Iwo Jima, had a powerful intellect and was a visionary, remained
close friends with Gray all through active duty and retirement. Haynes was transferred
to Korea to fulfill a crucial United Nations billet shortly after this picture was taken.[53]

Early one morning, around 0430, General Beckington swooped in on one of the
sub-units of the 2ⁿᵈ Marines, but was surprised to find the Regimental Commander
also there. Beckington had little to say to Lieutenant Colonel Al Gray other than to
ask cursory questions about the state of the sub-unit, since it was obvious to him that,
at least in the 2ⁿᵈ Marines, supervision was not lacking. It was not clear which officer was more astonished to meet the other; the early morning encounter provided
the basis for profound mutual respect between the two men. One thing was clear,
General Beckington had no future need for pre-dawn visits to the 2ⁿᵈ Marines.

Beckington would also soon learn to recognize when Lieutenant Colonel Gray arrived at the Division Command Post. Captain Zinni had remained General Pollion's aide, and Al Gray still created a buzz in the Headquarters Building. After all, generals' aides were among Lieutenant Colonel Gray's favorite targets. A typical visit would go something like this:[54]

> *Al Gray walks into the Aides' Office, punching Captain Zinni on the arm, asking, "What are you doing Zinni, making coffee?"*
>
> *Zinni, smiling, "Among other things, sir."*
>
> *Gray's retort, "I thought you wanted to be a real Marine?"*
>
> *Zinni, "Yes, sir."*
>
> *Gray: "Well, come on down to the 2nd Marines and we'll give you a real challenge."*

Then Lieutenant Colonel Gray would budge the junior aide, or the clerk-typist, or the Sergeant Major and continue the routine until he finally arrived at his destination, which could be anywhere though it was not likely to be the General's office. Al Gray only went to see general officers when summoned to them. Unlike many "careerists" that populated the Marine officer ranks in those days, Gray received enough notoriety and renown without drawing attention to him by hanging out around the flagpole. After all, the next higher headquarters is one's natural enemy! Zinni realized, of course, that Al Gray was actually encouraging him and showing him a fair amount of respect by singling him out for a punch on the arm and good-natured repartee; if Al Gray disliked someone, he ignored them.

But Gray was neck-deep in pursuits much more intellectually challenging than light-hearted banter with the general's aides. His old office at HQMC, AO2F, still ran the cryptologic-related activities of the Marine Corps. In 1972, the officer charged with leading the SIGINT-related issues of that office was Lieutenant Colonel James Quisenberry, affectionately (and widely) known throughout the service as "Q". Gray and Q had a long history of collaboration, interaction and, sometimes, argumentation. Their relationship dated to their times as captains, when Gray was at HQMC and "Q" was the Commanding Officer of 2nd Composite Radio Company at Camp Lejeune during the Cuban Missile Crisis. Later in Vietnam,

Lieutenant Colonel Quisenberry replaced Al Gray as CO of Radio Battalion units when Gray returned to the United States on emergency leave in January 1968.[55]

When Gray had first worked to establish Tables of Organization for the enlarged Radio Battalions and the Marine Support Battalion, the MOS that the Marines were assigned was purposefully nebulous. In those days, no one spoke of "cryptologists" and even the acronym "SIGINT" reeked of classified materials or top-secret work. Thus, "special communications" was much more acceptable, and it did not cause unknowing people to ask too many questions. Gray, and those helping him, decided that putting the new cryptologic specialties within the Occupational Field for Communications (25XX) was the fastest and most expedient way to get approval for their efforts. However, the success that Radio Battalion operations had during the Vietnam War opened the field to much broader acceptance; most if not all Marine general officers were well aware of the operational excellence reflected in the work of cryptologists, and there was a growing acceptance of the need for more Marines to understand SIGINT and cryptologic matters. Thus, there was much less aversion to bringing cryptology out of the shadows.

The personnel branch at HQMC, the G-1, was responsible for the manpower needs of the service; in the early 1970s, the G-1's Office of Manpower Utilization undertook a new effort related to cryptologists. A mustang captain, who had worked mostly in engineering billets, was assigned to the G-1 and tasked to work with Lieutenant Colonel "Q" and his AO2F section to study cryptologists. Don Whisnant, who thought he had seen and heard most of what the Marine Corps had to offer, was hardly prepared for the idiosyncratic "Q". Working with Captain Whisnant was a Master Sergeant named Hayes. After their first day working within the AO2F spaces, Hayes remarked that, "The lock on the door is not to keep people out of that office, but rather to keep the occupants in!"

But Q had the good sense to recommend that Whisnant, who had never been around cryptology before, go to Camp Lejeune to interview Al Gray about his study effort. Lieutenant Colonel Gray was in the field with his regiment when Whisnant arrived. True to form, and predictably, Gray met with the mustang captain in regimental field headquarters – for several hours. Whisnant was a quick study and realized the best thing he could do was keep quiet and take notes, voluminous notes! While Whisnant's basic instincts toward the study were good and he thought on target, the Captain got a major boost in confidence when Gray's ideas seemed to reinforce Whisnant's own thinking. Whisnant had been a Marine for 15 years, but he had never met an officer like Al Gray. And he never met another whose professionalism matched that of the Commanding Officer of the 2nd Marines.

As a result of the study, cryptologists were given their own Occupational Field, 26XX. The work that Al Gray had laid the foundation for in the early 1960s was completed, at least administratively. Whisnant's effort was the first that resulted in a new occupational field, and it was quickly approved at HQMC by then-Major General Sam Jaskilka.[56]

MARINE CORPS BASE, TWENTYNINE PALMS, CALIFORNIA, JULY 1972

Perhaps the most interesting thing Al Gray did while a regimental commander at Camp Lejeune involved *Operation Alkali Canyon*, a maneuver held clear across the country at the Marine Corps Base, Twentynine Palms, California. In the summer of 1972, in accordance with the Division's master schedule, it was the turn of the 2nd Marines to send a battalion for desert training, something one regiment at Camp Lejeune did annually. It was part of the Marine Corps cycle of desert, jungle and mountain training. The Division's training schedule dictated the unit rotation, but annually one infantry regiment, and its usual supporting arms attachments, would send a battalion to the sprawling base in the California desert. The base, now called the Marine Corps Air-Ground Combat Center, is by far the Marine Corps' largest.

Though leading a regiment is a colonel's billet, Lieutenant Colonel Gray still had not been promoted. That did not stop him from advancing the idea that instead of simply doing battalion-level exercises, the Division ought to have a regimental-size event in order to more fully utilize the space available at 29 Palms. Such an exercise would permit testing of expanded command and control, permit the use of greater maneuver over wider distances, and address issues not commonly encountered in the course of regular training evolutions. Gray's new boss, General Poillon, liked the idea of both a larger and longer exercise for the regiment, and forwarded the idea to his boss, Lieutenant General George C. Axtell at Fleet Marine Force, Atlantic. Axtell was also Commanding General, II Marine Expeditionary Force. An aviator who had earned a Navy Cross on Okinawa during World War II while serving as a 23-year-old major, Axtell not only liked the idea, but also he greatly expanded upon it.

The Marine Corps had long been divided by the continent that separated the Atlantic forces from those in the Pacific. Although it was the Marine Corps' intent that each force operates like the other, nonetheless it was easy for minor differences to have arisen and some did. So while Commandants liked to speak of one Marine Corps, within the service everyone knows that Hollywood Marines refers to those serving in California. Hollywood Marines tend to mock their brothers-in-arms who have to endure the snakes, mosquitoes and other pests and pestilence associated with Swamp Lagoon (Camp Lejeune, North Carolina.) Thus, Axtell viewed the idea as one that would permit a ground unit from the 2nd Division to work with air and ground units from I MEF as well as the logistics group already in place at 29 Palms. Axtell was quick to coordinate with his counterpart in the Pacific, the newly arrived Lieutenant General Louis Wilson.

General Wilson also liked the idea, and for more than the fact that it came from his former recruit, the man he often boasted that he had swept off the streets of New York, Al Gray.[57] Major General Wilson and Gray had earlier in the spring renewed their ties when Wilson, then the Deputy Commanding General for Education at Quantico, accompanied a class of Basic School lieutenants to Camp Lejeune to observe maneuvers there. As it would happen, the 2nd Marines were the demonstration unit. As Colonel Gray moved around among his troops, he espied Wilson's formidable figure standing on a piece of high ground. Gray strode over to the General, only to be met by, "I see they let anyone command my regiments these days!" It was Wilson's way to humor officers with faint praise. Of course, a 6'4" general wearing a single ribbon of five white stars on a blue field, representing a Medal of Honor earned on Guam in World War II, really did command all in his view. Now Wilson carried three stars on each collar and commanded all Marines in the Pacific, and he was enthusiastic in his support for a brigade-sized exercise at 29 Palms.

Generals Axtell and Wilson had expanded Gray's initiative to one that would include a six-week workup with small unit training prior to the formal exercise, a weeklong maneuver period, and then a four-to-five day wrap up. The designation *Alkali Canyon* was given, and Gray was frocked to Colonel to be in charge of the brigade-sized exercise.[58] It was going to be a big deal.

The East Coast contingent had hardly arrived before the first administrative dust up occurred. A general took exception when a Marine driving a 6x6 truck had the misfortune to accidentally drive his rig into a portion of the base designated as "officers country," the area where the officers' housing was located. Before he could extract himself and his large truck from the prohibited portion of the base, he hit a sign and ran over a yard. The local general was furious and wanted to immediately court-martial the young Marine. Gray patiently explained to senior officers that the Marine in question was part of II MEF, and that disciplinary action would have to wait until their return to Camp Lejeune. While the general was hardly mollified, the incident passed and the chastened young man in question stayed with his unit during the exercise.

Two round trips by 26 giant Air Force transports were needed simply to get the Camp Lejeune contingent to California. In addition to the 1st Battalion, 2nd Marines, their supporting artillery from 1st Battalion, 10th Marines, and attached engineers, the exercise would include fixed-wing Marine aircraft and helicopters from El Toro, a reinforced infantry battalion from Camp Pendleton, and the logistics unit from 29 Palms. During the exercise itself, a fourth ground maneuver element was simulated in a Command Post Exercise mode.

For the weeks of smaller unit training period before the exercise started, Gray used the ideas first implemented at Timbakion, Crete. Each company, the artillery battery, the tank or the amphibious tractor platoons or helicopter detachment was to request whatever training its commanding officer deemed necessary. The reaction of the subordinate commanders was easily predictable – they loved the chance to actually do what they thought important. Major Jack Sheehan, the S-3 of 1/2, coordinated all individual component training. It was no small effort for Sheehan and his assistants to coordinate, integrate, schedule and ensure that all subordinate element training went well, as planned by their commanders.

Gray and his S-3, in the meantime, planned the weeklong brigade exercise. Given the units would be free moving, collecting their own intelligence and reacting without a script, the planning had to be thorough. A highly competent and well-led Echo Company from the 2nd Battalion, 7th Marines provided the enemy force – the Sandonians. The aggressor name had more to do with the principal ground cover at 29 Palms, i.e., sand, than it did with a future irritant to U.S. policy in Nicaragua, the Sandinistas.

Each general in the chain of command wants something stressed during any exercise like *Alkali Canyon* and Louis Wilson was no exception. General Wilson wanted Colonel Gray to emphasize the responsibility that jets play in supporting Marine ground troops. The General always referred to the jets as the "white ones" and often would remark his Marines got to see the "green ones" (helicopters) often enough but it was essential that the "white ones" have a prominent role. While the Marines of that era were better at close air support than anyone else, they had lots of room for improvement. General Wilson knew all of that, and he wanted his infantry to understand the "white ones" were there to support them, Mostly, he wanted the entire force to get better. Gray made sure the General was pleased; there would be lots of "white ones" flying low above the maneuver area.

The exercise exceeded everyone's expectations. In an article in the Marine Corps Association professional magazine, *Leatherneck*, a number of captains, sergeants and Staff NCOs called the training the best they ever received. Interviewed by *Leatherneck*, Gray was typically low key:

> *"Exercise commander (and CO of RLT-2), Col A.M. Gray, tried out what he terms "centralized control, with decentralized execution," by having his subordinate commanders operate independently within the framework of the exercise.*
>
> *"We presented problems to the commanders," explained the colonel, "and let them solve them for themselves. That way, they could use their command capabilities and resources to their fullest."*
>
> *"I gave them a lot of slack," he added, "and they did a fine job."*
>
> *In one instance, a helicopter faked being shot down after flying over guerrilla positions. The guerrillas rushed out to claim the chopper. Once in the open, friendly forces struck out with simulated artillery barrages. Under cover of a helicopter gunship, the friendlies retrieved the chopper crew before the Sandonians could close in.*
>
> *Remarked one commander: "My men received three years' training in just three weeks." His statement typified those of all units in Aklali Canyon.*
>
> Excerpt from "Leatherneck Magazine."[59]

Gray may have been low key, but the exercise was truly historic. It marked any number of firsts, even though there were bumps and a few bruises along the way. Before it started, Gray had to convince the G-3 at I MEF that the exercise really would be free of constraints normally associated with large-scale, highly-planned events. "Planning" for the next part of the operation was indeed another part of the exercise that Gray had in mind; however, free-form exercises involving large numbers of troops spread over expansive tracts of terrain were not something staff officers were used to dealing with. They expected highly controlled movements that closely followed a script. However, those officers would have to learn new techniques, because such control was not seen during *Alkali Canyon*!

In the first Marine Air-Ground Task Force exercise of its type at 29 Palms, on the first day a motorized-mechanized task force covered 60 miles, an unprecedented achievement for a Marine ground force. The next night an infantry battalion conducted a helicopter assault with live, though offset, artillery fire and air strikes (from the white ones!) Adding to the complexity of events, the temperatures at the desert Marine base were so hot that eggs could be fried on the LVT-5s! [60]

Figure 4.19
In the midst of Alkali Canyon: Al Gray middle, Jack Sheehan in shorts.[61]

Yes, *Alkali Canyon* was indeed a big deal, so big and so effective as a training exercise for Marines of all ranks that it was repeated again in future years.

Figure 4.20
Tanks and Amphibious Vehicles in the initial armor/mechanized/
helicopter-borne task force operations.[62]

Figure 4.21
Tanks and Amphibious Vehicles in the initial armor/mechanized/
helicopter-borne task force operations.[62]

Figure 4.22
Helicopters from the 3rd Marine Aircraft Wing.[63]

Figure 4.23
Tanks and Amphibious Vehicles in
the initial armor/mechanized/heli-
copter-borne task force operations.[64]

Figure 4.24
A portion of the "enemy" personnel at their headquarters.[65]

Figure 4.25
Pictured here are two
of the air-delivered
seismic intrusion devices
(Ad-Sids) used to detect
enemy movements. [66]

Figure 4.26
Field Artilleryman of the 2nd 175mm Gunn Battery from Camp Lejeune, North Carolina
are undergoing desert training at the Marine Corps Base, Twentynine Palms, California,
with huge artillery pieces such as this 175mm self-propelled weapon. Sgt James D. Moss
and LCpl Jeff E. Brown atop the gun barrel, are section chiefs with the battery.[67]

Alkali Canyon was an unscripted free maneuver. To include both sides being required to conduct their own intelligence, surveillance, and reconnaissance operations.

Following the conclusion of *Alkali Canyon*, the Close Air Support tests for the Marines' new "jump jet," the AV-8A Harrier, were held at Camp Lejeune. Major General Tom Miller, Gray's old commander from the exercise in Turkey, specifically asked for the 2nd Marines to be the exercise support unit. During these critical tests, Gray deployed his regiment in the vicinity of helicopter landing zones and landing sites, including hiding along Lyman Road, a major thoroughfare that crosses Camp Lejeune. At the sites, the harrier pilots would be briefed verbally by the regimental forward air controllers on the precise targets and weapons to be supported by air strikes. The 2nd Marines ensured that the Harriers were put through their paces. It was the first time the Harriers worked with a ground unit to develop both tactics and support requirements. Gray and all the officers included in the exercise became vocal proponents for the new and unique aviation capability.

THE MED, AGAIN, UNDER UNHAPPY CIRCUMSTANCES, DECEMBER 1972

In addition to training in the desert at 29 Palms, it was also routine for Marines from Camp Lejeune to conduct jungle training in Panama and cold weather training at Camp Drum, New York. By this time, Gray had brought Major Sheehan up to be the S-3 of the regiment, and together they had planned the cold weather exercise for December. While at Camp Drum, however, Gray received an urgent phone call. His presence was needed immediately at Norfolk.

3rd Battalion, 2nd Marines was in the Med and there had been major troubles aboard two of the amphibious ships, the USS *Trenton* and the USS *Iwo Jima*. The confluence of bad timing, bad characters, and poor leadership conspired to put all the good work that Gray's BLT 1/2 had done in jeopardy. There was fighting on the mess decks of the *Trenton* and weapons had been drawn.

As it turned out the Battalion Commander, Major John Adams, was on emergency leave away from his command. When the trouble arose, neither the MAU commander nor anyone else took positive control to stop the violence. Major Adams was a fine Marine and someone Gray respected, but in his absence, Adams's chain of command, both above and below, let him down. The 6th Fleet Commander, Vice Admiral Miller, had called the Commandant requesting immediate help. Admiral Miller, of course, knew of Al Gray and his abilities from Gray's recent deployment with BLT 1/2. General Cushman, who had as a colonel commanded the 2nd Regiment, asked who the current commander was; after all, the unit involved was 3/2. Learning that his former subordinate from 1st Radio Battalion in Vietnam, Al Gray, was in command, Cushman directed that Gray proceed immediately to the Med.

Gray flew first to the Gaeta, Italy, homeport of the USS *Coronado*, the 6th Fleet Command Ship. The Admiral met and briefed Gray on additional details regarding the incidents; furthermore, and importantly, the Admiral promised his full cooperation should Gray need additional resources – or anything! Colonel Gray's first stop was the *Trenton*. By now Gray had been without sleep for more than a day, but he immediately ordered a gathering of the Marines on the hangar deck of the LPD. Gray read the troops the riot act in no uncertain terms. He also collected a dozen or so of the instigators and put them ashore under armed guard. He made sure that the officers and Staff NCOs realized that leadership, firm leadership, was required and that meant going into the berthing areas regularly to determine exactly what was transpiring and what the mood of the troops was. The troops could tell by the arrest of the 12 or so Marines who had been up to no good that this Colonel meant business.

Gray's next stop was the LHA, the *Iwo Jima*, a far larger ship that carried many more troops. Again, he met with all the Marines aboard in a series of assemblies and made sure everyone got the message, especially the officers and Staff NCOs. By the time Gray was done, he had been up for more than 48 hours. But the tinderbox was averted and no further problems ensued – proof that aggressive leadership was still effective.

His report to the chain of command was interesting, and showed that Gray was no martinet oblivious to the plight of other officers who encountered such incidents. He wrote, in part, "Those of us who live and lead in this environment understand…" Indeed.

In keeping with the notion that no good deed goes unpunished, Gray's reward for putting a lid on the troubles in the Med was the loss of his regiment. General Poillon needed a new G-3, Colonel Redman had departed, and the General had just the right man in mind: the junior colonel in the 2nd Marine Division.

HEADQUARTERS, 2nd MARINE DIVISION, CAMP LEJEUNE, NORTH CAROLINA. JANUARY 1973

General Poillon was so impressed with the results of *Operation Alkali Canyon* in 1972 that the General made sure that he had the opportunity to lead the Operation in 1973. General Poillon and Colonel Gray enjoyed a close and harmonious relationship, and even though Gray was his junior colonel the CG made him the Division G-3 (Operations, Plans and Training). The General gave Gray increasingly more responsibility and considered his staff assistant in the top 5% of Marine colonels, despite the fact that Gray had only recently been promoted. It is unsurprising that Lieutenant Colonel and then Colonel Gray was considered exceptional during his time at Camp Lejeune; all praised his professionalism and his leadership skills, and many made note of him being a good shipmate, someone well liked by his men and his contemporaries. One of Al Gray's great strengths was his ability to do unpleasant things while maintaining a pleasant disposition.

Of course, over the years some Marines, usually officers, felt Gray's displeasure; but they mostly became non-entities to him. Al Gray would much rather spend his time and energy with people and situations that he thought had a chance of being successful. Once someone had earned their way onto his ignore listing, they had to be especially dedicated and always professional if they were to get different status.

If Al Gray was going to be the G-3, well the least he could do was raid the Commanding General's personal staff to acquire the services of the senior aide, Tony Zinni.

Captain Tony Zinni had been an aide long enough. He was ready for a new assignment. General Poillon honored his request by assigning him to the new G-3. Some subordinate officers were known to take out their personal frustrations with generals by harassing their former aides, and Poillon wanted to foreclose on the possibility of that happening to Zinni. He thought Al Gray would take the Captain under his wing; Poillon, of course, was not privy to the relationship Gray and Zinni already enjoyed.

Indeed, it is highly doubtful that any Marine learned about any relationship Al Gray enjoyed with anyone except by the other party disclosing it. It is safe to say that Al Gray never divulged anything about others, particularly if they were his seniors, to third parties. Of course, as Zinni often saw, it would not be at all unusual for then Colonel Gray to show up at the Infantry Training Center with some sergeant, or gunnery sergeant or some junior officer in tow; he would then proceed to introduce his visitor to Zinni and the staff. On such occasions, Gray would report, "We served together in the 12th Marines, " or "Sergeant Smith worked with me in cryptology." The sheer numbers of Marines who knew of or served with Al Gray fascinated Zinni.

Captain Zinni checked in with the G-3 for duty thinking he would have some obscure, staff job, jockeying some desk at the Headquarters; his first audience with his new boss obliterated that impression. Colonel Gray did not tell Zinni what his job would be, but rather asked, "If you could construct your own billet description, and thinking outside the box, what would you want to do? Don't answer right away, but take your time and think about it." Zinni was thrilled. And he knew just what he wanted to do.

As a rifle company commander Zinni was frustrated by the lack of training resources and opportunities available to troop leaders. He was very interested in what in those days were referred to "special operations" – cold weather, mountain, jungle, etc.[68] He wanted something along the lines of an Advanced Infantry School that units could attend, where commanders could get the training they wanted complemented by experts in the areas of tactics, weapons, and special operations. There was an almost abandoned, largely rundown area of Camp Lejeune where during the Vietnam War a typical Vietnamese village had been constructed; but the village was dilapidated and the area mostly unused. Zinni thought it would be perfect for his intentions.

When the Captain took Colonel Gray out and showed him what he proposed, Gray liked the idea but admonished Zinni to "do it right, don't goldbrick anything, just the essentials."[69] The Generals in the chain of command loved what became the Infantry Training Center. The G-3 encouraged the infantry regiments to make use of Zinni's school, and before long every machine gunner, every 106mm recoilless rifleman, every mortar man and all other crew-served weapons teams in the 2nd Marine Division had been trained and certified by the Center. Al Gray, the officer who took what he got and made what he wanted, provided Tony Zinni with the same opportunity. The Marine Corps, at least the 2nd Division, was much better because of it.

Being the G-3 did not change the Gray Ghost's modus operandi. He still showed up unannounced, visited out of the way units and offices, and was seen by as many people as any officer of his rank – or any other rank. Force Troops, Atlantic, the organization that was home to the 2nd Radio Battalion, the 2nd Amphibious Tractor Battalion, the 2nd Engineer Battalion and the Shore Party Battalion and others, was separate from 2nd Division, and had its own Commanding General. Nonetheless, the two units had much in common in addition to both being located at Camp Lejeune. And the Commanding General, Force Troops, Atlantic, was an officer whom Al Gray respected very much. Gray had first met Robert L. Nichols at Quantico, when he briefed then-Colonel Nichols about intelligence programs at the Development Center. Now a Brigadier General, Nichols was very interested in the morale and disciplinary issues facing the Marine Corps.

The management system in vogue in Marines Corps of the 1970s stressed charts, graphs and the visual display of all sorts of data related to the unit's personnel and equipment. Each command from battalion on up had a room filled with such items. General Nichols actually paid attention to the data, however. He realized that there was a strong correlation between those Marines who did not finish high school and those Marines who deserted, left repeatedly on unauthorized absence (UA) or simply got into trouble time and again. Though later others made the same correlation, and it eventually formed the basis for the Marines demanding that at least 98% of its recruits be high school graduates, Al Gray always thought it was General Nichols who should have gotten credit for the high school graduation initiative. As was his fashion, Gray stored away the Nichols information for later use, though he probably had no idea that in less than two years he would be taking advantage of General Nichols's work in a very significant and unusual way.

Although Al Gray was the G-3 only eight months or so, he tried hard to make a difference, though he had many challenges while doing so. Gray always thought that staff leadership was every bit as important as leading while in command. Seldom did a day pass without him visiting a regiment or one of the Division's separate battalions, i.e., the reconnaissance or communications battalions. The purpose of these visits was not to hold official, inspection type meetings but rather to find out what the Division could do to assist subordinate commanders in their everyday challenges – of which there were many. In those days there were daunting requirements for human relations training dictated by no lesser authority than the Commandant of the Marine Corps. Besides HQMC, the 3-star general at FMFLANT added his ideas of what training needed to be accomplished, and of course, the Division piled on with yet more things that took the time and effort of small unit leaders. All these flowed down to the company commanders and platoon leaders, who lacked the time and capability to juggle it all while keeping their Marines active, engaged and motivated. Gray did what he could to help the local commanders. In the process, of course, he got to know and interact with the commanders and their key staff members, continuing his practice of knowing what was happening throughout his sphere of influence, and even beyond it.

As a young officer at HQMC, Gray had observed the interactions among generals, and he followed Charlie Beale's advice to a "T." He had learned to stay out of the way when the elephants were rumbling. As the G-3 he received an advanced course in Marine politics. The Commanding General at Norfolk, George C. Axtell seldom interacted with Generals Jacques Poillon, CG of the 2nd

Division, or General Lloyd (Bud) Wilkerson, CG of Marine Corps Base, Camp Lejeune. All were fine officers and well respected, and all knew Al Gray. But it was left to Gray, the junior colonel, to try to implement Axtell's directives while keeping both Poillon and Wilkerson happy. It was a fine line to walk, and one that required sensitivity and respect to both senior officers. Gray was intent on not choosing sides and not believing he was anything more important than the G-3. He made sure that Generals Poillon and Wilkerson were never upstaged and that he never acted as General Axtell's direct spokesman.

At one point General Axtell decided that the Marine security force at Guantanamo Bay, Cuba (Gitmo, as Marines invariably call it) needed to be reshaped. The 8th Marines had long maintained a whole battalion at Gitmo, and that commitment had a negative impact on the parent regiment, limiting it in many ways both training and operationally, and personnel wise. Consequently, Axtell reached down and personally directed that Gray accompany his own G-3, Colonel Jack Ivins, to Cuba to determine a new security arrangement that would reduce the number of Marines assigned there while satisfying the national security concerns related to the base. Ivins and Gray knew each other from the "helicopter incident" in Turkey, when General Tom Miller had accused Gray of hot-dogging over the beach. The two professionals got along well, and they proposed a viable solution to the issue, everyone throughout the chain of command was happy.

In addition to dealing with General Axtell, Gray was the recipient of recurring Saturday morning phone calls from the CG, 2nd Marine Air Wing – that same Tom Miller, though now he was a major general. Miller was very concerned about the coordination between the division and the wing. Whenever the infantry requests air support, it uses what is called a "TAR" – i.e., a Tactical Air Request. As if on schedule, each week General Miller would call Gray, rather than his general officer counterpart, to tell the G-3 how well, or not so well, the TARs had been during the previous week. It was just a minor additional duty for the young colonel to work through. Though it was seldom easy to accomplish, not choosing sides was something Al Gray took very seriously, and it served him well. [70]

In July 1973, Major General Samuel Jaskilka became the Commanding General of the 2nd Division. The new CG knew very well Colonel Al Gray, the Division's G-3, from previous assignments. When Lieutenant Colonel Gray was student at the Command & Staff College, freshly promoted Brigadier General Sam Jaskilka was the Director. He had been at the table during the class mess night when Commandant Leonard F. Chapman had apologized to Lieutenant Colonel Gray about the issue of Marine cryptology. General Jaskilka had long been a key Al Gray supporter, but Jaskilka would not get to take advantage of the Colonel's skills for more than a month before Gray was off to another assignment far from eastern North Carolina.

General Robertshaw's comment on Gray's Officer Qualification Record during the 1969 Top Level School Board selection process resulted in him going to Army War College.

The period 1971 through 1975, while the Vietnam War was winding down, would afford Al Gray ample opportunity to display his already legendary leadership skills. Never in its long history had the Marine Corps faced such significant, internal, societal-driven personnel issues. While his relationship with Lieutenant Pedrick and his family showed one side of Al Gray to best advantage, there were other sides to his complex personality, and they, too, were often on display. Gray always took care of his Marines and Sailors as best he could, but accomplishing his mission was the vital component that drove him. Many drug-abusers, petty and not-so-petty criminals, and even generally unmotivated officers and men found themselves either out of the Marine Corps or serving in new commands. Indeed, the personnel actions that Gray started while in the 2nd Marines in the early 1970s would become the norm for the Marine Corps by the middle of that decade.

Figure 4.27
General Sam Jaskilka, shown here as a Lieutenant General, was a strong supporter.
of Al Gray's leadership. This picture, which shows Doc Smith in a recruiting officer's
uniform, was probably taken in late 1976, just before Al Gray received his first star. [71]

VIETNAMIZATION IN FULL SWING

WASHINGTON, 1970 - 1971

Even before the Americans and South Vietnamese had been withdrawn from their Cambodian incursion, the Congress imposed the Church Amendment restrictions on future American operations. No longer could American advisors accompany their South Vietnamese counterparts if they left the borders of South Vietnam. Of course, Richard Nixon complained (rightfully so) that the Amendment limited his military options, but they hardly slowed the White House's appetite for influencing military operations in Southeast Asia.

Nixon and his principal foreign policy advisor, Henry Kissinger, had opened secret negotiations with the North Vietnamese, but the communists repeatedly balked at any compromise that left President Thieu in power. But the Nixon Administration, at least initially, remained loyal to its ally. Nixon and Kissinger did, in some ways, show some pragmatism in the negotiations when they dropped the requirement that the North withdraw its forces as a pre-condition to American withdrawal. After all, the Americans were intent on reducing the footprint of American ground combat forces. Nixon was gearing up for his re-election in 1972 and he appreciated that those prospects depending on him showing progress on ending the war, or at least ending American casualties.

With General Creighton Abrams touting the advances being made by the ARVN, the White House latched onto any plot intent on keeping the pressure on the North Vietnamese Army. The White House was particularly happy with the results of the Cambodia Incursion of April-June 1970. To politicians, and Al Haig, it looked as though the ARVN really were improving, just as General Creighton Abrams had been saying. While it is impossible to say exactly who and where the operation was initiated, but by late winter 1970-71, the Nixon Administration wanted further demonstrable success of their policy of *Vietnamization* by going into southern Laos.

By successfully attacking there, the Washington strategists presumed they could push back any future communist attacks for a year or more. During the late fall and early winter of 1970-1971, plans for Laos took shape. Unfortunately, and it was an oft-repeated situation that hurt the American war effort, the folks outside Vietnam did not appreciate the facts inside as well as their Commanding General did.

While attempting to negotiate from a position of strength, Nixon had shown some restraint on the bombing of North Vietnam, even as he expanded the use of B-52s against targets in Cambodia and Laos. But with the Marines out of Vietnam except for advisors and staffers, Nixon's emphasis on *Vietnamization* - using the ARVN to take the fight to the enemy – remained the keystone of his approach.

There were some revisions that affected the conduct of the war. First and fore-most among them, Congress put severe budget limitations in place. While not yet severe enough to impede operations, the financial aid needed to conduct the war, it was an ominous first step for what would later become a dire circumstance for President Thieu's government. Still, Thieu had the sense that the Americans were simply adjusting on the margins, not pulling out support for his country.

Admiral Thomas Moorer replaced Earle Wheeler as the Chairman of the Joint Chiefs of Staff. And while the Admiral represented a new leader for the JCS, he had little influence over the war. Nor did Moorer's civilian boss, Mel Laird, show the way with respect to Vietnam; he remained well in the background behind Kissinger. The role of providing military leadership in support of General Abrams fell to the Commander-in-Chief, Pacific. Regrettably, a military man inside the White House, Kissinger's aide, Brigadier General Alexander Haig, United States Army, became a strong counterweight to both Abrams and the Pacific Admiral.

While military policy remained ambiguous the domestic situation in the United States spiraled toward more and more violence and greater dissatisfaction with the war. In the Midwest, on 4 May 1970, the Ohio National Guard opened fire on anti-war demonstrators at Kent State University. Four students were killed in carnage that shocked the nation. The television pictures were both vivid and compelling. Nixon was appalled, though it was he who also received most the criticism as a result of events. It was an American tragedy.

I CORPS, REPUBLIC OF VIETNAM, 1971

In 1968, about the time that Creighton Abrams took over MAC(V), there was a change at CINCPAC. The Commander-in-Chief, Pacific is the top American military officer in the entire Pacific region. CINCPAC commanded even Abrams. Of course, Abrams as did Westmoreland before him, responded directly to the President and Secretary of Defense more than they did to CINCPAC. Nevertheless, the new CINCPAC was an unusually aggressive and determined-to-win-the-war type of officer. In that regard, he was much like Al Gray! The new CINCPAC was Admiral John S. McCain, Jr., the son of a Navy admiral and the father of a Navy pilot held in the Hanoi Hilton, Lieutenant Commander John S. McCain III, a future senator from Arizona and Presidential candidate.

Although diminutive in size, in that respect he was not much taller than Brute Krulak, McCain was a forceful advocate and strong supporter of Abrams's policy of seizing and holding the population centers. But he also backed the Army general when Abrams wanted to make cross-border incursions to attack NVA logistics bases, the kind of operation that had proven so successful in 1970.

By 1971 the drawdown of U.S. Forces was at full speed, and with the ARVN doing well the Washington crowd had formulated yet another cross-border attack as a means to deal with North Vietnamese logistics and supply dumps. If the ARVN could successfully destroy such supply centers, combined with Abrams emphasis on maintaining a strong ARVN presence throughout the rice-growing areas, then NVA plans would be seriously disrupted if not defeated.

Lam Son 719 was an operation that targeted the occupation and destruction of NVA materials around the Laotian town of Tchepone. The target lay just across the border west of Khe Sanh along old National Route 9, which the French had built. It had been a potential objective for American and South Vietnamese planners as far back as 1964 when Al Gray brought his Signals Survey and Engineering Unit to Tiger Tooth Mountain. Unfortunately, impassable mountains to the north and a river to the south bordered the main supply line for the projected operation, Route 9. The valley through which the road runs is very narrow. It is not optimal ground for any attacking force. Plus, the NVA had been in the area since the start of the war, and knew the region extremely well.

But politicians are very clever people and do not permit their lack of tactical or even strategic understanding to color their decision making. South Vietnam had been relatively quiet from the summer right through to the New Year, 1971. Abrams's emphasis on building a new brand of leadership among the senior ARVN had indeed shown impressive results, not because President Thieu had chosen new leaders but because the old leaders were growing into their jobs and responsibilities, and a generation of company and field grade officers were coming along – a generation committed to their country.

Even though the major professional military issues identified by Abrams remained, Laird, Kissinger, Haig and even Admiral McCain failed to acknowledge them. Abrams recognized that things were better in almost every area, but he also appreciated that the South Vietnamese were far, far from ready to take on their NVA counterparts in a toe-to-toe slugfest. The ARVN remained reliant on American artillery and American airpower, both in terms of close air support for ground units and helicopters for mobility, resupply and command and control. Abrams feared, rightfully, that pushing the ARVN to take on complex, highly problematic operations outside of South Vietnam was an invitation to disaster. The White House felt otherwise.

While the ARVN's Cambodian Incursion of 1970 featured a very capable, highly respected tactician, General Thanh as the Corps Commander, *Lam Son 719* featured a politician masquerading as a commander. General Hoang Xuan Lam, coincidently, was one of President Thieu's favorites. The operation would be very complex and take place in stages. It was all far beyond Lam's ability to guide, plan, lead, execute or, perhaps, even to understand. Below the Corps level, many South Vietnamese officers and units performed brilliantly, bravely, but too often futilely. [72]

Awaiting the South Vietnamese attack was a well-prepared North Vietnamese Army fighting for its life. If its supply routes and caches were destroyed, it would take years to rebuild. But the NVA had long ago demonstrated their tenacity and fighting capabilities, and *Lam Son 719* gave them the opportunity to bloody the emboldened ARVN. The NVA commanders were tough, experienced and resolute. Despite that, the NVA endured an estimated 13,000 casualties. Many of those can be attributed to the numerous B-52 strikes made in the area, but many more can be credited to American helicopters and helicopter gunships. The Americans lost over 100 helicopters during the operation as pilots and flight crews performed courageously, often going gun-to-gun against emplaced communist anti-aircraft weapons systems. American pilots also were more than heroic in resupplying or evacuating desperate ARVN units on the battlefield. Thus, while some ARVN units fought well, without American airpower *Lam Son 719* would have been a real disaster.

Despite the prominent role American airpower had in the operation, no American ground advisors were able to accompany their units into Laos as a result of the Church Amendment. Without American advisors to call air strikes and coordinate helicopters, the language gap proved an additional burden on the attackers; ARVN officers could not make their situations, often critical, understood by the American pilots, resulting in wasted opportunities or worse. Again, America fought the battle with one hand tied behind its back and its feet tied together.

As it was, the ARVN lost over 8,000 total casualties including 3,800 KIA. Perhaps the most significant as all the losses was the death of Lieutenant General Do Cao Tri. Tri had commanded the Cambodian Incursion in 1970 and was perhaps the ARVN's finest field commander. When the operation in Laos started to stall, President Thieu had ordered Tri forward to take command, but he died in a helicopter crash before reaching Laos. Again, the excursions outside the country had cost South Vietnam a fine leader at a time when such a loss was nearly irreplaceable.

Abrams had thought that the operation was a premature adventure given the quality and readiness of the ARVN units. And so it was. Precious advances in the quality of the ARVN's battalion and lower units in northern I Corps, which still needed more seasoning, were wasted, never to be rebuilt. The White House reaction? *Lam Son 719* was another victory demonstrating the efficacy of *Vietnamization*. Only people safe in their beds in Washington could possibly have come to such a conclusion.

Among Americans only Creighton Abrams had been proven correct about the outcome – McCain, Haig, Kissinger and Laird all had pushed, too hard as it turned out, for the attack. Of those who had optimistically encouraged Abrams into action, probably only McCain learned the lesson that military efficiency could not be force fed to the South Vietnamese. But McCain was soon gone; though he offered to and wanted to remain at his Pacific post, the crusty Admiral retired in 1972. Abrams lost an ally and the President lost a valuable, caring officer.

In the aftermath of *Lam Son 719*, the ARVN 1st Division, the country's finest Army division, could hardly be counted upon to defend an area that until 1970 was occupied by 80,000 American troops, including two Marine divisions. The government had to reinforce the area, which still faced significant amounts of NVA's firepower and multiple NVA divisions. Unfortunately, General Lam remained in charge and corruption remained the order of the day. Indeed, with the United States reducing the amount of supplies sent to South Vietnam, the black marketers needed to be more efficient and pervasive; added to the fact that ARVN pay and allowances were reduced because of the drop in aid. It is not surprising to note that ARVN morale in the region was suffering.

After considerable pressure from Abrams and the American advisors, reinforcements in the form of the new constituted 3rd ARVN Division, commanded by Brigadier General Vu Van Giai were added to I Corps. Giai had been a captain when Al Gray arrived in northern I Corps in 1964. By 1967, when Gray was at Gio Linh, Giai commanded the 2nd Regiment of the 1st ARVN Division, stationed just down the road from his old Marine friend. By 1969, when the 3rd Marine Division departed, Giai was a Colonel commanding the ARVN 1st Division Forward, which was responsible for protecting the DMZ area. His force included the 2nd Regiment and a single brigade of Vietnamese Marines. Al Gray knew General Giai very, very well, and knew him to be a fighter. And far from any possibility of Giai being disloyal, it was Giai and Gray who ran at least one communist defector turned agent who fed them information about the NVA's plans north of Dong Ha in 1967. But in late 1971, General Giai had an impossible task – defending northern I Corps while serving under the inept Corps Commander, Hoang Xuam Lam. Nonetheless, Giai threw himself into the task.

The 3rd ARVN Division was largely built on the rejects of other units. It suffered serious desertion rates and it found itself defending the most critical ground in South Vietnam, the old *McNamara Line* stretching from east of Gio Linh all the way to Khe Sanh. General Giai demonstrated what a fine officer he was by keeping his men active and demanding vigorous patrolling all along the front. He never permitted his troopers to become happily ensconced in defensive positions, and he moved battalions frequently as a means of offsetting a defensive mindset and ensuring his men learned the terrain they were covering. But it was far too much ground for a second-rate unit to protect, no matter how professionally led it was, or no matter how courageous its commander.

While *Lam Son 719* had proved to be a South Vietnamese failure in planning and execution, the North Vietnamese soon displayed their own capacity for military over-confidence, and in less than a year. Unfortunately, the ARVN would also lose.

1970 had seen several ARVN successes; 1971 was dominated by the failure of *Lam Son 719* to achieve its objectives and by the resulting loss in morale among the ARVN's northernmost tactical units. 1972 in I Corps would be lose-lose for the combatants.

WASHINGTON, 1972

By 1972 the combination of communist propaganda and left-wing claims of American atrocities in the war had reached their penultimate levels. Among the most brazen claims related to American bombing over North Vietnam. Never in the history of air warfare had a country gone to such great lengths, and placed its Airmen in such great peril, in order to avoid casualties to enemy civilians as did the United States throughout the Vietnam War. While his book deserves criticism in many areas, Stanley Karnow at least got the bombing of North Vietnam correct. When American anti-war activists and some reporters declared that the United States was "carpet bombing" North Vietnam, and killing thousands of innocent Vietnamese civilians, Karnow correctly – and to his eternal credit – ridiculed both the reports and the anti-war crowd. [73]

NOTES AND REFERENCES

1. A "mustang" is an officer with prior enlisted service.
2. Email from William Pedrick to author, January 2009. Al Gray connected with his Marines, and the lower the rank the more likely Gray was to take the time and make the effort to really learn about the Marine and his life. If he determined that the Marine in question had potential, shared a portion of Gray's value system, was interested in becoming the best professional possible, then Gray would do almost anything to provide assistance. And once any Marine entered Gray's orbit, he or she would never

be forgotten. Gray received outstanding loyalty from his Marines, loyalty that was repaid with interest many times over. Several years after then-First Lieutenant William Pedrick, USMC, 0302 had departed 1/2, he was assigned to the Security Platoon at the Pentagon; while there, he and his new wife attended one of the mega Marine Corps Birthday Balls held in the D.C. area. Then, Brigadier General Al Gray was conversing with what seemed to be an unending stream of generals and colonels, each of whom seemed determined to become the focal point of General Gray's evening. Lieutenant Pedrick finally caught General Gray's eye, and Gray quickly came to greet him. Pedrick asked if the General could take time to meet his wife, Diane, who was seated at a distant table. Gray not only excused himself from his far more illustrious conversationalists, but also took several minutes to tell Mrs. William Pedrick of her importance to the Marine Corps family. Gray's common courtesy and friendly repartee with all members of the Pedrick family reflected his lifelong sensitivity for and interest in Marine families. Bill Pedrick continued, "I have always greatly admired Rudyard Kipling's poem *If*. My father gave me a laminated, small copy of this poem when I graduated from high school (which I still carry, yellowed and all). There are a series of passages in there that go... 'if you can walk with crowds and keep your virtue...or walk with Kings - nor lose the common touch... if you can fill the unforgiving minute...with sixty seconds worth of distance run...Yours is the Earth and everything that is in it, and which is more, you'll be a man my son.' General Gray has always reminded me of those passages, or conversely, those passages remind me of him."

3. One McNamara social experiment and pet policy, called "Project 100,000," permitted many unqualified enlistees were to join the services. These men became a burden on small unit leaders who were required to try to train, and usually retrain, them to the standards of the other men. When that intellectual situation was combined with rampant drugs and alcohol abuse, particularly in rear areas, the situation was explosive. See, for example: http://www.vietnam.ttu.edu/resources/mcnamara/. Link checked, July 2012.

4. During World War II, African Americans who joined the Marine Corps were trained at Montford Point, North Carolina, at a facility separate from white Marines, and thus the reference.

5. Cosmas and Murray, *U.S. Marines in Vietnam: Vietnamization and Redployment, 1970–1971*, p. 352. Indeed, the entire Chapter 20 of the Cosmas and Murray volume, entitled "Morale and Discipline," gives a straightforward, unvarnished account of the issues the leadership faced in 1970. It is essential background for anyone interested in that aspect of the war.

6. Cosmas and Murray, *U.S. Marines in Vietnam: Vietnamization and Redployment, 1970–1971*, p. 352.

7. Cosmas and Murray, *U.S. Marines in Vietnam: Vietnamization and Redeployment, 1970–1971*, p. 369.

8. While in Korea, Gray won an acquittal for a Marine facing a special court-martial. When the word got out during that era, several Marines charged with various offenses sought his counsel. Fortunately, key operational assignments precluded such duty.

9. Led by the populist Jacob Coxey, "Coxey's Army" was a Washington D.C. protest march by unemployed American workers in 1894, during the worst economic depression in United States history until that time. It was the first significant popular protest march on Washington. Officially named the *Army of the Commonwealth in Christ*, the expression "Enough food to feed Coxey's Army" originates from this march. Few Marines know the origins of the phrase, but almost all have heard it used at one point or another during their active service as a Marine.

10. Author interview with Colonel Malcolm E. (Doc) Smith, Jr., USMC (Retired), September 16, 2010. In addition to consenting to an interview about his time with General Gray, Doc Smith was kind enough to share his autobiography with the author. *It's a Piece of Cake, The Making of a Marine: The Life of Doc Smith, a Memoir* is a very

detailed account of Colonel Smith's time as a Marine, and includes many letters he wrote and received while serving abroad or away from his family. Much more researched and well written than many self-published autobiographies, the reader gets an insightful view of this superb officer.

11. Rock Chandler was indeed an expert shooter who commanded the rifle range at Camp Lejeune when Major General Al Gray commanded the 2nd Marine Division.

12. Author telephone interview with Colonel James Magee, USMC (Retired), July 11, 2012.

13. In the early 1970s, Marine Corps end strength was tied to the Assistant Commandant of the Marine Corps (ACMC) keeping his fourth star. The Commandant of the Marine Corps (CMC) and ACMC were the only four star Marine generals.

14. As Commandant, General Gray well recalled his personnel and training difficulties in 1/2 and implemented a "School of Infantry" on each coast. The first director of the school was Lieutenant Colonel Vic Taylor, who as a young lieutenant in 2/4 had taken part in the Battle of Dai Do. The School of Infantry remains (as of 2014) one of the most prestigious and important schools in the Marine Corps.

15. Each officer is on a "lineal list" according to his date of rank. Then, each year the Marine Corps publishes the lineal numbers for the officers who will be "in the zone" for promotion. Officers who were in the zone the previous year, but not selected, are said to be "above the zone." Officers who will be considered for promotion but not in the zone, are said to be "below the zone." If an officer "below the zone" is selected, he or she is "deep selected." Only a very small percentage of selectees come from "below the zone." Being deep selected is a rarity and indicates the officer is exceptional. Gray was deep selected for colonel, the only time he was selected out of the zone.

16. General Gray jokes that until he was deep selected for colonel, his plan to retire as a lieutenant colonel was right on track. But for his unexpected appearance on the promotion list he and Jan could have lived happily while he managed 7-Elevens! Certainly in the author's opinion such expectation was unfounded based on his fine record. But, of course, General Gray never read his record book at HQMC!

17. For more about General Zinni's early professional life, see: Tom Clancy and Anthony C. Zinni, *Battle Ready*.

18. E.F. Hutton was one of the country's leading brokerage firms and during the 1970s and 1980s, it ran many television commercials that ended with this line: "When EF Hutton talks, people listen!"

19. From General Gray's private collection.

20. From General Gray's private collection.

21. A Marine Amphibious Unit consisted of a Battalion Landing Team (the ground element), an air element built around helicopters, and a logistics element. The MAU would be spread across three to five amphibious ships The BLT HQ, H&S Company and a rifle companies were normally assigned to an LPH (landing platform helicopter, a small aircraft carrier type of ship, which also carried the most the air wing personnel;) an LPD – landing ship dock – which typically carried a rifle company with the tanks, amphibian tractors, engineers and other equipment attached to the BLT.

22. Photo from: *Long Ago and Far Away*, LANFORSIXTHFLT 2-71, 1971-1972: HQ. 34 MAU Tiffany Pub. Co: Norfolk.

23. The captain of any ship, and any person holding the Navy or Marine rank of captain, is often called "skipper" by those serving with them. It is a term of respect.

24. As might have been expected, other units in the 2nd Division had sent less than their best Marines in the trickle draft; in fact, those sent were terrible. What was not anticipated was Gray's reaction. Replacements for future BLTs were much more closely screened at Camp Lejeune before being sent to the Med. The lesson learned was never assign poor performers to another unit!

25. From General Gray's private collection.

26. From General Gray's private collection.

27. From General Gray's private collection.

28. Captain Foley rose in the Navy to become Commander, U.S. Pacific Fleet. He and General Gray formed a great friendship that continues today, well after their

retirements from active service. They did have one personnel issue that arose between them, however. Admiral Foley's son was a midshipman in the Marquette University NROTC unit when he made a summer cruise to the Norfolk area. Then Brigadier General Gray was CG, 4th MEB at the time. Gray, among all the flag officers in the area, took time to meet with and speak to the midshipmen on evening. The younger Foley thereafter decided to become a Marine, and the source of a humorous friction between the two older officers.

29. *34th Marine Amphibious Unit Cruise Book*, 17 September 1971 – 15 March 1972.
30. ASIS is the acronym for the Amphibious Support & Intelligence System. SMLS is the acronym for the Seaborne Mobile Logistics System. Early computer-based military systems were highly problematic. Humans could still "remember" more than the amount of data the computer storage contained, yet entering the data required massive labor-intensive efforts. But through such experimentation systems requirements evolved, and soon the computers had the capacity to actually make things better. Now, of course, the military cannot operate without computers either operationally or logistically. But in the 1970s, it took much patience by everyone to get something useful from the systems.
31. Photo from: *Long Ago and Far Away*, LANFORSIXTHFLT 2-71, 1971-1972: HQ. 34 MAU Tiffany Pub. Co: Norfolk.
32. From General Gray's private collection.
33. From General Gray's private collection.
34. From General Gray's private collection.
35. From General Gray's private collection.
36. From General Gray's private collection.
37. From General Gray's private collection.
38. From General Gray's private collection.
39. Photo from: *Long Ago and Far Away*, LANFORSIXTHFLT 2-71, 1971-1972: HQ. 34 MAU Tiffany Pub. Co: Norfolk..
40. From General Gray's private collection.
41. Author telephone interview with Colonel James Magee, USMC (Retired), July 11, 2012.
42. As a Brigadier General, Al Gray commanded the 4th MEB during exercises in Europe. Upon the return of the unit to Norfolk, the officers held a "roast" that featured the expressions, attitudes and activities of General Gray. Both his mother and Jan Goss attended the roast, which Jan Gray described as one of the most fun evenings of her life – there were endless laughs. It is all memorialized in a "roast book" that General Gray still has.
43. A "5-paragraph order" was a shorthand way for Marines to give orders, especially in a tactical situation. Small unit leaders at every level from lance corporal to colonel were well schooled in recalling the acronym "SMEAC": Situation, Mission, Execution, Administration and Logistics, Communications. It provided a means to ensure the leader gave critical information before each mission. Gray added the constant reminder of Safety.
44. Author telephone interview with General John Sheehan, February 2011.
45. From General Gray's private collection.
46. From General Gray's private collection.
47. From General Gray's private collection.
48. The DRAGON is a medium-range, wire-guided anti-tank missile that is light enough for a single infantryman to carry and fire. Its lethal striking power means the DRAGON can destroy most armored vehicles and reinforced battlefield targets. Because of its light weight, the DRAGON is advantageous in airborne and airmobile operations. The DRAGON was first deployed in 1975. The basic TOW Weapon System, fielded in the early 1970s, is designed to attack and defeat tanks and other armored vehicles. It is primarily used in anti-tank warfare, and is a command to line of sight, wire-guided weapon. The system will operate in all weather conditions and on the "dirty" battlefield.
49. The Harrier Jump Jet, (known formally as the "Harrier" or informally as "the Jump Jet") is a British-designed military jet aircraft capable of Vertical/Short Takeoff and

Landing (V/STOL) through thrust vectoring. The Harrier family is the only successful design of this type from those emerging in the 1960s.

50. From General Gray's private collection.

51. As a Brigadier General, Gray was assigned by Commandant Wilson to conduct a study of Marine Reserve Forces. There was much clamoring against Gray's appointment until a reserve Brigadier General, the same man who had commanded the MAU exercise at Camp Lejeune, pointed out that Al Gray knew far more about the Reserves than he was given credit for knowing, thereby ending the complaints.

52. Many commanders would fill the days of their men by having the grass mowed much more often than was necessary. But perhaps the worst use of time was having Marines paint the rocks outside each unit's headquarters area, a practice that was anathema to Marines like Al Gray.

53. From General Gray's private collection.

54. Telephone interview with General Anthony Zinni, February 2011.

55. See Volume 1, Chapter 7 for the full story.

56. Email correspondence with Major Donald Whisnant, USMC (Ret.), 2013. Whisnant knew little of Gray's earlier story before reading Volume 1 of *Al Gray, Marine*. But when Whisnant learned of the longstanding relationship between General Jaskilka and Al Gray, he speculated that perhaps Gray was helping his study more than just a little behind the scenes, given Whisnant's work was so quickly approved.

57. There are many Al Gray stories: some true, many embellished, many completely untrue. In the author's opinion, if General Louis Wilson could embellish his "Al Gray Story," then all of us ought to be able to emulate that great Commandant.

58. Frocking means promoted without pay. Gray could wear the silver eagles of a colonel but until he was formally promoted he would be paid as a lieutenant colonel. Frocking was usually done in order to avoid situations where the "selected for promotion" officer might have to command another officer of the same rank who was senior in terms of their respective dates of rank.

59. Marine Corps Association, *Leatherneck Magazine*, December 1972, p. 43-47.

60. LVT-5 is Landing Vehicle Track- 5, the Marines' ubiquitous amphibious vehicle of the time.

61. From General Gray's private collection.

62. From General Gray's private collection.

63. From General Gray's private collection.

64. From General Gray's private collection.

65. From General Gray's private collection.

66. From General Gray's private collection.

67. Photo by Sgt Greg Smith.

68. In the early 1970s "Special Operations" did not have the connotation that term has had since the first Gulf War. Author telephone interview with General Zinni, January, 2011.

69. Author telephone interview with General Zinni.

70. Upon his promotion to Brigadier General, Gray received a hand-written note from Lieutenant General E.J. Miller, the President of the Promotion Board. The note read, "Congratulations Al, well deserved. You are beholden to no one."

71. From General Gray's private collection.

72. An excellent account of the operation from the South Vietnamese perspective can be found in Andrew Weist's *Vietnam's Forgotten Army: Heroism and Betrayal in the ARVN*. New York University Press, New York, 2008. Weist does a thorough job of both research and analysis and any American veteran who does not think the ARVN fought well or courageously against terrible odds needs to read his book.

73. Karnow, p. 653.

CHAPTER 5

ARMY WAR COLLEGE

EASTER OFFENSIVE

ARMY WAR COLLEGE

For the first time in many years, the Marine chewed his beloved Red Man in relative anonymity. The Army War College, at Carlisle, Pennsylvania, had a rich tradition in military education, surpassed only by the service academies at West Point and Annapolis. Colonel Alfred M. Gray had previously attended an Army school at Fort Sill, and he had dealt with soldiers during many artillery exercises and war games at Fort Bragg and during his years of service in Vietnam, but this was his first extended contact with so many senior officers from a sister service. The class consisted of 225-odd officers and government civilians, including eight Marines and a scattering of Air Force, Navy and international officers. Further, the class was divided into smaller groups of eleven officers, with each having at least one officer from the naval services and the Air Force as well as one civilian from various national and defense agencies; the Marine Colonel was the senior officer in his seminar group.

Colonel Al Gray had been a Marine for 23 years, and he had seldom taken off his pack. Even a previous assignment to the Marine Corps Command & Staff College had been anything but routine. At the War College, though, Gray was just another senior officer learning about high-level policy matters and other things the Army felt important. Gray loved reading and delighted in exposure to the best minds in the government and industry, and the War College provided lots of opportunity for such pastimes.

Al Gray was perhaps the only officer in attendance who did not have a bachelor's degree.[1] So while many of his contemporaries worked on master's degrees on the side, Gray opted to complete the military-oriented tasks assigned to his seminar group and to take graduate-level courses of interest, such as analytic decision making and economics. He always valued professional knowledge ahead of academic laurels, but the War College provided time to reflect and enrich his already prodigious reading list.

The capstone exercise for each class is the preparation and presentation of a research paper. Fittingly, as a just reward, while the rest of the class leisurely prepared to leave for their next assignments, Gray and his group, whose work was deemed the best, worked extra hard to prepare presentations for various officials from throughout the Department of Defense, other agencies and the National Security Seminar. Only when the presentations had been completed could Colonel Al Gray, anxious to get to the Far East and back to commanding Marines, leave Carlisle.

CAMP LEJEUNE, NORTH CAROLINA – AUGUST 1973

Colonel Al Gray had had a very successful tour at Camp Lejeune. Commanding an infantry battalion meant that after almost 20 years of commissioned service he had achieved his primary goal as an officer. The icing on the cake was subsequently commanding the 2nd Marine Regiment while still a lieutenant colonel, though he had been selected for promotion. When finally frocked as a bird colonel, he commanded a brigade in one of the most ambitious exercises ever held (to that point) at the Marine Corps Base, 29 Palms, California. His "reward" for defusing a serious racial situation in the Mediterranean was a lateral appointment as the G-3 (Operations, Plans, and Training Officer) of the 2nd Division, a billet seldom awarded to such a junior colonel – not that Gray wanted to leave the regiment. As G-3 he got to practice shuttle diplomacy to keep his Force Commanding General apprised of what was happening at Camp Lejeune, while also ensuring that his Commanding General knew what was expected of him. Gray also got to interact with the Base Commanding General, an officer he had met in Hawaii, when the General was a major and Gray was still a captain looking to organize and fund training for the Composite Radio Company.

For certain, Gray had accomplished much since his arrival in June 1970. He recalled those early days in 1st Battalion, 2nd Marines, when any number of decisions – if not backed by his seniors – could have jeopardized his professional prospects. He was always busy while in command. Occasionally, he would go to Washington over the weekend for discussions with friends in the intelligence community. While in the area, he would also stop to see Jan Goss. Jan was patient, as she knew she had to be. Convinced that her future would be with Al Gray or no one, she was prepared to play second fiddle to his Marine responsibilities. Emily Gray lived with her son Al during his time at Camp Lejeune, a situation that had become the norm since the death of Al Gray, Sr., in early 1968. And, of course, the Gray household included a couple of omnipresent black Labrador retrievers – including Lucky II, who was getting up there in years but still enjoyed a full life.

The note that Lieutenant General Louis B. Robertshaw had added to Al Gray's Officer Qualification Record at HQMC in 1969 ensured that Gray was not permitted to evade the war college as he had so successfully avoided high-level schools for so long before being required to attend the Marine Corps Command & Staff College. Thus, on a hot and humid August afternoon at Swamp Lagoon, Al Gray packed his mom and his labs into his Ford station wagon and set off for Carlisle, Pennsylvania and the Army War College. He could stop thinking about his pack for a while, though he surely would not forget his Red Man chew.

Figure 5.1
Colonel Browning, the senior Marine on staff at Carlisle, cuts the cake at the
Marine Corps Birthday celebration with some of his fellow Marines attend-
ing the War College. The Marines prided themselves on having the best of all
the formal parties, which were held monthly at the War College.[2]

Figure 5.2

Colonel Pat Howard, who would meet Al Gray again in Saigon in 1975, is on the far left as together they lead the Birthday Ball ceremony held in November at the Army War College.[3]

Figure 5.3
Colonel Corbin W. Ketchersid, US Army, Chaplain of the Army War College and Al Gray
were long time friends from the Point Pleasant Beach/Bay Head, New Jersey area.[4]

ARMY WAR COLLEGE, CARLISLE BARRACKS, PENNSYLVANIA, SEPTEMBER 1973 - MAY 1974

For the first time in a very long while, Al Gray was beyond the reach of seniors interested in having his unique skills address a variety of problems and situations. Having settled into the Army War College, he could be fairly sure that General Nickerson would not require his presence to conduct an intelligence-surveillance-reconnaissance assessment, or that Ray Davis would not interrupt his studies to accompany the General on a nationwide speaking tour, or that General Cushman would not pluck him out of a scheduled cold weather exercise to make an emergency trip to the Mediterranean to smooth over racial issues. No, for the first time in a very long time, Al Gray was quite content to be just another officer.

Each service was represented in Gray's war college class. The Army, of course, dominated the numbers, with officers from each of its many branches – infantry, artillery, ordnance, intelligence, military police, logistics, aviation, air defense, etc. Of a total of 225 students, the Navy and the Air Force each had a contingent of 15 to 20, and the Marines sent two colonels and six lieutenant colonels. And there also were a small number of foreign officers and Department of Defense civilians. It was an eclectic but highly capable group.

The Grays moved into a small but nice rental property about five blocks from the college. Coincidentally, there was a large adjacent field perfect for exercising the Labs. The other Marine colonel, an aviator named Pat Howard, resided not too far away, and Gray never forgot the many kindnesses that Mrs. Howard and her children showed toward Emily. Happily, he would be able to repay their thoughtfulness, with interest, less than a year after graduation.

While the War College involves work requiring mental clarity and full use of one's brainpower, it also has physical and social aspects. Gray, the former all-state athlete in multiple sports, loved the football, softball, basketball and other sports competitions. And he was still competitive enough that winning was not only fun, but also expected. On the social front, and on a revolving basis, each branch of the Army hosted a formal dinner dance each month. That gave Al Gray the opportunity to drive to Washington and pick up Jan, who still worked at the Defense Communications Planning Group, though the name had been changed to the even more vague Defense Special Projects Group.[5] They would spend the weekend at Carlisle with Emily and then Gray would take Jan home on Sunday evening. Of course, the social highlight of the year would be the Marine Corps Ball in November. The Marines loved putting on a real show for their service counterparts.

The first six months of the curriculum was directed toward strategic studies and high-level operations; those well-presented topics were combined with required courses in Army administration, which Al Gray found ineffectual. The second half was broken into individual and group studies with more required electives; each study required preparation of a research paper. Since the majority of students were also taking masters degree courses from Penn State or Shippensburg State, those students typically killed two birds with one paper – they worked independently while getting their thesis work and their war college research paper done concurrently. Others, who were not working toward advanced degrees, worked as part of a study team. Gray was asked to lead one such team, and he did.

In addition to the required graduate-level electives taken each semester, Gray decided to add other graduate-level courses on subjects about which he had not studied or read about, such as Economics and Analytic Techniques of Management, taught by a distinguished Princeton professor, Dr. Robert Kuenne. Dr. Kuenne was an World War II army veteran and had an abiding interest in defense matters. Gray found him fascinating and took two electives each semester from the economist. However, not all the students were as committed to things so esoteric. Another officer, surprisingly, decided that rather than spend his time reading and analyzing, he would rather build a television set from scratch, and that became his elective project.

During the early days of the first semester, one of the lecturers began with a joke – a common practice among those who taught at military schools. This joke, about the ability to tell time, was directed at Marines and questioned their intellectual capabilities. Al Gray sat patiently through the long presentation, but when it finished he made it abundantly clear to his contemporaries that the next time a lecturer used the Marines as a butt for a joke, he would walk out. Not just the Marines, Gray believed no service should be ridiculed in a public forum where inter-service cooperation and professionalism were the by-words for personal conduct.

A month or so passed before another guest speaker, a Marine lieutenant general from HQMC, addressed the class. As the general began his presentation, he delved into a time joke – about Marines. Gray, who was seated in the front of the classroom as was his habit, got up and left without hearing the rest of what the general had to say. Later, away from the lecture hall, the general and Gray met, the general asking if anything was wrong? Gray explained his behavior and his rationale for leaving, which the general accepted.

The incident quickly became lore in the far reaches of the Marine Corps, and added to Al Gray's growing legend. And it would not be the last time Gray confronted more senior officers about topics he felt were outside of bounds of acceptable speech.[6]

Gray also volunteered to attend monthly special presentations given by outside speakers. The Marine colonel would not only gladly attend, but he would happily serve as the dignitary's escort for a day or two. Through this program, Gray met, for example, Max Lerner, the controversial columnist and author of *America as a Civilization: Life and Thought in the United States Today*, which was published in 1957. Lerner had a real impact on Gray, who vividly remembered the writer's comments more than 35 years later. One of the themes of the class was the discussion of the "National Purpose," which was interwoven into many classes and seminars. In addition, each guest speaker was invariably asked to comment on his or her idea of the "National Purpose." Lerner said, "my notion of the national purpose is "to survive as a nation and per chance flourish economically.""[7] Gray used the time to learn new things, listen closely to the opinions of a variety of distinguished visitors and his contemporaries, and simply educate himself. In his opinion, there was a real joy in learning in such a setting, and he took advantage of it.

Al Gray found his experience and that of his soldier colleagues differed in two significant respects. First, because he had spent so much time in the field, he had much more relevant, meaningful troop leading expertise than his contemporaries. Even though he found them to be good officers, their lack of knowledge of allied or joint operations was also somewhat disquieting. In Gray's mind, the best prerequisite to higher command – which was the purpose of the War College, after all – was leading troops, participating in an array of operational situations, and working with allies.

The second difference was just as surprising to the Marine who worked closely with and respected the South Vietnamese. The Army students with whom Gray interacted, almost to a man it seemed, had no admiration for or the least amount of empathy for the South Vietnamese. Discussions with his contemporaries revealed that the situations in the II, III and IV Corps areas of Vietnam were much different than that Gray had experienced in the five northern provinces that constituted I Corps. Al Gray, the man who was interested in foreign languages and who studied foreign cultures, held a minority position vis-à-vis the South Vietnamese.

As opposed to the majority of his colleagues, Al Gray was a tireless supporter of the South Vietnamese. He found the attitudes of his Army counterparts troubling, even disconcerting. Given that Army combat units, especially when General Westmoreland was in command, had essentially no interaction with the ARVN, then, perhaps, the attitudes of American soldiers were at least understandable. It was a shocking and highly disappointing upshot of that General's policies. Al Gray, on the other hand, went to great measures to promote harmony and cooperation, and he had a genuine respect for South Vietnamese leaders such as Marshall Ky and Generals Truong and Giai. In the final analysis, it was a heck of a way to fight a war that many, perhaps even a majority, of the officers assigned to the theater of operations did not trust or even respect the host country as an American ally. When the attitude of those officers was combined with the fact that the US advisors had provided the host country with trucks, heavy equipment and even tactical advice more suitable to the Fulda Gap than to conditions in Southeast Asia, successful *Vietnamization* of the war was problematic at best. Surely, however, Gray and others thought that if the Americans had stressed counterinsurgency training and doctrine early on during the American buildup in the mid-1960s, the South Vietnamese could have been successful in the end.

While following the curriculum, Colonel Gray had a unique experience – one he could have only had at an Army base. He was made the senior member of a group of students who were assigned the task of improving the astonishingly poor financial status of the base officers' club. While he disliked the subject matter associated with club administration, Al Gray, Marine, was happy to contribute to increasing the profitability of the officers' club at Carlisle Barracks while there. Instead of becoming regular patrons, Gray's group made several beneficial suggestions that the Club's executives accepted and instituted.

Beyond working on officers' club finances, a far more meaningful exercise dominated the second semester. Because of Gray's background in long-range studies, a skill he perfected while leading the Intelligence, Surveillance, and Reconnaissance Division Section of the Development Center in 1969, he was asked to lead in a group study to envision a military strategy for the period 1990 – 1995. The then-Army Chief of Staff, General Creighton Abrams, and the Commandant of the War College, Major General Franklin Davis, had expressed a concern for conducting long-range systematic strategic thinking.[8] At the time, the U.S. Army had no systematic way to conduct long-range studies, and Generals Abrams and Franklin Davis were anxious to redress the situation. Exactly how or why Al Gray was asked to participate is not exactly known, but it can be speculated about at least with some confidence.

Creighton Abrams had been the Commanding General, Military Advisory Command, Vietnam, when Ray Davis was Commanding General of the 3rd Marine Division in I Corps. Abrams wrote that of the fifty or so generals who commanded divisions during the time he was in Vietnam, Ray Davis was the best. Although Ray Davis had retired as Assistant Commandant of Marine Corps before Gray was assigned to the War College, there were few officers who knew of Al Gray's capabilities more than General Davis; somehow that admiration reached Army Generals Abrams and Franklin Davis; alternatively, perhaps it was simply Gray's performance during the first semester that caused the senior Army leaders to take note.

The members of Gray's study group included an Army colonel with a military intelligence specialty, three Army lieutenant colonels (one each from infantry, ordnance, and armor) and an Air Force lieutenant colonel.[9] To ensure balance, each group always included at least one officer from the naval services. Gray was the senior man in his group, and he used his background in long-range studies to shape the research. In that regard, the group's research leader (part of the staff) was Lieutenant Colonel Lewis S. "Bob" Sorley, United States Army. Sorley, a third-generation West Pointer, has written several books related to the history of the Vietnam War and the Army in general. He became a lifelong friend of the future Marine Commandant.[10]

The overarching purpose of the study was look at a military strategy for the period 15 to 20 years in the future; in other words, a strategy for the 1990s. It was the kind of effort Gray had witnessed and been part of at Quantico before he attended Command & Staff College, when Commandant Chapman had re-instituted Mid-Range and Long-Range Planning in the Marine Corps. The study was ground breaking in many respects. The fact that it anticipated several international situations that came to pass showed the advantage of long-range study as a practical tool for the military. In viewing the future, the group suggested that technology would play an important role in the military strategy, though the group's

Al Gray and Bob Sorley got together again in December of 2014 at the Army War College when Gray was inducted as a distinguished graduate.[11]

vision of long-range supersonic aircraft circling the globe in a single day was a little too Rube Goldbergish even for 1974. But the study did yield positive results, and timely. For example, the group predicted there would be a breakup of Yugoslavia following the death of Marshall Tito, and the resulting chaos would be highly problematic for the western world. That analysis was spot on. It was another prediction, however, that was perhaps the most insightful.

In another area the group's study was perhaps even more perspicacious. In 1969, the President had announced the Nixon Doctrine. It had three principles: America confirmed all its treaty commitments; America would offer a nuclear shield to its allies or to countries vital to America's security; but most importantly, America would assist allies with economic and military assistance when called upon by its treaty obligations, *but America would look to the nation directly threatened to assume the primary responsibility for providing the manpower necessary for its own defense.*[12] In the world of unintended consequences, Nixon created a power vacuum in Africa, where few countries on the Dark Continent were well enough established to withstand threats using their own manpower. The Gray-group study anticipated that there would be Sino-Soviet adventurism in Africa and that America would have to respond. The prediction came true throughout the late 1970s and 1980s when both Soviet and Chinese disruptive activities in Africa became evident. Thus, the group recommended establishment of a "Vacuum Force" able to react and deploy quickly to offset such activity by the nation's enemies. The report published by Gray's group was entitled *A National Military Strategy for 1990–1995: The Problems of Power Projection.*

Five years after publication of the study, the United States Rapid Deployment Force (RDF) was activated in 1979 by President Jimmy Carter, with Gray's old friend, then-Lieutenant General P.X. Kelley, as its first commanding general. The RDF did exactly the role envisioned by Gray's "Vacuum Force." There is a well-known saying in military circles, something to the effect that a good idea has many fathers, while a bad one is a bastard. The Rapid Deployment Force (now, in 2014, known as Central Command) was one of the former. But there is documentation that Gray's study group presented the idea in 1974. [13]

It is small wonder that the Group's research study was selected by the War College to be the basis for the presentations to various Department of Defense and Department of the Army dignitaries. First and foremost it was an excellent example of how a well-researched and well-reasoned long-range study could be effective in shaping future policies and actions. Creighton Abrams and Franklin Davis must have been pleased. Second, despite the miss on the 1990 capabilities of highflying, supersonic aircraft, there were a sufficient number of specific insights and suggestions to give military planners much to think about when pondering the future. Third, the value of having a diverse group of officers who skills and knowledge complemented each other, and who followed a rigorous development model, could readily be seen. The War College was a perfect laboratory for incubating the Army's nascent long-range study program.

When Gray looked back and compared his recent experience as a student at the Marine Corps' Command & Staff College with the top-level Army War College, he thought the Marine instruction measured up very well. Historically there has been at least one significant difference between Army and Marine approaches to professional education. It boils down to mission of the school: the Army sends captains to an infantry course for captains with the goal of making them the best possible captains of infantry. The Marine Corps sends infantry captains to junior school, or Expeditionary Warfare School, to prepare them to be field grade officers – majors and lieutenant colonels. At the major and lieutenant colonel level, the Marines concentrate on giving officers the perspective they will need to operate effectively on high-level staffs, i.e., division or corps, or even joint.

Thus, the Marine Command & Staff College was extraordinary in Gray's opinion in giving its students a perspective far beyond their military experience to date. Graduates of C&SC were well prepared for any war college, and the strategic aspects of the instruction were every bit as good as that taught at Carlisle. An added plus, from Gray's viewpoint, was that there were no administrative subjects for the Marines during their Quantico curriculum; however, at Carlisle the Army colonels and lieutenant colonels (and all the students) were taught chapter and verse about the administrative aspects of running mess halls, officers' clubs and other tenant units of an Army base structure.

HEADQUARTERS MARINE CORPS, APRIL 1974

During the course of the academic year, Al Gray was mystified by the frequency and duration of the discussions between the Army students and their monitors – the officers in charge of future assignments. Gray had no such discussions, nor had he ever witnessed the degree of interaction his contemporaries had with those responsible for their future assignments. However, when fellow Colonel Pat Howard was summoned to Washington to be briefed on his impending assignment to Saigon, Gray accepted an invitation to accompany his classmate for the short drive down to Northern Virginia and HQMC. Howard was to be the aviation advisor to the South Vietnamese and his billet required a special consultation. The aviation colonels' monitor, whom Howard was to see, was located in close proximity to the monitor for ground colonels like Al Gray. The ground monitor, himself a Marine colonel, was happy to see Al Gray.

Much to Al Gray's surprise, his monitor suggested that Gray might be able to return to the Fleet Marine Force in the Western Pacific a year early. Normally, Gray's rotation tour date – the date at which he could expect to be sent overseas – would not come up until 1976 or so. Further, the monitor explained that by going overseas a year early, upon his return to the United States Gray could expect to receive just about any assignment he desired. The monitor went on to suggest that Gray might be able to get a three-year posting to the Defense Security Group in Washington. It would be an assignment that would permit him to live comfortably, take care of his mother and be one from which he could easily retire. All that sounded very promising to Al Gray. Getting another Fleet Marine Force job as a colonel was way beyond his expectation, and he could not wish for more. He readily agreed to the plan.

Since Howard was still tied up in discussions, Gray, as he habitually did, wandered the halls and on the second deck of the building he knew so well. By chance he ran into Lieutenant General Herbert L. Beckington, his former Assistant Division Commander at Camp Lejeune. Gray thought very highly of Beckington and considered him an officer whose counsel he respected. Beckington had been brought to HQMC by General Cushman and quickly rose to three stars. He was assigned as the Deputy Chief of Staff for Plans and Operations. The General was happy to see Gray and invited the Colonel into his office to chat.

Without much ado, Beckington launched into his plan to bring Gray to HQMC following Gray's graduation from the War College. He discussed how an assignment to the Plans or perhaps the Operations branch would be very career enhancing. Gray needed such an assignment, the General thought, to prepare him for higher rank. Al Gray listened patiently, flattered by the General's kind remarks about his future. But in Gray's mind, going to the sound of thunder, serving in the Fleet Marine Force, trumped any possible HQMC billet. He explained the plan outlined by the monitor, and indicated his desire to execute it. General Beckington was stunned, even angry, that Gray would forego a career-enhancing staff position that Beckington considered essential to the Colonel's future promotion opportunities.

But Gray was hardly thinking about promotion; he well knew that the South Vietnamese military situation was deteriorating quickly. And on a personal level, Gray also realized that Beckington not only respected him, but also he would accept Gray's decision. Not that it mattered, as it turned out. Within a year, General Louis Wilson would be sworn in as the new Commandant and General Beckington would retire.

BACK TO THE FLEET MARINE FORCE, JUNE 1974

Gray was pleased that he would be returning to the operating force, though he had no way of forecasting the numerous challenges that awaited him. He would find it ironic that the first time the Nixon Doctrine would be violated – less than six years after it had been enunciated – would be when the American government would refuse to apply its principles to assist its former ally in Saigon. Gray had been part of the group that pointed out how implementation of the Nixon Doctrine would cause issues in Africa; soon he would find himself in Southeast Asia dealing with the consequences of failing to apply it.

Before departing for Okinawa, Al Gray took his mother to Florida. He maintained the condo that he and his father had purchased years earlier, and he knew that some runs on the beach would be beneficial. General Wilson, still in command at Fleet Marine Force, Pacific (FMFPAC), was well known for having colonels stop through Hawaii on their way to Okinawa. General Wilson wanted to see for himself that his senior officers met his personal appearance standards, and Al Gray wanted to be in the best of shape when he met his old mentor. Yes, some beach runs in Florida would do him well.

Figure 5.4
Gray saying goodbye to Lucky 2 and Pepper at Camp Lejeune in Jacksonville, NC. [14]

How well did Al Gray do at the Army War College? In an exceptional class, one that had more future general officers than any other until that time, Gray's performance was not bad for a plain spoken, field Marine more comfortable with his men than entertaining dignitaries or making conversation at cocktail parties. He also proved to be highly effective while attending one of the nation's premier war colleges. One only need read these two sentences from his academic review: "He was an aggressive unadulterated achiever who produced outstanding results in all student course performances... This is a superior officer who should be rapidly promoted to general officer."

EASTER OFFENSIVE

SAIGON, EARLY 1972

Unknown to most American students of the war, by early 1972 South Vietnam was essentially at peace. One could drive throughout the country without a military escort. A no more objective critic of the war than John Paul Vann, the former U.S. Army officer turned senior political advisor, announced that 95% of the South Vietnamese preferred their government to that of the communists.[15] Van's comments were shown to be accurate by the fact that indigenous Viet Cong guerrillas played essentially no part in the coming NVA offensive – they had been neutralized.

Leading the charge toward progress in the countryside was the cooperation among the U.S. Ambassador, Ellsworth Bunker, the Commanding General of MAC(V), Creighton Abrams, and the government of President Thieu. However, when evaluating the war, consider this: the period after which Abrams took command (mid-1969) through early 1972 was the only time since the Americans had entered the war that the three major factors – the American administration through the Ambassador, the U.S. military through General Abrams, and the South Vietnamese and its political leaders and military – were aligned and complementary. The results were extraordinary. Of course, there were still some of the same old problems, but they were significantly reduced.

The Nixon White House still wanted to influence ground operations and control air power. President Nguyen Van Thieu still made all the personnel decisions related to corps commanders and district chiefs. The great majority of American advisors still did not speak Vietnamese beyond a few rudimentary words (despite America having been deeply involved for nearly eight long years), and the South Vietnamese Air Force (VNAF) was still in its infancy. Moreover, the VNAF, of all the Republic of Vietnam's services, had serious, even daunting, limitations.

America ensured that South Vietnam had virtually no way to threaten North Vietnam. The only jet aircraft in the VNAF was the F-5, a converted trainer. It had practically no capability for use as a fighter or in any ground support (bomber) role. It might have been fun to fly, but was useful for little else. The planes the VNAF did have for close air support, the A-1 and A-37, were both extremely vulnerable to shoulder-fired anti-aircraft missiles that the NVA increasingly used in large number, the SA-7. The VNAF did have C-130 cargo planes and used them very effectively, but they were transport aircraft and had no offensive capability. VNAF helicopters were highly effective and bravely flown, but they too were vulnerable to fire and after 1972 spare parts became increasingly problematic. Even if spare parts had been available, the VNAF capacity to repair and maintain its fleet never approached full effectiveness. It is fair to say that even as late as 1974 and 1975, the VNAF remained in its infancy. That anyone extolling the virtues of *Vietnamization* expected the VNAF to be as effective as American air power had been was ludicrous in the extreme.

The lack of the capabilities within the VNAF and the diminution of artillery support that accompanied the American withdrawal in 1971 and 1972 meant that ARVN forces no longer had the fire support they had grown accustomed to in previous years. Despite these shortcomings, the future of the Republic of Vietnam looked safe so long as Americans maintained their commitment to the Nixon Doctrine. And so long as American spare parts and, particularly, American air power could be used. After all, that is what the Paris Peace Accords, signed by Henry Kissinger, pledged.

President Thieu, to his country's peril, bet that the Americans would keep their promise.

SOUTH OF THE DEMILITARIZED ZONE, 30 MARCH 1972

General Vu Van Giai was a personally courageous, particularly able leader who led his men from the front. He had been assigned command of the 3rd ARVN Division following the ARVN's near rout during the campaign named *Lam Son 719* in 1971. One consequence from *Lam Son 719* was the appreciation in Saigon that the 1st ARVN Division, the country's finest, was not able to control I Corps without significant reinforcement. General Creighton Abrams had been pushing President Thieu and the Chief of the RVN General Staff, General Cao Van Vien to make changes in the area where Al Gray and the Marines had operated in the late 1960s. Slowly, Thieu made the necessary alterations, though his dithering foreshadowed the inevitable disintegration of his forces in the northernmost sector of the country.

The 3rd Division had been hastily assembled from groups of rejects and ne'er-do-wells given up by other ARVN commanders. Giai, however, did not take time to despair his fate; rather, he went to work trying to ensure that his beleaguered force was as well trained and as combat ready as he could make it. Strung out south of the DMZ, and occupying many old Marine positions such as Con Tien and Camp Carroll, Giai got little support from his Corps Commander. Lieutenant General Hoang Xuan Lam was a poor choice to command South Vietnam's most exposed region, and he had displayed his incompetence during *Lam Son 719* in 1971. Despite that incompetence, Thieu had remained loyal to his old friend, and then multiplied his error of not reinforcing I Corps with a top-notch division to augment General Truong's 1st ARVN.

The North Vietnamese had forcefully defended its Laotian supply lines along the Ho Chi Minh Trail and had thoroughly whipped that ARVN attack during *Lam Son 719*. When those results, combined with the Americans' self-imposed restrictions in bombing North Vietnam, restraint shown by Nixon as an incentive to the communists to negotiate, the NVA was well poised to attack southward and gain the final victory. There was never a pause in North Vietnam's intent to overwhelm the South, regardless of what their negotiating position had been. With Soviet and Chinese supplies and equipment pouring into Haiphong and other communist ports, the NVA focused on building up their air defense units that would accompany ground forces attacking toward Hué, the target of the offensive.

President Thieu had lots of intelligence in advance of the communist buildup. The South Vietnamese, however, thought the NVA would attack through the Central Highlands, their old invasion routes. Thieu and others discounted the idea that the NVA might brazenly attack straight through the Demilitarized Zone, but that is exactly what the NVA did.

On Easter, 1972, the communists aggressively and in force attacked south in a multi-division assault led by armor protected by mobile air defenses. The attack was preceded by three days of artillery preparation that put the command and control capabilities of the ARVN under great strain; indeed, it overwhelmed the ARVN ability to communicate and learn what was happening across the front.

The NVA attack toward Dong Ha, straight down National Highway 1 past Al Gray's former stomping grounds at Gio Linh, would have been even more successful but for the heroics of the 3rd Vietnamese Marine Battalion (VNMC) and its American advisor, Captain John W. Ripley, United States Marine Corps. Also sent north to defend Dong Ha at all costs was the 20th ARVN Tank Battalion and its advisor, Major James E. Smock, United States Army.

Smock gave Ripley a ride toward the major highway bridge north of Dong Ha, a bridge vital to the NVA advance. They arrived at the bridge simultaneously with the appearance of the lead NVA tank. Ripley watched as a VNMC sergeant stood alone in the middle of the span with a light anti-tank weapon. The sergeant's first shot went high, but the second found its mark at the juncture of the turret and the body of the tank, which prevented the tank commander from moving the turret. At this critical juncture, when moving forward was still an option, the NVA commander decided to back away. The sergeant had proven to the others that the NVA armor could be stopped.

By then the two Americans saw that the South Vietnamese preparations to blow the bridge would not be successful. Ripley, well trained in explosives, realized that unless the dynamite was placed under the girders, the bridge would remain standing. What followed was extraordinary. Braving direct fire from distances as close as 50 yards, Ripley spent three hours swinging hand over hand beneath the bridge, carrying explosives to where they were needed. While Ripley performed his heroics, the Vietnamese Marines poured fire into the NVA across the river. Finally, Ripley's efforts were triumphant and the span fell into the river, essentially halting the NVA advance until a detour to the west could be found. It was a delay vital for the South Vietnamese.[16]

No pause in the attack could save the 3rd ARVN Division, however. The division was essentially wrecked the first few days of the offensive.[17] Despite the heroics of the VNMC unit at Dong Ha, the NVA's two divisions overcame their adversaries and rushed south, seizing the key city at Quang Tri. General Giai and his American advisors barely escaped capture there before being flown to Da Nang. Regrettably, the South Vietnamese needed a scapegoat for losing Quang Tri, and his name was Giai. The popular, courageous and very capable ARVN officer was tried for malfeasance and sent to prison. The ARVN lost a good man and brave leader, while the actual party responsible, General Lam remained in command of I Corps.[18]

Despite the presence of air defense in depth, American air power finally stopped the advance, assisted of course by epic defensive brawling by the ARVN. General Truong and his force fought extremely well against great odds. The communists were contained short of their objective, though they had seized Quang Tri, and clung desperately to that important provincial capital.

Truong, however, having regained the initiative after air power had severely damaged the NVA ground forces, decided to use the VNMC brigade to attempt to recapture Quang Tri. The VNMC lost about 150 men per day during this counter-offensive, again disputing any notion that the South Vietnamese would not fight for their country.[19]

Nixon was outraged by the barefaced communist aggression that violated the DMZ. He felt that the North Vietnamese showed great disrespect for his moderation in the use of air power; that moderation reflected Nixon's willingness to negotiate rationally. However, with communist intentions clearly demonstrated, Nixon unleashed his formidable air forces. Furthermore, Nixon opened targets heretofore off limits to American pilots. The North Vietnamese had never seen air power like they would for the remainder of 1972.

Operation Linebacker, May through October 1972, came close to bombing North Vietnam back to the Stone Age, as General LeMay had threatened nearly a decade earlier only to be constrained by President Johnson. Almost every significant military target was hit, and all the harbors were mined. The advent of precision-guided munitions kept collateral damage and civilian casualties to a minimum; and with the professional military planners in charge of target selection, in relatively short order the North Vietnamese defenses were crushed. With no ships willing to enter dangerous harbors, and with no trains moving south from China, the North Vietnamese quickly learned that America had far more capabilities than they had previous seen. NVA logistics were thrown into utter turmoil, and public morale sagged.

When Nixon tried to press his advantage by starting another bombing operation, *Linebacker II*, over Christmas a near U.S. disaster ensued. Communist surface-to-air missiles knocked down 15 B-52s, six in one day. Fortunately, the communists ran out of missiles long before the United States lost sufficient bombers to call off the attacks. Indeed, the combination of new tactics by the attackers and North Vietnam's inability to resupply itself with missiles left the American crews largely free over the skies of Hanoi, Haiphong and anywhere else the pilots cared to fly.

Though the NVA still held significant portions of northern South Vietnam, including Quang Tri and Dong Ha, the communists were again highly motivated to parley. *Linebacker II* had demonstrated that Nixon was indeed willing to hang tough in the negotiations; the communists decided that concluding a peace treaty was a far easier way to finally gain their objective. Perhaps the U.S. could have achieved the same treaty results without losing so much during Linebacker II; indeed, the price paid for an incremental advantage was probably not worth the cost in American lives.

WASHINGTON, 1972 AND EARLY 1973

A significant event that dramatically affected the outcome of the Vietnam War happened thousands of miles from Southeast Asia. In the run-up to the elections of 1972, which would result in a crushing victory for Richard Nixon over the Democrat candidate, Senator George S. McGovern of South Dakota, the Republicans had authorized a criminal breaking and entry into McGovern's campaign headquarters. It was not only a stupid error in judgment, it was also completely unnecessary – there was never the slightest doubt that Nixon would prevail in the election. "Tricky Dick" was Nixon's moniker among the press and his enemies, and the break-in would turn the epithet into a mockery, engulfing the Presidency.

Before Watergate became the national scandal, however, negotiations to end the war were concluded in early 1973. Kissinger and the North Vietnamese lead delegate, Le Duc Tho, reached a breakthrough following the conclusion of *Linebacker II*, the B-52 strikes against the communists in late 1972. Prior to that, Kissinger had given his adversary many incentives to conclude a treaty. As early as 1970, the Americans had backed away from demanding the NVA withdraw from the areas around South Vietnam while the Americans drew down their combat forces. The stumbling block for the North Vietnamese, however, was the American requirement that President Thieu remain in office. Now, in early 1973, with NVA units still occupying significant areas of northern South Vietnam, and with communist sanctuaries intact in Cambodia and Laos, Kissinger dropped demands that the NVA withdraw as a precondition to a settlement.

Perhaps no other factor so clearly showed the American lack of will and Kissinger's utter contempt for his South Vietnamese allies and the Nixon Doctrine. By permitting the NVA to remain in place, combined with the Congressional action to essentially stop providing military aid to Thieu's government, the Paris Peace talks amounted to a death sentence for the Republic of Vietnam. Thieu tried to forestall the settlement, but Nixon and Kissinger held all the cards and crushed any opposition to the negotiation from the South Vietnamese. It would have been nice in retrospect, at least for those who fought in the war, if they could at least blame the fact that Nixon and Kissinger caved in to Le Duc Tho's demands on the exigencies associated with Watergate; however, the Paris Peace Accords pre-date the public's knowledge of the burglary authorized by "Tricky Dick". No, Nixon, Kissinger and the Congress simply walked away from the South Vietnamese; Watergate had nothing to do with it. Abandoning an ally during wartime had never before happened in American history; and no one should be proud to reflect on it happening in late January 1973.

The communists were in no condition to renew their offensive inside South Vietnam. Indeed, by the time the Peace Accords were wrapped up, late January and early February 1973, North Vietnam's economy was in a shambles and no supplies were arriving from China or the Soviet Union. Further, there was some indication that the Nixon Administration believed neither communist super-power would be sending either the volume or the breadth of military supplies to North Vietnam, though that turned out to be an empty wish rather than any result of "secret negotiations."

President Thieu was most dejected over the outcome of the Peace Accords, but with Nixon's assurance that America would not permit the communists to break the treaty, Thieu had few cards to play, and none higher than a deuce.

NOTES AND REFERENCES

1. Lieutenant General Alfred Mason Gray applied for and was granted his Bachelor's Degree from the State University of New York (later renamed the University of the State of New York) in 1986, just months before becoming the 29th Commandant of the Marine Corps. He had completed the academic requirements for his degree over a decade before, but, as many other things that General Gray thought were not germane to his professional performance, taking the time to complete them were unimportant and not worth his time. During this period, General Gray was serving as Commanding General, Fleet Marine Forces, Atlantic. How ironic that the man who cajoled Larry Bangs, Ed Kitt, and the other members of the 1st Special Communications Platoon in Japan in the mid-1950s to work toward their college degrees was probably the last to actually receive his.
2. From General Gray's private collection.
3. From General Gray's private collection.
4. From General Gray's private collection.
5. Dickson, p. 123.
6. Author videotape interview with Major General J. M. Myatt, USMC (Ret.) While still a colonel, Myatt heard a general telling jokes about Marines and confronted the senior officer with his displeasure. He credited his knowledge of Al Gray's actions at the War College as the basis for his own deed: if Al Gray could take on a Marine general about inappropriate speech, Myatt felt he must confront a general from another service on the same basis.
7. Author videotape interview with General Gray dated 18 August 2009.
8. The study is available at Carlisle. Army War College Group Research Project, AD785489, *A National Military Strategy for 1990–1995: The Problems of Power Projection*, Multiple authors, 6 June 1974.
9. The group included: Lieutenant Colonel Andrew P. Chambers (Infantry); Lieutenant Colonel Michael F. Connolly, United States Air Force; Colonel Alfred M. Gray, Jr., United States Marine Corps; Colonel John L. Heiss, III (Military Intelligence); Lieutenant Colonel William M. Stokes, III (Armor); Lieutenant Colonel Howard C. Whittaker (Ordnance). Lieutenant Colonel Lewis S. Sorley, III (Armor) was Research Leader.
10. While doing research on this book in February 2011, General Gray received a note from Lewis Sorley indicating that Sorley was in the process of finishing a monograph entitled *Westmoreland, the General Who Lost Vietnam*. The book provides new information about the man whose name is synonymous with the war.
11. From General Gray's private collection.
12. The Nixon Doctrine was articulated by the new President in an address to the nation about the war in Vietnam. It had three tenets: First, the United States will keep all of its treaty commitments. Second, we shall provide a shield if a nuclear power threatens the freedom of a nation allied with us or of a nation whose survival we consider vital to our security. Third, in cases involving other types of aggression, we shall furnish military and economic assistance when requested in accordance with our treaty commitments. But we shall look to the nation directly threatened to assume the primary responsibility of providing the manpower for its defense. If there ever were circumstances under which to apply the doctrine, South Vietnam in early 1975 were they. So much for

Presidential pronouncements; even Nixon's successor would not follow through. See Karnow, p. 594-600 and Langguth, p. 565-7, 643.

13. Group Research Project, AD785489, p. 44.
14. From General Gray's private collection.
15. Sorley, p. 348-9.
16. There are many accounts of John Ripley's heroic actions at the bridge. Perhaps the most detailed is John Grider Miller's *Bridge at Dong Ha*.
17. For a detailed, first-hand account of the loss of the 3rd ARVN Division, see Weist.
18. For an in-depth look at the Easter offensive from the ARVN perspective, see Weist, Chapter 9. There are many other books about the communist offensive in 1972. See for example, Gerald Turley, *The Eastern Offensive*. Then Lieutenant Colonel Turley was the senior Marine advisor to the VNMC.
19. Weist, p. 269-70.

CHAPTER 6

BACK TO THE FLEET MARINE FORCE
THE DEATH OF THE REPUBLIC OF VIETNAM

BACK TO THE FLEET MARINE FORCE

The graduates were all present, caps and gowns in place, teachers and staff seated in the rear. "Houghton" High School, nicknamed for the Commanding General of the 3rd Marine Division, was ready to present diplomas to its first class. And there is little doubt that these graduates were among the most emotional ever to earn their diplomas.

Camp Hansen, Okinawa, was the scene of tremendous racial strife in the mid-1970s. Blacks, whites, Hispanics, Samoans and other ethnic groups rarely mixed other than when in formation at various Marine Corps happenings. Liberty in the local Okinawan villages was divided along strict racial lines; blacks frequented bars in one section of town, whites in another, and neither entered the others' spaces without the probability of a serious incident. Fights, even stabbings, were more than occasional occurrences. The Japanese officials on Okinawa did not permit the use of Marine Shore Patrols or military police type of activity of discipline or security purposes. Any leaders who ventured out could not move without peril throughout the village. Officers and Staff Non-Commissioned Officers, those who remained in the quarters aboard the base rather than spending their nights in town, slept with entrenching tools nearby. Drugs, everything from marijuana to heroin, were readily available. Unit and personnel discipline was inconsistently applied, problematic and oft times simply missing.

The Commanding General, Fleet Marine Forces, Pacific was worried. He knew the relationship between his Marines with both the government officials in Japan and the people in Okinawa would continue to deteriorate at an alarming rate. Further, the American political leadership in certain quarters was beginning to wonder if the Marine Corps could be counted upon to successfully encounter its nation's future enemies. A new commander for the legendary 4th Marine Regiment stopped in Hawaii to receive his orders from the Commanding General. "Al, I know you can command that regiment. It's the problems of the base and these racial incidents that you have got to solve!" After their hour-long meeting, there was no doubt as to Lieutenant General Louis H. Wilson's priorities for Colonel Alfred M. Gray.

Given the high number of non-graduates among his Marines and Sailors, Gray knew what had to be done. Organizing his officers throughout Camp Hansen (as Commanding Officer of the camp, all tenant units reported to him), Gray soon had a new high school in the works. American military wives with teaching credentials were hired. Assistance from the Department of Defense school system on the island was sought and readily provided. Resources were mobilized and a plan executed. Foremost among the decisions that Gray

made was that attendance in school was considered more important than any other duties
a Marine might have. High School became the driving priority for those who had no
diploma; nothing was more important.

The transformation of those who attended was extraordinary. Grizzled gunnery
sergeants were seen accepting their high school diplomas with tears of joy streaming down
their face. Young Marines, whose previous personal achievement highlight was complet-
ing boot camp, accepted the congratulations of their Division Commanding General with
glee. Everyone benefited, most especially the Marine Corps. The school was a testament to
Al Gray's understanding that educational achievement was a critical element in what had
to be done to finally make many of his men into Marines.

III MARINE AMPHIBIOUS FORCE HEADQUARTERS, OKINAWA, SPRING 1974

Long before Al Gray arrived on Okinawa, the discussions about his future had
begun. The enthusiastic Colonel's reputation as a professional, can-do, willing-to-
take-any-assignment officer preceded him. The generals, all of whom sought his
services, anticipated his summer arrival after his name had shown up on the colonel's slate.

Major General Fred Haynes had returned from Korea and commanded the 3rd
Marine Division. Haynes, who most recently had seen Gray in action in the 2nd
Marines at Camp Lejeune, had a longstanding relationship with the younger officer that went back many years through numerous assignments. He wanted Gray to
command one of his regiments.

Major General Herman Poggemeyer, the Commanding General of III Marine
Amphibious Force (III MAF), and Haynes's boss, wanted Al Gray to head up one
of the Marine Amphibious Units (MAU) that would be going afloat to possibly
encounter serious, deteriorating environments in Vietnam or Cambodia. General
Poggemeyer, an artilleryman, first met Al Gray during his first tour in Korea when
Poggemeyer was the Executive Officer of the battalion in which Gray served. As
the senior officer on Okinawa, Poggemeyer, had the inside track. At that point,
however, Lieutenant General Louis Wilson, the Commanding General, Fleet
Marine Forces, Pacific applied the trump card. General Wilson had been in the
Pacific long enough to realize that the Marine Corps, and indeed all the services,
had overarching problems that needed solving, and they had nothing to do with
running regiments or potentially complex operations in Southeast Asia. General
Wilson would personally assign Al Gray to precisely the duties the Commanding
General knew were by far the most important.

Figure 6. 1 and 6.2
Colonel Gary Wilder, USMC, passes
the Fourth Marines Regimental
Colors to Al Gray at Camp Hansen,
Okinawa. Colonel Wilder was a
battle-tested commander who served
with distinction throughout his career.
In addition to being one of the initial
advisors to the fledgling Vietnamese
Marine Corps in 1958, he also served
in a special assignment in Laos and
commanded a battalion during the
Khe Sahn hill battles of 1968.[1]

Figure 6.3
The generals on Okinawa were not unanimous in exactly where Colonel Gray should
be assigned. Of course, it was Lieutenant General Louis Wilson, Commanding
General, Fleet Marine Forces, Pacific, who made the final decision. Here,
Colonel Gray is shown with Major Generals Herman Poggemeyer and Kenny
Houghton. Then-Lieutenant Gray had served with then-Major Poggemeyer in
Korea, and he often served with Kenny Houghton earlier in his career.[2]

KIN VILLE, TOWN OUTSIDE MARINE CORPS BASE, CAMP HANSEN, OKINAWA, JUNE 1974

Al Gray would never approve of anyone calling him predictable. Indeed, operationally speaking, being predictable is usually highly problematic, something sure
to draw Al Gray's ire. However, if the issue is determining the lay of the land and
finding the circumstances driving situations, then one can expect with 100% accuracy that Al Gray will conduct a personal reconnaissance and predicate his course
of action of what he sees with his own eyes and hears with his own ears. Not that
he did not value the opinions and evaluations of others, but Al Gray whenever
possible verified things personally. And so it was following his arrival on Okinawa.
His meeting with General Wilson in Hawaii left his priorities crystal clear. But
before meeting Marines, Al Gray confirmed the situation on the island for himself.

Even before the Marines had withdrawn from Vietnam, racial tensions, drug and alcohol abuse and other forms of disciplinary issues had plagued units assigned to Japan's southernmost island. The need for strong, aggressive leadership, just the kind that Al Gray had demonstrated at Camp Lejeune in the 2nd Marines, could not be over-emphasized. During their meeting in Hawaii, as Gray traveled to the Far East, General Wilson had stressed, re-stressed, and then stressed again that Al Gray's primary duty on Okinawa was to end the racial tensions and the alcohol and drug issues that threatened both the relationship with their Japanese hosts and the ability of the Marine Corps to effectively respond to future contingencies. The General would permit his former recruit to also run a regiment while commanding the Marines' largest camp, but ending the many disciplinary problems was to be the focus of main effort!

Prior to Al Gray's arrival things were often out of control, even on the Marine bases. One indication of the poor state of affairs in Okinawa was that former Marines – even those who had been given Dishonorable Discharges were still permitted to enter Camp Hansen. Once on the base, these criminals, who had been kicked out the service, could enter the barracks and openly deal drugs. They also were a prime source of discontent and racial strife. And no one seemed to do anything about their access or their presence.[3]

The first thing Al Gray did after arriving on the island was to make his way to the large town complex adjacent to Camp Hansen, called Kin Ville. When Gray left the camp to go into town, the military police manning the gate tried to dissuade him from going into town alone. Then, when he proceeded despite the warning, he chose to go specifically where the MPs had told him not to go – into the area where the black Marines congregated. Over the course of a couple of days, Gray quickly regained his mastery of spoken Japanese, and he used his language skills to best advantage. He repeatedly spoke to bar owners, shopkeepers, and most importantly, the local Japanese police force. He learned much. The situation was described as a "powder keg ready to blow at any second!"[4] General Wilson's grave concerns were well founded; the local situation had been festering for years and the need for corrective action paramount.

Among the most serious of the conditions Gray noted was the segregation present in the bars. Customer preference turned the local establishments into black bars, white bars, Samoan bars and Hispanic bars. There were no Marine or Sailor bars where everyone freely mixed. Gray also found that while there were some older Marines out in town, they were in civvies. These were the officers and Staff NCOs, Gray knew.

By making the bar owners understand that he wanted his Marines treated fairly and respectfully, and in return he would stop the fighting, the drunkenness, and the damages caused by such behavior, Gray earned the locals' commitment to cooperate. That he also spoke their language added significantly to his credibility. Just like he had done years before at Sakata, Al Gray understood that Americans living and training in a foreign land had to do so with the respect of the local community; he also realized that respect must be earned, that it was not simply granted. And before earning the respect of the Okinawans, he must first show respect to them. That part was easy for the personable, considerate, Japanese-speaking Colonel of Marines.

On the base, Gray noted that the only formations he observed were riot-control drills. The Marines were anticipating riots instead of taking measures to prevent them. Al Gray would change that, and soon after the change of command.

One of the battalions of the 4th Marines, his new command, would deploy within a week to the Philippines, to conduct a series of exercises there. Gray was determined to observe those exercises as a means of evaluating the readiness of his unit. However, if he did that, he would only have a few days on Okinawa to start the process of re-establishing good order and discipline among the units remaining on the island.

Gray's 4th Marines' headquarters was at Camp Hansen, where Gray was also the Camp Commander. Consequently, the artillery regiment and large independent battalions such as the Division Supply Battalion, the Engineer Battalion and the Communications Battalion all reported, as far as General Houghton was concerned, to Al Gray. Thus, instead of commanding a regiment of approximately 4,000 Marines and Sailors, Gray commanded a base filled with about 8,500 officers and men that included eight separate battalions in addition to his 4th Marine Regiment. His problem was how to get his new directives out quickly, so that he could go to the "P.I."[5]

As a result of discussions with the local staff, Gray learned that the base theater held roughly 1,000 people. With that information, a plan came together. Gray would schedule nine separate briefings in one day, each separated by a ten-minute break. First up would be the officers and Staff NCOs.

Figure 6.4
Al Gray on the field. Gray observing his Camp Hansen football team in action in the Fall of 1974.[6]

In typical Al Gray style, speaking without notes, slides or any other aids, Gray read the riot act to the officers and senior enlisted men. These were the leaders and Gray knew he had to get their attention, immediately. The new Commanding Officer's message was relatively simple, "Lead, follow or stand aside." To those who wanted to become part of the solution, it was a welcomed though long overdue message. Very few had joined the Marine Corps thinking they would experience the situation that existed, and most wanted a way to change it.

Al Gray was never a moralist who judged the personal choices made by others with respect to drinking and carousing. Some of the Marine Corps' most legendary leaders were not exactly role models for Christian behavior while they were on liberty, especially far from home. Included in that number were some whom Gray respected the most, professionally speaking. Al Gray well knew and clearly recognized that how others lived their lives had no affect on him, at least normally. However, in the summer of 1974 on Okinawa, and especially at Camp Hansen the state of affairs was very difficult and far from normal.

In that clime and at that place, how officers and Staff NCOs were living their lives did affect Marines, and too often adversely. Never in the Marine Corps' long and proud history was the need for high quality leadership more evident than it was in July 1974 at Camp Hansen and on Okinawa in general. Many officers and Staff NCOs, both married and single, had been living in town instead of their assigned quarters aboard the camp. The so-called leaders would leave the base at night and return the next morning. With much of the leadership absent at night, there was not the supervision needed to maintain good order and discipline among the Marines. Exacerbating the issue, alcohol abuse was rampant and drug abuse was at a very high level. One of the first announcements that Gray made to the officers and senior enlisted was, "Move back aboard Camp Hansen by 1600 (4 P.M.) today or be off the island tomorrow." Gray directed that leaders spending their nights off base was no longer an option. To emphasize the point, Colonel Gray announced a midnight curfew for Camp Hansen.

Gray went on to mention to his subordinates that there were many things being done wrong, and that he demanded these be stopped, or in some cases, started. Things like not supervising the troops, not being seen in town in uniform, not fully utilizing the training areas, and not motivating the troops – all that would end or he promised to find new leaders. He announced that henceforth there would be officer and Staff NCO courtesy patrols nightly in Kin Ville, the large Okinawan community just outside Camp Hansen. Further, they would be working in concert with the Japanese police to ensure proper conduct and to take care of their Marines and Sailors. Having gained the attention of the officers and Staff NCOs, Al Gray was ready for the troops. While the new Commanding Officer briefed the troops, many of the recently censured leaders hurried into town to recover their personal belongings.

His message to the troops was very similar, though Gray – while forceful in his interaction with the troops – understood that the most junior of Marines usually reflected the values and priorities they observed in their leaders. Gray let them know that there was a new sheriff in town, and that he would be watching, correcting, and, if necessary, eliminating problem Marines from the Command. While the Marine Corps still had not adopted the personnel policies that Al Gray had first implemented a few years earlier at Camp Lejeune in the 2nd Marines, Gray well knew how successful his actions there had been.[7] Troublemakers did not want to be sent home to uncertain civilian futures; almost immediately, the bottom 20% of agitators who commanded a big majority of the leadership's time and efforts became a much smaller percentage. The worst cases were, indeed, sent off the island. The message resonated; Gray, everyone soon realized, meant business.

Fights, in particular, raised the dander in Al Gray. He could not understand how Marines reached the point of physically harming each other. He was intent on eliminating such behavior in the future and his actions reflected common sense, basic leadership. Gray met with the Chief Hospital Corpsman who ran the dispensary at Camp Hansen. Anytime a Marine was brought in seriously injured as the result of being in fights, Al Gray wanted to be called. As if on cue, the next night Gray received a phone call from the Chief Corpsman announcing there was a fight victim in the dispensary. It turned out the injured Marine was from 7th Communications Battalion; Gray had the Commanding Officer awakened and ordered to come to join him at the sick bay to see his Marine. Almost immediately he had everyone's attention on yet another issue.

The Commanding General, Marine Corps Bases, Okinawa met the idea of courtesy patrols and a nightly curfew with initial disbelief. Brigadier General Harold A. Hatch, when he learned what Gray proposed, told the new Base Commander that he could not do that – the Japanese authorities would not permit it. Gray informed the General that the Japanese had already approved the plan even before he had announced it. Gray's informal, highly personal liaison with all levels of Japanese society earned him both their confidence and their cooperation. After all, fights, public drunkenness and drugs benefited no one who operated a business or ran the local government. Recalling the event and the General's reaction, Gray thought that perhaps General Hatch never forgave him for his unilateral decision to implement a curfew. On the other hand, General Hatch also became a bona fide admirer of the Camp Commander, and soon gave Gray wide discretion in dealing with the Japanese government and civilians.[8]

Within a week of storming aboard Camp Hansen, Al Gray was off to the Philippines to evaluate the operational readiness of his subordinate commanders. He knew that a very important Brigade-level exercise was planned for November 1974, and he was determined that it would be successful.

KUBASAKI HIGH SCHOOL, SEPTEMBER 1974

In August, Major General Kenneth Houghton, who first met Al Gray in the early 1950s when he was still an enlisted man, had replaced General Haynes in command of the 3rd Marine Division. Later in the 1950s, Houghton again served with Gray on Hawaii when Gray was a young captain implementing the activation and training for the 1st Composite Radio Company. Still later, in 1967 in Vietnam, Colonel Houghton was the III MAF Intelligence Officer when Lieutenant Colonel Gray commanded the Radio Battalion in country. Houghton, it is fair to say, greatly admired Al Gray.[9] General Houghton also knew that keeping General Wilson, his big boss in Hawaii, well satisfied was among his highest priorities.

Both Lieutenant General Wilson and Major General Houghton realized that Al Gray had bitten off a very big piece of leadership pie. Commanding a regiment, especially one with battalions in active training cycles preparing for contingency operations in Southeast Asia, was more than a sufficient challenge for even the best Marine colonels. To command the 4th Marines while also running, de facto or otherwise, the largest Marine Corps Camp in Japan was particularly daunting. Or so thought the Generals involved. Not that Gray was complaining, he never did – even if he ever thought there might be someone who cared to listen!

Al Gray had learned of the correlation between non-high school graduates and Marines with disciplinary issues during previous discussions with Lieutenant General Bob Nichols when both were at Camp Lejeune. Gray held General Nichols and his analysis in extremely high esteem. He now would take Nichols's findings and turn them into action. Given that nearly 55% of his Marines lacked a diploma, Gray knew there were lots to do.

Having confirmed that the 4th Marines and all the other units at Camp Hansen were filled with individuals who did not complete high school, Gray envisioned a radical course of action. Discussions with the leadership of the Department of Defense (DoD) School System, which operated schools from elementary through high school for the American dependents living on Okinawa and other parts of

Japan, led to an agreement that the DoD schools would provide curriculum, testing, some teachers and the overarching framework for a high school at Camp Hansen.[10] Gray also finagled assistance from dependent wives, usually Air Force dependents from Kadena Air Base, who had teaching credentials but were not employed by the DoD School System, as well as other interested parties. While setting up the school at Hansen, Gray also collaborated with the Commanding Officer of the 9th Marines, Colonel James Woodring, who established a similar facility at Camp Schwab. Woodring was a superb officer, and one of Al Gray's favorite contemporaries dating back to their service together in Vietnam.

Perhaps the most important aspect of Gray's idea for a high school for his Marines was the need to convince the subordinate commanders that he really meant to give education the top priority. He got their attention by announcing that any school-nominated Marine's first duty was to attend high school; classroom attendance trumped field exercises or any other duty that commanders or their first sergeants might assign to the troops. Gray assigned the responsibility for ensuring that all commands at Camp Hansen actively participated in the program to his Deputy Camp Commander, Lieutenant Colonel Don Morris, a gifted infantry leader who also had a strong background in computer science. Infantry units got a week in school, and then a week in the field; there were no exceptions. There might have been bickering, snickering and outright complaining about losing their men to attend high school, but attending school was exactly what the Base Commander wanted to happen – and it did.

Gray's new Regimental Executive Officer, Lieutenant Colonel Robert White, recently joined from FMFPAC in Hawaii, was looking forward to being back in the field with Marines while serving with one of the Corps' best known troop leaders. He was stunned by his first project: ensure the 4th Marines' portion of Kubasaki High School up and running, and produce graduates! Of course, it was not Bob White's only task. The official name of the school was the Camp Hansen Learning Center and it was opened on 16 December 1974 with General Houghton as the guest speaker; another speaker was Mr. Betchel, the area coordinator for Department of Defense School, Far East Division. The third speaker was Colonel Al Gray, the camp commander, who also served as the Master of Ceremonies.[11]

Creating the school was a remarkable endeavor, and it took all of Al Gray's by now legendary powers of persuasion to keep the vision on track and make it into a reality. Every Marine who was not a high school graduate or who had not earned a General Equivalency Diploma (GED) would attend class five days a week so long as his unit was at Camp Hansen (or Camp Schwab). It was hardly that simple.

Indeed, just the administrative requirements were huge. This was much more than a GED program; this was a veritable high school. Testing put the students into classes they needed and permitted the staff to align individual requirements with the course offering – English, mathematics, science, history and government, all the subjects were offered. Twenty-six Quonset huts were fitted for air conditioning and turned into classrooms. School was in session!

The educational records of all those Marines had to be collected, processed, verified and evaluated in order to know what courses they had to pass in order to graduate. The process began when Marines checked into Camp Hansen; if they did not have a diploma, their record was tagged and a request sent to their high school(s) requesting records. Thus, records were sought from countless high schools back in the United States. Tutors and classroom aides were recruited from among the other Marines or dependents. When Colonel Gray encountered a group of company commanders whining and moaning at Friday Night Happy Hour at the Officers Club – complaining that they did not have their Marines to train – Gray decided that he had heard enough. He told his subordinates, "Until you commanders learn to use time effectively, like holding crew-served weapons drill while you are awaiting transportation to the field, I don't want to hear any more complaining." Taking an additional step, Gray then required each commanding officer who had troops in school to serve on the newly formed "Parent-Teacher Association." Further, he made each officer meet with the teachers weekly to be informed as to the progress being made by their students. Very quickly no one was grousing about losing his troops to education. The Marines of 2nd Battalion, 4th Marines (2/4), the Magnificent Bastards (2/4's nickname since 1966), were the first infantrymen to attend classes every other week.[12]

The weeks that the troops were not in school, they were training – training hard – throughout the island. It was normal for the units to go to the field on Monday and return late Thursday evening or even Friday. Regular maintenance of personal and unit equipment occurred on Saturdays. Despite the priority put on school for the non-graduates, they routinely went to the field and were always busy. This high level of activity had the very positive effects of reducing alcohol and drug abuse, while also limiting the amount of time troops spent on liberty in Kin Ville.

There were other untold advantages to having created high schools at Camps Hansen and Schwab, though they accrued at the expense of young officers and Staff NCOs learning their profession. Instead of being in the field leading various tactical exercises or firing weapons, or learning how to maneuver, officers had other duties. They were in town keeping a damper on race relations or they were tutoring their men on the vagaries of English or the logic of geometry. But those officers were also learning key lessons in leadership, especially of the advantages, the benefits, and the rewards of putting others ahead of self. Another gain was that everyone was engaged in the effort – the infantry, artillery, engineers, communicators, everyone. It provided a means for the disparate units to bond together with the common goal of achieving something highly tangible for many of their troops, and that included some Staff NCOs and NCOs. They were also teaching each other about their profession through classes and field work. The young officers discovered the joy of helping people who previously had little reason to rejoice; the young officers learned the real meaning of leadership.

NEW NORMAL IN KIN VILLE, FALL 1974

Colonel Gray quickly developed a close relationship with the Okinawan police. As a result, the police became actively involved in promoting the Colonel's agenda of reducing drug and alcohol abuse. That, of course, did not mean things always went smoothly. Two captains from 2/4, out in town to relax and unwind, and mindful of their regimental commander's edict to get involved, pay attention and take action when they saw anything illicit taking place, were walking between bars when they spotted a local Japanese covertly engaged in selling drugs to several Marines. Captains Joe Betta and Ed Gerstner, the Battalion S-4 and Communications Officer respectfully, ran toward the car and placed themselves in front and back, yelling and disrupting the drug trade. The driver was able to back up and then speed away before the two officers accomplished anything other than disputing a drug trade.

The next morning Captain Betta was summoned to the regimental command post. On the way he met up with Gerstner and they pondered their fate. Each was sure they had done nothing wrong, but when Lieutenant Colonel White suggested that "they were in trouble," both felt the pangs of uncertainty. They reported to Colonel Gray, who announced, "You guys screwed up last night. We had that drug deal set up with the local police and were waiting at the end of the block." Of course, Gray could hardly be upset that his officers had intervened, as he fully expected them to do, and he quietly dismissed the pair, only adding that they keep up their good work while paying attention to their surroundings. Gray never tried to stifle initiative, yet both officers left with new respect for the widespread dealings of their Regimental Commander.

The troops in the Marine Corps of 1974 were much different from the Marine Corps of the early 21st century. The 1974 enlistees far too often were educationally challenged; they were not men and women who, in the 2017-version of the Marine

Corps, might have earned some college credits or be enrolled in distance learning courses. One clear indication of the problem was reflected when 2/4 tested its men to determine their reading level. Fully 25% did not read at the fourth grade level, including some who were high school graduates! Many of the rank and file in the infantry and other units on Okinawa had been losers in life. Lots of them only joined the military after having dropped out of school, or having been forsaken by a girlfriend, or being encouraged to join by not-so-lenient judges.[13] That was not true of all the troops, of course, but without the draft the Marines needed men, lots of them. Almost any enlistee was welcomed into the service at a time when beggars (the military services) were seldom choosers (those who were qualified to enlist).[14]

As a result of the high school, Gray and every other officer could see blacks helping whites, macho Samoans learning American history from small female teachers, and Chicanos (and many others) learning the joys of algebra. It was an uplifting experience for all concerned. Perhaps it was not what happened in the classroom that turned the tide, but rather what happened after class, during study periods. One-on-one mentoring built unit cohesion. While teaching each other, or learning from their cohort, Marines learned that their similarities, their goals and desires, were much stronger than their racial differences. Gray thought the trade-off between education and restrained professional development of the junior officers and men was more than worth the effort. The proof would be fast coming.

While the high school would prove to be a tremendous success for all involved, it was Gray's attention to another matter that fully complemented his priority on education. While there were drug problems on Okinawa (and really everywhere military units served and throughout the civilian communities in 1974), this challenge was somewhat mitigated by the harsh Japanese laws prohibiting illegal use of drugs. Gray realized that alcohol abuse was the much more important culprit in creating problems related to fighting, unauthorized absence, dereliction of duty, insubordination and other leadership issues. As a result of his analysis, Colonel Gray established an aggressive program both to identify probable alcohol abusers and then to abate their bad habits, or worse, their addiction.

Al Gray personally led counseling sessions with Marines and Sailors in need of help. His personal example spawned a wide following of officers and Staff NCOs who found that preventing alcohol abuse was more productive, and far more personally rewarding to the leaders, than picking up the pieces after alcohol-induced incidents occurred. On August 19, 1974, Gray published a letter to all the commissioned, non-commissioned and petty officers of the regiment; it was entitled personal awareness and it was prompted when a young, black sergeant died in his arms on a street in

Kin Ville. The letter described the process by which the combination of drugs and alcohol combined to be fatal to anyone who used them, and it sought to have leaders at every level become vigilant for signs that others might be affected. It also showed the anguish that such deaths caused the Commanding Officer of the 4th Marines. The letter is reproduced below:

Headquarters
4th Marines, 3rd Marine Division (-) (Rein), FMF
FPO San Francisco 96602

AMG:wmt
1700
19 Aug 1974

From: Commanding Officer

To: All Commissioned, Non-commissioned and Petty Officers of the Regiment

Subj: Personal Awareness

On 16 August 1974, a young Marine of this Regiment was found dead. Although all post mortem reports are not available at this time, it is almost a certainty that this individual died by drowning in his own vomit. This is the FOURTH such incident in the Regiment in almost as many months.

Without presupposing the medical findings in the particular case, I feel certain that this Marine fell victim to a dangerous circumstance which prevails on Okinawa. Below is the cycle of events that may very well have led to this man's death:

A. Barbiturates, in the form of non-prescription menstrual tablets, easily available in KIN VILLE and other local communities, are bought and ingested. This medicine acts as a depressant on the central nervous system, short-circuiting natural body reflexes such as coughing.

B. An individual who has taken this medicine experiences a state of euphoria. Then, in the totally uninhibited state, he drinks beer or some other form of alcohol and becomes intoxicated. In other words, he is both "high and drunk."

C. Upon returning to his quarters, he literally passes out. While asleep, his body performs a natural reaction to the overindulgence and he vomits. Since, however, the barbiturates he had taken have negated his natural life-saving reflex to cough, his vomit passes into his lungs and he literally drowns.

In each and every case of such a death, the people sleeping near the dying Marine state that he sounded as if he were snoring.

Responsibility for this tragic happening rests, to a degree, with each of us. Had we, the commissioned, non-commissioned and petty officers who are leaders, been a little more aware of the pitfalls that present themselves to our men; had we taken extra time to instruct, re-instruct and then supervise them on and off liberty; had we listened more closely to the sounds of a dying man; this Marine and three others might be alive today.

I have heard it said of those who might fall into the cycle of events I have described: "if they want to mess around with that stuff, they deserve to die." Such a statement not only shows a callous disregard for the value of human life, but is in itself an admission of failure to lead.

I charge each of you to think long and hard and seriously about this sad event. I ask you to reflect on what your feelings would be if this were your son or younger brother who had just died. Would you feel that his leaders had done everything they could to keep him from injury and death? One element common to all good leaders of whatever rank is their AWARENESS of the needs of those they are privileged to lead. Deaths and injuries to our Marines and Sailors almost inevitably mean that some leader was NOT aware. See to it that you are not one of those! Instill awareness in the men you lead by the example you yourselves set.

Once again, I have used this type of correspondence to apprise you of my views. This is a very expensive way to communicate with you; but if the word gets out and even one life is saved, it will indeed have been worth the expense.

A.M. Gray

Al Gray always thought, and took measures to ensure, that any Marine or Sailor who left the service after their initial enlistment should re-enter society a better person than when he or she came into the service. As far as Al Gray was concerned, that was the real meaning of leadership and the essence of John A. Lejeune's writings about the relationship between officers and enlisted. It was one thing to lead Marines while storming up hills or conducting night reconnaissance patrols; it was quite another, and no less important, to teach Marines how to read, how to handle bank accounts, or how to rid themselves of the demons caused by alcohol. In the end, for Al Gray it was the source of great self-satisfaction when other officers and Staff NCOs learned the joys associated with giving, helping, and encouraging the men to achieve more than the men themselves had previously thought possible. As important, Gray's personal denial of alcohol when serving abroad became something other officers adopted, and they thanked him for his example. Al Gray knew that his Marines were much more likely to follow officers who walked the walk, and not just talked the talk.

When BLT 1/4 returned to Okinawa in October after spending several months in the Philippines, the Staff NCOs and troops recognized that many changes had been made. In addition to Kubasaki High School, the troops noticed that they spent much more time in the field. Lance Corporal Ken Crouse had flown onto the island with a Staff NCO who turned out to be his Company Gunnery Sergeant in Alpha Company. Calvin Lynn was a veteran Staff NCO who was none too happy about what he found upon his arrival. When Lynn found the younger Marine in his Company, he made Crouse the Company driver – good duty if you could get it! Now, returned from the P.I., Gunny Lynn was happy to take the troops to the field, even if they had to sober up while marching there. The Gunny had positioned himself at the rear of the Company column to collect stragglers, including many Marines who seemed more than slightly incapacitated. He was encouraging the men when out of nowhere the Regimental Commander appeared. "What's going on here, Gunny?" asked Al Gray. Lynn replied that he was herding the stragglers to the Company position, where those who might need treatment for minor aches and pains, or blisters and the like, would be seen by corpsmen. Gray looked around, nodded his approval, and disappeared. Lynn had never spoken to any Regimental Commander while in the field, and the experience left quite an impression on him. Crouse recalled that going to the field made a lot of sense to him because, "Marines don't get in trouble rolling around in the mud." BLT 1/4's absence meant neither Lynn nor Crouse had heard Gray's opening speech; but both recognized that "Okinawa was different." [15]

The whole situation at Camp Hansen reinforced one of Gray's favorite dictums: *take what you get and make what you want.*

MORE LOCAL CHALLENGES, 1974-1975

Although the transformation wrought by Al Gray both in the village and on the base was significant, it would take a few months before the makeover was complete. However, before that happened, a couple of situations arose that proved good leadership is long remembered, and that often it is as important to be lucky as it is to be good.

Gray had been doing his usual roaming around in town, observing what was happening and encouraging the men. One of his first directives was that officers and Staff NCOs be assigned to town each evening. They would also walk, in uniform, throughout the village helping ensure good order and discipline. Within a month, no one was better known in Kin Ville than Al Gray; the locals, the Marines and Sailors, everyone knew the Base Commander. Often they knew him because he would stop them to chat, to find out how things were going, to find out what could be done better. Few people were as good a listener as the stocky Marine Colonel.[16]

Everyone with whom he spoke was sure that the Colonel had his or her personal interest ahead of anything else then happening. Gray's ability to speak the local language cannot be underestimated, either. That he took the time to try to master the local language or even the local dialect everywhere he went was a signature of his service, but one few have emulated. Respecting the local people starts with trying to learn their language, difficult as that might be. Gray's natural affinity for languages gave him a great advantage over most others, and attempting to master the local dialect costs nothing while yielding significant benefits.

Gray normally traveled alone in civvies, however, and one night he found himself surrounded by a large group of black Marines. It turned out that the Marines were in Kin Ville though they were assigned to Camp Schwab, a more northern base that was home to the 9th Marines. These Marines did not recognize Al Gray nor know what he was doing. They only knew that he was in a section of town that blacks had long partitioned as their own. As Gray jostled with and traded barbs with the men from Schwab, he heard a voice in the back say, "What's going on, Colonel? Can we help?" It turned out that a bunch of African-American Marines from Camp Hansen had surrounded the crowd from Schwab. Gray realized at that moment that insofar as race relations at Hansen were concerned, he had turned a big corner. The situation was diffused as the Hansen Marines explained that "their Colonel" was okay, that he treated people fairly and squarely, listened to valid complaints and deserved everyone's respect.

One night Colonel Gray met alone, off base, with a group of dissident Marines from Puerto Rico who were causing trouble. They complained about many items, most notably about the way they were treated by other Marines. Gray promised them fair treatment. However, in return, he required that their conduct improve considerably or he would send them off the island with their discharge records appropriate to their offenses. Apparently the issues were resolved because the group caused no more trouble.

That was all good, and even promising, but there were other ethnic groups that still required attention. On another night, Gray, again in civilian clothes, was again in the village when he was recalled to the base on an emergency basis. The Officer of the Day reported that "something big" was happening in the area behind the Headquarters of 1st Battalion, 4th Marines, which was afloat. Gray hurried to that location.

What he found was a large gathering of Samoans, who appeared to be forming a war party. They had set ablaze a large bonfire around which they were dancing and whooping. They had collected about 80 men from all over the island, but mostly from outside Camp Hansen; they were agitated because of their relationship with blacks. There had long been bad blood between the two groups, and the Samoans were determined to extract some measure of revenge for past slights and fights, perceived or actual. And that was when good luck, perhaps even better timing, came to Al Gray's assistance.

"What are you doing here, Lieutenant Gray?" asked one of the older Samoans.

Over 20 years before, when then-1st Lieutenant Al Gray commanded Able Company, 1st Battalion, 7th Marines on the Main Line of Resistance in Korea, he had three Samoans in the second platoon of his company. All were indeed large, and all named Sam. They were nicknamed, appropriately, Big Sam, Middle Sam and Small Sam. All three were boxing champions in the division's smokers.[17] They all liked and respected their former company commander, and he liked them.

On that night at Camp Hansen, Big Sam was the chief in charge of the gathering. It only took a short conversation between the old boxer and Colonel Gray to scatter the setting and disperse the assemblage. Good leadership from long ago saved considerable trouble from arising; certainly, as Al Gray often says, what goes around comes around.

While Al Gray was on Okinawa in 1974, the island reverted to the control of the Japanese government. Since the end of World War II, the island was operated as a protectorate of the United States. With reversion came a realignment of the currency, and overnight the cost of beer – and everything else – went up. Instead of the troops having lots of spending money when on liberty, their entertainment dollars shrunk considerably. With Japanese control, new political agitations began. The Base Commander periodically encountered demonstrations and protest marches outside the main gate. These were usually organized and paid for by the socialist agitators from the main island of Japan. The protests had a common theme: they demanded the return of the training areas and bases to the Okinawans so that the locals would have more land to use and cultivate.

Gray responded to these events just he would any encounter – directly. He walked right out into the demonstrators and engaged them in conversation. It helped immensely that Gray could speak the language, and even better he could discern the differences between an accent from Honshu, the main island, and one from Okinawa. Just like knowing if you are speaking to someone from New York or Mississippi, knowing if the speaker was a local or from Tokyo earned Gray extra respect. He could use the local dialect to appeal to the local people for reason. Gray understood that the average Okinawan had little more love for the Japanese than they did for the Americans. The mainland Japanese had long treated the Okinawans as second cousins, and the locals now returned the favor by giving the Japanese Self Defense Force no more respect than they gave the Marines. Even before he left the island permanently in August 1975, the locals considered Al Gray the "Mayor of Kin Ville."

TOKYO AREA, JAPAN 1975

While Colonel Gray's later travels to Cambodia and South Vietnam got the attention of most high-ranking military officers in the Pacific area, it was a secretive trip that garnered no attention that revealed a side of Gray that most have never seen, and few know about. During his interactions with the Okinawan police force, which was almost a daily event during the first few months that Gray was on the island, he had learned of an American Marine imprisoned in the Tokyo area. Quietly Gray gathered information about the man. The prisoner faced a long prison term because of an accidental, though drug-related, killing of a local Japanese. Gray determined that while the young man was clearly guilty of the crime committed, the tragedy of events leading to the accident were breath-taking. This was a fine American who had a momentary lapse in judgment, for which he faced a severely long time in a Japanese prison where conditions could be described as harsh and primitive - at best. Typically, inmates are not given blankets or other accoutrements of normal living unless they are supplied by the inmate's family. And in terms of quality of food, recreational or sports pastimes, and other measures of modern living, the Japanese prisons of the 1960s and 1970s were unforgiving by even the standards of 19th Century America. This Marine, Gray knew, would suffer long under extremely difficult conditions even if he even survived his sentence.

Gray quietly arranged to visit Japan by taking normal leave from his duties on Okinawa. At his own expense, he traveled to Honshu and met with the Marine to hear his story and evaluate for himself the Marine's truthfulness and his degree of remorse for his actions. Convinced that the man's life could be turned around if he were given a second chance, Gray worked to gain the prisoner's release. Discharged from the Marine Corps but returned to the United States, the man became a positive, productive citizen.[18] But few ever knew of Colonel Al Gray's involvement. That Gray had earned the trust and confidence of the local Okinawans, and before that of Japanese at Kami Seya and Sakata, no doubt played a significant role in the events surrounding the story. In Gray's retirement, it was one seemingly insignificant episode in his long professional life. But it clearly demonstrated that Al Gray *did as much as he could, for as many as he could, for as long as he could.* And getting credit was never a consideration.

OPERATION MABLEX 1-75, PHILIPPINES, SEPTEMBER THRU DECEMBER 1974

Like he did in the 2nd Marines, Gray benefited by being surrounded by good officers who supported and reinforced his style of leadership. Initially, the battalion commanders of his three infantry units were Lieutenant Colonels Carl E. Mundy, Jr., a future Commandant; Edwin J. Godfrey, a future Lieutenant General; and Bill Davis, Jr., another outstanding officer who retired as a Colonel. Gray welcomed the efficiency and effectiveness of his subordinates, because the Regiment was assigned the task of providing the afloat battalion which was ready for combat anywhere in Southeast Asia, while a second battalion was in the final stages of readiness training before going afloat, while the third battalion was reconstituting itself and beginning the deployment and readiness cycle. It really was left to the regimental commander to juggle all three balls.

Lieutenant Colonel George P. Slade soon replaced Carl Mundy as the Commanding Officer of the Magnificent Bastards, Gray's 2nd Battalion.[19] It would be George Slade, the recruiting poster image of a Marine officer, who led 2/4 into contingency operations in Southeast Asia.[20] And the prelude to all the operations that would occur in 1975 was called Marine Amphibious Brigade Landing Exercise 1 (MABLEx 1-75) that took place in December 1974.

Figure 6.5
The 29th and 30th Commandants of the Marine Corps served together in the 4th Marines on Okinawa in 1974. Colonel Al Gray, center, with Lieutenant Colonel Carl Mundy, the outgoing CO of 2/4 on his left. Others are, from the left, LtCol George Slade, incoming CO of 2/4, Lt Col Jack Godfrey CO of 3/4 (on Gray's right), and LtCol Bill Davis, CO of 1/4 on the far right.[21]

There had been no major exercises in the Pacific since the end of the Vietnam War. General Wilson wanted to have one, no doubt realizing the benefits of *Operation Alkali Canyon* at 29 Palms in 1972 and 1973. Those, the first of which Al Gray organized and led, proved to be immensely successful in terms of improving unit effectiveness, providing relevant experience for the troops and their leaders, and beginning the process of mastering combined arms environment. General Louis Wilson wanted those exercises duplicated in the Pacific to the greatest possible extent.

The planning for the exercise began at Camp Hansen in September. Al Gray's 4th Marines would be the major ground unit. A provisional air group from nearby Marine helicopter squadrons was formed, as was a logistics group that was carved from units already on Okinawa. One of Okinawa's major advantages as a base for Marine operations was that it was centrally located and there already existed a huge logistics establishment from which to draw. The Assistant Division Commander, Brigadier General H.L. Coffman, was designated to be the MAB Commanding General.

Gray worked exceptionally well with General Coffman, who from the start leaned heavily on his ground component commander.[22] They did something unusual for the time: they gathered the key staff officers from the ground, air, and logistics units and put them together in the same offices at Camp Hansen. As a result, for example, the ground logistics officer, the air logistics officer and the S-4 of the logistics group worked in concert; similarly, operations officers with each component shared facilities. Right from the get-go the MAB staff would be in sync. The close coordination eliminated one of the main criticisms of Marine operations of the time – that being that the staffs met only at the exercise, executed their assignment, and went home. They never had an opportunity to know each other or understand each other's problems and challenges.

A Marine Amphibious Brigade exercise also has another essential component – a U.S. Naval Force. Colonel Al Gray's forces were assigned to an ARG under the command of Rear Admiral Donald B. Whitmire. Whitmire's Navy units, like their Marine counterparts, had not conducted amphibious operations since Vietnam, and they could use the experience every bit as much as the MAB. The exercise also had tremendous value going forward. Admiral Whitmire, his staff and ships' personnel would be mostly the same that would support Marine forces in the forthcoming contingency operations to be conducted during the Spring of 1975. After becoming familiar with each other during the MABLEx, when real operations loomed the Navy and Regimental Landing Team-4 (RLT) could concentrate on their assignments and not have to learn how to work together. The mutual respect stemming from a close-knit relationship between the naval forces would provide a substantial advantage in the months to come.

Figure 6.6
Brigadier General H. L. Coffman commanded the first major
MABLEx after Gray arrived in the Pacific.[23]

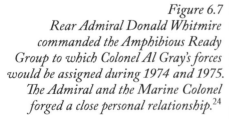

Figure 6.7
Rear Admiral Donald Whitmire
commanded the Amphibious Ready
Group to which Colonel Al Gray's forces
would be assigned during 1974 and 1975.
The Admiral and the Marine Colonel
forged a close personal relationship.[24]

Figure 6.8
Major General Kenny Houghton speaks with the troops during the
exercise in the Philippines while Colonel Gray watches.[25]

Following MABLEx 1-75, Regimental Combat Team-4 returned to Okinawa and Camp Hansen. The conditions aboard the base and in Kin Ville were in stark contrast when compared to those Al Gray encountered when he arrived in June 1974. There were no troops practicing riot-control drills; instead there seemed to be a happy undercurrent as both the troops and their officers hurried to and from their tasks. Classroom learning and after hours studying with related tutoring continued apace. Perhaps the biggest changes were in town, however.

No one needed to walk with a group in order to have protection from other Marines whose complexions were different. Individuals moved freely about the entire town, and calls from the Chief Hospital Corpsman alerting commanders that their Marines had been injured in a fight were practically non-existent. It was the best Christmas present that General Wilson, still in Hawaii worrying about the future of his Corps, could have received.

With General Wilson on Okinawa in consultations with his commanders about the increasingly serious happenings in Southeast Asia, Colonel Gray was getting more tasking.

In keeping with the idea that if one wants something done, give it to someone already very busy with other tasks, Gray had been given yet another important posting. Despite General Wilson's admonition that Gray was to focus on cleaning up the racial and drug-related issues facing Marines on the island, his operational duties were expanded. Already the Camp Commander at Camp Hansen and the Commanding Officer of the 4th Marines, in the late fall of 1974 Gray was appointed Ground Security Officer (GSO) for Phnom Penh and Saigon. Colonel Sidney H. (Tom) Batchelder, the Logistics Group Commander, was designated as the Alternative GSO. This arrangement ensured that Major General Houghton, the CG of the 3rd Division, had two of his best operational commanders available to head up contingency operations, regardless of who commanded the MAU when or if the balloon went up. Further, it permitted a single officer to oversee planning and coordination for each capital city while MAU commanders could concentrate on the myriad duties associated with daily operations and other contingencies.

American leadership had long worried about the situation in Cambodia and many thought the Cambodian capital, Phnom Penh, would fall. As part of the planning process undertaken by the Pacific Forces, Major General Michael Ryan, the Commanding General, III Marine Amphibious Force in Okinawa, briefed his staff in early April of 1973 about the situation.

At that time, evacuation planning for American personnel would commence immediately under the code name *Eagle Pull*. The Third Marine Division began monthly "fly away" drills involving the 1st Marine Aircraft Wing and the Air Force Base at Kadena under the supervision of the III MAF. Colonel Steve Olmstead, later a Lieutenant General, who commanded the 9th Marines was designated Ground Security Officer on 30 June 1973. Olmstead, a seasoned combat veteran of Korea, including fighting in the epic battles of the Chosin Reservoir as an enlisted man, briefed both CINCPAC and FMFPAC in mid-July. On the 4th of August, General O'Keefe, who headed the USSAG in Nakom Phanom, Thailand, convened an *Eagle Pull* planning conference. Veteran Marine Corps planner, Colonel Ed Bronars, another superb officer, who would later rise to Lieutenant General, was the Director of Plans and Operations and the de facto point of contact for the GSF. Other key personnel included Colonel Wally Wessel, a veteran Marine aviator and Marine Major "Pony" Baker, who was the USSAG Action Officer for *Eagle Pull*.

The next day, the GSF commander participated in an evacuation Command Post Exercise (CPX) at the American Embassy in Phnom Penh with the Charge d'Affaires and the senior military officer, Brigadier General John Cleland, U. S. Army. Various options for the evacuation were considered including fixed-wing transport out of Pochentan, the international airport, or helicopters operating out of landing zones from Phnom Penh.

In December 1973, the GSF Commander and his command team checked the security of the evacuation sites and confirmed communications with both the American Embassy and the USSAG Headquarters in Thailand. On 23 January 1974, Colonel Olmstead and his command team were ordered to Thailand where they reviewed the USSAG plan and conferred with Colonel David Twomey, who commanded the 31st Marine Amphibious Unit. The 31st MAU was the ready force in the South China Sea area. They then went to Cambodia and reviewed the plan, validated the movement routes and selected evacuation sites. At that time, none of the selected sites required extensive preparation time. The GSF command team conducted meaningful liaison with the Embassy and returned to Okinawa in mid-February, 1974.

With the experience gained in planning and executing the evacuation of US citizens from the Dominican Republic in April of 1964, and supported by a group of dedicated and talented people, the Olmstead team was confident that they could successfully conduct *Operation Eagle Pull*. Colonel Olmstead had his change of command with the 9th Marines on 7 May 1974 and rotated to the United States. Also, there was change of command among U.S. Army personnel in Cambodia.[26]

As is sometimes the case when senior personnel and other key people within the chain of command rotate, a gap in continuity for evacuation contingency planning occurs. This becomes particularly acute when conditions in a particular country or region deteriorate rapidly, as was happening in late 1974 in Cambodia. Exacerbating the issue, there were changes of command at the III MAF and both the Third Marine Division and the 1st Marine Air Wing, and there was a new USAF commander at the USAAG in Thailand.

Soon after his arrival in Thailand in September 1974, Lieutenant General John J. Burns requested that Colonel Gray, as the designated Ground Security Officer, visit him. USSAG, headquartered at Nakhon Phanom, was in charge of all operations in Southeast Asia.

General Burns had reviewed the new evacuation plan for Phnom Penh and wanted to get another opinion about its potential effectiveness. Burns asked Gray to go to Cambodia, conduct an in-depth operational review and report back. Gray immediately went to work; he found the recently revised evacuation plan far too complicated to be readily implemented, especially if the evacuation force were also under pressure to work quickly while facing attack from a determined enemy. The existing plan, developed by in-country U. S. Army Special Forces, envisioned establishing five landing zones throughout the city. That arrangement would have required trees to be cut down at a variety of points, and for helicopters, with supporting ground security, to then operate from a series of landing zones that were not connected and not mutually supporting.

In the course of his analysis, Gray took the time to meet several times with the Ambassador, John Gunther Dean. The Marine Colonel took the time to patiently explain to the diplomat the need to make things easier related to evacuation procedures. The Ambassador, who had served in several posts in South Vietnam as an advisor on civil affairs but remained wary of military officers, grasped the state of affairs that would challenge any rescue attempt. As it turned out, it would not be the last time that Gray met Ambassador Dean, though their future encounter would be half a world away and take place only after Gray wore a star on his collar.

Fortunately for Gray's preparations, Phnom Penh had two large soccer fields. The newly appointed Ground Security Officer explained that everyone who needed to be taken out would have to go to one or the other. Ground security requirements were to be minimized and the whole operation greatly simplified. As ordered, Gray revisited General Burns, who immediately approved Gray's new preparations. As fate would have it, neither officer could have foreseen how quickly the new plan would be tested.

TROUBLE IN SOUTHEAST ASIA, JANUARY 1975

Events in both Cambodia and the Republic of Vietnam were deteriorating daily. Intelligence reports had become alarming and the threats to American interests in both countries became more imminent. While there were only about three hundred Americans in Phnom Penh, there were many thousand, in Saigon. These were diplomats, CIA operatives, American contractors and the rump of the Military Assistance Commands as well as other civilians who would need to be evacuated in the event of communist aggression. Evacuations appeared to be the inevitable ending in both Phnom Penh and Saigon.

As the situations in both countries deteriorated, American and Vietnamese military leaders were well aware that the tremendously reduced levels of supplies from the United States had worsened the already bad military situation that the ARVN faced. Conditions were not only untenable in South Vietnam, but worsening elsewhere.

In Cambodia, the North Vietnamese Army was on the move. Americans had long thought the Cambodian capital, Phnom Penh, would fall. In late 1974, though, there was an apparent lull in the fighting as the NVA regrouped, reformed and resupplied, but every American military planner expected the North Vietnamese to resume their offensive sooner rather than later, perhaps during the winter dry season. The circumstances were grim, and the tip of the spear that would have to come to the rescue, wherever the assistance would be needed, would be the Marine force on Okinawa.

Much like in the Mediterranean, where Marine Amphibious Units (MAU) operated year-round, prepared for various contingencies (as discussed in Chapter 4), Al Gray and Marines on Okinawa encountered a similar situation in the Pacific. Usually one MAU was afloat aboard an ARG; the MAU consisted of a Battalion Landing Team and Helicopter Squadron and Logistics Support Unit. When Al Gray arrived on Okinawa, his 1st Battalion, 4th Marines (1/4) served as the BLT aboard the ARG.

In August 1974, another of Al Gray's subordinate units replaced 1/4 as the afloat BLT. Lieutenant Colonel Edwin J. Godfrey's 3rd Battalion, 4th Marines (3/4) assumed the responsibility, which by that time considered the evacuation of Phnom Penh as a most likely mission. Given the missions of 1/4 and then 3/4, Al Gray immediately had immersed himself in various Southeast Asia contingency plans. While 3/4 was afloat, the training regime of 2/4 was adjusted to prepare that battalion to go afloat in December 1974, to replace 3/4. As a consequence, Gray and his staff ensured that Lieutenant Colonel George Slade and his Marines saw much of Lieutenant Colonel James L. Bolton and his heavy helicopters of HMH-462. Only Marine or Air Force heavy helicopters – the CH-53, or the Air Force's HH-53 variant – had the range that would permit a round trip from ships offshore to the Cambodian capital. The close ties developed during the training cycle between the infantry and air wing Marines paid significant dividends within months.

Figure 6.9
Colonel Gray looking at something, and his Sergeant Major trying to discern exactly what.[27]

Figure 6.10
Colonel Al Gray had come a long way since 1950, when he enlisted. A most professional officer, he was poised to lead Marines while reacting to a major crisis in Southeast Asia.[28]

Gray also insured that the intense training on Okinawa including making sure that all Marines learned how to use close air support. He insisted that his Marines saw a lot of the "white ones," as General Wilson called the jet attack aircraft. Air control and support operations were stressed on all levels. This too, was one of his Force Commander's points of main effort. Concurrently, things were so improved at Camp Hansen that when Lieutenant General Louis Wilson visited in February 1975, his attention was diverted to a much different, and lower, priority. With Al Gray in the front seat of a staff car, Generals Wilson and Houghton sat in the back while the Commanding General, FMF Pacific, was given a driving tour of the base. Wilson, while pleased with the remarkable turn around that was obvious to even casual observers, remained ever on the alert for Marines who were over-weight. Plus, it was General Wilson's personality to not permit his subordinates to feel overly content by what they might have already accomplished. As the car moved around, Wilson espied what he considered to be an overweight Marine. The General started grumbling about the need to make sure the men were in shape and ready to fight. Thinking quickly, Al Gray directed the driver to pause near the individual in question as he walked along the street. Rolling down his window, Gray said, "Good morning, Doc, fine day on Okinawa, isn't it?" Gray then ordered the driver to continue, not waiting for "doc's" reply. There was noticeably less grousing from the rear seat.

That visit marked the last time that Al Gray saw Wilson until after the General had become Commandant of the Marine Corps in June 1975. They would have lots of time to reacquaint themselves in the years to come. Al Gray might joke about General Wilson's rich southern drawl, but there was no other officer that Al Gray held in higher esteem. [29]

DUAL CRISES IN SOUTHEAST ASIA, MARCH 1975

As the flames of war spread across Southeast Asia, the situation in Phnom Penh appeared that it might burst even sooner than the deteriorating chaos that was enveloping South Vietnam. As a result, Colonel Sydney H. (Tom) Batchelder, was designated Ground Security Officer for Cambodia, while Gray (who had spent time in Phnom Penh at the behest of Lieutenant General John Burns of USSAG) focused on South Vietnam and Saigon. Burns' headquarters would exercise over-all command for any future operations in Southeast Asia. Even though Gray had developed the new evacuation plan for the Cambodian capital during January, 1975, it would be Tom Batchelder who would be responsible for the overall security of the Phnom Penh evacuation.

The American presence in Cambodia was never more than a small fraction of the size it had been in South Vietnam, although the North Vietnamese Army's existence in that troubled country had always been significant because of the presence of the Ho Chi Minh Trail. Lon Nol had established a pro-American government in Cambodia in 1970, just before a combined United States-South Vietnamese incursion into border regions near the so-called Parrot's Beak. The combined US-ARVN operation was stunningly effective, restrained only when the indecisive American President, Richard M. Nixon, pulled the reins. Internally, however, Lon Nol's presence gave rise to the Khmer Rouge, a communist insurgent group backed by the North Vietnamese.

The Khmer Rouge and NVA made an unlikely pair, given the Vietnamese' openly hostile treatment of Cambodians over the years. But from the very beginning, the Khmer communists outnumbered and outgunned the pro-government forces, who maintained power only through the support of American airpower. By 1975, the communists had cut the main supply line into Phnom Penh, the Mekong River. The Lon Nol regime was bound to fall unless America changed the passive policy enacted by the U.S. Congress. When Lon Nol left the country in January, the situation lurched from crisis to crisis, each of which seemed to announce the fatal chapter. By early 1975, two years after Paris Peace Accords had essentially ended the American presence in South Vietnam, only a couple hundred Americans remained in Cambodia.

BORING HOLES IN THE SOUTH CHINA SEA AND GULF OF THAILAND, MARCH 26 THROUGH APRIL 11

The 31st MAU embarked into ARG Alpha, which consisted of the amphibious assault ship USS *Tripoli* (LPH 10), the amphibious transport dock USS *Vancouver* (LPD 2), and the tank landing ship USS *Peoria* (LST 1183). Initially, 2/4 was the ground combat element and Marine Medium Helicopter Squadron (HMM) 164 was the air unit, both supported by Landing Support Unit (LSU) 2/4. That remained the organization until the advent of the dry season in January 1975. In January, the USS *Okinawa* (LPH-3) relieved the *Tripoli* as the ARG's Landing Platform Helicopter (LPH). The LPH at the time was by far the best helicopter support ship in the amphibious force.

Coincidental with the turnover of ships, Lieutenant Colonel Bolton's HMH-462 relieved HMM-164, thereby giving the MAU a long range, high lift helicopter that could make a round trip from the ships in the Gulf of Thailand to Phnom Penh and back. No sooner had the new squadron been taken aboard when the ARG made a high speed run back to its loitering point ready of operations within 96 hours. From January until April 12, ARG Alpha/31st MAU would remain offshore near Thailand on alerts that varied from 96 hours to six hours. The Marine commanders got ashore periodically to attend planning and coordination conferences, but for the Marines and Sailors it was a long three months of shipboard boredom; so much so that Commander, 7th Fleet, Vice Admiral Steele, worried about their readiness.[30]

OPERATION EAGLE PULL, PHNOM PENH, CAMBODIA, 12 APRIL, 1975

The 31st MAU had been continuously at sea nearly 30 days when orders were given to stand by to evacuate the Cambodian capital. That meant that after April 4, the ARG Alpha and the BLT 2/4 stood ready to conduct operations on a 6-hour response time. Simultaneously, the fixed-wing C-130 airlift from Cambodia was expedited and the Ambassador called for the Ground Security Officer Command Element to be placed ashore inside the capital. From then until the final evacuation, Americans on the ground were exposed to desultory rifle, mortar and rocket fire. Fortunately, there were no casualties. However, it would be more than a week before the Ambassador determined that the Embassy should be closed on April 11. As that date drew near, however, as the result of the anticipated arrival of the aircraft carrier USS *Hancock* and another squadron of Marine CH-53s (HMH-453), the evacuation was pushed back to April 12. The additional Marine squadron meant that the United States Air Force's HH-53s could be held in reserve.

When the order finally came to evacuate Cambodia and close the Embassy, it would be Colonel Tom Batchelder, who had been in Phnom Penh for a week with his command element, who implemented a slightly different version of the plan Al Gray had prepared in December 1974. Given the fixed-wing effort to take people out of the country, the final phase of the operation would need to use only a single soccer field, and security could be provided by a total of 360 troops, not a full battalion.

The very capable MAU commander, Colonel Roche, decided to use HMH-452 to land the Marines from George Slade's 2nd Battalion, 4th Marines (2/4) and then use those aircraft to remove the evacuees, while assigning HMH-453 the task of extracting the Marines. The plan was executed with only very minor flaws, even though the soccer field permitted only three of the huge helicopters to be on the ground simultaneously. The long and hard joint training on Okinawa between BLT 2/4 and HMH-452 proved extremely beneficial in Cambodia.

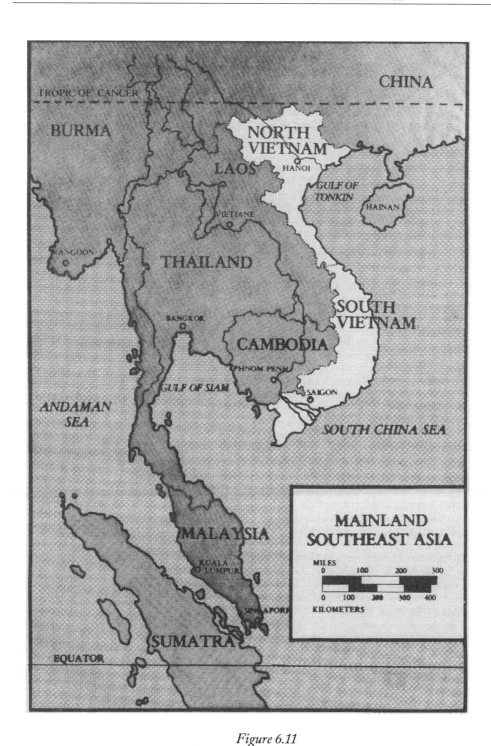

Figure 6.11
In order to be closer to Cambodia, ARG (A) was usually positioned well into the Gulf of Siam (Thailand). From there, the large CH-53 helicopters could make the roundtrip to Phnom Penh. For the Saigon portion of the operations, the Navy shipping was located southeast of Saigon about where the "SOU" of South China Sea is shown. [31]

Marine commanders were told that they had about two hours to execute the evacuation before the communists would take action. The almost 300 evacuees were staged at the designated soccer field and there were no pressing issues related to crowd control; indeed, the nearby crowds displayed more curiosity than panic. The well-trained Marines conducted a textbook operation. The CH-53s landed in three-ship flights on the designated landing zones and the entire operation lasted just under the prescribed 120 minutes. After the Marines were out, two Air Force Jolly Green Giant HH-53s from the 40th Air Rescue and Recovery Squadron picked up Colonel Batchelder's command element, which was last to leave.

The intelligence proved prophetic, however. As the last Marine helicopter lifted off from the soccer fields, communist forces took a potshot with a rocket propelled grenade (RPG) that flew wide of its intended target. Subsequently, the last two HH-53s were hit by small arms and 12.7mm anti-aircraft fire, which caused note-worthy damage on the second helicopter's tail rotor, though both made it safely back to Ubon Air Base in Thailand. However, the near-miss RPG and the 12.7 mm machine gun fire reminded everyone that there is the potential for chaos in almost any military operation. Specifically, the plan needs to be as simple to execute as possible. Had the "evacuation" lasted minutes longer, or had the Khmer Rouge hit their targets with earlier salvos, *Eagle Pull* would have quickly turned into a military operation, not a humanitarian one. Putting an unnecessary layer of complexity into the planning process seldom results in fewer casualties or a quicker positive outcome. Al Gray always thought, and preached, that a good plan violently executed was far better than the perfect plan delayed; the operation at Phnom Penh proved him right.

With respect to BLT 2/4, it was interesting to note that the battalion had been the original test case for Kubasaki High School on Okinawa. Its men had been the first to experience a week in the field followed by a week in school. But Lieutenant Colonel George Slade's men performed their mission in an exemplary fashion, proving that the trade-off between education and professional development made good sense, at least in the timeframe of 1974 and 1975.[32]

While Colonel Batchelder and his force were involved in Phnom Penh, an even more ominous development was taking place in South Vietnam. Whereas *Operation Eagle Pull* resulted in slightly fewer than 300 Americans being taken to safety, there were literally thousands of potential evacuees remaining in Saigon, along with multitudes of South Vietnamese nationals who would receive sure death sentences if the communists captured them. As soon as the operation was completed, ARG Alpha set sail for Subic Bay, Republic of the Philippines. The troops deserved some time off the ships, though they would barely get to the Marines' favorite liberty port in the Far East before being put on alert in Southeast Asia.

In Cambodia, predictably, the government officials and supporters who remained behind were executed within weeks of the communist takeover, victims of America's inability, or unwillingness, to honor its commitments. There were no repercussions for the American politicians, however.

33rd MAU ACTIVATED MARCH, 1975

III MAF Commander activated the 33rd MAU, to be commanded by Colonel Al Gray, for operations and deployment off the South Vietnamese Coast with Amphibious Readiness Group Bravo (ARG Bravo). Initially, 33rd MAU was comprised of Battalion Landing Team 1-9, Logistics Support Unit 3-9, plus two helicopter squadrons, HMM-165 and HMM-463 and they set sail for the operating area. ARG Bravo shipping included the amphibious transport dock USS *Dubuque* (LPD 8), the amphibious cargo ship USS *Durham* (LKA 114), and the tank landing ship USS *Frederick* (LST 1184).

Concurrently, the 9th Marine Amphibious Brigade, under Brigadier General Richard E. Carey, a Marine aviator who had served in Korea as an infantry officer, was activated for planning in order to participate in a long-anticipated training exercise designated MABLEx 2-75. Originally intended for the entire MAF, the absence of the 31st and 33rd MAUs aboard ARG shipping in the South China Sea, meant the MABLEx would be downgraded to a Brigade-level event. It would resemble the exercise Al Gray had participated in the previous November and December, MABLEx 1-75. The ground combat element of 9th MAB would be Al Gray's Regimental Landing Team (RLT) 4, composed of BLTs 2/4, 1/9 and 3/9.

However, the 9th MAB staff soon was planning for more than an exercise: Southeast Asia was ablaze.

Soon after General Carey and 9th MAB were activated for planning, however, the situation in Vietnam went from bad to critical. During his initial planning conference, Carey warned everyone to be prepared to conduct night operations, thinking darkness might provide a significant advantage for the American helicopters.[33] At the time, however, 9th MAB remained a planning unit, with no operational control of any subordinate units. Rather, it was Al Gray and the 33rd MAU which became the focal point for all Marine Corps-related operational activities directed toward Saigon.

Figure 6.12
Company D and elements of Headquarters and Service Company march down the pier
at White Beach, Okinawa on 25 March 1975, to embark in USS Blue Ridge *(LCC*
19). As members of the Amphibious Evacuation RVN Support Group, these Marines spent
the next 13 days at sea recovering refugees evacuating northern South Vietnam.[34]

Figure 6.13
U.S. Marines Board CH53 Sea Stallions for flight to Cambodia.[35]

Figure 6.14
Evacuees from Cambodia arrive aboard USS Okinawa. *U.S.* [36]

Figure 6.15
Acting Cambodia President, Saukham Khoy depearts USS Okinawa. *He's flanked by wife*
and son, Saukham Van Roeunn (left) and Long Botha, Cambodia Minister of Culture.[37]

Figure 6.16

American Ambassador to Cambodia,
John Gunther Dean arrives
aboard USS Okinawa.[38]

Figure 6.17

American evacuee from Cambodia arrives aboard
UUS Okinawa *clutching prized poodle.*[39]

Figure 6.18

Cambodian evacuees in
berthing compartment
aboard USS Okinawa.[40]

Despite the close cooperation between the ambassador and the military in Cambodia, which resulted in a successful evacuation, the story in Saigon was far different. The American Ambassador there, Graham Martin, had thrown up road-block after roadblock in order to deny visits by military commanders. That was despite the fact that the situation in Saigon was much more complex and fraught with many more potential problems than those in Phnom Penh. In the fall of 1974, the III MAF G-3, Colonel John M. Johnson, Jr., had been able to make a quick trip to Da Nang and other cities. He returned with a dire assessment of conditions there. Johnson's report, combined with the continuously poor appraisals made by Vice Admiral George Steele, the Commander, United States' 7th Fleet, and ominous intelligence reports being received from sources inside and outside South Vietnam gave Al Gray and every other Marine good reason to expect, and plan for, the worst.

In the Republic of Vietnam, on the other hand, there were potentially millions of evacuees who would need to be taken from the jaws of the advancing North Vietnamese. At his original planning meeting for Saigon and South Vietnam, Colonel Gray was struck by the enormity of the humanitarian challenge that the 33rd Marine Amphibious Unit would face. Gray's planning guidance foretold of up to one million people would be need of assistance and evacuation. While indications were that a fixed air evacuation would start soon, there was no way that air transports could fly out a million refugees. While Gray met with the III MAF staff, and his friends within the intelligence community, to get current intelligence estimates and operational briefings, the North Vietnamese Army was slicing through northern South Vietnam. Several divisions of NVA regulars were in the process of rolling up the ARVN units that opposed them. While no one knew exactly how the NVA forces would react to a humanitarian evacuation, Gray knew he had to plan for the worst.

Facing the NVA challenge, III MAF had at most six infantry battalions that could be made available to the Ground Security Officer for Saigon. Of the six, only two or three were optimally ready to deploy south. Marine combat units on Okinawa go through an annual training cycle that begins with new officers and men being assigned to a unit, then starting pre-deployment training in earnest before being tested to ensure they were ready to deploy. Following a several month deployment aboard ship, the unit was returned to Okinawa where the unit would be in reserve as it began to transition personnel back to the U.S. and new people arrived, thus starting the process anew. Gray well understood that only a single infantry battalion would be part of the 33rd MAU. However, in his estimate of the situation, he recognized that if, indeed, the worst-case humanitarian disaster might unfold, that is, embarking a million people while under attack from the advancing NVA, then a Marine Amphibious Brigade or even a Marine Amphibious Force size unit would be needed. Thus, much of his planning involved making the 33rd MAU the nucleus for a much larger force.

The Marine Corps invented close air support prior to World War II. Gray realized that if the evacuation came under fire from the NVA, he would have overpowering air support for his ground forces. Not only would the naval air assets of the U.S. Navy's 7th Fleet, but USAF aircraft in Thailand could easily reach the Saigon area. As Gray studied the situation, he became increasingly confident that the combination of air power and Marine ground forces would be sufficient to stop the NVA. As the planning for the operation advanced, Gray continually revised his estimates, but throughout he remained confident of Americans' ability to handle the military threats that might arise.

As Colonel Gray went through the planning process, he also quickly determined that current, accurate tactical intelligence would be of the essence. Of course, the Americans in South Vietnam were passing intelligence to the U.S. military, and Americans were monitoring activities from listening posts throughout Southeast Asia; nevertheless, the situation on the ground was changing so rapidly that no one had a good handle on precisely what was happening in the old I Corps area of South Vietnam. Al Gray, who always tried to make a personal reconnaissance in advance of any operation, knew that he would have to diligently and persistently gather tactical intelligence at every opportunity, from every source.

One of the very serious challenges facing the Americans was related to the anti-air threat. Everyone knew the NVA had a very capable anti-air capability; that was made abundantly clear during the entire war from 1965 through 1972. One question, for example, not readily answered was whether the NVA would deploy the newest Soviet anti-air systems.

The Yom Kippur War of 1973 introduced the world to a new family of Soviet anti-aircraft weapons that had played havoc with the Israeli Air Force, despite which Israel had prevailed in the end. Given that the Soviets were the leading arms supplier to the NVA, American commanders were unsure of what capabilities awaited them. The entire Vietnam War had been one of action and reaction with respect to American air power and North Vietnamese anti-air defense, and at various times each side had held the advantage. Now, in early 1975 the Americans again faced uncertainty as its intelligence sections attempted to weigh the enemy forces.

With ARG Alpha and ARG Bravo already at sea, there normally would have been a dearth of backup naval vessels. In 1975 that was not the case because, periodically, the Navy would extend the stay of outgoing amphibious ships in the Western Pacific (WestPac) in order to have sufficient shipping to conduct the planned MAF level exercise. Without the extension, the Navy could support only a brigade-level event. When the ships' time in WestPac was lengthened, there was a relative wealth of amphibious lift available to the Marines, permitting heightened flexibility to Pacific Region commanders. On April 3, the USS *Midway* (CVA 41) had been alerted for operations and was ordered to prepare to be sent south from its home base in Japan; when *Midway* steamed past Okinawa, she took on Marine Helicopter Group (MAG) 36.

MILITARY PLANS EVACUATION, EARLY APRIL, 1975

Although Ambassador Martin remained vehemently opposed to taking any action that might suggest Saigon would be evacuated, by April 1975 it was clear to many military professionals that the chances of the South Vietnamese holding off the NVA aggression were nil.

In early April, Colonel Gray, as Commanding Officer of the 33rd MAU, and four of his officers were assigned to augment the 9th MAB staff. Gray accompanied General Carey on a quickly arranged trip to the Philippines to meet with the Commander Task Force (CTF) 76, Rear Admiral Donald B. Whitmire on April 4th.[41] General Carey had not previously worked with Whitmire, the big, gregarious former All-American lineman at both the Naval Academy and the University of Alabama. But Gray knew both the Admiral and his staff very well as the result of participating in MABLEx 1-75. The Admiral liked the hard-charging Marine Colonel, and usually referred to him, in private of course, as "Al Baby."[42] They forged a close professional relationship. Though the situation was very clear for Al Gray, it was somewhat confusing to historians. The 9th MAB was still not operational, though Gray and his staff provided concurrent, parallel planning that forecast the requirements for both the MAB and 33rd MAU.

By April 8th, Al Gray found himself triple-hatted. He was the Ground Security Officer (GSO) for Saigon, the Commanding Officer, 33rd MAU, and Commanding Officer of the ground combat element (RLT-4) under 9th MAB. In his role as the MAU Commander, the only operational headquarters then activated for operations, Al Gray controlled all the Marine Corps helicopter assets then located in the South China Sea. Gray was also assigned to augment 9th MAB on General Carey's staff, but 9th MAB was still in a planning status. Shortly after the 33rd MAU was activated, III MAF planners and Commander, 7th Fleet drew up preparations for the

35th MAU. An exception to Gray's control was the 31st MAU then positioned in the Gulf of Thailand in anticipation of operations in Cambodia.

Al Gray was still in Subic in the Philippines when the USS *Hancock* (CV 19) arrived on April 6, 1975. Operating from a large deck attack carrier was a highly unusual occurrence for a MAU, and Gray wanted to ensure that things went smoothly. There were, indeed, problems to be solved. *Hancock* was one of the Navy's attack carriers, meaning that it normally carried a mixed air wing consisting of attack jets, fighters, refueling and electronic warfare aircraft, and a single helicopter used for safety during flight operations. Some of *Hancock*'s air wing had been left in San Diego when the carrier left port. Then, when the ship was transiting through Hawaii, Marine Medium Helicopter (HMM) Squadron 453 had flown aboard. On the approach to Subic Bay, the remainder of the carrier's air wing flew into the Naval Air Station at Cubi Point; subsequently, additional Marine helicopter assets were placed aboard. Besides the helicopters, about 500 Marines from 1st Battalion, 9th Marines, part of BLT 1/9, the 33rd MAU's ground combat element, went aboard the big flat top.

Hancock was under orders to transit to the Gulf of Thailand to support ARG Alpha and the 31st MAU, awaiting operations in Phnom Penh, but first Al Gray went aboard to coordinate with the Captain and check on requirements that would be needed to transform *Hancock* for an amphibious role. There were several issues, and the ship's Commanding Officer seemed none too happy about his orders. His ship was an attack carrier, and he would have preferred to keep it in that role.

The captain raised an objection to conducting helicopter operations, citing the fact that he did not have a "helicopter direction center" (HDC). Even though the ship was well equipped to conduct fixed-wing operations – it had been doing so dating back to World War II - and while every carrier has a helicopter aboard for flight safety purposes, the captain was concerned about launching and recovering multiple rotary-wing aircraft in a safe manner. Gray took action that satisfied that deficiency by arranging to have a HDC flown out from Hawaii on an emergency basis. The HDC was an air-transportable shelter operated by a Marine Air Control Squadron that could be carried by cargo planes and then placed where needed, afloat or ashore; in this case, the HDC would be located on *Hancock*'s flight deck. Colonel Al Gray diffused captain's second issue in a much more straightforward, much more direct, some would say "Al Gray" way.

The Commanding Officer of the *Hancock* had locked all the officers' (pilots) staterooms when the *Hancock*'s aircraft wing was sent ashore. Consequently, when the Marines pilots flew aboard, they had no place to rest. The squadron personnel, including the pilots, were directed to use the metal surfaces in the hangar deck as their berthing area. The situation was completely unacceptable to Al Gray. He understood that BLT 1/9's infantry, who typically carried "rubber ladies" with them, could obtain a modicum of rest while sleeping on the hangar deck, but pilots and air crewmen required real cots and beds.[43] Those aircrews, Gray knew, would be flying long hours under stressful conditions, and he demanded that the unused staterooms be made available to the Marine aviators. The captain refused.

Al Gray directed a MAU officer who was accompanying him "to go and retrieve some primer cord." When the captain asked why he needed primer cord, Gray responded that he intended to blow the locks off the stateroom doors. The naval officer suddenly saw the situation in a new light, this time from Gray's perspective. A crisis was averted and Marine pilots were made comfortable. But there was always something else to do. With the berthing settled, *Hancock*, with Gray aboard, departed Subic for Vietnam. Upon arrival off Vung Tau, South Vietnam, Gray cross-decked to the 33rd MAU flagship, the USS *Dubuque*, while the *Hancock* continued on to the Gulf of Thailand.

On 9 April, six additional Marine helicopter squadrons were placed under Gray's command. He remained the senior Marine whose command had been activated for operations. On 13 April, 33rd MAU reported to 9th MAB for planning, but Gray remained responsible for all helicopter operations except those of 31st MAU, just returning from operations in the Gulf of Thailand. Despite the hectic activities and overall uncertainty of impending events, Gray and Carey, and their superb staffs, worked meticulously to prepare for the worst-case scenarios that might arise. The continuous, concurrent, parallel planning was greatly assisted by the fact that most of the team knew each other and had worked together before the previous fall, during MABLEx 1-75. Indeed, there was a great rapport and sense of camaraderie among the Navy and Marine staffs. It had been Gray's suggestion that they work together before and after exercises, and that idea paid tremendous dividends when push came to shove in Southeast Asia. When the American components in Thailand were added to the planning, Gray's exceptional professional knowledge not only of Navy and Marine capabilities, equipment and procedures, but also those of the United States Air Force, went far to ensure efficient use of the staff's time and resources.

ARG Bravo and BLT 1/4 had returned from their humanitarian operations off northern South Vietnam. Thousands of Vietnamese and many Americans had been picked up at sea and taken to a small island near Thailand. Lieutenant Colonel Charles E. Hester's men had performed an arduous, demanding and often dangerous job with aplomb and professionalism. Along the way the Marines also assisted several American commercial ships that had no military presence aboard, in one case saving the ship from being commandeered by ARVN soldiers who had run amok. When the ships finally put their displaced guests ashore, ARG Bravo hastened to Subic Bay to pick up the remainder of 33rd MAU's ground element, Lieutenant Colonel Royce L. Bond's 1st Battalion, 9th Marines. [44]

Also on April 9th, the *Hancock* had departed for the Gulf of Thailand while the rest of the 33rd MAU, now embarked on ARG Bravo shipping, sailed for the seas off Vung Tau. BLT 1/9 would serve as the reserve for the Cambodian operation. Al Gray, having moved aboard *Dubuque*, immediately arranged to visit the capital. It was never too early to start intelligence gathering.

Figure 6.19
*Colonel Gray with a friend from Air America, Tan Son Nhut, 1975. In
a huge coincidence, Gray had met a man whom he had previously
known during an earlier Vietnam tour while visiting Laos.* [45]

Because of the restrictions placed on American military visitors to Saigon by Ambassador Martin, getting to and from the Vietnamese capital was not straight-forward. Indeed, it turned out to be tortuous. Ambassador Martin was reluctant in the extreme in permitting military officers into South Vietnam; Al Gray was forced to conduct all his personal reconnaissance trips in civilian clothes. Whenever he was within helicopter range of Saigon, which included each day after April 10th, Al Gray went ashore. And while liaising with 9th MAB was something he naturally did during the first half of April, Gray actually worked for Admiral Whitmire, the CTF 76 Commander.

Figure 6.20
Air America helicopter. Helicopters were indispensable in the planning,
preparation, and execution of the Saigon evacuation.[46]

Going ashore meant flying in aboard an Air America helicopter, usually a UH-1, that was designed for flying over land, not over water. The Air America birds were all single engine aircraft flown by pilots not familiar with open sea flying. There is good reason that Navy and Marine Corps helicopters are dual-engine; such configuration means that a single point failure does not doom the crew and passengers to a watery grave. On several occasions an anxious Al Gray was pleased to see the gray topsides of the Navy ships. Once, for example, after Gray had departed Tan Son Nhut for his return to *Blue Ridge,* the Admiral had decided to move his force further out to sea; no one checked with Al Gray to find out his position or expected arrival time. Gray, happily, made it aboard, thanks to the professionalism of his Air America pilot.

The typical day for Colonel Gray started with an early morning intelligence briefing of what had happened overnight. The Cambodian operation, *Eagle Pull,* was nearing a climax, and Gray was eager to hear how the results of that operation and how the enemy had reacted. He would also meet with the S-3, S-4, and logisticians to determine what cross-decking operations were needed. The 35th MAU and its ARG had joined CTF 76 and 9th MAB at sea and was not optimally loaded, and Gray took the lead in planning major cross-decking requirements essential to effective MAB operations. There was no finality to how the evacuation would proceed, or even what the size of the force needed ashore might be. Thus, Gray and his staff had to plan for every contingency, including an amphibious landing in the Vung Tao region. If, in fact, there were to be a million evacuees, there was no way helicopters alone could bring such a number to safety; amphibious landing craft would have to be used.

After the intelligence and logistics briefings, the Air America chopper would arrive. Initially, the Colonel maintained his Headquarters aboard *Dubuque,* but after 9th MAB moved to the Vung Tau area on April 10th, Gray moved to the *Blue Ridge,* where Whitmire and Carey were collocated. Gray would make the approximately 90-minute trip to Saigon, always ensuring to look over the ARVN and Vietnamese Marine bases at Vung Tau and the river access to the capital, as well as trying to spot any large formations of ARVN or NVA near or around Saigon.

Figure 6.21
Newport Pier Complex.[47]

Once the helicopter reached Tan Son Nhut, Gray usually landed at the DAO Compound, but he also visited the Embassy, the ARVN Command Center and other key locations. Typically, he begged or borrowed a car, often a sedan with a driver from United States Aid for International Development (USAID). In that form of transportation Gray could readily move around the city and its environs discretely causing no alarm, thus satisfying Ambassador Martin's inflexible limitations on visits by military officers. On one occasion, Gray decided to see how far he could get driving from Saigon to Vung Tau, almost 75 miles by car, along the route that took him near Bien Hoa, which had been a large U.S. Army base in earlier years. Gray and driver arrived at the peninsula without incident, confirming in Gray's mind that the ARVN still controlled that vital access route although he noted considerable Viet Cong activity along the way.

Returning to *Blue Ridge* each night was not Al Gray's choice. Both flag officers were hungry for news, and there was no better source than a first-hand report from the CO of 33rd MAU. The three elephants in the process, as far as the Navy-Marine planners offshore were concerned, remained these questions: (a) how many evacuees could be brought out, (b) how would the NVA react to the presence of American forces, even though their mission was humanitarian, and (c) when would the operation kickoff. Each passing day seemed to complicate those issues, not resolve them.

One of Gray's early stops in Saigon had been to visit the detachment of the National Security Agency. NSA had approximately 30 analysts spread throughout South Vietnam in April 1975. Of course, events around Da Nang and the former I Corps area, and the attacks in the Central Highlands, had sent all Americans, not just NSA representatives, scurrying for safety. There were no Americans advising ARVN or Vietnamese Marine tactical units – indeed, there was a specific prohibition against such activities – though there were a number of Americans from the USAID, the Central Intelligence Agency, and American civilian contractors left throughout the country. From the NSA representatives, Gray sought the technical information about enemy communications that would permit his embarked SIGINT/EW detachments to perform their work more effectively. However, the Marine was surprised to learn that the Americans had turned over all responsibility for the technical aspects of SIGINT to Unit 15, the ARVN *Dancers* with whom he had worked closely in 1967 and again in 1969. Moreover, Gray learned that Unit 15 was still functioning effectively, still flying airborne missions against the NVA and still processing tapes and radio intercepts. But things were changing fast, and not for the better.

Ten days before Gray's arrival in Saigon, Commander-in-Chief, Pacific, Admiral Noel Gayler, had issued a warning that the Republic of Vietnam could fall in as few as five days. Admiral Gayler recommended to the Defense Attaché, Major General Homer Smith, United States Army, that the evacuation of non-essential Americans and Vietnamese begin in earnest.[48] General Smith had directed Brigadier General Richard M. Baughn, United States Air Force, to take charge of evacuation planning. Baughn and his staff, aware that there was no useable evacuation plan, began working at a frantic pace, with the full knowledge of the Embassy's staff. Baughn had been frustrated about the lack of evacuation planning for months, but Gayler's warning finally prompted action, even at the Embassy. On April 11, Gray flew into Saigon and met with General Baughn.[49] Gray was also happy to see an old friend.

Among the officers that Gray encountered from the Defense Attaché Office (DAO) was his former classmate from the Army War College, Colonel Pat Howard. Howard, the senior Marine on Major General Homer Smith's staff, was working for General Baughn, the Deputy Defense Attaché and senior Air Force officer. General Baughn was anxiously trying to establish evacuation plans and procedures, and Howard was assisting, having relieved Colonel Paul L. Siegmund, USMC, in March 1975. In addition, Lieutenant Colonel Bill McKinstry, an old friend that Gray had known when McKinstry was a Lieutenant in the 1st Force Reconnaissance Company in the late-1950s, Major Jamie Sabater, and Captain Anthony (Tony) Wood, both in Saigon, were deeply involved in evacuation planning, as was Major Ed Grimm, who was Lieutenant General Burns' Action Officer Planner in Nakhon Phanom, Thailand. Everyone on the staff was doing yeoman work related to getting people out of the country.

Though Baughn's assignment at the DAO was logistics oriented, as were all his American counterparts then assigned to Saigon, Dick Baughn was a proven combat leader. As a young officer, he flew P-51s in Europe during World War II, and at the start of the American phase of the Vietnam War he was a squadron commander tasked with bombing North Vietnam. Dick Baughn had a good feel for combat and for war, and he realized in early 1975 that South Vietnam was losing its fight for survival, though that view was not one that the Embassy permitted to be promulgated or even discussed openly. Baughn was happy to see Colonel Al Gray, even if Gray was obliged to wear civilian clothes in accordance with Ambassador Martin's wishes.

General Baughn, however, while loyal to and trying to abide Martin's orders, soon ran afoul of the Ambassador's wishes. Baughn recalled that Al Gray was most interested to learn the total number of Americans and Vietnamese to be removed from country, a number Baughn had long tried to discover, though the powerful figure in charge of the American Embassy had thwarted his efforts. Baughn recalled, "The Marines were very concerned about the number of Americans still in Vietnam and an unknown number of loyal Vietnamese who would have to be evacuated. They believed that if they had to evacuate such large numbers it would be a high-risk situation for everyone concerned." Besides evacuees, there was another pressing issue related to Air America pilots. There simply were not enough pilots to support the clandestine trips into Saigon by the Marines, and Al Gray sought to have some of the MAU pilots augment those at Tan Son Nhut, and sought permission to accomplish that action. Action on several fronts was needed: General Baughn and Al Gray prepared a message for release to the world; it addressed the growing security needs at the DAO Compound and included the call for evacuation.

"I asked the Colonel to show the message to Martin's DAO monitor, so the monitor could designate who in the Embassy should see the message before its release. Keep in mind, now," Baughn said, "the monitor was the person who was supposed to insure that Martin was kept informed of all DAO actions. But for some reason, he (the monitor) did not see fit to show this message to Martin, although it had to be the hottest topic on the embassy's list."[50] When Dick Baughn heard that the message had not been shown to Ambassador Martin, he was happy; after all, Martin might not have approved its release. The enigmatic Martin did, however, read the communication later that night.

At 2 A.M. the next morning local time, General Baughn was awakened to learn that he had an urgent personal communication. A message from Lieutenant General John W. Roberts at Headquarters, United States Air Force, in Washington directed Baughn to be on the next airplane out of South Vietnam. Martin had called the Secretary of Defense, James Schlesinger, and demanded General Baughn's removal.[51] As a result, Al Gray would be working even more closely with Pat Howard going forward.

As General Baughn knew, and Al Gray quickly confirmed, the number of South Vietnamese who might need to be taken out of the country remained potentially very large. But with Ambassador Martin still reluctant to show his hand that the Americans were leaving, removing all the Vietnamese who worked for America and who would be in grave danger was almost impossible. Already the number of abandoned children (mothers tossed babies over the fence where they were caught and taken to the bowling alley, which became a nursery) was producing significant problems, and the staff at DAO was increasingly overwhelmed. The crash of a plane in what was called *Operation Baby Lift* was tragic, but it did not deter Vietnamese mothers from trying to get their babies out of the country.[52] By keeping a virtual lid on the fact that the United States was withdrawing, Martin condemned many former allies to horrible fates.[53] The Ambassador's actions, or rather his lack of action, also appreciably complicated the potential for a looming disaster.

With Baughn no longer the point of contact, Al Gray worked with four Marines extensively. Colonel Pat Howard along with Lieutenant Bill McKinstry, were now filling the key evacuation-planning roles for General Smith, while Major Jaime Sabater and Captain Tony Wood were doing yeomen's work outside the DAO Compound and inside the city of Saigon. They had arrived at a series of contingency plans involving the Newport Dock area along the river, where seagoing vessels could safely reach the city from Vung Tau. Additionally, Sabater and Woods had conceived of a series of rooftop landing sites on some buildings downtown; the idea was that small Air America UH-1 helicopters could land atop the buildings to take out refugees who would unite at those points. Al Gray thoroughly checked all these sites, and spent a great deal of time figuring out how to defend the area around the Newport Dock. The rooftop landing sites were of less concern because Marine choppers were too large to use most of them, while securing the sites would have been largely impossible. Sabater and Wood tirelessly reconnoitered land routes from the city to the DAO Compound, and they were out each night ensuring the routes were still passable. A central part of the evacuation plan was that anyone requiring evacuation, including those at the Embassy, would go to the DAO Compound. There was no thought given to defending or evacuating the embassy compound, because Ambassador Martin had agreed to the plan to move everyone to the DAO Compound.

A fourth Marine, Lieutenant Colonel Anthony Lukeman, another of Gray's classmates at Quantico, was the senior advisor to the South Vietnamese Marine Corps. He spent most of the final month ensuring the defenses at the seaside base at Vung Tao were in order, an important assignment that took him away from the capital. As home to the Vietnamese Marines, Vung Tao and its surrounding peninsula represented the most formidable and challenging evacuation site in terms of its size and complexity. While during the planning process it received a large percentage of the attention of the staffs, Vung Tao never became the focus of the evacuation.

Can Tho, a large town 50 miles southwest of Saigon along the Bassac River, was yet another possible evacuation point for up to 2,000 people. Can Tho was reachable by either river craft or helicopters, and Gray made sure to overfly the area during his frequent visits to Saigon. However, Can Tho never became a hub for 9th MAB efforts.

The Newport Dock area of Saigon would be used if ships were needed as a result of large numbers of Vietnamese requiring evacuation. Almost two weeks after Admiral Gayler has issued his dire warning, Marine planners still had no idea of the numbers of Vietnamese to be evacuated! The whole tactical scenario at the docks would be fraught with multiple dangers. Because that eventuality might come to pass, however, Gray took extra time to ponder exactly how he would defend the area, as well as the river egress routes. Such a scenario, combined with helicopters to be used to take Americans out of Tan Son Nhut, surely would demand more than a single Battalion Landing Team.

It should be emphasized that at no time did the U.S. Embassy and its grounds figure into evacuation planning. The Ambassador had agreed that in the event Americans would leave Saigon, only he and perhaps a small staff would remain at the Embassy. Everyone else would withdraw by bus or other means to the DAO Compound. No one foresaw the possibility that the Ambassador might change his mind at the last minute.

Gray did almost all his reconnaissance work in and around Saigon unaccompanied, but for his driver. There was more than sufficient work for all involved, especially the beleaguered DAO Staff, though Al Gray did not need assistance. Colonel George Slade, the Commanding Officer of 2/4, remembered Al Gray during the operation with this quote, "Al Gray did not need a staff. He carried 3x5 cards in his pocket and as he looked around or asked questions, he would jot things down on those cards. I never saw his notes, but I think Al Gray could have run the whole operation without a staff, just by relying on those cards." Slade, a Command & Staff College graduate, also remarked, "Al Gray knew more professionally than all the Command & Staff College instructors combined."

Throughout his professional life, it was not unusual for Gray to operate independently, without staff or aides. In fact, when Lieutenant General John H. Miller was interviewed about his remembrances of Al Gray, he said, "Do you know that Al Gray was a renegade general? Yes, as a general officer he would go months without having an officer aide, he would just use his enlisted driver as an aide." Thus, it was hardly abnormal or in any way out of the ordinary for Al Gray to roam around with neither aides nor attendants.

During one of Gray's initial visits to Saigon, he went to the Embassy to liaise with the wide variety of people who operated there. Lance Corporal Kenneth Crouse was manning Post #4, the vehicle entry gate. Crouse was relatively new to Saigon, having arrived in February 1975 with several other recent graduates of the Marine Security Guard School. With things looking more and more sobering in the north, the Marines at the Embassy were no longer rotating their posts. Each Marine was assigned to a specific post, and each typically served 12 hours on duty and then 12 hours off, but always at the same post. When a sedan with USAID marking approached the gate, Crouse was surprised to see Al Gray in civilian clothes sitting in the front seat. Without requiring Gray to show his Identification Card, the young Marine waved the car through the gate. Gray stopped, however, and approached the Lance Corporal asking, "Why didn't you check my ID, Marine?" Crouse replied, "Sir, I recognized Colonel Gray from my time in the 4th Marines on Okinawa last year." With that, Gray gave the younger man a punch on the shoulder and went inside to do his business.[54]

While the physical challenge of the schedule Gray maintained was formidable enough to wear out most men, the stress of the evacuation planning was even more taxing. There were so many unknowns. The timing of the operation and the number of Vietnamese remained worrisome, ambiguous and unsettled. Although *Blue Ridge* was off Vung Tau on April 10th, Gray was critically short of a ground maneuver element for 33rd MAU. BLT 2/4 was conducting *Operation Eagle Pull*, with BLT 1/9 in reserve. BLT 1/4 was in Subic, and did not have its heavy attachments. If the Republic of Vietnam collapsed during the period April 10 through April 15, things would have been mighty sticky for Al Gray and the Marines who were charged rescuing people.

On April 13, General Carey, accompanied by Gray, made his only planning trip into the capital, where they held a brief, and thoroughly unproductive, meeting with the seemingly irritated American Ambassador. The trip did serve to provide Carey with a first-hand view of the areas where operations would most likely occur – the DAO Compound, the Newport Docks and the Vung Tau peninsula. They also met with General Smith and the CINCPAC "observer," Rear Admiral Hugh G. Benton. Neither Smith nor Benton provided any tactical or operational insights to the forthcoming events, however.

NVA ATTACKS TOWARD SAIGON, APRIL 1975

While Al Gray pondered a plan, NVA columns streamed toward the capital; the ARVN defenders to the north of the city had simply collapsed. At Xuan Loc on April 9th, the NVA attacked the 18th ARVN Division, which fought well and hard though outnumbered and outgunned. Indeed, a week later the NVA push appeared to be stopped, at least temporarily. While President Thieu remained in the city, and the ARVN high command spoke of making a stand, none of the Americans had any confidence in a positive outcome; still, Ambassador Martin remained intransigent against permitting any mention of evacuation planning. Had not the Marines arrived offshore, and had not the Defense Attaché permitted, even encouraged, his staff to plan for the worst, the situation would have eventually been far more appalling. However, ongoing evacuations using Air Force transport aircraft continued despite the tragedy of *Operation Baby Lift* and the number of Americans remaining in the Saigon was going down daily.

The daily trips to the capital provided significant benefit to the Americans, however. Gray knew many of the South Vietnamese officers and quickly befriended those he did not know. As a result, he was able to obtain the best information – intelligence – possible related to the positions and capabilities of the enemy units located near and around Saigon. Adding to this intelligence, more American resources began to arrive.

On 16 April, a 26-man detachment from 1st Radio Battalion arrived aboard *Blue Ridge*. The SIGINT/EW detachment, led by Captain John J. Folan and Master Sergeant Albert S. Harvick, had taken a route that can only be described as circuitous to reach the ship. Folan had previously been the Officer-in-charge of the Marine Detachment on the ship, and for him it was like old-home week. The cryptologists barely had time to get settled, however, before the *Blue Ridge* was on the move.

The conditions in South Vietnam had seemingly stabilized, at least to those viewing the situation from afar. *Operation Eagle Pull* had been successful though Cambodia had been relinquished to the communists, though without the loss of American lives. Al Gray was proud of the efforts put forth by his 2nd Battalion, which aboard ARG Alpha shipping was on its way to Subic Bay for some much deserved liberty. With the NVA apparently stalled at Xuan Loc, Admiral Whitmire received permission for *Blue Ridge* to return to Subic for much-needed engineering repairs to the ship. Al Gray, still functioning independently of the 9th MAB, transferred to *Dubuque* and remained off Vung Tao.

THE DEATH OF THE REPUBLIC OF VIETNAM

WASHINGTON, 1974 AND 1975

Saigon fell on April 30, 1975, and that date generally marks the death of the Republic of Vietnam. Believing that to be true would be a mistake. The death of the Republic of Vietnam should be marked by the date that the United States signed the Paris Peace Accords, which supposedly stopped the fighting in South Vietnam while achieving peace with honor. That date was January 27, 1973. No one objectively assessing the military situation that came into being immediately after the Accords were signed would ever doubt the eventual outcome, given that the United States refused to live up to its obligations under the Accords to provide military support to its former ally.

Despite President Thieu's strong protests against the Accords, Nixon, Kissinger, and the American Congress rendered Thieu's position completely untenable. Notwithstanding the gains made during the period that Creighton Abrams was in command in Saigon, and regardless of the flood of equipment, much of it useless, provided to both the Army of Vietnam (ARVN) and the Air Force of Vietnam (VNAF), neither force was sufficiently mature to meet the NVA threat. No doubt that the South Vietnamese shared a large degree of the responsibility for their lack of readiness, but in the opinion of many senior Marines, the principal problem had been the lack of focus by General Westmoreland and the American commanders during the period 1965 through 1968.

Westmoreland's primary efforts were directed at defeating the North Vietnamese and Viet Cong on the battlefield. Among the American military and civilian hierarchy, improving the efficiency and effectiveness of the ARVN and VNAF were little more than afterthoughts. Further, when Americans advised their allies on the composition and organization of the Republic's armed forces, they schemed to have the South Vietnamese imitate their American counterparts, an unbelievable blunder. There was never, during that early period before General Abrams took command, any attempt to coordinate operations or gradually improve ARVN tactics and supporting arms techniques. While the American military commander in Saigon practically ignored his counterparts, two American Presidents consistently and passionately stressed their everlasting support to South Vietnam's government and their South Vietnamese counterpart. Perhaps the confusion and lack of focus by the South Vietnamese President in Saigon was at least a little understandable.

After the events of Watergate broke into the news in April 1973, President Nixon paid very little attention to South Vietnam. He was not only trying to manage the consequences of the burglary, he was also moving ahead in developing new relationships with China and the Soviet Union. Even before the Paris Peace Accords were concluded, Nixon was determined to leave a legacy that involved opening China to American trade and establishing a new bond with that communist regime. Nixon's trip to Beijing in February 1972 and his meeting with the Chinese communist leader, Zhou Enlai, had been historic. Indeed, Nixon and Kissinger calculated that by improving U.S.-Chinese relations, they could further isolate the primary political target for American foreign relations, the Soviet Union. Following a policy called *Détente*, Soviet-American tensions were eased and the high water mark of the relationship between the two superpowers reached in June 1973 when Nixon and his Soviet counterpart met at a summit hosted by the Americans.

While most of Nixon's admirers stress his foreign policy achievements, he was equally active on the domestic side of politics and had many notable accomplishments in that arena, including the establishment of the Environmental Protection Agency and the Department of Energy. Certainly, Nixon was preoccupied by many things other than events in Southeast Asia, and why not? Henry Kissinger had assured him that the Peace Accords represented the best deal possible for the Americans. Besides, the easy, politically expedient thing to do was to declare victory and leave the South Vietnamese to their destiny; and that, to his everlasting dishonor, is precisely what Nixon did.

Even if Nixon had wanted to support his former allies, the Congress was intent on ending the drain on the American treasury. After all, it was not any senator or congressman who had declared their undying support for America's ally. Plus, cutting off funding to the South Vietnamese earned the Congress the admiration and support of that all-important faction in the Fourth Estate – the American Press. Between 1973 and 1975, Congress reduced funding for the South Vietnamese by over 60%. At the same time, North Vietnam was receiving an increase of up to 70% in the assistance they got from China and the Soviet Union. Clearly, the highly emotional Congressional critics of President Thieu, led by Senator Edward Kennedy of Massachusetts, were determined that getting United States troops out of the war was not enough. Only by also starving the government in Saigon would those critics be happy.[55]

Nixon, increasingly trapped by Watergate and having moved on to focusing on China and the Soviet Union, appeared oblivious to the rapidly deteriorating military conditions that faced President Thieu. Kissinger? Well, the illustrious Secretary of State had suggested that the Nixon Doctrine, which supposedly would protect South Vietnam in the event of exactly what was happening at the end of 1973 and into 1974 – North Vietnamese aggression – was something that he had concocted and something he could change! So much for being loyal to a longtime ally.[56] While Nixon and Kissinger repeatedly hyped the Paris Peace Accords by touting the end of the war as having achieved "peace with honor," in fact they had done neither. South Vietnam faced 150,000 NVA inside its borders, and on the attack.

As Nixon increasingly became the target of the 6 o'clock news and congressional investigations, he grew more isolated and less involved. His first Vice President, Spiro T. Agnew, had been forced to resign over allegations of corruption while he served as Governor of Maryland. On November 27, 1973, the Senate confirmed Nixon's appointment of Gerald R. Ford, the House Minority Leader, as Vice President. When Nixon's fatal flaws drove him from office on August 9, 1974, it would be Gerald Ford who was left holding what remained of the American position in Vietnam. Kissinger, by then the Secretary of State and the de facto National Security Advisor as well as Chairman of the Joint Chiefs, continued to lead the U.S. policy toward Southeast Asia.

In December 1973, as a result of the Paris agreement, Henry Kissinger and his North Vietnamese counterpart, Le Duc Tho, were awarded the Nobel Peace Prize even though peace was far from settled. There would be thousands of deaths throughout South Vietnam within 16 months after the Paris agreement. Signing the Paris Peace Accords was simply a means to an end; the communists never intended to abide by the agreement.

When in late 1974 and early 1975 the communist invasion plan crystallized, Ford was unable to muster any support in the Congress to defend South Vietnam in any way, shape or form. Why South Vietnam had earned the enmity of many in the American Congress, the American media, and the American people, is inexplicable.

SAIGON AND SOUTHEAST ASIA, 1973 - 1974

Even after the peace agreement, South Vietnam was under attack from North Vietnam. As early as the end of 1973, the ARVN were losing up to 100 casualties per day in fighting in the Mekong Delta, while in that area of South Vietnam that had been I Corps when the Americans were still engaged, the fighting grew in intensity as 1973 turned into 1974.

The communists were never sure of the reaction of President Nixon to their open aggression. After all, Nixon had proven surprisingly decisive after their *Easter Offensive* of 1972, and the resulting bombing campaign had both shocked and confused the communist leadership while reducing North Vietnamese infrastructure to rubble. No, the communists were not uncertain as to what Nixon might do, but the NVA was intent on probing, especially in the Central Highlands and the Mekong Delta. While they continued attacking, they also all the while kept an eye to the sky, fearing the return of American air power.

President Thieu was committed to protecting all the territory of South Vietnam. In 1974 alone, he lost 31,000 of his best troops trying to do just that.[57] By ordering his forces to defend his entire country, Thieu fell into the same trap strategically that Jefferson Davis made in the American Civil War. Thieu simply lacked the resources to defend everywhere against an invader who both outnumbered and outgunned his defenders. The ARVN, though fighting well and courageously when properly led, had committed all its strategic reserves, the Airborne and Vietnamese Marine forces, long before 1974 came to an end. The Central Highlands were largely held by the NVA, along with areas north of Quang Tri City. In addition to dwindling supplies, an over-extended Vietnamese Air Force (VNAF) was incapable of providing the support necessary. Thieu and the senior ARVN staff simply had not be given enough time to develop the next generation of combat leaders needed at the regimental and battalion levels.

While President Thieu struggled to devise a strategy to meet the North Vietnamese aggression, the NVA became ever bolder. By 1974 they had constructed a petroleum pipeline into South Vietnam, and what had been footpaths in early times of the war became paved, all-weather highways. The critical weaknesses that had exposed the communists during their offensives in 1968 and 1972, namely their inability to logistically support their forces, had been eliminated. Furthermore, it was becoming more and more apparent to the leadership in Hanoi that American air power – so decisive in supporting earlier ARVN operations – was now missing from the battlefield.

The bigger mistake that Thieu made was putting his trust in American leadership. As the events of the Watergate scandal swirled out of control, forcing Nixon to resign in August 1974, the Congress became increasingly, even more stridently anti-war. Thieu clung to the repeated, though privately given, assurances Nixon had conveyed to him that the United States would not permit South Vietnam to fall. Unfortunately, neither the Congress nor the Department of State were aware of Nixon's promises. Perhaps Thieu would have taken alternative measures in defense of his country, or perhaps South Vietnam would have collapsed more quickly had Nixon not made his grand gestures to the Vietnamese President. Almost certainly the U.S. Congress was not going to come to Thieu's rescue regardless of the circumstances. Thieu, unlike his predecessor, Ngo Dinh Diem, was not adept at reading the American tea leaves.

As the American politicians dithered, the South Vietnamese government alternated between denial that the North Vietnamese could defeat them and hope that the Americans would never abandon them. American military leaders, on the other hand, were trying to realistically plan for various contingencies. But throughout 1973 and 1974, and even well into 1975, Ambassador Graham Martin in Saigon worsened the difficulty of such planning with respect to the Republic of Vietnam. All the while, new President Gerald R. Ford thought Martin was planning for a large-scale evacuation of those Vietnamese whose lives would be in danger in the event of a communist takeover. That was simply not happening, whatever those in Washington thought.[58]

Indeed, in retrospect it seems that the U.S. Department of State and Ambassador Marsh thought the worst outcome in Saigon would be a coalition government where the South Vietnamese would share power with the communists. However, anyone familiar with Vietnamese history, and the persistence of the communists, should have discounted that possibility.

Throughout the summer of 1974, Vice Admiral George P. Steele, the Commander of the 7th Fleet, and Major General Herman Poggemeyer, Jr., Commanding General of III MAF, tried to determine the effectiveness of the Embassy's evacuation planning. The Ambassador repeatedly denied permission for American military officers to enter Vietnam to gather information, stating that planning for such an eventuality would create the fall of Vietnam that he was there to prevent. Nonetheless, after many requests, Martin relented and Colonel John M. Johnson, Jr., the III MAF G-3, was permitted to visit the country in September 1974. What Johnson found, in almost every category, was appalling. Johnson's report pushed Admiral Steele to visit Saigon personally. The Admiral concluded that the Defense Attaché, Major General Homer D. Smith, United States Army, was both competent and helpful; but Steele also thought the Ambassador's attitude was unrealistically ambivalent toward the rapidly dissolving military situation.

Throughout 1973 and 1974, the United States Support Activities Group (USSAG) at Nakhon Phanom, Thailand, had been developing contingency plans for the possible evacuation of South Vietnam, Cambodia and Laos. The USSAG had also formerly had the designation 7th Air Force, but a coup against the military government of Thailand had raised Thai sensitivities toward the United States conducting offensive operations into bordering countries; as a result, the 7th Air Force designation had been dropped. USSAG, though, had been selected as the command responsible for future operations anywhere in Southeast Asia.[59]

Admiral Steele, who well understood it would be his subordinate units, not USSAG's, that provided most the forces should an evacuation be ordered, asked to be designated the primary commander for such operations. Despite that, Admiral Noel A. Gayler, Commander-in-Chief, Pacific, confirmed that USSAG should command future operations in Saigon and Phnom Penh, leaving Admiral Steele nothing but to commit to his best efforts to support USSAG. Gaylor's decision certainly complicated future ventures in and around Saigon.

As 1974 faded, the military situation in South Vietnam and Cambodia could not have been worse.

NOTES AND REFERENCES

1. Official Marine Corps photograph.
2. Author interview with Colonel Richard L. Jaehne, USMC (Ret), June 2011. Jaehne had just arrived and been assigned to 2nd Battalion, 4th Marines shortly after the arrival of Al Gray. He was told of the situation in the barracks by those who had been there before Gray assumed command.
3. CG, THIRD MARDIV, message dated 280330Z Feb 75. General Kenny Houghton used a 6-page message to recommend Colonel Al Gray for the 1974 John Paul Jones Award given each year for outstanding leadership by the Naval League. The message enumerates all of Gray's accomplishments while at Camp Hansen. From General Gray's private collection.
4. In common Marine slang, the Philippines are called the "P.I." – short, of course, for the Philippine Islands.
5. From General Gray's private collection.
6. See Chapter 4, this volume.
7. Understanding the roles of all the "Commanding Generals" at a place like Okinawa can be difficult for civilians, and even Marines. Colonel Gray reported through two chains of command. As CO of the 4th Marines, his immediate boss initially was Major General Fred Haynes, Commanding General of the 3rd Marine Division. General Haynes was responsible for the training and readiness of the Division. Initially, Major General Herman Poggemeyer was the Commanding General, III Marine Amphibious Force, and therefore Haynes's boss. General Poggemeyer commanded and was responsible for any Marine units actually deployed in the Far East; all Marine Amphibious Units and Brigades were General Poggemeyer's to command, and that included the 3rd Division and the 3rd Air Wing at the Marine Corps Air Station, Futema, Japan.

During Gray's time on Okinawa, General Poggemeyer was relieved as III MAF by General Carl W. Hoffman in December 1974; General Haynes was relieved in August 1974 by Major General Kenneth J. Houghton. On the other hand, Brigadier General Harold Hatch was the Commanding General, Marine Corps Bases, Japan. General Hatch oversaw all the bases, their physical assets like the barracks and the buildings, the mess halls and clubs, all the administrative things necessary to operate bases in Japan. Lieutenant General Louis Wilson, Commanding General, Fleet Marine Force, Pacific, commanded all the operational forces in the Pacific region. On the bases and administrative side, another general, at that time it was Major General John N. McLaughlin, was Commanding General, Marine Corps Bases, Pacific.

8. In General Gray's oral history at National Security Agency (NSA), dated 30 August 2010, speaking of the curfew, General Gray is quoted as saying. "And General Hatch, he never forgave me for that, but he went along with it, but that's the way it was." On one occasion General Hatch noted, "Although periodically assigned various other tasks which took him away from the camp, he was able to constantly provide the guidance and supervision necessary to keep everything working smoothly. He is a tireless worker that has spent nearly every night of his 13-month tour concerning himself with what the troops of his camp were doing, and making every effort to keep them out of trouble. He has given major emphasis to totally successful secondary education programs and to establishing outstanding rapport with the civic and business leaders of Kin-son." General Hatch might not have forgiven Al Gray for implementing the curfew, but he also thought extremely highly of his camp commander.

9. General Houghton repeatedly referred to Gray as the "premier colonel" in the Marine Corps.

10. The DoD schools fulfilled the needs of the dependents of predominately soldiers, Sailors, and Airmen; there were few Marines assigned to Okinawa with dependents. All Marines in the 3rd Marine Division and III MAF, for example, were on unaccompanied tours of duty. But there were major Air Force and Navy installations and most the Airmen and Sailors assigned to them had their families on Okinawa.

11. Marine Corps Base, Camp Butler, Base Bulletin 1560, 48/RWF/sab, 12 December 1974.

12. Jaehne interview. Jaehne was skeptical at first about troops losing training time to school, but was soon convinced of the benefits.

13. As late as the 1970s, a common alternative to criminal prosecution was enlistment into the military by the accused.

14. The author was an instructor at The Basic School during the period August 1973 to July 1974. Many of the second lieutenant students, who were all college graduates and who had recently entered active service, would not have been permitted to re-enlist in the Marine Corps if they had been enlisted men. Their General Classification Test scores were not high enough. It was not just the enlisted ranks that suffered from the lack of educational achievement that General Gray's actions to establish a high school on Okinawa addressed.

15. Author interviews with Sergeant Major Calvin Lynn (2011) and Ken Crouse (2011). Sergeant Major Lynn would serve again with General Gray in the 2nd Marine Division in the early 1980s, and General Gray was present for his retirement ceremony at Camp Lejeune in 1988. Crouse would see General Gray again much sooner, even though Crouse left Okinawa in January 1975.

16. Gray not only stopped and talked, he also assisted his men when they needed money. Enclosed in a letter dated January 31, 1975, was $25. L/Cpl Michael A. Babincsak of Bravo Company, 1/4, penned the letter which read in part: "Dear Colonel Gray: I am the young Marine that you ran into last week in town. I would like to extend my appreciation for your help in person, but it is rather hard to do so, you being a Colonel in the Corps. Therefore, I would like to extend my gratitude from the bottom of my green

Marine heart; and I hope we don't have to meet again under the conditions which prevailed that night. I hope to meet you, Sir, when I make NCO. Than you very much, Sincerely, ..."

17. "Smokers" were hugely popular boxing matches held within various Marine and U.S. Navy units. Aboard ship, there were often matches between the embarked Marines and the fleet Sailors. The champion from all the Marine units would box the champion from the amphibious squadron. Cheers and jeers, bets and catcalls, accompanied the matches. The preliminary matches, usually between troops that had little boxing experience and even less expertise, were particularly popular; winners earned the respect of their peers while losers were treated sympathetically, if not sensitively. Becoming a division boxing champion was no small thing.

18. From General Gray's private collection.

19. In those days, individual, not unit, replacement was still the norm. Officer and Staff NCO rotation to and from Okinawa normally occurred during the summer when Marines' dependents are out of school.

20. When George Slade was a young Captain, the Marine Corps photographed him as a 1st Lieutenant in order to make a recruiting poster using Slade's image, in dress blues carrying a sword.

21. From General Gray's private collection.

22. General Coffman stated that Colonel Gray was exceptional and specifically mentioned Gray's skills at planning and executing the events, and he went on to say that he "would be honored to serve with him at any time, in any place or war." They had a great relationship.

23. From General Gray's private collection.

24. Picture courtesy of the Alabama Sports Hall of Fame: http://ashof.org/index.php?src= directory&view=company&srctype=detail&refno=169&category=Football.

25. From General Gray's private collection.

26. Colonels Steve Olmstead, Ed Bronars and David Twomey had many exceptional staff officers involved in the process.

27. From General Gray's private collection.

28. From General Gray's private collection.

29. Many exaggerate and embellish their "stories" about Al Gray. Even General Louis Wilson, Medal of Honor recipient and retired Commandant of the Marine, embellished his "Al Gray story." General Wilson had been Gray's recruiting officer, but after his retirement, whenever General Gray's name came up, Louis Wilson would proclaim, "I recruited Al Gray off the streets of New York." Author telephone interview with Mrs. Jane Wilson, March 2009.

30. *The Bitter End*, p. 107.

31. Map adapted from History and Museums Division, Headquarters, United States Marine Corps original.

32. Author interviews with Colonel George P. Slade, USMC (Ret) 2008-2010, and Colonel Richard L. Jaehne, UMSC (Ret), May 2011.

33. *The Bitter End*, p. 66.

34. *The Bitter End*, p. 86.

35. U.S. Navy photo by PH3 Paul Salesi.

36. U.S. Navy photo by Lt. Cmdr. Tony DeMarco.

37. U.S. Navy photo by PHC Don Hays.

38. U.S. Navy photo by PH3 Paul Salesi.

39. U.S. Navy photo by PH3 Paul Salesi.

40. U.S. Navy photo by PHC Don Hays.

41. Task Force 76 encompasses all the amphibious shipping that is part of the U.S. 7th Fleet.

42. Author interview with Colonel Lloyd Earl (Jerry) Goodwine, United States Marine Corps (Ret), September 2010. As a Lieutenant Colonel, Jerry Goodwine was the senior

Marine officer on Admiral Whitmire's staff in 1975 during *Operation Frequent Wind*. An unabashed Al Gray acolyte, Colonel Goodwine also has many interesting stories about Admiral Whitmire, an officer he greatly admired and respected.

43. "Rubber ladies" are air mattresses and many grunts carried them for use in the field. Even in combat, more than a few Marines chose to rely on their rubber ladies and not sleep on the often cold or wet ground.

44. For an in-depth look at the humanitarian efforts conducted by the "Amphibious Evacuation RVN Support Group" see *The Bitter End*, pp. 85-98.

45. From General Gray's private collection. On one of his early trips into Saigon in 1975, Colonel Gray was surprised to hear someone say, "Major Gray, it that you?" Turns out that the man calling him was a Cambodian who worked for Air America and met "Major Gray" during operations in 1964.

46. U.S. Navy photo from the USS *Hancock* (CVA-19) 1975 Cruise Book.

47. From General Gray's private collection.

48. Larry Engelman, "The End of the Golden Chain," interview with Brigadier General Richard Baughn (September 2009), *Pushing On*, http://lde421.blogspot.com/2009/09/general-richard-baughn-2.html. Dr. Larry Engelmann has a very interesting series of three interviews with General Baughn. Unfortunately, there was no love lost between CINCPAC, Admiral Gayler, and Ambassador Martin. Baughn heard Martin refer to Gayler as "that polo-playing admiral." Gayler never visited Saigon except when Martin was out of the country. When on April 1 Gayler issued the warning that the country might fall within five days, Martin ignored it. Both General Gray and General Baughn express great respect for Admiral Gayler; however, their views of Ambassador Martin are more divergent.

49. Engelman interview with General Baughn. *Pushing On* Internet blog.

50. Engelmann interview with General Baughn. *Pushing On* Internet blog.

51. "Later General Baughn heard from General Roberts that Martin had telephoned the Secretary of Defense and asked him to get rid of Baughn immediately. Martin had read the Baughn message in his file that night and called for his removal. Baughn concludes, "If I had it all to do over again I would do exactly as I did before. I was determined to avoid any further risk to the thousands of Americans and loyal Vietnamese and I was determined to avoid at all costs grandstand plays for lost causes, bureaucratic face-saving schemes, dim-witted intrigue or senseless demonstrations of bravado. The longer we continued Martin's head-in-the-sand policy, the further we put thousands of Americans and loyal Vietnamese at risk. "In complete disgust," Baughn said, "I decided to retire early." "Some thought that Martin had a vested interest in hanging on in Vietnam," Baughn says, "because it would be his last hurrah. Others thought he would try to avoid being chased out of Vietnam at almost any cost due to his arrogance and irrational determination to establish his place in history. Representative Paul McCloskey, who visited Saigon while I was there, said that he thought Graham Martin was demented. General Louis L. Wilson, who was with the Commander-in-Chief of the Pacific Air Forces, once visited Martin. "As General Wilson and I drove away from the Embassy, Wilson shook his head and said, 'I have now met my first egomaniac.'" One official, Baughn remembers, who knew Martin well, said that 'Martin was one of the few men who could stand in the shadow of a corkscrew.'" Engelmann interview with General Baughn, *Pushing On* Internet blog. Al Gray never was told why General Baughn was suddenly gone.

52. On April 4th, a C-5 Galaxy crashed shortly after takeoff from Tan Son Nhut. The flight, dubbed *Operation Baby Lift*, killed 138 of 314 passengers, including all but one of 37 women from the DAO staff who had volunteered to accompany the babies. Besides the horrific loss of life, the crash significantly affected morale at the DAO Compound. Soon after, more children were being dropped off at the Compound as parents sought to get their kids out of the country. Incoming flights afterwards included baby formula and pallets full of diapers. *Bitter End*, p. 156-7.

53. General Baughn's Vietnamese maid knew that Ambassador Martin had sent many of his most valued personal belongings out of the country, so many were aware that Martin's personal actions did not reflect his public stance. Engelmann interviews with General Baughn.

54. Author interview with Ken Crouse, October 2011.

55. James H. Willbanks, *Abandoning Vietnam: How America Left and South Vietnam Lost Its War*. University Press of Kansas, 2008. Dr. Willbanks, a retired U.S. Army officer and Vietnam veteran, provides both the most compelling and the most thorough treatment of the last years of the Republic of Vietnam, 1968 through 1975. For discussions about the U.S. budget, see pp. 213-7.

56. Langguth, p. 565.

57. Willbanks, p. 223.

58. Douglas Brinkley covers in some detail the American politics related to Congress and the Nixon and Ford Administrations and their affect on the war in Vietnam.

59. *Marines In Vietnam: The Bitter End*, p. xxx.

CHAPTER 7

THE END OF A LONG WAR
THE DEATH OF THE REPUBLIC OF VIETNAM

THE END OF A LONG WAR

Colonel Al Gray listened intently as Rear Admiral Don Whitmire and Brigadier General Dick Carey told him the news. The powers that be, probably as the result of pressure exerted by civilian leadership, demanded that only a single rifle company provide the security for the helicopters that were to be used to evacuate unknown numbers of Americans and South Vietnamese from Saigon. The evacuation operation, which might start at any moment, had been planned, refined, and evaluated continuously for the past month.

Al Gray had personally visited Saigon numerous times during the past three weeks. He very well knew that since the end of the fixed-wing flights out of Tan Son Nhut airbase, the Marine and Air Force CH-53 and Air Force HH-53 helicopters, would be the mainstays for the planned mass departure. Gray had personally reviewed and supervised the establishment of 18 landing sites for the big helicopters in the area near the Defense Attaché Office Compound and DAO Annex, and the ground in between them at the mammoth airbase.

Gray also was aware of the panic that would likely greet the news of the American departure from South Vietnam. No one knew precisely how many evacuees there would be, nor could anyone predict how the rank and file of the South Vietnamese armed forces might react. In other words, the potential for a crowd control disaster existed, and in spades.

Moreover, Gray was sensitive to the potential for a military confrontation with the North Vietnamese Army that was streaming toward Saigon from three directions. Though the South Vietnamese Army had bloodied the NVA noses at Xuan Loc, the ARVN loss there was the final straw that caused President Thieu to flee his country on April 21st. Al Gray could not be sure how the NVA, supremely confident and drugged by the success of their recent string of victories, would react to the presence of a fleet of American helicopters – even if they were on a humanitarian mission.

More thoughts rolled through his mind; after all, it was Al Gray, not Admiral Whitmire or General Carey, who was charged with the responsibility of Ground Security Officer. At some point every evacuation turns into a military operation, and it would not be the Secretary of State, or politicians, or even senior military commanders whose lives would be at risk. No, it would be Al Gray's Marines, Sailors, and Airmen who would be called upon to display grace under pressure, and perhaps face an aggressive enemy while completing their planned humanitarian mission.

Al Gray certainly would follow his orders and the very tight Rules of Engagement, which were designed to minimize any potential military confrontation with the NVA, but he would not abide putting his Airmen, and his Marines and Sailors on the ground, into harm's way with an inadequate force to protect them should trouble arise. A single rifle company could not even begin to protect the two designated CH-53 landing zones at the DAO Compound and the DAO Annex. More importantly, a single company could not provide crowd control while having sufficient maneuver capability and firepower to deal with the immediate threats. Furthermore, the close encounter with an enemy rocket propelled grenade during the flights out of Phnom Penh was a constant reminder of the dangers lurking at the edge of the landing zones. No, a single company would never do to complete this mission.

"Sorry, sirs," Al Gray replied to the flag officers, "we either conduct this mission as planned, or we don't go at all."

9th MAB ACTIVATED, APRIL 18, 1975

Conditions in Vietnam had deteriorated almost as soon as *Blue Ridge* reached Subic, to undergo engineering repairs on the April 16. Colonel Gray with his 33rd MAU and ARG Bravo shipping remained off the coast of South Vietnam in the vicinity of Vung Tao peninsula. The Navy was ordered to leave Subic within 48 hours of arriving in port. The battle of Xuan Loc finished badly, and NVA columns were approaching Saigon from two other directions.

With 9th MAB staff on *Blue Ridge*, ARG Alpha shipping, augmented by the aircraft carriers *Hancock* and *Midway*, all in or around Subic, the Commanding General, III MAF, decided to reorganize his forces. First among those actions was to activate 9th MAB for operations. With the activation, Brigadier General Carey assumed command of all Marine forces assigned to conduct evacuation operations.

Simultaneously with the commencement of 9th MAB operations, Major General Houghton, acting in General Hoffman's absence, ordered that the ground combat element be constructed around Colonel Al Gray's Regimental Landing Team 4, which would consist of BLT 2/4, BLT 1/9, and BLT 3/9. Colonel Hans G. Edebohls, who had been Commanding Officer, 35th MAU, was assigned to command the Brigade Logistics Support Group, while Colonel Frank G. McLenon headed the Provisional Marine Aircraft Group 39. While the organization of units became streamlined, there was still much work to be done. The 9th MAB had to literally be formed at sea, which had never been done before, with 3 Marine Amphibious Units as part of its core capability.

Only the 31st MAU, aboard ARG Alpha and just returned from *Operation Eagle Pull*, was "combat loaded." Combat loaded refers to the way the Marine forces and their equipment are carried on the ARG ships; it means the ships are ready to conduct amphibious operations ashore. Conversely, "administrative loading" is usually done for speed and efficiency with little thought to amphibious operations. The speed with which 33rd MAU loaded out and the fact that the 35th MAU was administratively loaded from the very start (its communications equipment, for example, was stored in the bottom of the ship and could not be off-loaded if needed ashore in a timely fashion), meant Gray and his staff had the ships' crews and Marines continuously moving supplies, ammunition and equipment while at sea. After all, no one had ever formed a Naval amphibious taskforce, of this size, while at sea. The fact that there were two aircraft carriers available, and two Marine heavy lift helicopter (CH-53) squadrons that would be augmented, on April 20, by eight CH-53 and two HH-53 variants from the United States Air Force, provided great flexibility for any helicopter-heavy operation. While the ten USAF helicopters added significant lift capability, they took all the available space aboard *Midway*. The fact that the Air Force aircraft did not have foldable rotors, as Marine versions of the CH-53 do, meant that only the large deck aircraft carrier, with its larger elevators could move them to the hanger deck for maintenance.

There still was no clear indication of the type of operation that would be conducted, though it was increasingly obvious that an evacuation would be required. If saving large numbers of Vietnamese refugees became the final goal, then conducting operations ashore on Vung Tau Peninsula would probably be required. That implied substantial numbers of landing craft would be employed, and that a much larger number of Marines would be needed ashore, possibly having to defend the evacuation force against NVA attacks. Any operations at Vung Tau would be equipped much differently than if only a helicopter evacuation from Saigon was necessary. But what if both helicopter operations from Saigon and seaside evacuations were required? Gray and General Carey kept the planners busy making preparations for whatever eventuality would be encountered, still planning for the worst case.

Major John F. Guilmartin, USAF, led the flight of two Jolly Green Giant HH-53s from the 40th Aerospace Rescue & Recovery Squadron. Major Guilmartin and his USAF cohort were all highly experienced pilots and not in any way intimidated about flying off an aircraft carrier. However, when one of the more junior aircraft commanders forgot that he was taking off 40 feet above water level, and momentarily disappeared below the level of the flight deck before recovering, the Air Force pilots were reminded of the differences between carrier operations and those ashore.

The situation aboard the CTF 76 ships became so frenzied that Admiral Whitmire often would rub his hands together and ask, "What are we moving today, Al Baby?" Then-Lieutenant Colonel Jerry Goodwine, as the senior Marine assigned to Admiral Whitmire's staff, had a ringside seat to the inner workings of the CTF 76 and Brigade staffs during the run-up to operation. There was no doubt in Goodwine's mind who was driving the train: the energetic, hard-working, highly-professional Colonel of Marines, Al Gray. Though Gray served as Commanding Officer of RLT-4, he was also acting de facto as the Chief of Staff, 9th MAB.[1]

Figure 7.1

BGen Richard E. Carey hosts one of many planning sessions over Saigon contingencies conducted on board the USS Blue Ridge *(LCC 19). Seated to Gen Carey's right, from left, are LtCol Royce L. Bond, Col Frank G. McLenon, and Col Alfred M. Gray.*[2]

As 9th MAB returned to the seas off Vung Tau, no one was sure what kind of venture was in the wings. Gray planned on being able to meet whatever arose, still having to envision the worst, and such preparation involved lots of work. And by April 20th or so, it was clear that a MAB-level evacuation would be required. The result was that creating the MAB at sea had become an absolute necessity. There was no chance to return Subic Bay to combat load the ships, given the dire straits then existing in Saigon. Consequently, moving equipment among ships, or even within a ship, would usually require "cross decking." Helicopters would pick up equipment from one ship and carry it to another, where it might be stored temporarily while the first ship moved things around. When the first ship was ready to reload the original gear that had been removed for temporary storage elsewhere, it was returned. The entire logistics operation required detailed analysis of what the various MAUs had in the way of stores and gear, and moving it required close coordination among ships' captains and crews, the air wing and the Marine logisticians.

The RLT staff, consisting of the Administrative and Personnel Officer (S1), Captain R.D. Moran; his Intelligence Officers, Major Ray Porter and later, Captain R.D. Moran; the Operations Officer (Major James E. Livingston); his S-4 Logistics Officer, Major J.A. Murray; and his Air Liaison Officer, Captain J.F. Davis; his Fire Support Coordinator (Major J. Miller); and his versatile Communications Officer, Major John Whalen had done a superb job meeting the expectations of their very demanding, very operationally oriented Commanding Officer. This was despite the fact that the RLT Executive Officer; on April 13, Lieutenant Colonel Robert D. White had been assigned to serve on the MAB staff as the G-3 because he was an experienced planner. To fill that void, Gray double hatted John Whalen because of his overall professionalism and experience. However, building a doctrinally sound MAB while at sea could not have been achieved without the great work done by the Sailors aboard all the CTF 79 shipping, and the air crews who moved supplies, equipment and materiel among the various ships. The Marines could only say where they wanted things; the Navy had to perform the exertions necessary to execute the plans. In that regard, Al Gray was thankful that such a fine officer as Rear Admiral Don Whitmire led the Naval Task Force. Gray also had a deep appreciation for the superb professionalism of Whitmire's Senior Marine Staff Officer, Colonel Jerry Goodwine, who played a critical role in helping to create a MAB at sea. The Admiral, and his entire staff, were enthusiastic, positive and quite willing to "get on with" whatever needed to be accomplished.

One of the key decisions made during the final preparations involved communications. By 1975, American military commanders had the option to use either "secure" or plain-voice communications when talking over radio links. Earlier in the war, Americans' (and North Vietnamese's) only option was to use "plain voice" when talking on field radios or from aircraft. Plain voice is susceptible to enemy exploitation, and that is precisely the vulnerability that 1st Radio Battalion had used to great advantage. But make no mistake, the NVA were equally adept at exploiting American and especially ARVN radio communications.[3]

The technological advances made during the war permitted field and aircraft radios to operate in a "secure" mode. When the secure mode was used, the enemy had no idea when transmissions occurred, much less what was being said. Al Gray was by far the most knowledgeable officer in the operation when it came to both tactical communications and communications exploitation. Gray theorized that by using plain-voice mode, the NVA would know precisely what the Americans were doing and that there would be much less chance for confrontation with the enemy, whom Gray was sure would be monitoring American radio frequencies. Plus, by operating in the plain-voice mode, corrective action and necessary coordination could be accomplished more readily if, as it almost invariably happened, the communications should fail at some critical juncture. Consequently, Gray recommended that all the U.S. forces involved in *Operation Frequent Wind* place their radios in the plain-voice mode. Admiral Whitmire and General Carey readily agreed.[4]

In addition to operating in a plain-voice mode, Gray ordered that every unit down to the infantry squad level carry extra radios. Gray had long been an advocate of good communications and communications planning, and he had worked to ensure every unit he commanded, dating back to his days in Korea, had reliable, effective communications. In Gray's mind, better that the troops carry extra radios than have a circumstance where a single radio failure caused a problem.[5]

While building the ground component of a MAB while remaining at sea might have been more than sufficient to keep most commanders busy, it was far from all Al Gray had on his plate. In the days leading to the evacuation General Carey had the opportunity to visit Saigon only once, (on April 13), just prior to CTF 76 and CTF 79 returning to Subic Bay on the USS *Blue Ridge* for repairs and further coordination. The planning conference that ensued in Saigon had introduced the large cast of characters to each other, though the meeting left more issues than it provided answers. Additionally, President Thieu had fled the country and the NVA had been victorious at Xuan Loc. It was left to Al Gray to continue his daily business in Saigon to assess the situation and report back to the Commanders and Staffs on the flagship each evening. On one trip, Gray quietly evacuated Ambassador Martin's wife and her poodle to safety aboard the USS *Mount Whitney*. Throughout the ordeal, the Ambassador and Embassy still did not provide an estimate of refugees, though by then everyone knew there would be many.

Based on his extensive personal reconnaissance missions, and his contact with key military and civilian officials ashore, Gray's overall concept of operations as it evolved from a MAU to a brigade conducting joint operations was for RLT-4 to reinforce and secure the DAO Compound, the adjacent Air America complex and the entire Tan Son Nhut airbase. The plan included provisions for evacuating up to 100 people from the Embassy in the event some personnel did not make it to the DAO area. (It is critical to understand that the Ambassador had promised that the great majority of personnel would leave from the DAO compound and that it was never considered that the Embassy become a major evacuation point.) In addition, Ground Security Force elements had to be ready to deploy to the Newport Dock area if required, as well as to locations Can Tho and Vung Tao. Of course, all three areas would greatly complicate the operation and require a larger portion of the Brigade to be committed ashore. GSF units would have to be introduced by both waterborne and helicopter means. Indeed, if the situation at Vung Tao deteriorated, up to a brigade-sized unit would be landed over the beaches there by both sea and air assets.

On the bright side, Carey and Gray realized he had extremely capable air power at their disposal. Also, in addition to the Airforce Airborne Command, Control, and Communcations (ABCCC) capability that would be supervising the operations ashore, General Carey had taken steps to ensure that a USMC aircraft, with a Direct Air Support Center (DASC) aboard, would be available to help control air support. The Navy and MAB assets alone were significant, and the Air Force in Thailand could provide extraordinary capabilities in a very short time. There was also naval gunfire available to support operations in the Vung Tao region. That combination of firepower helped offset the critical absence of Marine artillery.

Although an estimate of the total people to be evacuated was never provided, it was apparent that a significant American military force might be needed to enter South Vietnam in order to bring its citizens and its allies to safety. RLT-4 had four infantry battalions standing by, with a total of six that could be called if events turned really ugly. BLTs 2/4, 1/9, and 3/9 were in the immediate area and ready to deploy ashore on order. BLT 1/4 was in Subic, but could be brought to Vietnam quickly: 3rd Battalion, 4th Marines and 2nd Battalion, 9th Marines, standing by on air alert on Okinawa, also could be rushed south in an emergency. With up to six battalions of reinforced infantry and a vast armada of aggressive, highly capable airpower overhead, Al Gray was comfortable that he had at hand sufficient firepower to meet any NVA threat.

In retrospect, Al Gray recalled the tremendous efforts of the staffs of RLT-4, 9th MAB and CTF 76. The 9th MAB/RLT-4 Operations Plan, the highly complex RLT-4/MAG 39 Helicopter Assault Tables and all related scheduling activities, were first promulgated on April 20th and continually refined thereafter, consistent with the dynamic, ever changing situation ashore. It was an extraordinary effort made possible only by the close working relationships all the staffs had developed, dating to the MABLEx the previous December. It is interesting to note that despite the enormous complexity and uncertainty of the situation that encountered the planners, General Carey and Colonel Gray directed execution of a simple operation order that was a page and a half, double-spaced, message. This op-order provided for a battalion-sized force to be landed simultaneously at 18 sites in the DAO Compound for security and commencement of the evacuation. These initial waves were followed by a daisy-like chain flow of helicopter operations and security personnel as required. The number of people to be brought ashore could be readily stopped, changed, or augmented as the situation dictated.

Consequently, as a result of endless staff planning and the hard physical work of Sailors and Marines throughout CTF 76, a restructured and powerful MAB had been formed at sea under General Carey. The superb orchestration of ships, helicopters, combat equipment, supplies and personnel had been conducted brilliantly, and the Americans stood ready for any eventuality. But over the final days in April 1975 events accelerated at an even more hectic pace as the NVA tightened their grip around the South Vietnamese capital.

THE FINAL DAYS, APRIL 20-25, 1975

As part of the 9th MAB's activation, III MAF had assigned Colonel Wylie Taylor, the Commanding Officer of the 9th Marines, as Deputy Commander of the Brigade and ordered him into Saigon. Taylor arrived there on April 21. Taylor's assignment was to coordinate with the DAO Staff in arranging the evacuation, but there was at least one major problem. Taylor was not familiar with any of the specifics of the MAB, from any proposed schemes of maneuver to how the ships were loaded and organized. With the operation likely to kick off any moment, Al Gray sent ashore his Operations Officer, the very capable and highly energetic Major Jim Livingston. Livingston, who had earned a Medal of Honor while leading Echo Company, 2/4 at the battle of Dai Do in April 1968, was both talented and thorough. Meanwhile, operating from the USS *Dubuke* and the ARG Bravo shipping that had remained on station off the Vung Tau peninsula, Al Gray had maintained his daily visits to Saigon even while the *Blue Ridge* had been in Subic. With the command ship now back on station off of Vung Tau, Gray moved back aboard the *Blue Ridge* on the 19th of April to keep the senior officers and their staffs current.

One trip to Saigon was decidedly unusual. Gray assisted the VNAF to load 55-gallon fuel cans into the back of their C-130s. The aircraft proceeded to overfly the NVA columns traveling down Routes 1 or 2 and kick the cans out the back. Though the results were not sufficient to turn back the assault troops, such tactics did give the NVA pause to consider whether U.S. bombers had returned. In fact, the NVA reaction gave Marine SIGINT personnel at least a little excitement as the enemy's communications security posture broke down in the face of the possibility of new *Arc Light* attacks from the Americans.[6]

One of the first things that Colonel Taylor and the DAO Staff requested was reinforcement of the DAO Compound by a platoon of Marines. This was much the same as the request that Al Gray had crafted and which had gotten General Baughn fired only 10 days earlier. After a four-day delay, on April 25, the request was approved and a platoon from Charlie Company, BLT 1/9 landed at the DAO Compound. In keeping with Ambassador Martin's wishes, they arrived in civilian clothes, though the platoon changed to utilities shortly after landing. The delay in granting the request, combined with the extraordinary circumstances of the Marines' attire highlighted how out of touch the American decision-makers were. Thousands of North Vietnamese were overrunning South Vietnam, yet Ambassador Martin, Secretary of State Henry Kissinger, Secretary of Defense James Schlesinger, even the Joint Chiefs of Staff, were seemingly oblivious to the situation.

President Gerald Ford made an attempt to put together a support package for South Vietnam, but the Congress was uninterested in lending a hand to a former ally, or, for that matter, in having America live up to its treaty obligations. If, indeed, there were going to be a humanitarian operation to remove countless Vietnamese who had assisted U.S. forces, it would have had to start immediately upon Thieu's departure. Instead, Martin and his bosses at Foggy Bottom dithered.[7]

9th MAB and Al Gray could do little but await orders. Meanwhile, General Smith, acting on his own initiative, had expedited the evacuation of thousands of American civilians and dependents of Americans and their relatives. Smith, for example, canceled the Post Exchange privileges of American retirees living in and around Saigon; the retirees, at least most of them, got the hint. The Department of State also approved the evacuation of orphans, especially those of mixed heritage who probably had been fathered by Americans.

In the meantime, in other areas of Vietnam, several acts of courage, dedication and professionalism were unfolding.

In the seas off the former I Corps area, an extraordinary event had been occurring. The Amphibious Evacuation Support Force (AESF) was saving literally tens of thousands of South Vietnamese – civilians and former military members. The AESF was the brainchild of Major General Carl W. Hoffman, the Commanding General, III MAF, who activated the unit on April 17 and attached it to 9th MAB. Earlier, in late March and early April, BLT 1/4 and the ships of ARG Bravo had saved thousands of Vietnamese, and General Hoffman realized an impending humanitarian disaster was in the making. Major General Kenny Houghton, Commanding General, 3rd Marine Division, had been tasked to organize and staff the AESF, and to command it he chose Major David A. Quinlan, the 9th Marines Operations Officer (S-3). Quinlan was a fine staff officer and his appointment turned out to be an exceptional selection. Quinlan organized ten 72-man detachments, each led by a captain or 1st lieutenant; the AESF also included a headquarters detachment and two 20-man sections. Each detachment was assigned to a United States Navy Ship (USNS) that was going to receive refugees.

The organization of the AESF was superb, but the execution of its assignments was even better. Quinlan benefited greatly from the experience that Lieutenant Colonel Charles Hester's BLT 1/4 had in late March and early April. Discussions with Hester and Al Gray led General Carey to assign the majority of his military police, interrogator-translators and counter-intelligence specialists to the AESF. Communication with harried, frightened and bewildered refugees was essential, and the interrogator-translators performed a vital service in keeping the evacuees calm and generally under control. The entire process, from the time the AESF picked up the refugees, usually at sea and under a wide variety of circumstances, until the time they were resettled, usually in the United States, was exemplary and made Americans proud, despite the other dismal circumstances in Vietnam. Quinlan, his Marines and Sailors could not have performed better.[8]

At sea, Vice Admiral George Steele's 7th Fleet was the major command, though Admiral Maurice F. Weisner, the Commander-in-Chief, U.S. Pacific Fleet, was also often nearby. In addition, there was ARG Alpha and ARG Bravo shipping, supplemented by many United States Naval Ships (USNS), which were manned by civilian crews. The USNS ships provided the capability for humanitarian rescues that AESF supported. In addition, the Navy not only provided the aircraft carriers *Hancock* and *Midway* to serve as helicopter platforms, but also the USS *Enterprise* (CVAN 65) and USS *Coral Sea* (CV 43) and their embarked air wings to provide round-the-clock air support. It was a formidable naval force, yet no details were overlooked. For example, although its air wing was in Subic (and San Diego) the *Hancock* provided its embarked Marine EA-6B aircraft to the *Coral Sea* in order to provide jamming and Electronic Warfare support for *Frequent Wind*. But not just the Navy would be supporting the evacuation force.

Because of the decision made months earlier by CINCPAC, Admiral Gayler, Lieutenant General John J. Burns, United States Air Force, Commanding General of the United States Support Activities group (the former 7th Air Force) in Nakhon Phanom, Thailand would have overall command of all forces ashore. Al Gray had known General Burns since Gray's visit to Nakhon Phanom and Cambodia in 1974; furthermore, Gray's detailed knowledge of USAF tactical capabilities and procedures aided the planning and coordination process immensely. Besides providing CH and HH-53 heavy helicopters used for the evacuation, the Air Force also provided an AirBorne Command & Control Center (ABCCC), commanded by a Brigadier General, codenamed "Cricket." Cricket ostensibly was to control helicopter ingress and egress routes, and among, other things, keep count of how many evacuees were carried out, and then pass the information back to General Burns in Thailand. USAF transports, mostly the ubiquitous C-130 Hercules but also including C-141 Starlifters and even some mammoth C-5 Galaxies (it was a C-5 that had been lost during *Operation Baby Lift*) would evacuate thousands of Americans and Vietnamese from Tan Son Nhut before the events of April 28 ended fixed-wing operations. Supporting the helicopters, transports and the ABCCC, General Burns's force could count 193 fighter/attack aircraft to assist the Marines ashore. When combined with the 125 sea-based fighter/attack planes the Navy made available, 9th MAB would benefit, if necessary, from overwhelming air support. Gray was not worried about the lack of naval gunfire or artillery; his men would have staggering amounts of air power ready and willing to take on NVA tanks and artillery. Still, things were not going as well in Saigon.

ALMOST GONE, THE AMERICAN PRESENCE IN SAIGON, APRIL 26, 1975

Almost gone, but not quite. By April 26, the Marine evacuation force knew that the chances of a very large-scale exodus of thousands more Vietnamese civilians was probably not going to happen; there was not sufficient time to organize the logistical effort that would be required. Getting ships upstream to the Newport Docks, or downstream to Can Tho, or moving thousands of civilians to Vung Tau were also increasingly less likely to occur. About this time, Gray's RLT-4 had been ordered to prepare to support a C-141/ C-130 fixed-wing evacuation. But the orders to execute never came, and as events rolled forward, the staff's focus began to narrow to a helicopter operation centered at the DAO Compound.

On the 27th, during yet another trip ashore, Al Gray knew it was time for the NSA representatives working with the ARVN's Unit 15, the *Dancers*, to leave. There was nothing the NSA personnel could do to stem the tide, and it was time to get its people taken to safety. Gray personally went to the combined NSA/Unit 15 operations center to tell the Americans it was time to leave. The first person that Gray saw after knocking down the "green door" was someone he knew well, Ralph Adams. Adams recalled that never was he so happy to see anyone as he was to see Al Gray that April morning. The NSA civilian had not known that Gray led the Marine evacuation force; he remembered Gray saying, "Ralph, we've come to take you out."[9]

Indeed, NSA's last representative in Saigon, Tom Glenn, had been quietly recalling his far-flung detachment ever since late March. Gray's appearance put a close to NSA activity in South Vietnam, and Adams was able to fly out on one of the last fixed-wing flights from Saigon. Adams vividly recollected that the *Dancers* were still at their posts, working against the NVA, when he departed later on the 27th. Tom Glenn and two communication technicians kept the NSA communications center open even after Adams and the other analysts had departed. Glenn, who also had a longstanding professional relationship with Al Gray dating back to the early 1960s, also was not aware that it was Gray who commanded the Marine infantry force, though during his final days in Saigon Glenn was seriously ill and not operating at peak efficiency.

By April 28th things were even more depressing, but still Ambassador Martin would not announce the evacuation. The government of the Republic of Vietnam had been in a shambles since the departure of President Thieu on the 21st. On the 28th, the Presidency had devolved to General Duong Van "Big" Minh. Not long after the ceremony installing Minh, NVA artillery started landing throughout the area; to add insult to injury, a flight of VNAF A-37 jets, flown by defectors, bombed Tan Son Nhut. Had there been any remaining question about the future of the Republic of Vietnam before April 28, there was none after. Without a shadow of a doubt, South Vietnam was lost.

Then, in the early morning hours of April 29, NVA rockets and artillery landed in and about Tan Son Nhut. Two Embassy Marines who had been assigned to augment security at the DAO Compound were killed instantly when a rocket exploded directly on the checkpoint they were manning. Corporal Charles McMahon, Jr. and Lance Corporal Darwin D. Judge were the last Americans killed on the ground in South Vietnam. At first light, their bodies were removed from the DAO Compound to the Seventh-Day Adventist Hospital; the decision was in accordance with the American Embassy's standard operating procedures for handling remains. Although these casualty reports were made to the CTF 76 and CTF 79 Chains of Command, no one told Colonel Gray about any Marines from the Embassy being killed until after the evacuation had been completed.

The same attack wreaked havoc on the airfield; one of three USAF C-130s waiting to be loaded with refugees, was destroyed on the runway. The other two departed immediately, empty. Indeed, soon all the runways were littered by bombs, weapons and abandoned equipment jettisoned by the South Vietnamese who had commandeered aircraft to fly to safety in Thailand. General Smith reported to the Ambassador that they must close the air base to fixed-wing operations. Still, Ambassador Martin, perhaps because he was ill, could not bring himself to make a decision to call for the departure of the Americans. Instead Martin went to Tan Son Nhut to get a personal briefing.

During his trips into Saigon, Gray often met with ARVN officers that he had known over the years. In almost every case, he offered to take these officers to safety, and in almost every case they would refuse. Gray was able to see some South Vietnamese soldiers and their families to safety. The "friend" he met at the airport (and seen in Chapter 6, Figure 6.19) being one. The Vietnamese culture placed a high value on family ties, and most Vietnamese were unwilling to leave their families for safety. Indeed, most ARVN officers, and certainly those in special units like the Rangers and Vietnamese Marines, were committed to fighting for their country – even if their senior leadership was not. That will to fight was seen to the bitter end, and the coming evacuation would have been much more difficult, and likely more American casualties would have been inflicted but for the fact that the ARVN around Saigon fought to the end. Former Premier and Vietnamese Air Force General Nguyen Cao Ky had flown his family out to the American naval force aboard a VNAF helicopter, but only did so when it was apparent Saigon would fall. Other brave South Vietnamese were not so fortunate.

Finally, on the morning of April 29 – after days of waiting and several hours wasted – Martin called Washington for instructions. The evacuation was ordered. Gray strongly believed the order came at least a day too late.

USS BLUE RIDGE, SOUTH CHINA SEA, APRIL 29, 1975

The operational decisions made in the final days before *Operation Frequent Wind* were critical. Al Gray made or influenced many of them.

The basic scheme of maneuver was fine tuned by Major Jim Livingston ashore of the DAO Compound, as required by events. The Air Officer, Major J. Miller, also did yeoman work throughout the operation. The Marines of BLT 2/4 were well prepared, right down to the fire team level. Each company commander, each platoon leader and squad leader, indeed, each fire team leader had been given pictures of his assigned position, pictures which included what the fields of fire for each unit would look like. Though none of the BLT officers or men had been on the ground physically, they knew the layout of the DAO Compound and the surrounding area much like the back of their hands.

Basically, the thrust of Al Gray's plan was to put as many Marines on the ground, with as much firepower, as was needed during the initial flights. Because the fixed-wing flights had evacuated many Americans and Vietnamese, and because fixed wing was no longer an option, Gray's scheme of maneuver was to land two rein-forced rifle companies and the BLT Command Group aboard the large CH and HH-53s as quickly as possible.

More than 800 Marines and Sailors would be on the ground in 8 minutes. The number of evacuees waiting at the DAO Compound was significant, but well within the total number that 24 Marine CH-53s, eight Air Force CH-53s and two Air Force HH-53s could manage during multiple sorties. The helicopters would land, dispatch the Marines and Sailors, then fill with refugees to return to their ships offshore.

The plan for the Embassy was simple, because at most 100 people were expected to be taken out from there: two CH-46 Sea Knights would land and take out the Ambassador and remaining staff. After all, according to the Ambassador's own plan, most the Embassy people would be taken to Tan Son Nhut aboard busses. Captain Gerry Berry would lead the flight of four Sea Knights, which included two aircraft loaded with Sparrow Hawk Marines.[10] The 9th MAB planners, and those of CTF 76, 7th Fleet and USSAG Thailand envisioned that the only major thrust for the evacuation would be at the DAO Compound adjacent to the large air base that supported Saigon; everyone was supposed to have departed the Embassy but for a very few personnel.

Early on the 29th, CTF 79 and 9th MAB were ready to go. Everyone knew that conditions in Saigon were deteriorating rapidly. Further, everyone knew that the longer the delay before launching *Operation Frequent Wind*, the greater the danger to all. When the relief force had arrived back in the seas off Vung Tau, 9th MAB was on a "six-hour" alert. However, the night of the 27th, Admiral Steele had lowered the response time to a single hour before sunrise on the 28th. As events seemed to stall, Steele relaxed the readiness to six hours. But later in the day, Admiral Gayler confirmed the urgency of the forthcoming operation by again reducing the response time to a single hour. That meant the Marines, helicopter aircrews, Sailors across the Fleet, fighter/attack crews in Thailand and at sea, everyone, had to be able to begin operations one hour after being notified.

Unfortunately, there remained major confusion about what "beginning operations" meant. To naval forces, "L-hour" designated the time helicopters or amphibious landing craft arrived at their destination. To the Air Force, "L-Hour" meant the time the aircraft lifted off from their bases. That there was confusion between the Air Force commander in Nakhon Phanom and the naval forces in the South China

Sea was perhaps the major planning failure leading up to the start of operations. The implications of the differing understanding of the term "L-Hour" had far-reaching repercussions both in Southeast Asia and, of course, in Washington, D.C.

Given the distance the Fleet was located offshore, it would take the aircraft a minimum of 30 minutes to fly to Tan Son Nhut. Loading the Marines would take additional time. The scheme of maneuver called for the troops to be carried ashore aboard CH- and HH-53 helicopters, and all those aircraft were located aboard large deck shipping – either aircraft carriers or landing platform helicopters (LPH). But the troops were berthed aboard smaller ships, where the H-53s could land only one at a time. Then, considering the time spent loitering while waiting their time to land on specific ships, the helicopters burned precious fuel. The concept was that after the troops had been loaded onto the aircraft, each would be refueled so that it left for Saigon topped off. Such action would permit the big choppers to make a round trip without having to refuel ashore. The complexity that extended the time needed to load the Marines was crucial to the goal of landing overwhelming force as quickly as possible. Otherwise, the Marines would have been fed piecemeal into the landing zones, offering a reduced footprint that could have been overpowered in detail.

General Carey received General Burns' order "to execute" at 1215 local time.[11] There had been an inexplicable delay from 1052 local time when Burns had actually issued the order before it appeared aboard *Blue Ridge*. Predictably, the howls from the armchair quarterbacks in Washington started almost immediately: what is taking so long? After having procrastinated for days, Washington now insisted upon instantaneous execution of the evacuation order.

After the directive had been given, every level in the chain of command from D.C. to *Blue Ridge* was demanding that 9th MAB provide a time for "L-Hour" (the time the helicopters would land at the DAO Compound.) The longer it took for the Marines to give an answer, the more pressure there was that the information be provided. Finally, Al Gray, doing some "back of the envelope" calculations based on his knowledge of the Helicopter Flow Table and flying time to Saigon, announced that "L-Hour" would be 1400. General Carey and Admiral Whitmire passed that information back up the chain of command; inside CFT 79, where everyone was already busy; indeed, things became frenetic.

At 1315, General Carey and Colonel Gray departed *Blue Ridge* aboard two UH-1N helicopters. They proceeded inland using the prescribed routes. Gray, as had been his custom dating back to his time in the Mediterranean, rode in the portside crew seat of his chopper. He was wearing his flight helmet and connected to various internal aircraft communications and could choose to listen to various tactical radio links. The trip to Tan Son Nhut was very familiar to him; after all, he had been making it daily since April 10. As the flight section started over the city center, Gray suddenly yelled "break left, break left" into the radio. Fortunately, both pilots immediately responded to the RLT Commander's firm order.

The UH-1Ns had been headed directly for the Presidential Palace, and Gray knew from his many liaison trips to the city that the Vietnamese had very capable anti-aircraft artillery emplaced all around the Palace with orders to shoot any aircraft attempting to invade the air space above the Palace. The security procedure had been implemented a few years before when a Vietnamese Air Force defector had attempted to bomb President Thieu's residence. Gray had briefed the UH-1N pilots about the danger, but on April 29 those pilots were not at the controls. More senior pilots, who probably thought it necessary to fly the mission since General Carey was aboard, had replaced them. Having escaped the danger over the Palace, as the pair of helicopters approached Tan Son Nhut, all could see that the airfield was under attack from artillery, rocket and small arms fire. Though neither aircraft took direct fire, the circumstances reinforced to both senior Marines that there was danger aplenty for the young men who would be following them.

One of the UH-1N pilots was Captain William A. Whitlow. Whitlow would rise to become a Major General before retiring from active service, but on April 29, as he flew into Saigon, with Colonel Al Gray, the pair heard an unusual voice on the radio. Gray's informal but almost always-used call sign was "Papa Bear." There was always lots of the radio chatter whenever Gray was on the move and various units checked in with Papa Bear. A thick German accent asked, "Who is this Papa Bear?" Gray could see the co-pilot who turned and watched as Gray gave him the "slashing throat" sign to kill the radio; Whitlow calmly changed the frequency and the Marines continued on their mission, unhampered by discussions with the powerful American Secretary of State. Kissinger would have to bother someone else to find the answer to his question.[12]

The hazard averted, the section of helicopters arrived at the DAO Compound at 1350, where the Marine commanders established an austere command post. While they were inbound, Admiral Whitmire had declared that L-Hour would slip an hour, and was scheduled for 1500. The Admiral had based his decision on the ongoing complexity associated with moving the helicopters around the task force. However, within minutes of landing, General Carey was notified that the first wave of 12 CH-53s was inbound to the DAO Compound. Delaying the first wave by an hour would greatly complicate matters, including adding the requirement that the big choppers refuel before making the return trip. Besides, the initial planeloads of refugees were formed and ready to go. After consulting with Gray, General Carey made the decision to land the first wave, and at a couple minutes after 1400, Marine helicopters from HMH-462 were spilling out the *Magnificent Bastards* of BLT 2/4. Not by coincidence, the same air-ground team that had performed so splendidly in Phnom Peng seventeen days earlier began securing the landing zones around the DAO Compound.

DEFENSE ATTACHÉ OFFICE COMPOUND & ANNEX, 1400, APRIL 29

There were 18 landing sites for the big CH and HH-53 helicopters. Each was assigned a specific site in accordance with the final plan promulgated by 9th MAB. And while the initial landings went off exactly as planned, almost immediately circumstances changed. The big choppers began to load evacuees after discharging their Marines. Helicopters were quickly loaded and the evacuation proceeded smoothly.

Figure 7.2
The first section of CH-53s approaches the DAO landing zones. At 1506 the first helicopters of HMH-462 touched down at the Alamo, officially beginning Operation Frequent Wind.[13]

After the second wave hit the deck, helicopter pilots landed their aircraft in any landing space available, and the simple "Daisy Chain" flow of helicopters proceeded to and from the amphibious shipping. As soon as each big bird was loaded at the Compound it took off to return offshore; not surprisingly, as the day progressed the passenger loading became more and more dense in terms of the number of refugees aboard each aircraft. Air Force Major John F. (Joe) Guilmartin thought during one flight his aircraft had almost 100 Vietnamese aboard.[14]

As the Marines flew ashore on the early waves, many saw the same incoming fire that General Carey and Al Gray had observed before landing. Despite being veterans of the Cambodia operation, the Marines of BLT 2/4 were, for the most part, new to combat. Several officers and Staff NCOs had, of course, seen action in Vietnam before the Marines departed in 1970, but most the men were nuggets, as they say – new to combat.

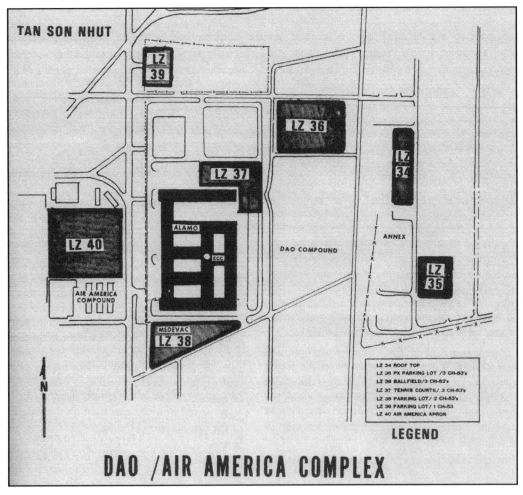

Figure 7.3
Preparations had long been made to ensure that the big H-53 choppers could safely operate in the immediate vicinity of the DAO Headquarters and DAO Annex. [15]

With the arrival of the second wave of 12 CH-53s, Lieutenant Colonel Slade reinforced his perimeter. And while the tall, calm, and cool Texan deployed his men in accordance with the original plan, it was the thorough preparation of each small unit that ensured efficiency. Though the helicopters had safely brought the grunts to the area safely, some were in the wrong landing sites. Despite the confusion, each commander knew where his men were supposed to go, and they took them there.

Second Lieutenant Tom O'Hara was the Executive Officer of Fox Company and reported this experience:

> *The pilot of the aircraft, an Air Force CH-53, he says we are going into LZ Bluebird and I looked at my map and realized that was Tan Son Nhut Airport and that was not where we were supposed to go. And he said we're landing. And I passed a message back up and said, "No we are not landing." Or rather, "We may be landing, but we're not getting off this thing." Sure enough they landed but we refused to get off. Then they took off again and took us to the DAO. I had argued with the crew chief. The crew chief said he was a major in the Air Force and I said, "I'm a 2nd Lieutenant in the Marine Corps and they're not getting off cause I'm not telling them to get off here." And I told him we wanted to go into the DAO compound and that is where he took us.*

> *I took my folks out and split them up into four groups and then we augmented the different platoons that were already there. The perimeter was already established. I was shocked to see the volume of people. As we were getting off, people were getting on, we were going one way and civilians were coming the other way. I was amazed it was that fast. I saw Colonel George Slade and asked him where Fox Company was and he pointed that way and we took off.[16]*

Captain William R. Melton, a company commander, also shared his landing zone experience:

> *We landed in the DAO compound and it was just a matter of getting out of the aircraft. It was the wrong place and I told the pilot but he said we would have to get out there and we so[sic] got out and went around to another spot, near the annex. The pilot just wasn't going to say, "Whoops!" and get up and go somewhere else.[17]*

Captain Richard Jaehne, the BLT's Assistant Operations Officer, recalled flying into Saigon with a platoon of young Marines, none of whom had ever seen combat. As the helicopter approached the area around Tan Son Nhut, the pilot reported that the landing zone would be "hot," which meant there was incoming fire. Jaehne vividly remembered that when he passed the word, it appeared that each individual Marine's eyes got a little wider, but as the command to lock and load their weapons was given, Jaehne also recalled that everyone was calm and looked very determined. The man who as a Lieutenant had earned a Navy Cross in Vietnam years earlier was sure that the men would be just fine.[18]

For the men new to combat, the circumstances were both bizarre and gut-wrenching. Lieutenant O'Hara gave this account:

> I didn't think we would ever go to the DAO because so many Vietnamese came out. But about 1400, however, we finally took off (from the ship). There was a break in the people coming in and we heard our number for going in.
>
> A couple of events stand out from that day. First of all we had LAWS, light anti-tank weapons that we kept crated in the boxes. We hadn't busted them out. We had the 106s, too. A buddy of mine called in on the radio and said, "You're not gonna believe this, we have tanks sitting right here, and the barrels are pointed at the building. North Vietnam tanks."
>
> They were sitting out there and all of our LAWS were crated up and we hadn't even busted them out and given them to the troops. So I went high tailing it over there and got a quick glimpse of this. And there they were. They were their's all right. They could really have handed it to us at that moment. Then an artillery battery that had been captured started taking out the airbase with 8-inch artillery. Apparently, they strayed and shot at something near some of our people and our airplanes were stacked up at the time and they went at the battery, and the battery exploded, then the planes pulled back up in the air and there was no more firing.[19]

Despite the issues concerning landing zones, there was no sense of alarm or panic among the officers and men, which was a testament to the groundwork that Lieutenant Colonel Slade and his staff had trained, drilled, and re-drilled into the subordinate leaders of the BLT. Everyone remained unruffled, found their assigned position or adjusted on the fly. The demeanor of the Marines started and remained exemplary throughout the operation. Indeed, as Gray, who was constantly moving around throughout the area, observed the actions of the ARVN military police and the South Vietnamese units outside the Compound, he recommended to Carey that the two additional BLTs (1/9 and 3/9) remain in reserve aboard ship.

Of course, the reason that Al Gray was not overly worried about the NVA tanks was because he knew that American air cover would take them out at the first provocation, just like the enemy artillery position had been hit. But the Marines on the ground were not the only Americans in harm's way. Major Guilmartin was the lead pilot for a section of HH-53 Jolly Green Giant helicopters that had supplemented the big Marine choppers. Guilmartin was a very experienced pilot who had earned two Silver Stars picking up downed pilots (one USAF and the other U.S. Navy) over North Vietnam earlier in the war. As he and his wingman began the long run into Saigon, his surface-to-air (SAM) missile early warning detector went crazy, indicating that there were many threats in his immediate area. Things got so loud, and so distracting, that later Guilmartin simply turned the threat-warning receiver off, rather than continue to listen to the alarms.

But on his first run in, Joe Guilmartin listened intently as a flight of Air Force F-4 fighter/attack aircraft took out an NVA SAM site. The NVA were set up north of Saigon, and made the mistake of lighting off their acquisition radars. The American planes immediately detected the threat and one flight was vectored toward it. Nearly simultaneously, the NVA radar closed down, but it was just a moment too late because the Air Force plane had launched precision-guided munitions against it. Guilmartin listened as the American pilot yelled, "Protective reaction. Protective reaction" over the radio. Guilmartin was leading an experienced flight crew that had lots of prior combat, and while they understood the rules of engagement, they also were quick to return fire when they saw tracers racing skyward in their direction.[20]

Things remained hot inside the American perimeter for the remainder of the day. 2nd Lieutenant Thomas Linn recalled:

> *The compound was bracketed by enemy artillery. I got the feelings that rounds were coming in along the perimeters. I am of the opinion that they did it because they wanted us to know that they could bring fire in. And we heard that the compound that we were in had taken over 100 rounds of artillery fire during the night. It would stand to reason that if they wanted to they could easily have brought rounds in on the compound. Artillery fire or mortar fire.*

For those of us seeing combat for the first time, these rounds would come in and we would all hit the deck, except for the old hands. I remember Colonel Al Gray, rounds came in and everybody hit the deck, all the green guys, and old Al Gray was standing there and his ears could apparently gauge the distance by the sound of the shells. [21]

Of course, to young Marine lieutenants there are no colonels who are not "old," though perhaps by this time Al Gray might have been showing his age (46) – he had been awake for at least 36 hours. Still, as would be expected, Al Gray appeared wherever there was trouble or the sense of trouble. Lieutenant Linn continued:

There were quite a few Vietnamese around the fence. There were instances where they tried to get over the fence line. And there were refugees lined up in the compound. I remember this guy, a white fellow with an afro-type haircut, he was in some leisure suit that he had been in for about five days, I expected that the guy was a CIA type, he was ushering these poor refugees, he was actually controlling them and explaining procedures. He would shout to them in Vietnamese, and a number would get up and go to the helicopter. When the helicopter would come in, all of these refugees would get up and he would shout to them in Vietnamese and wave this .38 at them. I later on sent over additional Marines to give him an hand. I also gave him two beers. I asked him his name and he told me, Ephraim Bloch. He said he was a Major in the Marine Corps Reserve.

The crowd inside was all squatting. The ones on the outside would come up to the fence in order to try to get in. And in one particular instance I recall, some Vietnamese military – I don't know what service they were with, but it looked like they might have been Marines, relatively high ranking since they had shoulder boards with three or four stripes – they were trying to come over the wire in my perimeter, and my men came up and passed the word to me that we had some Vietnamese military were trying to come over and so we prepared to push them back and as we prepared to push them back, Al Gray came up and said, "Let them come in" and he let them over the wire. There were about 4 or 5 of them climbing over the wire. Then a few minutes later MPs began firing into the compound, South Vietnamese MPs, at these guys who had just come through. We all locked and loaded. They were firing with an M1 carbine at these guys. Al Gray came up and saw that it was a hot scene, and he started speaking in

Vietnamese to them. We were ready to go, to exchange rounds, but Gray asserted himself and soothed the ruffled feathers, and everything died. The incident died. [22]

The fact that Al Gray had a battalion of Marines backing him permitted his "discussions" with the Vietnamese Military Police to end well. Despite the incident, Gray remained respectful of the performance by the now leaderless ARVN units around the base. As for the people he had permitted to enter, they had shown him identification indicating they worked for the American government, and Gray made the decision on the spot to permit them to be evacuated. Indeed, the whole air operation was going remarkably well, due in large part to the expert Marine ground controllers who kept the helicopters coming into the zones without any significant problems, and of course, the superb airmanship exhibited by all the pilots and aircrews. Slowly but surely the number of refugees in the DAO Compound was dwindling.

Gray attributed the smooth operations at the DAO to the highly professional efforts by advanced party of Army and Marine planners. All the evacuees were carefully screened and briefed, then they were placed into groups appropriate for a single aircraft and their personal needs were attended to. The fact that most remained very calm during the ordeal was a tribute to the professionalism of those charged with organizing the effort, and the fact that there were a few isolated incidents did nothing to detract from that professionalism. The GSF personnel working in concert with ARVN personnel outside the Compound promptly and efficiently handled those incidents.

Things at the Embassy, however, were not going nearly as well, though Al Gray had no clue exactly why. Carey and Gray had repeatedly been given every assurance from Ambassador Martin that there would be no large-scale evacuation from the Embassy.

About 1600 Gray received a call on the tactical radio net from Major Jim Kean at the Embassy. Kean was the senior Marine officer with the detachment, having only recently flown into Saigon from his post in Hong Kong. He knew to be where he was needed most, and that surely was Saigon. Kean enjoyed a good working relationship with Ambassador Martin, though, perhaps, no military officer had Martin's full confidence. Kean asked Colonel Gray to send some "Fleet Marines" to the Embassy to provide additional security. He provided no other information and implied that the presence of the Fleet Marines would assist in the evacuation, as many Vietnamese were pressing against the barriers and walls, trying to get their chance at freedom. Gray quickly responded by sending BLT 2/4's highly capable Reconnaissance Platoon, which had been in reserve at the DAO Compound.

Later, another platoon was sent to the Embassy in support of Major Kean by the 9th MAB Headquarters. It should be noted that all of the senior officers from the DAO Compound, including Colonel Taylor, had been evacuated on the early flights out. Indeed, Taylor and the two admirals from CINCPAC and CINCPACFLT were among the first evacuated when the operation was put into action.

The additional platoon of reinforcements was taken over to the Embassy aboard a CH-53, but not without some angst on the part of the their platoon leader, 1st Lieutenant Thomas Ochala:

> My platoon was in a reserve role. We flew into the DAO compound and were to go wherever there were problems.
>
> We landed at the DAO and were deployed there. We were to go wherever we were needed. Probably an hour and a half after we landed the Embassy got hot and we flew over there.
>
> My understanding was that there were too many people for them to handle at the Embassy. They needed somebody to control the crowds.
>
> They took us over in a CH-53. They landed us in the parking lot at the Embassy.
>
> There were some problems with the coordination of the helicopters. I was sent to arrange for a helicopter to fly us there. I went to arrange for it and it took a long time to get there. The people who were controlling it were up on the DAO building. I got up there and told them who I was and told them I needed a helicopter to get to the Embassy. There was a helicopter sitting down in the parking lot below us and they said, "That's your helicopter and your people are in it, go get in it." And so I went running back out of the building, about a five-minute process, and when I got there they took off with my platoon. So Air America was flying out of the LZ right next to us, so I went in and told Colonel Slade what had happened, and told him I was going to try to hitch a ride with Air America. I went over and the Air America terminal asked for a ride, and they said, "Sure, where do you want to go?" and they took me right into the Embassy.

I thought I beat my own platoon in. They landed in the parking lot and I landed on the roof. I talked to some people there and said, "I'm looking for a platoon of Marines, have you seen one?"

They said no Marines had flown in there. I went down and reported immediately to Major Kean, who was in charge of the Marines there at the Embassy and he was elated that more Marines were coming in and told me where he wanted them deployed, and about ten minutes later I ran into my platoon sergeant. I said, "How long have you been here?" and he said, "Where have you been?"

The parking lot was filled mostly with Americans at the time and a few Vietnamese. It seemed kind of confused. They were landing helicopters in there and flying people out. It was normal confusion. Out around the gates people were packed, there was this huge crowd out there. And people were coming over the walls. [23]

There had been a giant banyan tree, which Ambassador Martin considered almost sacred, that stood near the Embassy parking lot which Al Gray had earlier arranged to be removed so that a CH-53 helicopter could land in emergency. It was at this emergency landing site that the aforementioned Lieutenant Ochala's platoon landed to provide additional security at the Embassy. Only CH-46 helicopters with their smaller footprint could land on the roof of the Embassy to evacuate any people at that location.

As the evacuation gained steam, more and more people, both Americans and Vietnamese, went to the Embassy, not the DAO Compound. Ambassador Martin without alerting anyone in 9th MAB or outside Saigon, was intent on saving as many as he could, so he simply had Major Kean and the Marines, assisted by three senior Army officers who appeared on the scene, form the evacuees into groups that were pushed aboard the CH-46s that were supposed to get the Ambassador and his small staff. Captain Gerry Berry was the lead pilot of the four CH-46s tasked with retrieving Ambassador Martin. Two of his section of planes were empty, to be used to pick up the final Americans from the Embassy, and two carried Sparrow Hawk teams, squads of Marines that would deploy around any plane that was forced to land in an area outside American control. After two trips to the Task Force with evacuees, Berry ordered the Sparrow Hawk units to get off at the Embassy and enhance security there, thus providing more lift capability for the refugees. But almost immediately, Kean realized that flights of four CH-46s would never clear the compound of the people jammed into it. Unfortunately, he never transmitted the depth of his problems to General Carey or Colonel Gray. The officers aboard ship knew something was amiss when Berry's 46s kept spilling out refugees, none of whom were the Ambassador. Only sparse information about the chaos at the Embassy finally reached the Commanding General and Al Gray at the DAO Compound sometime late in the evening.

Though there was a press of humanity at the Embassy, crowd control was not the issue causing problems; the issue causing the problem was the shear magnitude of the number of people to be evacuated. That number included diplomats and allied military officers. Many writers of the event have mentioned the South Koreans in particular. But Lieutenant Ochala, from his front row seat, made these observations:

> It was kind of controlled, it wasn't as if people were yelling and screaming. It was like they were waiting their chance to get in and when they saw their chance to get in, they came in. My platoon was deployed then in three different places. There was an annex that joined the Embassy compound, that was my hottest spot, I had a squad there. I had a squad that was out on the side that Tu Do street was on, about a block and a half away. Then another squad I didn't see because they were employed on the perimeter and then were plugged in with the other squad.

> We just pushed people back. People tried to climb over and we pushed them out. Some journalists said that their fingers were smashed or they were kicked. But I never saw any of that. There were a couple of occasions where people were climbing over the wall and they put their fingers up, and somebody would reach up and pry their fingers loose, but it would never be enough to cause any damage. It was just to let them know that they weren't supposed to do that.

> The situation was always under control, throughout the afternoon. There were times when it seemed people would rush us in waves, and eight or ten would get past, and we would push the others back. They'd start climbing up and run down the roofs and into the compound itself. It wasn't as if we were in danger from them, they were just trying to get in, that was it. We never pushed any women or children back over because they weren't physical enough to climb up and over the wall. It was usually just the men who were coming over the wall. The women or children had verification and came through the gate.

It was intense because it had a lot of potential. One thing that impressed me about the Vietnamese people that stays in my mind, was the way that we were able to control them. I thought in my mind, "Gee, they must not know how few of us there are. If they want to get inside the compound they could if they wanted to, really."

All of us were aware that there were too few of us. Our reinforcements were at the DAO compound.

If one helicopter had gone down in that courtyard landing zone it would really have slowed things down. But it went fairly well. As the helicopters were coming in, there were a lot of tracers coming up at them. A lot of them. I suspected that a lot of those were the ARVN because I don't believe the NVA or the Viet Cong were in the city in strength at that time. The ARVNs were probably shooting at them.

We were concerned about bicycle bombs or something like that. We had one incident that was strange, really strange, that to this day I can't explain.

We'd shut down the evacuation for a while. The helicopters had quit coming in for one reason or another. We told everybody to remain calm and that the evacuation was temporarily shut down. So they did, they calmed down and waited for us to say they could come in. It was a night.

At one point everybody, all the Vietnamese in front of us got up and just moved away from the wall. Like somebody told them there was a bomb ready to go off here. And so I got on the radio and said, "Something's happening here." And then all of a sudden they all got calm again and came back and sat down right in front of us again. It was the strangest thing. I'd love to know what the explanation was.

There was this American going around, about my age, speaking Vietnamese to the people. He said he'd been in Vietnam before and he'd come back to get his wife. She was Vietnamese, and she didn't want to leave. So he was just waiting for his turn to get on the helicopter. And he hung around my position and interpreted for me.

One problem we had was the identification of evacuees. When we went in it was the Embassy responsibility to tell us who was to be evacuated. And that had not been done. So were we getting such

*things as Embassy stationery with names of people typed on it. And
it was obvious that some people in the Embassy had used this as an
advantage, perhaps for monetary purposes or whatever. I remember,
for instance, this one black guy came up and he had a list of about
twenty people who were his relatives. He had a list of his cousins
and uncles and it was on Embassy stationery. And I told him, that
just doesn't wash.*

*The crowd never seemed to get any smaller, inside or outside the fence.
There was this annex to the Embassy compound. And in it was this
swimming pool. And in it was the marshalling area for the people.
And we had not enough people to keep the Vietnamese out. So they
kept filling the place up. It was a bottomless pit, really.*

*Later on in the evening the decision was made to move everybody
inside who was going to be evacuated, and we would move them
into the inner Embassy compound. And that was the first time that
we could cover the entire Embassy perimeter. And then we got orders
that only Americans would be evacuated. The Ambassador decided we
would fly out everybody who was in the compound, but Americans
could still come over the wall.* [24]

As events and conditions at the DAO Compound improved, it became obvious to Gray and General Carey that something had to be done at the Embassy. Communications between the Embassy and the DAO area had all but been eliminated. Likewise, they apparently were not good between the Embassy and Navy/Marine staffs aboard the flagship. Gray suggested to General Carey that the Commanding General should return to the *Blue Ridge* and ensure things at the Embassy were straightened out. About 2100 (9 P.M.) Carey turned the operation ashore over to Gray and left. Although darkness had fallen, the day was very overcast and a thunderstorm swept the area. There was also another issue worrisome to Gray.

As evening approached, the ARVN anti-aircraft artillery at Tan Son Nhut had fallen into enemy hands, and Gray worried that those guns might be turned against the American humanitarian effort. But the lowered visibility, and the generally poor weather, provided additional cover for the American aircrews, because they limited the ability of any NVA gunners looking to make trouble. Of course, on the flip side, the deteriorating weather added to the pilots' stress and significantly increased the possibility of an accident. Some helicopters turned on their top lights so other aircraft that might be above could see them. Despite the weather, the number of refugees was reduced, and Al Gray began to tighten his perimeter.

But herding the refugees onto the helicopters was not all that was happening in and around the DAO Compound. Lieutenant O'Hara had these memories:

> *One of the things the troops had to do in leaving there, we got the word from our company commander who said, "Tom, pick some people and make sure that none of these vehicles out here in the compound will run again."*
>
> *So I knew just the people to pick. I said, "OK, gang." I had about five or six of them. "These vehicles will never ever run again." And they said, "Sir, can we blow them up." And I said, "Don't blow them up cause we'll get burned to death. Do something else."*
>
> *Well, they had a field day. There were all these new pickup trucks and brand new Cherokees and jeeps and government vehicles. And these kids knew how to rip out the wires and smash the electronics and punch holes in the gas tanks. These guys had fun. See, I was the executive officer, and I really got to know who was who, the good, the bad and the ugly. So I picked the bad and the ugly. You know where they're from and I had the right guys for the job.* [25]

An hour or so after General Carey had departed, things seemed to be even more unsettled at the Embassy. The radio transmissions, and the fact that the airborne commander, *Cricket*, was diverting more CH-53s there, began to really worry Gray. General Carey had not been heard from, and with Lieutenant Colonel Slade's men in firm control of the DAO Complex, Gray decided to go over to the Embassy. He returned to the area where his UH-1N had been parked and found out that both UH-1Ns had been sent back to the Fleet for safekeeping. The GSF commander was furious. Gray had started his time in Vietnam awaiting helicopters to fly him off Tiger Tooth Mountain. But those helicopters remained safely in Da Nang, unavailable to fly when the weather cleared. Now, as Gray was in the final hours of his involvement with the Republic of Vietnam, the helicopter he needed was again away, safely parked aboard ship. With only CH-53s available to take him to the Embassy, Gray remained at the DAO area. He had learned in 1964 that at times the mission is more important than the safety of the helicopters; now as the American effort in South Vietnam was ending, he was again reminded.

At about 2300 (11 P.M.) the word was put out on the tactical nets that the CTF 79 helicopters would stop flying. Admiral Whitmire had determined that the pilots had reached the end of their daily flight time and for safety reasons he decided to order them to stop. Needless to say, that decision caused an uproar among Marines, and no more so than at FMFPAC, where Lieutenant General Lou Wilson went ballistic. General Wilson told Admiral Gayler that he would personally press charges against anyone who tried to interfere with Marine pilots rescuing the Marines remaining in Saigon. As a consequence of General Wilson's forceful intrusion the decision was reconsidered almost immediately. Despite the fact that men like Captain Berry had been flying almost continuously for 12 hours or more – under highly stressful conditions, and for the past five hours in darkness and extremely poor weather – the pilots continued their missions.

Aboard *Midway*, Major Joe Guilmartin did not realize that there had been a general stand down in flying. Since his Jolly Green Giant section was designed and configured for rescue missions, he thought it made sense for the Jolly Greens to stop flying and standby for any assignment to retrieve downed flight crews and other passengers. Guilmartin was, consequently, completely unaware of the "stop-flying brouhaha" until years later.

Everyone at the DAO Compound that was to be taken out had been and about midnight on April 29/30 Gray turned his attention to leaving the area, permanently. Then, Captain Melton remembered leaving in these words:

> At the DAO we had some small arms incoming fire or some mortar or artillery rounds, two or three. They hit within fifty or seventy five yards.
>
> Somewhere around six or seven I was told to withdraw my company and I would be followed. I was to go into a giant Butler Hut – a large metal building – inside this place there were supplies, I still have a little vase I took off a secretary's desk there. There we found 782 gear, better shape than we had, so some of the troops traded the stuff. They would go up to a pallet of Pepsi-cola, open it up, take one drink and throw it away. We stayed in there for a time.
>
> We came out right around midnight. We landed on the Midway. We left in the dark. I felt and was told that there were 16 to 18 divisions around the city at the time. And if they wanted to do something there wasn't a lot we could do about it. After being there I knew they had ample opportunity to do what they wanted.
>
> I remember a firefight in a park nearby. I was told that the South Vietnamese had dug in and were fighting to the death.[26]

Lieutenant Clough from Golf Company had a similar memory about leaving:

> *I recall seeing a couple of red flares going off pretty close to the area. You see red and you know that's something bad. I called up Major(sic) Melton and he indicated not to worry about it. There were a lot of things going on all around us.*
>
> *We started moving when it got dark. The annex was finished before the DAO. We marched back through the corridor to the DAO. We moved a couple of times waiting for transportation out. And we waited for the evacuation of the civilians.*
>
> *It was dark for a long time before we finally got out.*
>
> *What it impressed me that night was that the action started getting closer and closer. We could hear it. Helicopter gun ships were going over a ways off, and they were conducting gunfire. Every now and then a stray round came in, close enough for everyone to hit the deck.*
>
> *We went back on a Marine helicopter. I think it was maybe half an hour ride on the way out. I looked out on the way out and I remember, we were up pretty high, the crew chiefs were looking for SAMS. I had heard that there was some rumor of them being shot.*[27]

Lieutenant Linn's memories of the withdrawal were more philosophical:

> *We moved to the DAO Annex, while there was still a little light. I remember that vividly. I remember moving to the DAO annex. Then we staged in a certain area and waited, I can remember that it seemed to have gotten quieter, but there were many some(sic) instances of a random rifle shot or pistol shot into the compound. I remember a bus of refugees came crashing into the compound. A Marine officer had gone up to them and they took the bus back out.*
>
> *I don't think the crowd got smaller as the day went on, the people were still there, but in the dark you couldn't see them all. It seemed like the effects of the collapse of South Vietnam were not as notice-able in the dark.*
>
> *We were told that we would be going out around 10:30 or 11:00 that night and about 11:30 we finally got on the aircraft. When you are in an operation like that you don't have the luxury of reflecting on*

your place in history. In a situation like that it might get in the way. You are more concerned with accomplishing the mission and taking care of the men. Before the evacuation when we were waiting off the coast of Vietnam, we knew that it was a matter of time before Vietnam fell, we had gotten operations orders over and over again. And I remember standing out on the catwalk thinking about that. As a lieutenant I was quite excited because we were going to do something, do something that we had been trained for, a combat mission. And from that aspect it was very exciting. We really were up for this. But at the same time, you experience the sadness in knowing that (nearly) 60,000 lives had been spent for nothing. And you knew that this was not a great moment in history. This was something that was very, very sad. It was like being part of a great defeat. You wanted as a Marine to be part of a heritage or legend of Okinawa or Iwo Jima. But here we were part of a great defeat for America.

As we lifted off I looked out and could see fires burning in the city of Saigon. As far as looking for the sake of history, I didn't do that. I was more concerned with the mission. In retrospect I think just about what I was thinking at the time.

The men were very excited about what they had done. They thought they had participated in something important; they had trained and trained and trained, and they accomplished their mission. They were excited. [28]

Around 11:30 PM, Gray, along with Captain R.J. McManus and Master Sergeant W.V. East (his team of Explosive Ordnance Disposal [EOD] Marines), had an unusual job to perform. Gray thought the mission was winding down and it was time to execute the final steps of their plan – destruction of the DAO Compound, other vital areas, and equipment so as to deny their use to the enemy. Also, several days earlier, Captain Tony Wood had signed for the receipt of 8 million in U.S. currency that had arrived at Tan Son Nhut. Wood retrieved the cash and stored it 55-gallon drums at the DAO Compound. Gray, under specific orders to ensure the money was destroyed, had the drums rigged with thermite grenades, ignited, and watched as the money was burnt to a crisp. Gray also determined that there would be no NVA general living in the house where US Army General Creighton Abrams was quartered. That house, not far from the DAO complex, was also rigged with explosives and blown up prior to the departure of the Marines. There would be no inquiry about blowing up anything, except, of course, the money. Some bureaucrat in Washington had undoubtedly been assigned the mission to account for the cash. Despite the relative insignificance of the $8M, given the hundreds of millions that were being destroyed and lost by the fall of the Republic of Vietnam, one might have thought that the cash was the most important thing America had in Saigon.

Figure 7.4
There was much happening in Saigon that was very dangerous. ARVN units
were fighting the NVA who were moving closer to city center. [29]

Al Gray and George Slade, and indeed all Marines, could be proud of the things Lieutenant Linn and his Marines accomplished. For officers like Gray and Slade, and for the younger Marines like Tom Linn, Bill Melton, Tom O'Hara, Dick Jaehne, and countless others, there was nothing more important than completing the mission and taking care of the men. Adherence to those primary goals represented the qualities imbued in every Marine officer, Staff NCO and NCO, and clearly the performance in both Phnom Penh and Saigon demonstrated for all to see that officers and men of BLT 2/4 and, indeed, every other unit in 9th MAB, had returned to basic Marine values. Much of it was the result of the great leaders Al Gray was privileged to serve with on Okinawa in the weeks and months leading up to *Operations Frequent Wind* and *Eagle Pull*. Colonels like Jim Woodring, Tom Batchelder, and Hans Edebohls, Lieutenant Colonels such as George Slade, Jerry Goodwine, James Bolton, Bob White, and young Majors like Jim Livingston, T. H. Shannon, and J. Miller made extremely valuable contributions that were the result of their leadership traits and their enduring professionalism. But there is little doubt that the driving force behind not only changing the culture on Okinawa, but also making Marines into a highly-effective, well-trained fighting force for freedom in 1975 was Colonel Al Gray.

While things wound down relatively smoothly at the DAO, at the Embassy, things were still chaotic, though crowd control was not really the problem. American civilians, mostly newsmen but also others, climbed over the walls to reach safety. Included in that number was the Chicago-based reporter, Keyes Beech. Beech had been in Da Nang when Al Gray arrived in 1964 for the operation at Tiger Tooth Mountain. Now, in 1975, Beech would leave with the last Marines. Lieutenant Ochala had a bird's eye view as the evacuation from the Embassy closed down:

> *Later on in the evening the decision was made to move everybody inside who was going to be evacuated, and we would move them into the inner Embassy compound. And that was the first time that we could cover the entire Embassy perimeter. And then we got orders that only Americans would be evacuated. The Ambassador decided we would fly out everybody who was in the compound, but Americans could still come over the wall.*

> *Everybody in the compound was tired. It was obvious that they had been up for a long time. I heard the order, on the radio that I had, that the helicopter to bring the Ambassador out had landed, and the pilot said that he was not going to leave until the Ambassador got on the helicopter. I had the helos on the hand held radio that I had. I am*

not sure why that was. It seemed to be that the radio net was using the same frequency to talk to everybody. The helo was on the ground, and the pilot was talking to somebody who was in control. He said something about orders from the President, I believe, that he was not to leave until the Ambassador was on board.

The helo sat up there for about 20 minutes, and while he was up there he was being shot at. I remember seeing the tracers going up at this poor guy sitting on the rooftop. It was automatic fire, I could tell from the amount of tracers coming up. For about 20 minutes. Some of the helos had requested permission to return fire on ground fire, but they were denied permission...

Then Major Kean said, "We're going into the Embassy, and we're gonna get on the rooftop." And then I knew that nobody else was flying out but us at that point. And there were about 450 Vietnamese left in the courtyard at that time.

We formed a line between them and the Embassy, and so we had a defensive line, and on the word we just did a peel off and just ran right into the Embassy. The Vietnamese just sat there and they were looking at us, but it was as if they had no control over the situation. We got inside and barred the doors and went up to the rooftop on the same stairwell I had walked down earlier.

At that point I figured that we were going to go out and nobody else was going to be flown out of the Embassy. That was just the thing that was happening. It wasn't a moral question to me at the time. Decisions were being made at a higher level than me and I was just doing those things.[30]

Lieutenant O'Hara reported this experience:

On the way out, we had just gone over Saigon, over the harbor, and there were two ships out there duking it out. One was obviously North and one was South, and they were just handing it to each other. And there was a cargo ship left in the middle that was taking almost all of it, and all of these tracers just glaring off the water. And the first sergeant and the crew chief were hanging off the back looking at this, and we thought, "God, this is beautiful to watch, but I'd hate to be down there."

Then I saw something come from our right corner. I grabbed a crew chief and yelled," SAM!" And his eyeballs just opened. He took out his flare gun and started shooting flares at the missile and he grabbed his headset and called the pilot. I didn't think a helicopter could dive that fast. We went straight down, and the missile went up over us and it was a SAM. We were just shocked. I remember the first sergeant looked at me and said, "Oh shit!" Those were the only words that came out of his mouth. "Oh shit!" It was dark and you could see this orange flash and glow coming up at us. It looked like a flame coming up at us and the flares never took it out. We didn't know what to do at that moment. I saw it and the crew chief saw it and the pilot took immediate action and dove. They did not fire the smart version of it because that could have followed us.

After that we stayed very low over the water. I kept telling the crew chief and the pilot also that if they landed on any other ship than the USS Okinawa we were not getting off. I told them I want to see the number 3 on the flight deck. So we were very fortunate. Some of our friends got stuck on the Midway and we didn't see them for many weeks after that.[31]

But even after lifting off, it was not as though the flights out to the ships were routine. Major Guilmartin also recalled that on his last flight out of Saigon, his crew was on the receiving end of fairly accurate anti-aircraft fire. The Air Force helicopter, whose crew were all combat veterans, returned fire continuously. In fact, during their debriefs the intelligence officers told Guilmartin that his section of HH-53s had done the great majority of the firing against NVA (or the stray ARVN) who took the Americans under fire. Guilmartin's early warning receiver chirped loudly when it was turned on, though he did not recall any air strikes against SAM targets after the one he had observed on the first flight into Saigon.

The flight crews cannot be given too much credit for their efforts during *Frequent Wind*. They not only battled the threat of SAMs and more than occasional ground anti-aircraft fire, but they persisted though long hours in the cockpit, flying in marginal weather conditions without the usual ground flight controllers being able to assist them, and they conquered the stress of all that safely. No troops, and no refugees, were lost in accidents. The only grave mistake during the entire operation happened to a Marine helicopter that was providing Sea and Air Rescue duties. That tragic crash at sea was the only blemish on the tremendous safety record that the helicopter pilots and crew earned during the operation. Sadly, the CH-46 pilot and co-pilot, Captain William C. Nystrol and 1st Lieutenant Michael J. Shea, became the final casualties of America's long war in Vietnam.[32]

At the DAO Compound, in the early morning hours, Gray ordered the perimeter to be reduced completely and the extraction of Marines was completed as planned. Gray had heard nothing to indicate that the Embassy had not closed down, and he was completely unaware of the chaos still extant there. The last two Marines to board helicopters at the DAO Compound were Major Livingston and Colonel Gray. Standing in the rear of the helicopter, he watched as the NVA advanced and much of the area was in flames. For Gray, it was an emotional end to his long years fighting for Vietnamese freedom. Although extremely proud that all of the evacuation force had performed magnificently, he was deeply saddened that we abandoned our South Vietnamese allies and that our nation did not keep its word to help them. This still bothers him even today. Although they thought they were on the last helicopter to leave South Vietnam, it turned out not to be the case.

As luck would have it, General Carey had flown back to the fleet aboard a USAF helicopter, and it landed on the *Midway*. After some time there, Carey finally made his way back to *Blue Ridge*, arriving just before Gray arrived on the last chopper from the DAO Compound. As a result of that confusion, there was no finality at the Embassy until Washington ordered General Carey to ensure that Captain Berry did not fly any more people from the Embassy other than the Ambassador. At 0458 on April 30, Captain Berry executed his mission.[33]

As Al Gray and his cohort landed on *Blue Ridge*, he was surprised to find General Carey returning to the USS *Blue Ridge*, as well. That partially explained the reason for the continued confusion at the Embassy. But Al Gray discovered a far bigger surprise than the information about General Carey's travels. Lieutenant Colonel George Slade, who had flown out of the DAO Compound on an earlier helicopter, was in full battle dress and headed for a CH-46 that appeared ready to take off. Gray ran over to his BLT Commander and asked, "Where are you going, George?" As they walked toward the helicopter, Slade let Gray know that all the Marines were not yet out of the Embassy, and that he was going in to get them. Gray told Slade to slide over in his seat, the RLT Commander would be going too.[34]

Lieutenant Tom Ochala, whose platoon was still at the Embassy, recalled his flight out in these terms:

> On the roof everyone was milling about and there was mass confusion. It was all Marines, maybe 100 to 150, just walking around. I was worried that not everybody had got up there. So I told my men to get into a formation cause I wanted to get a head count, so I had

these three ranks stand over against the wall so I could get a count and make sure that I had everybody. Major Kean looked over and he said, "Who's that over there." And I said "That's the recon platoon," and he said, "Your[sic] gonna be the first ones to fly out." It was a matter of organization. He said, "Those guys are together, they'll go out first."

I laid up on the roof and watched the sun come up. It was beautiful that morning.

Only 15 got on our CH 47[sic] to get out. I saw the people in the courtyard as we lifted off. There was some people doing some looting and some people hot-wiring the vehicles outside the Embassy.

We saw the beaches, south of Vung Tau as we flew out. Off to the sides you could see vegetation that was just beautiful. The jungle is very beautiful. But the Delta portion to the Southeast of Saigon had been defoliated by agent orange and heavily bombed, and you know, this was my first time in Vietnam, and people had talked about these areas that looked like the face of the moon, and it literally looked like the face the moon. The Delta area had been defoliated for miles and miles and there were bomb craters all around, from the sea almost into the city itself. There had been an active VC battalion in there and so they had defoliated the area. And it was really like the face of the moon.

When we got out over the water the crew chief gave a thumbs up and pulled the ammunition out of his machine gun. And it felt like we had crossed the Rubicon when we got over the South China Sea.

We flew out into the rising sun.[35]

Following Lieutenant Ochala's platoon, the remainder of the Sparrow Hawk detachments and the BLT 2/4 men flew out, and finally, about an hour later, the last 11 men of the Marine Security Guard detachment, including Major Kean, were lifted off the Embassy roof by one of Captain Berry's pilots. Their departure marked the end of the American military mission in Saigon.[36]

Al Gray and George Slade, heading back into Saigon while the sun was rising, got word that all the Marines were finally all out of the Embassy. The two commanders exchanged "thumbs up" and smiled. Their aircraft turned and flew back to the *Blue Ridge* without incident. It was an anti-climatic conclusion for Al Gray's Vietnam experiences; although after being up for nearly 48 consecutive hours, the lack of further excitement was a very good thing for the Marine.

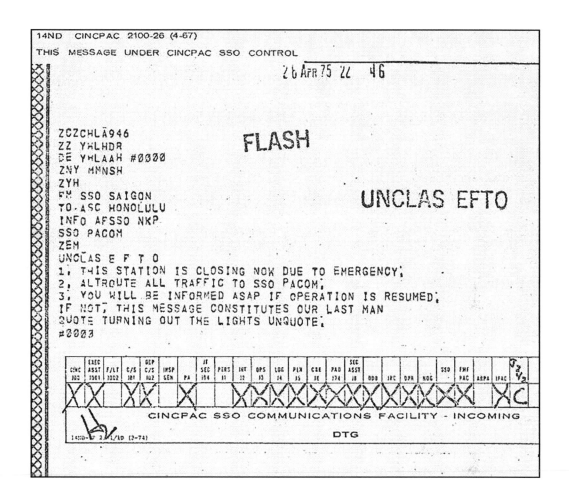

Figure 7.5
Last message sent from Communications Station, Saigon. Note the sense of humor! [37]

WASHINGTON, 1975

There was little sorrow in Washington following the fall of the Republic of Vietnam. In response to a new threat in Southeast Asia, President Ford had tried to react forcefully when Cambodian forces seized the *Mayaguez*, but the pressure that his Secretary of State exerted on the military to respond quickly – rather than smartly - came close to having a disastrous result. By the end of May 1975, for the first time in nearly two decades, neither American forces nor American allies were at war. The post-mortem analyses of the Vietnam Era could begin in earnest, and soon did.

Al Gray had observed the war up close and personally. While he had access to almost all the intelligence related to the war, Al Gray was only at the periphery of the policy-level decision making, even within the Marine Corps. But one of his best friends, someone with whom he had established a close bond and whom Al Gray respected as one of the finest Marines of his era, saw the war from a higher viewpoint.

In 1965, after having worked together at HQMC, when Major Al Gray left for Vietnam, Raymond G. Davis was a general officer serving as the Assistant Division Commander of the 3rd Marine Division, then on Okinawa.[38] Brigadier General Davis was there for the initial deployment questions related to putting ground forces into Vietnam, though he did not actually deploy. After that 13-month tour, Davis returned to HQMC and was promoted to Major General. He was active in support of Commandant Greene's and especially the Chief of Staff's initiatives. Davis clearly held Lieutenant General Leonard F. Chapman, the Chief of Staff, in highest regard. Thus, Davis had an insider's view as General Greene readied the Marine Corps for combat in Southeast Asia. After several years at HQMC, Davis returned to the war zone and led the 3rd Marine Division as its most successful commander during the entire Vietnam War. Al Gray had returned to Vietnam in 1969 on temporary additional duty and was there to see the fruits of General Davis's tactics.

Returning to the United States in the early 1970s, General Davis and Lieutenant Colonel Al Gray toured the country speaking about the war. During their speaking tour, the men had ample opportunity to discuss the war; after all, it was the very topic of the tour! General Davis was soon promoted to three stars and then four as the Assistant Commandant during the final years of the war. Ray Davis had a much higher, insider view of the conduct of the war than did Al Gray, and his comments about what went wrong are compelling. Moreover, the observations put forth by General Davis in a succinct, clearly understood way, are more forceful than authors who have written entire books on the subject.

In 1995, General Ray Davis, over two decades retired from active duty, succumbed to the long time, oft-repeated requests of Colonel William J. Davis (no relation) to write his story.[39] The resulting book, inexpensively produced with the proceeds going to the *Korean War Veterans Memorial Dedication Foundation, Inc.*, tells a straightforward story of a great Marine, and perhaps a better man.

Interestingly, the first topic that General Davis addresses in his book is the Vietnam War. He makes twelve points as to why it turned out the way it did; they are summarized here: [40]

1. Role for Military Forces

» *From the beginning, it was known that the real enemy would be 14 North Vietnamese Army regular divisions plus the Viet Cong main force regiments and battalions.*

» *The American buildup was much too slow, and never culminated until 1968.*

2. Limit on Funds

» *The Fiscal Year 1965 supplemental budget established $11.2B (billion) as the amount needed to deploy American forces. After internal debate between the President and the Congress, the decision was made to actually fund $1.7B. Recall from the second part of Chapter 5 that Johnson's first priority was his Great Society programs and the Vietnam never received a lion's share of even the military budget – which was targeted mostly against the Soviet Union.*

3. Withholding the Ready Reserve

» *The military was organized around active duty units and ready reserve units. When Johnson decided not to use the Ready Reserve, he upset the whole balance of forces, and put too much stress on the draft and individual replacements.*

4. Pacification in Reverse

» *The numerical lack of forces did not permit all population areas to be protected until finally, in 1968, all the originally planned for U.S. forces arrived in Vietnam. When the NVA units, the Viet Cong main force units, and the VC cadres were destroyed, people thrived.*

» *Progress came too late to show the people at home that the war was being won.*

5. Areas of Sanctuary Provided for Enemy Forces

» *The enemy had relative sanctuary along a 1,400 mile border, able to concentrate against weak U.S. or South Vietnamese positions, and able to flee to escape further losses when hurt.*

» *U.S. forces could not exploit tactical advantages because of the restrictions against crossing borders (which the NVA did not have).*

» *The sanctuary syndrome by American politicians extended even to Haiphong harbor, though at no time did the Chinese ever object to U.S. attacks against NVA supply positions. Aggressive attacks against the cross-border NVA supply and logistics centers in 1968 would have destroyed them while guaranteeing a South Vietnamese victory.*

6. The McNamara Line – A $6B Blunder

» *The sanctuary syndrome created a false need to a barrier to infiltration. But the U.S. was not concerned with infiltration when entire enemy divisions were entering South Vietnam at other border areas.*

» *Spending $6B for the barrier was outrageous.*

» *When restrictions were lifted in 1968 (when Abrams took command in Saigon) not only did morale among the troops go up, but also U.S. forces were must more effectively employed.*

7. Air Defense Buildup in North Vietnam

» *Although intelligence predicted and then followed the buildup of air defense positions around North Vietnamese airfield and military targets, fear of "disturbing" the Chinese prevented aggressive attacks against them.*

» *As a result, soon North Vietnam had the best air defense capability in the world and U.S. planes littered the country, and prisons were full of U.S. pilots.*

8. Cease-Fire

» *Periodically "cease-fires" were agreed to that ostensibly permitted Viet Cong soldiers to return home, but rather were used to expand VC presence in the countryside, recruiting, resupplying, reorganizing, etc.*

» *The attacks of Tet were a capstone of their deceptive use of a cease-fire.*

9. Artillery/Rocket/Bombing Halt

» *In 1968, the enemy had been badly hurt, so they wanted to talk. The Washington politicians were anxious to give them what they wanted, and so a pause in the bombing and firing into North Vietnam by U.S. artillery permitted the enemy to regroup.*

» *By 1968, computerized control of U.S. heavy artillery was particularly effective against NVA artillery north of the DeMilitarized Zone. Photos showed how counterbattery fire destroyed the NVA artillery almost every time it fired. The U.S. had also captured 3,000 rockets in the western mountains along the Laotian border. With no rockets to shoot, and their artillery under siege, the communists pleaded for a cease-fire, which Washington granted.*

» *1972, with American tactical aircraft clobbering North Vietnam, the enemy asked for a truce, which Kissinger granted. Even though the North Vietnamese promised to stop using the Ho Chi Minh Trail, they violated the agreement and invaded the South.*

10. South Vietnamese Army Regional Concept

» *Limited military resources and limited response syndrome led to a faulty concept in the organization and deployment of the South Vietnamese Army.*

» *The lack of experience among the ARVN became a factor in the defeat suffered in Laos in 1971, and later in 1975.*

11. Withholding of Support in Laos

» *After the successful expedition in Cambodia (in 1970), preparations were made to do the same against enemy concentrations in Laos (in 1971); however, the day before the operation was to start, the media broke the story in Washington. The enemy was given confirmation of precise details of forces, times and places. Worse, the clamor around D.C. caused some hurry up, disastrous decisions about participation (or lack thereof) by U.S. forces.*

» *The failures caused by limitations on U.S. participation and inexperienced ARVN leadership marked the beginning of the end. A successful operation would have eliminated the enemy threat from Laos, but Washington's wrong decisions made that impossible.*

12. Premature Withdrawal of U.S. Forces

» *Pressures to end the war, including the voice of Walter Cronkite, brought on a program of premature withdrawals. It was obvious the NVA was still strong and still in the field, though it had been badly hurt. What had been the mission of the U.S. military? American strength did not achieve its full commitment until 1968, then America began to rapidly withdraw a year later.*

» *The South Vietnamese were left without good options. When, in 1972, the U.S. denied its former ally 60,000 tons of ammunition that was already aboard ships sitting in Saigon, it was a death blow against an enemy who was always well-supplied by China and the Soviet Union.*

General Davis pointed out that the genesis for most of the 12 critical decisions came from Washington, half way around the world, and they produced but one result – total disaster. Despite the outcome, General Davis still thought supporting our friends in their quest for freedom to be a noble cause, but only if U.S. forces are permitted to win! He thought Vietnam, where Americans were committed and then support withheld, was a betrayal of those who served the country in the military.[41]

Clearly, General Davis considered that most of the bad decisions made during the war were made in D.C. General Gray echoed his former mentor's comments about the Chinese; they were never a threat to intervene militarily.[42] Korea had been a bad experience for American forces; it had been a disaster of the first magnitude for the Chinese. They had no desire to again lose millions in the Red Army to the air superiority, bombardment and overwhelming firepower of the American military. But American decision-makers had neither a sense of history, nor an understanding of the geopolitics of the region. Most Americans are surprised to learn that Vietnam and China fought a war against each other before the decade of the 1970s had ended. And in 2012, the Chinese and Vietnamese were again at each other's throats over the issue of oil in the South China Sea. It is interesting that the U.S. Department of State and the White House under two administrations worried about the Chinese threat, but apparently discounted the threat the U.S. posed if its forces were unleashed with the goal to win the war! Half-measures in defense of freedom, it can be learned from the Vietnamese experience, did not work despite the sacrifice of over 58,000 American lives and great expense to the U.S. Treasury.

NOTES AND REFERENCES

1. Author interviews with Colonel Jerry Goodwine. As Admiral Whitmire's senior Marine staff officer, then-Lieutenant Colonel Goodwine was present for many of the discussions between the Admiral and Colonel Gray.
2. Dept of Defense Photo (USMC A150913).
3. See *Al Gray, Marine Volume 1,* Chapter 7 for more details about the 1st Radio Battalion.
4. Author interview with Colonel Richard L. Jaehne, USMC (Ret), May 2011. Indeed, Colonel Jaehne thought the decision to use plain voice for communications to be one of the keys for the success of the operation.
5. The fact that BLT 2/4 would be carrying extra radios did not sit well with the BLT's S-4, who knew the logistics problems associated with PRC-25 radio batteries and who lamented the extra weight that the grunts would have to carry. After briefing for the operation, when questions were called for, Captain Joe Betta, in his then-inimitable fashion, asked, "Whose brilliant idea was it that the troops carry extra radios?" While speaking he noted that Lt. Col. Slade was giving him hand signals that indicated he ought discontinue his line of questioning. As he sat down, Colonel Gray rose and answered that indeed it was his idea that the extra radios be used. Betta, whose respect for Al Gray was by then already extraordinary, replied sheepishly, "It's a fine idea, sir!" Betta, who retired as a Colonel of Marines, recalled that George Slade and Al Gray taught him lots about how to more effectively question decisions as he progressed in his profession. Colonel Betta provided this anecdote to the author in 2013.
6. Arc Light refers to B-52 strikes, which would be devastating to troops caught in the open. President Nixon's unfettered use of B-52s in reaction to the NVA's *Easter Offensive* brought North Vietnam to its knees in 1972 despite the loss of numerous American aircrews. The NVA were very wary of American air power, and not sure that it might not be used to counter the NVA's current offensive.
7. "Foggy Bottom" refers to the area surrounding the Department of State's headquarters in the District of Columbia, though many think of the name as a double entendre that also reflects the thinking done inside the building.
8. For a full explanation of the organization and achievements of the Amphibious Evacuation Support Force, see *U.S. Marines in Vietnam: The Bitter End, 1973-1975.* General Richard Carey and Major David Quinlan also wrote a series of three articles about *Operation Frequent Wind* and the AESF for the *Marine Corps Gazette.* Both sources give much more detail about air operations.
9. Author interview with Ralph W. Adams, August 2011. See *Al Gray, Marine,* Volume 1, Chapter 4 to read about when Al Gray first met Ralph Adams.
10. Sparrow Hawk designates an infantry unit, usually a reinforced squad, which is ready to deploy around a downed aircraft to protect the aircrew and the aircraft until everyone can be evacuated, including the aircraft. Alternatively, the aircraft would be destroyed in place. Two of Captain Berry's four aircraft were empty but for flight crew, and two had Sparrow Hawk Marines aboard in the event they were needed for contingency operations.
11. All times will be local time in Saigon, using the 24-hour military clock. Thus, 0500 is 5 A.M., 1700 is 5 P.M., and 1215 is 12:15 P.M.
12. Author interview with Major General William A. Whitlow, USMC (Ret) 2009.
13. Photo by LtCol William R. Melron, USMC, see *U.S. Marines in Vietnam: The Bitter End, 1973-1975.*
14. Author interview with Lieutenant Colonel John F. Guilmartin, PhD, USAF (Ret) 2007-2011.
15. Map adapted from *U.S. Marines in Vietnam: The Bitter End, 1973-1975.*
16. Larry Englemann. Marine Memories of the Evacuation of Saigon, *Pushing On* Internet blog. 2012. Accessed 2017 at: http://lde421.blogspot.com/2012/12/marine-memories-of-evacuation-of-saigon.html.

17. Larry Englemann *Pushing On* Internet blog.
18. Author interview with Colonel Jaehne.
19. Larry Englemann *Pushing On* Internet blog.
20. Author interviews with Dr. Guilmartin, 2007-2011.
21. Larry Englemann *Pushing On* Internet blog.
22. Larry Englemann *Pushing On* Internet blog.
23. Larry Englemann *Pushing On* Internet blog.
24. Larry Englemann *Pushing On* Internet blog.
25. Larry Englemann *Pushing On* Internet blog.
26. Larry Englemann *Pushing On* Internet blog.
27. Larry Englemann *Pushing On* Internet blog.
28. Larry Englemann *Pushing On* Internet blog.
29. Picture courtesy *U.S. Marines in Vietnam: The Bitter End, 1973-1975*.
30. Larry Englemann *Pushing On* Internet blog.
31. Larry Englemann interview with Thomas O'Hara. *Pushing On* Internet blog.
32. For the most complete view of the helicopter operations in both *Frequent Wind* and *Eagle Pull*, see *U.S. Marines in Vietnam: the Bitter End, 1973-1975*. Some details between that historical record and our story vary. However, as any historian can attest, often the "record" and individual memories differ. One such variance is the time that the first flight of helicopters landed at the DAO Complex at Tan Son Nhut. The official history says 1506 (3:06 P.M.) local time, but General Gray's recollection was that it was 1402 (2:02 P.M.) local. Though Admiral Whitmire had indeed ordered "L-Hour" changed to 1500, the first wave of CH-53s was already over Tan Son Nhut at 1400, and General Carey, as General Gray recalls, decided to land them rather than wait. It was a good tactical decision, and saved much confusion that any delay would have surely caused. General Gray's memory is confirmed by the account given by Tom O'Hara, who recalls taking off on a later wave at about 1400, after some refugees had begun to return to the ships. In any event, our narrative is not meant to correct the official account; rather, it is intended to tell the story as accurately as General Gray, and others, remembered it.
33. Author interview with Lieutenant General Richard A. Carey, USMC (Ret), 2012.
34. Author interview with Colonel Slade.
35. Larry Englemann *Pushing On* Internet blog.
36. A recently published book, *Last Men Out*, tells the story of the happenings at the Embassy those final days in April, 1975. Though the book is well written, it contains numerous factual errors. Nonetheless, Major Kean and his Marine Security Guard detachment, Saigon, deserve lots of credit for a job well done under very stressful circumstances.
37. From General Gray's private collection. He might not have been the last man out of Vietnam, but General Gray was the last man out of the DAO Compound, where the message center was located. And he did more than simply turn the lights out, he made sure the place was blown to smithereens.
38. Gray and Davis first met when then Colonel Davis visited Captain Gray in Japan in 1957. The relationship grew at HQMC, where Davis served in the G-2. Davis went away to the National War College in 1961 and then on to Europe in the NATO J-2, but, as a new Brigadier General in 1963, he returned to HQMC for several months before going to the 3rd Division as Assistant Division Commander. He returned to HQMC before Gray left in December, 1965. After their joint speaking tour in 1969, the men remained close. Davis retired in 1972, but the Generals were in close contact until General Davis's passing in 2003. General Davis probably would have been a serious contender for Commandant of the Marine Corps but for the close relationship that President Nixon had with General Cushman, whom Nixon appointed to that post in 1972; that appointment prompted Davis's retirement. See *The Story of Ray Davis*.
39. Colonel William J. Davis is the same officer who commanded 1/7 during the actions at Charlie Ridge that are described in Chapter 7 of Al Gray, Marine, Volume I.

40. Larry Englemann *Pushing On* Internet blog.
41. Colonel Wm. J. Davis (Ed.), *The Story of Ray Davis*, p. 4-12.
42. Author videotape interview of General Gray dated January 12, 2010. "And I just never, never, never thought that the North Vietnamese would ever invite the Chinese into the war… China at that time, and historically before that, has always been really a – a regional kind of a power, thought process, where they wanted to protect their own borders and the like. They did not – they were not interested in expansion and – and that kind of activity."

CHAPTER 8

HQMC, BRIEFLY

HQMC, BRIEFLY

By June 1975, arguably the most respected man on Okinawa to both the local citizenry and to the Marines was Al Gray. The Colonel, who spoke conversational Japanese quite well, had changed the culture not only aboard Camp Hansen, but also in Kin Ville, the popular liberty spot just outside the Camp's gates. But the time had come for Gray to turn over his command to his good friend and contemporary, Colonel Robert Haebel.

For Gray, it was an emotional turn of events. He knew when he arrived on Okinawa in September 1974 that there was much to do. He also knew that events in Southeast Asia made a military confrontation with the North Vietnamese highly likely, almost inevitable. No matter how critical events might have become in Asia, however, the Marine Corps desperately needed a rejuvenation of spirit and purpose among the troops who would be called upon to meet potential adversaries. That Gray had completely transformed the ways of thinking and the morale aboard Marine bases could not be denied; indeed, his efforts were memorialized when he was awarded the John Paul Jones Leadership award by the Navy League. His Commandant, General Robert E. Cushman, thought so highly of the fruits of Gray's labors that he personally went to New Orleans to accept the award on behalf of his Colonel, who was then aboard ship still deeply involved with the events in Saigon. Gray was very proud of his Marines and how they performed in Phnom Penh and Saigon, and he knew they would meet future challenges just as well.

Al Gray was ordered to a new assignment in Washington, knowing that his former Commanding General in the Pacific, and his old recruiting officer, General Louis Wilson, was the new Commandant. Gray might have speculated as to how that change would affect his future, but that was hardly his style. He had orders to report to the Training & Education Division at Headquarters Marine Corps, and in accordance with his long-standing modus operandi he gave little thought to anything other than doing well in his new duties. But anyone who ever met him, or ever spoke at length with him about his profession, knew one thing was certain: Al Gray would take what he got and make what he wanted.

THE AFTERMATH, MAY 1, 1975

Al Gray was bone tired. The adrenalin was wearing off. When the helicopter carrying Lieutenant Colonel George Slade, Colonel Gray, and its crew had turned away from Saigon to return to the *Blue Ridge*, Gray began to relax for the first time in weeks. Yes, there were assorted administrative details that would require his attention, but his Airmen, Sailors, and Marines were no longer in harm's way, and he could look forward to getting some well-deserved rest. Content that the operation had gone just about as well as he or anyone could have envisioned, Gray congratulated the Commander of his 2nd Battalion for another exceptional performance as the CH-46 returned to the CTF 76 flagship. After quickly making the rounds to ensure things were really wrapped up, Gray proceeded to his cabin, intent on getting some much-needed sleep. Rest was not to be, however. Three issues arose, and each made Gray furious.

First, there was message traffic from CINCPAC indicating that there was to be a formal inquiry into all aspects of the operation. Despite private assurances via back channel communications that this inquiry was not intended to become an inquisition, the forthcoming affair quickly became referred to among the staff as the "non-inquisition inquisition."[1] Second, along with the information regarding the upcoming non-inquisition inquisition, there was additional message traffic indicating an Air Force colonel would soon be arriving at the flagship to interview Gray about the $8M that was destroyed before the evacuation was completed. He was keenly aware that a message had been sent through the chain of command to the CINC PAC stating that Colonel A. M. Gray and Captain R.J. McManus, and Master Seargent W. V. East had witnessed the destruction of the currency. Gray was completely astonished that anyone would come to personally question him about that event. He told the staff, "Keep that colonel away from me, because if I see him I will throw him overboard."[2]

Somewhere, of course, there was some high-level bureaucrat whose entire focus was to double-check and then triple-check that the cash had been destroyed and not stolen, but the urgency with which such assurance was sought made the effort more resemble something from beyond the bizarre rather than a rational investigation. And whichever "higher headquarters" had dispatched a colonel to personally interrogate Al Gray should have known much better. Not that Al Gray required special treatment, but any officer who just completed a complex operation certainly did not need to be harassed by investigators, especially after having already reported in official message traffic that the money had been burned.

The third event that raised Gray's ire was much more problematic, more serious and went to the core of the Marine Corps' ethos. General Carey had directed Major Kean, the Senior Marine from the Embassy Detachment, to brief Gray in his stateroom. For the first time, Gray was informed that two Embassy Marines had been killed by rocket fire at Tan Son Nhut prior to the evacuation, and that their bodies had not been recovered. Gray was shocked, and then became livid, as he learned of the events that conspired to create this most unsatisfactory state of affairs. Gray had been the Commander of the Ground Forces, and felt it should have been his responsibility to retrieve the bodies. He requested that General Carey appoint him to be the investigating officer to determine what had happened and what could be done to rectify the circumstances. Carey approved this action and Gray, through a rapid series of interviews and discussions with key personnel, determined that the bodies of the two Embassy Marines had been taken to the Seventh-Day Adventist Hospital in accordance with the then-State Department policy for handling these situations. Under normal circumstances, these bodies would have been removed from Saigon by airlift to the United States. This, of course, was not done since airlifted operations out of Saigon had been terminated earlier and the bodies had probably remained at the hospital.

There was no doubt that the 9th MAB staff knew of the casualties. What also became clear, however, is that no one took responsibility for retrieving the remains of Corporal McMahon and Lance Corporal Judge. In the early morning hours of the 29th, the senior Marine on site at DAO, Colonel Wylie Taylor, reported the casualties and their disposition to the MAB staff. That occurred hours before the evacuation was ordered to begin. Although it is inevitable that some details fall through the cracks while commanders and their staffs are preparing to conduct operations, there is no excuse for what happened. Had Colonel Taylor, who had not worked with the staff yet held the title Deputy Commander, not been thrust into Saigon as a representative of General Carey, perhaps Colonel Gray would have been alerted to the circumstances. But, for whatever reason, he was not.

Late in the afternoon, after the evacuation had begun in earnest, Admiral Donald Whitmire inquired of Lieutenant Colonel Jerry Goodwine if the Marine knew what had happened to the bodies? Goodwine replied that he did not, but that he would query the MAB staff. Goodwine approached Colonel Hans Edebohls, the MAB G-4, and told him that Rear Admiral Whitmire wanted to know about the remains of the two casualties. Edebohls chastised Goodwine with a reply to the effect that, "Tell the Admiral that Marines will take care of Marines." Then, as Goodwine turned away, Edebohls added, "The remains have been taken to the morgue on the Midway." Goodwine returned to the Admiral with that news. The next time Goodwine heard anything about the incident was when Major Kean came aboard *Blue Ridge* in the early hours of the 30th and reported that the Marines' bodies were still at the Seventh-Day Adventist Hospital.[3]

After addressing the issue related to the cash burnt in Saigon and reviewing the situation regarding the Marine casualties, Gray turned his attention to the movements of CTF 76 and ARG Alpha. With the operations concluded in Saigon, it was likely that 9th MAB would stand down and the 33rd MAU would be reconstituted. Gray recommended that ARG Alpha and the 33rd MAU remain in the South China Sea in the event future contingencies arose. The whole of Southeast Asia had been ablaze and there was no dearth of possible threats to American interests in the area. Despite Gray's concerns, the entire naval force sailed directly to the Philippine Islands. Everyone, it seemed, from flag officers to privates first class were ready for maintenance, upkeep, and liberty in Subic Bay.

Before the ships reached Subic, Ambassador Martin, aboard the *Blue Ridge*, held a hastily convened press conference. Martin was shocked when an angry Keyes Beech, the Chicago reporter, confronted him over the issue of the chaos that had resulted at the Embassy during the evacuation. "I thought we were friends," exclaimed the Ambassador to one of Beech's observations. "We were," replied Beech, "until I had to drag myself over the Embassy wall in order to reach safety."[4] In a war filled with coincidences, a minor one was that the newsman who was in Vietnam when Al Gray arrived in 1964 with Marine Detachment, Advisory Unit #1, also departed Saigon when that same Marine left Vietnam for the last time. Gray considered Beech one of the few American reporters who actually tried to present the story of the war objectively. As a combat correspondent, Beech had landed on *Tarawa* with the Second Marine Division; later, as a civilian he covered Korea. Unlike many of his contemporaries, Beech was not unduly influenced when David Halberstam won the Pulitzer Prize for his largely anti-war reportage.

The circumstances surrounding the bodies had upset Al Gray more than anything in quite a long time, and the recovery of the remains became his focus over the coming weeks. Had he known during the evacuation that these bodies were still there, he would have taken action to recover them. He knew the hospital location well and had been there many times during his reconnaissance of the area. It would have been difficult, but quite possible, to go there during the evacuation and recover the bodies for movement to the ships via helicopter.

During the return to the Philippines, he flew directly from the ship to Manila and consulted with Deputy Ambassador Ronald F. Lehman, who had been the number two diplomat in the Embassy. He also made met with French and other foreign diplomats whom he thought might be able to intercede with the North Vietnamese on humanitarian grounds to permit the bodies to be flown out of Saigon. Gray went so far as to quietly fly to other countries in the area though his meetings with diplomats there were no more successful than his efforts in Manila. Sadly, Gray's quest was fruitless. Finally, in 1976, due to the tireless efforts of Senator Edward M. Kennedy of Massachusetts, the bodies of Corporal McMahon and Lance Corporal Judge were returned to the United States for suitable burial.

SUBIC BAY, MAY 3–12, 1975

It was only fitting that following the withdrawal from South Vietnam that Al Gray would return to the Philippines. After all, it was from the "P-I" that Captain Al Gray made his initial foray into South Vietnam, back in 1961.[5] Assigned to the 1st Composite Radio Company, he had led a Flyaway Team to San Miguel to operate against live targets in Southeast Asia. When serving with such detachments, Gray traveled under orders designating him a "courier," and his orders which never really put limits on the locations where he might go. Learning that a Navy cruiser was making a port visit to Saigon and then immediately returning to Subic, then-Captain Al Gray hitched a ride. The North Vietnamese were targets for his detachment, but Gray was also interested in learning more about the situation in South Vietnam.

A thoughtful book by Ellen J. Hammer, *The Struggle for Indochina*, was one of the first works about the region that Gray read. It was Hammer's book, combined with future uncertainty associated with the new (Diem) government in Saigon, coupled with the increased emphasis that the Kennedy Administration had put on aiding the South Vietnamese regime that had piqued Gray's interest. Gray, in civilian clothes and operating far, far under the radar, quietly contacted the Marines at the Embassy, looked around the capital, and left when the ship's port visit ended. Now, 14 years later, Colonel Gray again returned from Saigon to the Philippines, under far different circumstances, and unable to escape the glare of the national spotlight.

The Sailors and Marines of the amphibious task force arrived in Subic on May 3. An Army general led the team that would conduct the inquiry into *Operation Frequent Wind*; Colonel Robert E. Haebel was the lone Marine representative. Haebel was then serving as the G-3 at FMFPAC; Al Gray knew Colonel Haebel to be an outstanding, highly respected officer. All concerned were confident that inquiry would be objective and fact-finding, and really would not have the air of an inquisition.

One embarrassing detail that was thoroughly investigated was why there had been a discrepancy between CTF 76 and USSAG Thailand over the issue of "L-Hour." In the final hours leading up to the launch of the evacuation force, General Burns in Thailand misunderstood that L-Hour meant the time the aircraft would leave the task force ships to begin their travel to Saigon, not the time the aircraft would touch down in Saigon. Since the flight time was about 50 minutes, the discrepancy had implications. The inquiry concluded that whatever the difference in the understanding of L-Hour, there was no delay from the time CFT 76 was ordered executed and time the Marine aircraft began the operation.

Admiral Whitmire directed that Lieutenant Colonel Jerry Goodwine, the senior Marine on his staff, attend the proceedings of the board of inquiry. Goodwine recalled that Al Gray personally answered 75 or 80% of the questions presented to those involved in the operation. Goodwine thought Gray demonstrated a masterful display of the facts related to a wide variety of issues that had been raised. Further, it was Al Gray who invariably provided the rationale for the decisions made before and during the operation. In Goodwine's professional opinion, while the evacuation might have been successful without Al Gray's personal involvement, there was no doubt who the central driving force for what was accomplished on April 29 and 30. But more than Jerry Goodwine knew of Gray's integral part in the evacuation. General Carey also heaped praise on the sturdy, highly professional commander of RLT-4, who also served as Carey's de facto Chief of Staff. The two men later served together for a number of tours as general officers, and few praised Gray's professionalism more than Carey.[6]

THE MAYAGUEZ AFFAIR, MAY 12–15, 1975

The non-inquisition inquisition had no sooner wrapped up than another situation developed. On the morning of May 13, Lieutenant Colonel Charles E. Hester, Commanding Officer of 1st Battalion, 4th Marines, called his boss, suggesting that Colonel Gray meet him at the Naval Command Center. On his way there, Gray encountered the Commander-in-Chief, Pacific Fleet, Admiral Maurice F. (Mickey) Weisner.

Figure 8.1
Gray meeting up with Admiral Weiser at the Subic Command Center. [7]

Admiral Weisner had been in the area during *Operation Frequent Wind* and he knew Colonel Gray dating back to even before the events of Saigon. Asking Gray what was happening, the Admiral led the Marine into the command center where together they would be briefed. It turned out that Cambodian pirates who were thought to be part of a Khmer Rouge military unit had hijacked an American flagged merchant ship, the SS *Mayaguez*. Someone at Commander-in-Chief, Pacific (CINCPAC) Headquarters, had placed Lieutenant Colonel Hester's battalion on alert. At the same time, elements of the 9th Marines on Okinawa had been notified to be ready to deploy.

The situation made Colonel Al Gray unhappy. Gray had wanted to keep the 33rd MAU in the South China Sea, ready to respond to an emergency such as this. On May 13 there was no seaborne unit ready to react. The aircraft carrier USS *Coral Sea* was diverted from a trip to Australia and two U.S. Navy destroyers were ordered to the area. The USS *Hancock*, was in Subic Bay with Marines embarked but could not get underway before May 15th due to maintenance requirements. Air Force Lieutenant General John Burns in Thailand was ordered to react forcibly and quickly. Also, by now there were two targets: the ship itself and the crew, which had been removed from the ship and taken ashore. Using a combination of Air Force CH-53s and Jolly Green Giant HH-53s, General Burns came up with a plan to use volunteers from the 56th Air Force Security Squadron to assault the *Mayaguez*. Tragically, that plan ended on May 13th when one of the CH-53s crashed, killing 17 security airmen and the helicopter's five-man crew.

Gray met with his battalion commander, and after finding that Delta Company, 1/4 would be the unit sent, Gray decided to add a field grade officer to the mission. His reasoning was that a field grade officer with Special Intelligence access would command better cooperation from the other services involved; he sent his Regimental S-2, then-Major Ray Porter, also an experienced infantry officer, to command the unit from 1/4. Although the Delta Company commander, Captain Lewis W. Woods, was an outstanding officer who had earned a Navy Cross in Vietnam, adding Porter was the proper move; he provided experience and knowledge for the mission. Another Gray directive that proved prescient was having his Marines carry two gas masks, after ensuring their filters were functioning properly. First Battalion, Fourth Marines had been deployed for several months and was both ready and capable. Concurrently, the 9th MAB Command Group, under General Carey, with a small, special staff, was re-activated at Subic Bay for planning contingency special operations. The Command Group with Gray as their Chief of Staff, embarked on the USS *Hancock* along with BLT 2/4 and HMM-462. LSU 3/9, along with an infantry company from 2/4, embarked on USS *Mobile*. Loading was completed on the morning of the 15h and the *Hancock* and *Mobile* left Subic Bay for the Coastal area of Cambodia. Initial planning considered four basic options: 1) seizure of Koh Tang Island, 2) seizure of the Poulo Wai Island complex, 3) seizure of Kampong Som Port, and 4) recovery of the SS *Mayaguez*. Early on the morning of the 15th, the concepts were modified to included reinforcement of Marine Ground Security Force (GSF) inserted by Air Force helicopters on Koh Tang Island, as well as continued planning to secure the Port of Kampong Som in Cambodia.

President Gerald R. Ford, Secretary of State Henry Kissinger, Secretary of Defense James Schlesinger, and the Acting Chairman of the Joint Chiefs of Staff, General David Jones, understandably, intended to show that despite the recent withdrawal from Saigon and the accompanying loss of South Vietnam, the United States remained strong and committed in Southeast Asia.

Accordingly, the 9th Marine Regiment in Okinawa received a warning order to have a battalion ready to deploy, the 2nd Battalion, which was currently located in the Northern Training Area of Okinawa preparing for deployment was ordered to return to base. On May 14th, the battalion, led by Lieutenant Colonel Randall Austin, boarded Air Force C-141 transport aircraft and flew to Thailand. There, Lieutenant General John Burns and his staff had crafted another hastily drawn plan to use 2/9, with Air Force CH-53 helicopters, to assault Koh Tang Island, where the crew of *Mayaguez* was thought to be held.

During the day of 13 May, attack aircraft from U.S. bases in Thailand had sunk several small boats associated with the *Mayaguez* attack. However, when the crew was taken off the ship and moved in the direction of the mainland, the U.S. had lost contact and really knew nothing about the crew's whereabouts. Unfortunately, the Americans also knew nothing about Koh Tang Island. The island was one of those whose ownership was disputed between Vietnam and Cambodia. With the Vietnamese communists threatening to occupy the island, the Khmer Rouge had fortified it and committed about 100 strongly armed men to its defense. The Cambodians feared an attack from Vietnam, not the United States.

Figure 8.2
Delta Company Assault. Marines from Delta Company 1st Battalion 4th Marines in the assault to recover the Mayaguez.[8]

The *Mayaguez* remained at anchor and on May 14th General Burns ordered the Marines of Delta Company, 1/4 to make a helicopter assault to retake the ship. However, intelligence remained fuzzy or non-existent, and the assault was called off. Later in the day, however, Burns received orders to attack the ship and Koh Tang Island simultaneously on the morning of the 15th.

Figure 8.3
Major R.E. Porter and Captain Walt Wood raising the flag on the Mayaguez *after its recovery.*[9]

Delta Company was embarked aboard the destroyer USS *Holt*, and shortly after dawn the company made the first ship-to-ship assault by Marines since the Civil War. After a furious barrage of tear gas covered the ship, the Marines, in gas masks, quickly determined the ship was unmanned. Volunteers from the Military Sealift Command got the ship underway following its recovery.

Early in the morning of 15 May, the complex and hastily drawn up plan for a helicopter assault on Koh Tang Island by the BLT 2/9 Marines commenced. It was fraught with high risk and danger on many fronts. First, intelligence estimates placed 20-30 enemy troops on the island, when in reality the number was over 100, not counting their family personnel. (Southeast Asian troops, like most warriors, will fight with extraordinary tenacity and heroism if their families are threatened). Second, the Marines were unable to acquire aerial photos of the island nor the two selected landing zones, which, in fact, were covered by accurate anti-aircraft fire manned by a determined enemy. Third, the Air Force pilots and crew were not experienced with the tactics used when encountering contested landing zones and heavily defended sites. And finally, the Air Force helicopters could not talk directly to the Marines forces because their radios used incompatible frequencies.

Of the eight helicopters involved in the initial assault, three were destroyed on or around the island, and four more sustained damage so severe they were out of action. Incredible airmanship kept the number of casualties from being even more severe than would have been expected given such damage. As a result of the carnage, the Marines ended up on East and West Beach, and at another location southwest of West Beach, where Lieutenant Colonel Austin and his command group and mortars had been landed. The heroism of the Air Force personnel and individual Marines largely kept a bad situation from becoming a terrible tragedy. Throughout the day about 100 Marines, split into two separate areas, fought to survive against a well-entrenched and aggressively-led enemy. Only the presence of an AC-130 gunship and the arrival late in the day of an OV-10 aerial observer dedicated to the island prevented more casualties.

While the Marines battled for their lives, and the Air Force scrambled to keep sufficient helicopter support in the area, the Cambodians announced the release of the crew of the *Mayaguez* on May 15. With the crew of the *Mayaguez* released and the ship recovered, the Joint Chiefs ordered offensive operations on Koh Tang suspended and the Marines evacuated. Unfortunately, the Khmer Rouge never received that order! A second wave of Marines who were approaching Koh Tang had been diverted back to Thailand when the stand-down order from Washington was received. Lieutenant Colonel Austin, whose men remained hard pressed by the enemy, and who were still scattered about the island, had to get permission from General Burns to receive reinforcements that were necessary to extract the Marines already on the island. When the additional Marines finally reached the island, Austin was finally able to start the extraction process, though never did that most difficult of military operations – withdrawing under heavy fire – ever achieve satisfactory status. Chaos reigned and for those involved, it was a bitter outcome and provided proof positive of the need for training and readiness. Austin was a brilliant commander, whose officers and men fought with great courage and tenacity throughout the ordeal.

Meanwhile, on the USS *Hancock*, following confirmation of the successful recovery of the *Mayaguez* and her crew, 9th MAB planning focused on the extraction of Marine ground crew from Koh Tang Island based on continuous monitoring of the tactical situation on Koh Tang Island over the ABCCC Command Net. The 9th MAB had nearly completed a detailed, flexible plan for landing by surface or air to conduct the required operations when word was received on the evening of the 15th that the GSF extraction had been successfully completed.

In the United States, President Ford's strong and decisive leadership went a long way toward restoring U.S. prestige in the region.

CAMP HANSEN, OKINAWA, MAY 20- JUNE 15, 1975

The Commanding Officer of the 4th Marines returned to Okinawa in late May. He knew his time in command was drawing down, and for officers who thrive on leading Marines, change of command ceremonies are not fun. The old saying among Marines is that you can tell who the outgoing commander is – he is the one not smiling.

Gray and Bob Haebel had known each other for years. No Marine was more highly respected than Haebel, and Gray knew the 4th Marines would continue to be in good hands. But Gray also took time to help others, continuing a trait that personified him since his earliest days as a Marine. Colonel William Weise was coming to Okinawa as the new Commanding Officer of the 9th Marines. Weise, an infantryman who had not previously had a lot of time interacting with Al Gray, was both quite surprised and highly thankful that Gray took time from his own schedule to fully brief Weise about all aspects of commanding troops on Okinawa in 1975. Weise never forgot the many courtesies Gray extended to him, although there was no apparent reason for Gray's actions – no reasons other than helping a fellow Marine and wanting all Marines on Okinawa to be successful.[10]

Figure 8.4
Colonel Robert Haebel relieved Colonel Al Gray as CO, 4th Marines.[11]

Figure 8.5
Led by Lieutenant Colonel George Slade, the Magnificent Bastards of 2/4 pass in
review during the 4ᵗʰ Marines Change of Command ceremony. Major Ramsey
Green is the second from the right in the formation behind Colonel Slade.[12]

Prior to leaving the Philippines Colonel Gray had received the following tele-
gram from then-Major John Sheehan:

```
PMS ICS IPMSFSD SFO
04909 (FT006 RELAY) 1-038698C176 6-25 1738 SUSPECTED DUPE NL
PMS 01075 NL NEWPORT RI 6:25 VIA FORTORD CA 06-27
COL A M GRAY COMMANDING OFFICER
4TH MARINE REG 3RD MARINE DIVN
FPO SAN FRANCISCO CA 96602
RECENT INFO FROM O-9 SOURCE INDICATES BONE STEEL-6 TO BE
ASSIGNED DUTY TO B G FLEMINGS (TNG) CURRENT BATTING ORDER
WEEK CAN BE ASSIGNED TO TNG IF SO DESIRED EXPECT TO REPORT
HOME ON AUG 15 REQUEST INSTRUCTIONS NEW CP AS OF 10 JULY
5302 POMEROY DRIVE FAIRFAX VA 22303 DOC SAYS BRAVO ZULU ON
YOUR RECENT ACTIVITIES
  J J SHEEHAN
```

Figure 8.6
Telegraph to Colonel Gray from Major Sheehan.[13]

It is obvious that Jack Sheehan was speaking in relative code to his former boss. The "0-9" source that he referred to was then Lieutenant General Sam Jaskilka, the soon-to-be Assistant Commandant of the Marine Corps. "Bone Steel-6" had been Gray's radio call sign when he and Sheehan served together in 1st Battalion, 2nd Marines at Camp Lejeune. So that sentence translates to "Colonel Gray can be assigned to work for Brigadier General Fleming in the Training and Education Division – should Gray want that assignment." If he did, Gray could expect to receive orders requiring him to report by August 15. Sheehan then gave his new address, and closed by saying Lieutenant Colonel "Doc" Smith, the former XO of 1/2, sends his congratulations for the success of Gray's recent operation. "Bravo Zulu" is shorthand in the naval services for "well done." Very few officers had a closer relationship with Al Gray than did Jack Sheehan.[14]

While Gray and his men had been deployed away from Okinawa, the *John Paul Jones Award* for leadership from the Navy League had honored the energetic Colonel of Marines. Major General Kenny Houghton, the Commanding General of the 3rd Division, had prepared a six-page recommendation that detailed the accomplishments Gray had achieved while restoring discipline and improving the atmosphere in and around Camp Hansen during the fall of 1974. Gray was informed by a HQMC message that his award had been approved and that he was authorized to return to New Orleans to receive it. He declined the invitation, saying he was off the coast of Vung Tao, South Vietnam, and preferred to continue planning for the evacuation. Besides the remarkable write-up that General Houghton submitted, his reports on the performance of the CO of the 4th Marines left no doubt that he believed Gray to be the best colonel Houghton had ever worked with during his long career. Of course, it is not unusual that given the turn around Gray had initiated on Okinawa his senior officers would hold him in high esteem, but it was a remarkable tribute that the Commandant of the Marine Corps chose to personally travel to New Orleans to accept the award on Gray's behalf.

Gray's relationship with General Robert E. Cushman had begun many years earlier when the General had been double hatted as the G-2/G-3 at HQMC and Gray was assigned to work with then-Lieutenant Colonel Charlie Beale in AO2F. However, after Gray's deeds in combat commanding the Gio Linh Outpost, and later the 1st Radio Battalion forces in Vietnam, plus his efforts in resolving the Mediterranean racial problems of 1972, the General was even more aware of Gray's leadership skills.

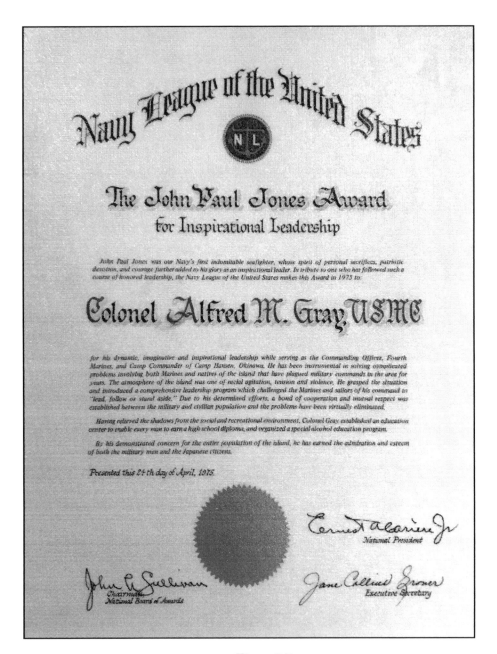

Figure 8.7
John Paul Jones Award. [15]

While most of Marine history is given to Gray's achievements on the operational side, as CO of the 4th Marines and the Ground Security Officer in *Operation Frequent Wind*, it was probably in his role as Commander of Camp Hansen that Colonel Gray made the more long-lasting impact on the Marine Corps, and indeed the country. A series of commanders had been unable to get the racial, drug and alcohol situations on Okinawa under control. It was a desperate time, and Lieutenant General Louis H. Wilson had well known of its seriousness when he summoned Gray to his office on Hawaii. General Wilson realized that future, often critical, deployments throughout Southeast Asia were dependent on a professional, well trained and highly motivated force of Marines. So long as racial tensions, the ravages of drug abuse, and the incipient degradations of alcoholism were rampant within Marine units on Okinawa, the successes of future deployments were in serious jeopardy. Al Gray's superb leadership, which others bought into hook, line and sinker, provided the impetus for an almost immediate turnaround at Camp Hansen. And as importantly, his actions were a blueprint for the Marine Corps to follow. Commandant Wilson and subsequently Commandants Barrow and Kelley, each put Marine readiness on an upward trajectory by their implementation of new policies related to separating troublemakers and addicts, increased emphasis on educational achievement, and simple professionalism as demonstrated by the energetic Commander of Camp Hansen and the unofficial mayor of Kin Ville. Gray's relationship with both the local people and their law enforcement can only be characterized as exceptional.

Figure 8.8
Letter from Japanese Police to Colonel Al Gray. [16]

Then-Major General Harold A. Hatch, the Commanding General of all bases on Okinawa, certainly warmed to Al Gray's methods and effectiveness during the year in which Gray worked for Hatch. General Hatch lauded Gray a tireless worker who spent nearly every night concerning himself with his troops while working to keep them out of trouble. His achievements came despite the fact that Gray was often away from the Camp for weeks at a time. Gray's personal example, especially his refusal of alcohol in all its forms, set a tremendous example that many officers and Staff NCOs followed. And Gray set the tone for the human relations program then so important within the Marine Corps by living the tenets of the program throughout all aspects of his life, a fact that did not go unnoticed by his seniors.[17]

Gray knew that Bob Haebel would do a great job leading the 4th Marines; indeed, there were no contemporaries that Gray held in higher regard than the tall Colonel who shared the change of command ceremony with him. Following it, General Houghton invited one of his favorite colonels – the premier colonel in the division according to Houghton – to his quarters to discuss events in Southeast Asia as well as events in Washington, where General Louis Wilson was to be the new Commandant.[18] While having the conversation with his old mentor, Gray, at Houghton's urging, had his first drink while outside the United States thirteen months ago – a scotch and water. And then Gray was off to his forthcoming tour at HQMC.

Figure 8.9
Then–Lieutenant Colonel Robert White and Colonel Al Gray
at Gray's farewell party on Okinawa.[19]

HEADQUARTERS MARINE CORPS, JUNE – SEPTEMBER 1975

Colonel Al Gray was part of a throng that crowded into the Commandant's briefing room. As usual, Gray sought a quiet place near the rear of the room, far outside the line of sight of the Commandant, General Louis Wilson. General Wilson leaned back in his chair, speaking calmly while his hands slowly moved back and forth, hands templed, touching his fingertips in rhythm with his speech. As the Commandant surveyed the room, his hand motion stopped, and he fixed his gaze on Al Gray, "Well, I see our great warrior has returned. When are you going to come and see your Commandant, Colonel Gray?" "Well, General, I usually don't enter carpeted offices unless I have been invited," responded Gray. General Wilson and the assembled officers smiled at the humor, but it was crystal clear that Gray would soon be on the Commandant's calendar.

Gray's assignment was as the Deputy to Brigadier General Lewis Fleming of the Training and Education Division at HQMC. General Fleming, a naval aviator, was quite busy coordinating an issue that the Marine Corps had long sought to solve – how to make its two Recruit Depots mirror images of each other. The General's absence left the day-to-day working of the section to Al Gray, and he jumped in with both feet. But he had other assignments thrust on him, as well.

Gray's old boss from his days as a battalion commander in the Med, now Lieutenant General Tom Miller, drafted him to participate in a broad reaching study of Marine fixed-wing aircraft. There were sure to be significant changes in the structure of Marine Aircraft Wings following Vietnam, and General Miller knew that Gray's fertile mind and vast professional knowledge of all things military would enrich the effort. Of course, Gray did not mind a bit joining the analysis; there were few Marines more interested in long-range studies and analysis than the sturdy New Jerseyan. And no sooner had the fixed-wing study concluded than Miller again tapped Gray to participate in a study of Marine helicopter requirements.

Gray, fresh from the evacuation of Saigon and familiar with the tragic use of Air Force helicopters on Koh Tang Island, eagerly accepted the assignment. Gray well understood the issues associated with Marine helicopters during the entirety of the Vietnam War. During that war, the equivalent of one and one-half Marine Aircraft Wings tried to support two and one-third Marine divisions, often with spotty results. Gray wanted very much to be part of finding a solution that would prevent future misunderstandings between the air and ground components.

But it was as much a credit to General Miller's professionalism as it was to Al Gray that he had been selected to participate in both studies. Miller had overcome his initial (but incorrect) impression of the ground colonel to become one of Gray's biggest supporters. It was proof that men used to flying at supersonic speeds could adapt, change and grow when they encountered new information about those far junior to them. Al Gray seldom altered from his own course and speed, but he was very happy to understand that his seniors were equally adaptable.

Within the T&E Division, a project that garnered a large share of Colonel Gray's attention was a new concept to establish a Marine Corps Combat Readiness and Evaluation System (MCCRES). From his time as CO of both the 2nd and 4th Marines, and from being the G-3 of the 2nd Division, Gray understood better than most the integral relationship between training and readiness. Before

MCCRES, the Marines did not have a good way to measure readiness and for the most part relied on Army-type tactical tests. Gray took the lead in preparing the necessary staff work to have the concept approved, and his recommendations to have LtCol Alex Lee and LtCol Mike Sullivan lead the ground and aviation efforts, respectively, was also approved. This long-term project was implemented in the operating forces in 1978.

Being at HQMC in the T&E Division allowed Gray to advance another of his favorite projects – exercise simulation. Dating from his days participating in the major Fleet exercises in Hawaii,[20] Gray had been interested in adding realism to exercises so as to give participants the best possible training. He had come to know a small Navy detachment near San Francisco's Treasure Island where an engineer was building a data entry and communication capability centered around a large cathode-ray tube. Gray made it a habit of visiting the detachment whenever he traveled near or through San Francisco. In 1969, while traveling from Vietnam back to his assignment in Quantico, Gray had arranged for the capability to be demonstrated at Camp Pendleton during an exercise there.

Gray's interest in simulation was piqued by one of his former battalion commanders, LtCol Bill Davis, who was working on a system at the Navy Yard called Tactical Warfare Analysis Evaluation System. Gray took the ball forward. As the acting head of T&E he brought the capability to the attention of then Lieutenant General Robert Barrow, at that time the head of Manpower. Gray subsequently briefed the idea to the Chief of Staff's committee, where it met opposition from the Quartermaster General, Major General James R. Jones, one of the Marine Corps most senior major generals. Though he was treading in deep water by taking on things under the purview of General Jones, Gray persuaded the committee that because the envisioned system would be a low-density item located in limited numbers at only a few locations, a complete logistics support package would not be necessary, and that all the parts needed could be procured within the research and development program. In this, Gray drew from his acquisition experience at HQMC during the early 1960s when he designed, procured and fielded a wide variety of SIGINT systems and equipment.

The seed had been planted, and within a couple years TWAES had been expanded, by adding simulation; it was renamed TWSEAS (Tactical Warfare Simulation, Evaluation and Analysis System.) By 1982, when Gray assumed command of the 2nd Marine Division, TWSEAS was not only fully fielded, it was fully integrated into regimental, division and force-level exercises. Logistics and electronic warfare modules had been added, and the system integrated into the command post. If the division deployed, TWSEAS would go with it to the field.

During the period when Gray was Commanding General, Marine Forces Atlantic, TWSEAS was a vital component in the exercises designed and led by Admiral Isaac Kidd, the Commander of all U.S. and Allied forces in the Atlantic area. Admiral Kidd was a strong advocate of wargaming, and used it as a tool to evaluate his subordinate commanders. The fact that Gray had personally participated in numerous wargames put him in good position vis-à-vis Admiral Kidd. TWSEAS became the backbone for simulation and wargaming within the Marine Corps through the early 1990s.

In 1987 and 1988, Commandant of the Marine Corps Al Gray put TWSEAS to continuous use by wargaming the American plan for throwing Saddam Hussein out of Kuwait. In an almost daily exercise, Gray would oppose a group of young majors from Quantico who fought as the Iraqis. Gray could not, of course, reveal the American intentions, but he could vary his tactics in a way to get a good feel for how that upcoming battle might unfold. In doing so, Gray became increasingly confident. TWSEAS, the simulation capability he had pushed in 1975, was a major component in perfecting American plans. TWSEAS was eventually replaced in the early 1990s by the Marine Corps Tactical Warfare System (MTWS), which was a greatly improved system that is still in use today.

During this period, Gray also took the lead in developing a concept for a new operations and training department at HQMC, which was eventually approved. Additionally, although not a formal member of the General Haynes Board, which was studying the force structure for the Commandant in response to a request of the Senate Arms Forces Committee, he spent several weekends assisting the study group at Quantico, wherein he championed the development of a mechanized armor regiment capability.

SELECTED FOR BRIGADIER GENERAL, SEPTEMBER 1975

The brigadier general's promotion board met not long after Gray's arrival at HQMC, and when its results were published Gray was surprised, and humbled, to find his name on the list. The President of the Board was Lieutenant General E.J. Miller, an officer whom Gray knew well and whom the entire Marine Corps held in highest esteem. A brief note that General Miller penned to Al Gray made the junior man feel even better, though that was hardly possible. General Miller's note read:

Dear Al:

Congratulations. You are beholden to no one.

Warm regards, E.J. Miller

For an officer who never asked any favors of anyone senior to him, and who tried throughout his career to assist others regardless of rank or situation, there could be no more positive affirmation that his approach was the correct one. General Miller's note is among General Gray's most prized personal papers.[21]

Figure 8.10
Commandant of the Marine Corps General Louis Wilson,
Al Gray, Mrs. Emily Gray, and Lieutenant General Sam Jaskilka on the
occasion of General Gray's promotion to Brigadier General.[22]

Also on the promotion list for new brigadiers, Gray was delighted to see the name of his old friend, Robert Haebel. Gray and many others considered Haebel the most prominent member of the new group that would be promoted to flag rank. At one of the early meetings of the new brigadiers, one of the senior civilians from the manpower section addressed the assembled officers. Manpower had studied the general officer selection process and was able to forecast that there was a good possibility that one of the newly selected brigadiers would become a future Commandant. In Gray's estimation, and he thought the opinion of most others, that officer was likely to be Bob Haebel.

Having been selected, but not yet promoted, there remained a plethora of things for Gray to accomplish at HQMC.

Figure 8.11
Jan Goss, Brigadier General Gray, and Mrs. Emily Gray, 1976.[23]

Among the most important was one personally assigned by the Commandant. When General Wilson required a study recommending a broad reorganization of the Marine Corps Reserve, its roles and mission, it was Al Gray who was given the job. Told that he could choose any officer in the greater Washington area to assist him, Gray adroitly grabbed then-Major Tony Zinni from his daily tasks at Headquarters.

The Marine reservists were at first very concerned about the selection of Gray to lead the study. After all, what did Gray know about the reserves? But then one of the reserve colonels who had supported Gray's 2nd Marines at Camp Lejeune, made it known that Gray was a good man to work with and was sure to give the reserves a proper study. It should be noted that the head of the Marine Corps Reserves at the time was the aforementioned Major General Mike Ryan, who was well aware of his background. Gray picked Major Zinni to give the final briefing to the Chief of Staff of the Marine Corps. The overall effort was well received and resulted in 53 recommendations being made for how to better train, use, organize and integrate the Marine reserves into the Marine Corps' overall mission. Fifty-one of the recommendations were adopted immediately, and the other two implemented after some discussion and minor changes.

With the reservists reorganized and the Commandant pleased, Brigadier General Al Gray made his way to Norfolk, Virginia, home to the United States Navy's Atlantic Fleet. It was back to the Fleet Marine Force for the highly professional, always-enthusiastic new general – but that is a story for another day.

NOTES AND REFERENCES

1. Author interview with Colonel Jerry Goodwine, 2010. Goodwine attended the "inquisition" as the representative of Rear Admiral Whitmire, CTF 76.
2. Author interview with Colonel Goodwine.
3. Author interview with Colonel Goodwine
4. Author interview with Colonel Goodwine.
5. Author interview with Colonel Goodwine.
6. Author interview with Lieutenant General Carey.
7. From General Gray's private collection.
8. Department of Defense Photo (USMC).
9. U.S. Navy photograph, by Michael Chan.
10. Author interviews with Brigadier General William Weise, USMC (Ret). 2008-2011.
11. From General Gray's private collection.
12. From General Gray's private collection.
13. From General Gray's private collection.
14. General Gray has often commented that when General Sheehan retired in 1997, he was the most highly qualified military officer on the planet.
15. From General Gray's private collection. That Commandant Cushman took the time to personally accept the John Paul Jones Award on Gray's behalf both surprised and honored Gray. He had first worked for General Cushman during his first tour at HQMC in the early 1960s. However, it was their time in Vietnam when Gray's Radio Battalion provided such magnificent support to Cushman's III MAF that cemented the relationship. See *Al Gray, Marine*, Volume 1, Chapter 7.
16. From General Gray's private collection. Al Gray consistently sought to create a close working relationship between his Marines and the local population, wherever he served: Korea, Japan, the Philippines, Turkey, Italy, France, Germany, Norway, the United Kingdom, Vietnam or any other country. He tried hard (and usually succeeded) to learn the local dialect, and he consistently set an example for his Marines and Sailors. He was also very well read with respect to each country's history, traditions and customs in addition to its military capabilities. He considered all that part of his education as a military professional.
17. The Human Relations Program was so important in the mid-1970s that each officer's fitness report had to include a statement as to whether or not the officer was compliant with the program.
18. General Houghton's reports on the topic of Colonel Al Gray make it perfectly clear that if Gray was not his favorite Colonel, then he surely was the one Houghton held in highest esteem. From General Gray's private collection.
19. From General Gray's private collection.

20. See Volume 1, Chapter 2, pp. 98-102.
21. From General Gray's private collection.
22. From General Gray's private collection.
23. From General Gray's private collection.

BIBLIOGRAPHY

BIBLIOGRAPHY

INTERVIEWS

The author has had the privilege to interview and communicate with many military personnel and colleagues of General Al Gray in the process of writing Volume 2, and thanks these individuals for the use of their contributions in this work.

Ralph W. Adams (NSA) (2011)

Brigadier General Richard M. Baughn (USAF) (2011)

Colonel Joe Betta, (USMC) 2013

Lieutenant General Richard A. Carey (USMC) (2012)

Kenneth Crouse (USMC) (2011)

Major Bruce Duderstadt, (USMC) (2008)

Thomas Glenn, (NSA) (2011-2012)

Colonel Lloyd E. "Jerry" Goodwine (USMC) (2010-2011)

General Alfred M. Gray (USMC) (2007-2014)

Mrs. Alfred M. Gray (2007-2014)

Lieutenant Colonel John F. Guilmartin, Jr. PhD (USAF) (2007-2013)

Colonel Richard L. Jaehne (USMC) (2011)

Sergeant Robert R. Jones (USMC) (2010-2011)

Colonel Donald Q. Lange (USMC) (2010)

Major General James E. Livingston (USMC) (2008-2011)

Sergeant Major Calvin Lynn (USMC) (2011)

Colonel James Magee (USMC) (2012)

Lieutenant General John H. Miller (USMC) (2011)

Major General J. M. Myatt (USMC) (2010)

Warren "Tom" O'Hara III (USMC) (2008-2011)

Major William Pedrick (USMC) (2008-2011)

General John J. Sheehan (USMC) (2010)

Colonel George P. Slade (USMC) (2009 and 2010)

Colonel Malcolm E. (Doc) Smith (USMC) (2010)

Major Richard T. Spooner (USMC) (2008-2011)

Brigadier General William E. Weise (USMC) (2008-2011)

Colonel Robert D. White (USMC) (2009)

Major General William Whitlow (USMC) (2009)

Mrs. Jane Wilson (2010)

General Anthony C. Zinni (USMC) (2011)

PRIVATE COLLECTIONS, PUBLIC ARCHIVES

Dr. Larry Engelmann

General Alfred M. Gray

Dr. John F. Guilmartin

General Alfred M. Gray Oral History, National Security Agency, 2010-2011.

Author videotaped interviews with General Alfred M. Gray, 2009-2011

BOOKS, ARTICLES

Berman, Larry. *The Incredible Double Life of Pham Xuan An,* Time *Magazine Reporter & Vietnamese Communist Agent.* New York: Collins, 2007.

Bernstein, Irving. *Guns or Butter: the Presidency of Lyndon Johnson.* New York: Oxford University Press, 1996.

Clancy, Tom, General Anthony C. Zinni, and Tony Koltz. *Battle Ready.* New York: G.P. Putnam's Sons, 2004.

Coram, Robert. *Brute: The Life of Victor H. Krulak, U.S. Marine.* New York: Little Brown & Company, 2010.

Davis, Colonel William J. (ed). *The Story of Ray Davis.* Varina, N.C.: Research Triangle Publishing, 1995.

Dickson, Paul. *The Electronic Battlefield.* Bloomington: Indiana University Press, 1976.

Drury, Bob, and Tom Clavin. *Last Men Out: The True Story of America's Heroic Final Hours in Vietnam.* New York: The Free Press, 2011.

Fall, Bernard. *Street Without Joy.* Mechanicsburg, PA, Stackpole Books, 2005.

———. *The Two Viet Nams*: A Political and Military Analysis (2nd Revised Edition). New York: Praeger, 1965.

Guilmartin, John F. *America in Vietnam: The Fifteen Year War.* New York: Military Press, 1991.

Halberstam, David. *The Best and The Brightest.* New York: Ballantine Books, 1969.

Hammer, Ellen J. *A Death in November: America in Vietnam, 1963.* New York: Oxford University Press, 1987.&

Karnow, Stanley. *Vietnam: A History.* New York: Penguin Press, 1997.

Kidd, Arthur. *My Life as a Marine*. Private Press, 2007.

Krulak, Victor H. *First to Fight: An Inside View of the United States Marine Corps* (Paperback). New York: Pocket Books, 1984.

Lansdale, Edward G. *In the Midst of Wars: An American's Mission to Southeast Asia* 1991. (Paperback).

Langguth, A.J. *Our Vietnam: The War 1954-1975*. New York: Simon & Schuster, 2000.

McMaster, H.R. *Dereliction of Duty: Lyndon Johnson, Robert McNamara, The Joint Chiefs of Staff, and the Lies that Led to Vietnam*. New York: HarperCollins, 1997.

McNamara, Robert Strange. *In Retrospect: The Tragedy and Lessons of Vietnam*. New York: Vintage Books, 1996.

Millett, Allan R. *Semper Fidelis: The History of the United States Marine Corps*. New York: The Free Press, 1980.

Millett, Allan R. and Shumlinson, Jack (ed). *Commandants of the Marine Corps*. Annapolis: Naval Institute Press, 2004.

Moyar, Mark. *Triumph Forsaken: The Vietnam War, 1954-1965*. Cambridge: Cambridge University Press, 2006.

Parks, W. Hayes "Rolling Thunder and the Laws of War," *Air University Review*, Vol. XXXIII, No. 2 (January-February 1982), 14.

Peterson, Michael E. *The Combined Action Platoons: The U.S. Marines Other War in Vietnam*. New York: Praeger, 1989.

Pribblenow, Merle L. (trans). Senior General Hoang Van Thai, et al, eds. *Victory in Vietnam: The Official History of the People's Army of Vietnam, 1954-1975*. Lawrence, KS: University Press of Kansas, 2002.

Robbins, James S. *This Time We Win: Revisiting the Tết Offensive*. New York: Encounter Books, 2010.

Sharp, U.S.G. *Strategy for Defeat: Vietnam in Perspective*. Novato, CA: Presidio Press, 1993 (Paperback).

Sheehan, Neil. *A Bright Shining Lie: John Paul Vann and America in Vietnam*. New York: Vantage Books, 1988.

Smith, Charles R. (ed). *U.S. Marines in the Korean War*. Washington, D.C.: History Division, United States Marine Corps, 2007.

Wicker, Tom. "Broadcast News." *New York Times* 26 January 1997. http://www.nytimes.com/books/97/01/26/reviews/970126.26wickert.html. Retrieved 2010-11-12.

U.S. Marines in Vietnam Series – All published by History and Museums Division, Headquarters Marine Corps, Washington, D.C.

U.S. Marines in Vietnam: The Advisory and Combat Assistance Era, 1954-1964. Captain Whitlow, Robert H., 1977

U.S. Marines in Vietnam: The Landing and the Buildup, 1965. Shumlinson, Jack; Major Johnson, Charles M., 1978.

U.S. Marines in Vietnam: An Expanding War, 1966. Shumlinson, Jack; 1982.

U.S. Marines in Vietnam: Fighting the North Vietnamese, 1967. Major Telfar, Gary L.; Lieutenant Colonel Roger, Lane; and Fleming, V. Keith, 1984.

U.S. Marines in Vietnam: The Defining Year, 1968. Shumlinson, Jack; Lieutenant Colonel Blasiol, Leonard A.; Smith, Charles R.; Captain Dawson, David A., 1997.

COMMAND CHRONOLOGIES

All Command Chronologies are available online at http://www.vietnam.ttu.edu/. Command Chronologies were published monthly by each unit during the Vietnam War.

III Marine Amphibious Force, 1965-1971

1st Battalion, 7th Marines, December 1968

1st Battalion, 12th Marines, 1965 through 1968

12th Marines, October 1965 through August 1967

2nd Battalion, 4th Marines, November 1965 through December 1968

INTERNET RESOURCES

http://www.2ndbattalion94thartillery.com/

Vietnam Studies, Riverine Operations 1966-1969, a monograph produced by the U.S. Army and available online at http://www.history.army.mil/books/vietnam/riverine/index.htm. Website checked March 2011.

http://www.time.com/time/magazine/article/0,9171,906068,00.html. *TIME Magazine,* June 26

http://www.afa.org/magazine/feb2007/0207tapes.asp, 1972.

http://www.tecom.usmc.mil/HD/PDF_Files/Pubs/Units/Brief%20History%20of%20the%2012th%20Marines.pdf. Smith, Charles R. *A Brief History of the 12th Marines.*

APPENDIX

APPENDIX

1/2	1st Battalion, 2nd Marines
1/4	1st Battalion, 4th Marines
1/9	1st Battalion, 9th Marines
1/12	1st Battalion, 12th Marines
2/4	2nd Battalion, 4th Marines
2/7	2nd Battalion, 7th Marines
2/94	2nd Battalion, 94th Artillery
25XX	Occupational Field for Communications
3/2	3rd Battalion, 2nd Marines
3/4	3rd Battalion, 4th Marines
ABCCC	Airforce Airborne Command, Control, and Communications
ACMC	Assistant Commandant of the Marine Corps
AESF	Amphibious Evacuation Support Force

AO2F	Signals Intelligence/Electronic Warfare Branch of the Intelligence Division at Headquarters, US Marine Corps
AP	Associated Press
ARG	Amphibious Ready Group
ARVN	Army of the Republic of Vietnam. Also referred to: South Vietnamese Army, Army of South Vietnam, and Army of Vietnam
ASIS	Amphibious Support and Intelligence System
BLT	Battalion Landing Team
C&SC	Command & Staff College
CG	Commanding General
CIA	Central Intelligence Agency
CINCPAC	Commander-in-Chief, Pacific
CINCPACFLT	Commander-in-Chief, Pacific Fleet
CO	Commanding Officer
COSVN	Central Office for South Vietnam
CPX	Command Post Exercise
CTF	Commander Task Force
DASC	Direct Air Support Center
DAO	Defense Attaché Office

DASC	Direct Air Support Center
DCPG	Defense Communications Planning Group
DF	Direction Finding
DMZ	Demilitarized Zone
DSPG	Defense Special Projects Group
DoD	Department of Defense
EOD	Explosive Ordinance Disposal
EW	Electronic Warfare
FMFLANT	Fleet Marine Forces, Atlantic
FMFPAC	Fleet Marine Forces, Pacific
G-1	Personnel Officer (on a general's staff)
G-2	Intelligence Officer (on a general's staff)
G-3	Operations Officer (on a general's staff)
GED	General Equivalency Diploma
GSF	Ground Security Force
GSO	Ground Security Officer
HDC	Helicopter direction center
HMM	Marine Medium Helicopter Squadron
HQMC	Headquarters Marine Corps

I Corps	I Corps: South Vietnam was divided into four military zones- I Corps (prounounced "eye corps"), II Corps, and III Corps
ISR	Intelligence/Surveillance & Reconnaissance
JCS	Joint Chiefs of Staff
KIA	Killed in Action
LCU	Landing Crafts Utility
LHA	Landing Helicopter Assault
LPD	Landing Ship Dock
LPH	Landing Platform Helicopter
LSU	Landing Support Unit
MAB	Marine Amphibious Brigade
MAC(V)	Military Assistance Command (Vietnam)
MAF	Marine Amphibious Force
MAGIS	Marine Air Ground Intelligence System
MAU	Marine Amphibious Unit
MCCRES	Marine Corps Combat Readiness and Evaluation System
MEF (II)	Marine Expeditionary Force II
MEU	Marine Expeditionary Unit

MOS	Military Occupational Specialty
MP	Military Police
N-2	Intelligence Officer (on an admiral's staff)
NATO	North Atlantic Treaty Organization
NCO	non-commissioned officer
NJP	non-judicial punishment
NROTC	Naval Reserve Officers Training Corps
NSA	National Security Agency
NSG	Naval Security Group (Name has evolved to Naval Warfare Command, Cyberforces)
NVA	North Vietnamese Army
OCS	Officer Candidate School
POW	prisoner of war
RDF	Rapid Deployment Force
RLT	Regimental Landing Team
RPG	rocket propelled grenade
RRU	Radio Reconnaissance Unit
S-1	Personnel Officer (on staff of a colonel or below)
S-2	Intelligence Officer (on staff of a colonel or below)

S-3	Operations, Plans and Training Officer (on staff of a colonel or below)
S-4	Logistics Officer (on staff of a colonel or below)
SAM	surface-to-air
SCAMP	Sensor Control and Management Platoon
SIGINT	Signals Intelligence
SIGSEC	Signals Security
SLF	Special Landing Force
SMLS	Seaborne Mobile Logistics System
SRIC	Surveillance, Reconnaissance Center
Staff NCO	Staff Non-Commissioned Officer
STEAM	Sensor Technology as Applied to the Marine Corps
T&E	Test & Evaluation
TACAN	tactical air navigation system
TAOR	Tactical Area of Responsibility
TAR	Tactical Air Request
TIPI	Tactical Information Processing and Interpretation
T/O	tables of organization

TWAES	Tactical Warfare Analysis Evaluation System
TWSEAS	Tactical Warfare Simulation, Evaluation and Analysis System
UA	Unauthorized Absence
UPI	United Press International
USAF	United States Air Force
USAAG	United States Army Artillery Group
USAF	United States Air Force
USAID	United States Aid for International Development
USMC	United States Marine Corps
USNS	United States Navy Ship
USN	United States Navy
USSAG	United States Support Activities Group
VC	Viet Cong
VNAF	South Vietnamese Air Force
VNMC	Vietnamese Marine Battalion
XO	executive officer

MARINE AND NAVY OFFICER RANKS

Marine (Army/AF) Officer Ranks		Navy Officer Ranks	
Second Lieutenant	2nd Lt	Ensign	ENS
First Lieutenant	1st Lt	Lieutenant, Junior Grade	LT (jg)
Captain	Capt	Lieutenant	LT
Major	Maj	Lieutenant Commander	LCDR
Lieutenant Colonel	Lt Col	Commander	CDR
Colonel	Col	Captain	CAPT
Brigadier General	Brig Gen	Rear Admiral (Lower Half)	RDML
Major General	Maj Gen	Rear Admiral (Upper Half)	RADM
Lieutenant General	Lt Gen	Vice Admiral	VADM
General	Gen	Admiral	ADM

INDEX

INDEX

A

Abrams, Creighton
    on ARVN improvements, 169
    on Davis, 47
    and Gray's Army War College
        research, 189, 191
    as U.S. commander in Vietnam
        and ARVN leadership, 171
        coordination of U.S. and South
            Vietnamese leadership, 195
        and defense of I Corps, 196
        and drawdown of U.S. forces, 90
        installment as, 25, 27–28, 73
        limited impact on U.S. policy, 170
        McCain's support for, 170–71
        and preventive strikes, 73–74
        strategy of, 73, 90–91
        successes of, 74, 261
        and U.S. progress, 73
        and Vietnamization, 90–91, 171,
            172, 173
Adams, John, 143, 161
Adams, Ralph, 283–84
AESF. *See* Amphibious Evacuation
    Support Force
Africa, Nixon Doctrine and, 190–91
Agent Orange, 310
Agnew, Spiro T., 263
Air America, *250, 251,* 252, 255–56, 278,
    296
aircraft, Marine Corps, study of
    requirements for, 340
air-delivered seismic intrusion devices
    (Ad-Sids), *159*
air power, U.S.
    and Soviet anti-aircraft weapons, 246
    withdrawal of, and fall of South
        Vietnam, 264

AK-47 rifle, 30
alcohol
    abuse in military, *See* drug and alcohol
        problems
    Gray's avoidance of while overseas, xxi,
        338
America as a Civilization (Lerner), 187
Amphibious Evacuation Support Force
    (AESF), 281–82
amphibious operations, Gray's expertise
    on, 139–40
Amphibious Support and Intelligence
    System (ASIS), testing of, 124,
    177n30
anti-aircraft weapons, North Vietnamese
    effectiveness of, 246
    U.S. unwillingness to attack,
        consequences of, 314
    vulnerability of South Vietnamese
        aircraft to, 195
anti-war movement
    civil rights movement and, 32–33
    and draft, resistance to, 27
    intensification under Nixon, 69, 89,
        173
    and Kent State protesters, shooting of,
        92, 170
    mischaracterizations of U.S. bombing
        in North Vietnam, 173
AO2F, military occupational specialty
    classification for, 151–53
ARG Alpha
    and evacuation of Phnom Penh,
        237–40, 248, 260
    and evacuation of Saigon, 275, 282
    return to Philippines after evacuation,
        324

NVA destruction of, 284–85, 288, 292
and *Operation Baby Lift* crash, 269n52
Taylor, Maxwell, 25–26, 27
Taylor, Wylie, 280, 281, 296
Têt Offensive (1968), 23–26
  detailed U.S. knowledge of
    preparations for, 23
  Gray on media reports about, 25
  Johnson's bombing pause prior to,
    23–24
  as military disaster for NVA, 24, 26
  NVA objectives in, 24
  as political victory for NVA, 24–26
  and U.S. press, biased and inaccurate
    coverage of, 24–25, 26, 35n19
  Viet Cong obliteration in, 26, 72
  Viet Cong role in, 24
Thailand
  U.S. Igloo White program and, 13, 20
  U.S. operations in, secrecy
    surrounding, 20
Thieu (president of South Vietnam). *See*
  Nguyen Van Thieu
3rd Force Reconnaissance Company, 50,
  52
III Marine Amphibious Force (MAF)
  command of, 266–67n7
  and evacuation of Phnom Penh, 230
  and evacuation of Saigon, 206, 230,
    241, 245, 247–48, 265
    and changes of command, 231
    helicopters available to, 275
    and operations off aircraft carriers,
      248–49, 275
    reorganization of forces, 274–77,
      280
  and I Corps surveillance,
    reconnaissance, and intelligence
    situation
    Gray's evaluation of, 39–40, 41, 43,
      48–55, *51*

success of integrated system for,
  55–56, 57–58
SIGINT/EW center established by
  Gray at, 43
SRIC for
  Army's dismantling of, 68, 78n36
  Gray's creation of, 40, 54, 56, 57
3rd Marine Division
  9th Regiment, mobility of, 47
  Sensor Surveillance Unit, 55
  and U.S. evacuation of Phnom Penh,
    230–31
31st Marine Amphibious Unit (MAU)
  and evacuation of Phnom Penh, 231,
    237–38, 248
  and evacuation of Saigon, 248, 275
33rd Marine Amphibious Unit (MAU)
  components of, 241
  under Gray
    and evacuation of Saigon, 241,
      245–50, 259, 274
      reloading at sea prior to, 275
      return to Philippines following,
        324, 325
    Gray's hope to maintain as ready
      force in South China Sea, 324,
      327
34th Marine Amphibious Unit (MAU).
  See also 2nd Marine Division,
  1st Battalion, deployment to
  Mediterranean under Gray
  commanding officers of, 116, 117
35th Marine Amphibious Unit (MAU),
  and evacuation of Saigon, 247–48,
  252, 275
Thrash, Gay, 87, 95n7
TIPI. *See* Tactical Information
  Processing and Interpretation (TIPI)
  program
tobacco chewing, Gray and, xxi, 181, 182